GLOBAL MIGRATION

Global Migration provides a clear, concise, and well-organized discussion of historical patterns and contemporary trends of migration, while guiding the reader through an often difficult and politicized topic. Aimed primarily at undergraduate and Master's students, the text encourages the reader to reflect on economic processes, politics, immigrant lives, and raises debates about inclusion, exclusion, and citizenship. The text critically highlights the global character of contemporary migration and the importance of historical context to current processes and emphasizes the role of gender, race, and national ideologies in shaping migration experiences.

Using over a decade of their own insight in teaching undergraduate migration courses in the US and the UK, and the knowledge and understanding of the subject they have acquired as migration researchers, the authors offer an accessible and student-friendly manner for readers to understand and explore the complex issue of migration. The book features numerous international case studies, a chapter dedicated to the perspective of the immigrants themselves, as well as key terms and a list of further readings at the end of each chapter.

Both theoretically and empirically informed, *Global Migration* examines the subject in an holistic and expansive way. It will equip students with an understanding of the complex issues of migration and serve as a guide for instructors in structuring their courses and in identifying important bodies of scholarly research on migration issues.

Elizabeth Mavroudi is a Lecturer in Human Geography in the Department of Geography at Loughborough University, UK.

Caroline Nagel is an Associate Professor of Geography at the University of South Carolina, USA.

GLOBAL MIGRATION

Patterns, processes, and politics

Elizabeth Mavroudi and
Caroline Nagel

Routledge
Taylor & Francis Group

LONDON AND NEW YORK

First published 2016
by Routledge
2 Park Square, Milton Park, Abingdon, Oxon OX14 4RN

and by Routledge
711 Third Avenue, New York, NY 10017

Routledge is an imprint of the Taylor & Francis Group, an informa business

British Library Cataloguing in Publication Data
A catalogue record for this book is available from the British Library

Library of Congress Cataloging in Publication Data
Names: Mavroudi, Elizabeth, author. | Nagel, Caroline Rose, author.
Title: Global migration : patterns, processes, and policies /
Elizabeth Mavroudi and Caroline Nagel.
Description: Abingdon, Oxon : New York, NY : Routledge, [2016] |
Includes bibliographical references and index.
Identifiers: LCCN 2015047341| ISBN 9780415683869 (hardback : alk. paper) |
ISBN 9780415683876 (pbk. : alk. paper) | ISBN 9781315623399 (ebook)
Subjects: LCSH: Emigration and immigration. | Emigration and
immigration—Economic aspects | Emigration and immigration—
Government policy. | Immigrants—Cultural assimilation.
Classification: LCC JV6033 .M38 2016 | DDC 325—dc23
LC record available at http://lccn.loc.gov/2015047341

ISBN: 978-0-415-68386-9 (hbk)
ISBN: 978-0-415-68387-6 (pbk)
ISBN: 978-1-315-62339-9 (ebk)

Typeset in Galliard
by Keystroke, Station Road, Codsall, Wolverhampton

To our wonderful daughters, Pippa, Georgia, and Nefeli,
who remind us, as only children can, to keep it real.

Contents

List of figures   xi
List of tables   xiii
List of plates   xv
List of boxes   xvii
Acknowledgements   xix

1 MAKING SENSE OF GLOBAL MIGRATION   **1**

Introduction   1
What counts as migration?   4
Why does migration matter?   8
In what sense is migration global?   14
Theoretical perspectives on migration   15
Overview of the book   21
Key terms in this chapter   24
Further reading   24

2 GLOBAL MIGRATION IN HISTORICAL PERSPECTIVE   **28**

Introduction   28
Migration and the emergence of a European-centred world economy   28
Migration and socioeconomic change in early modern Europe   30
Migration and the colonial economy   31
Migration and the Industrial Revolution   35
Migration and the upheavals of the 20th century   41
Migrations in the post-World War II era   44
Economic restructuring and a shifting migration system at the end of the 20th century   46
Conclusions   51
Key terms in this chapter   53
Further reading   53

3 MIGRANT LABOUR IN THE ECONOMY   **57**

Introduction   57
Matching workers to jobs: skills, education, and qualifications   58
Immigrant social capital in the labour market   59
Employer expectations, stereotyping, and segmented labour markets   65
The role of the state in shaping an 'unskilled' immigrant labour force 69
Labour market segmentation and skilled migration   73
Recovering migrant agency   79
Conclusions   81
Key terms in this chapter   83
Further reading   83

4 MIGRATION AND DEVELOPMENT   **91**

Introduction   91
What is development?   92
Migration and development: the view from the Global North   94
Migration and development: the view from the Global South   97
Evaluating migrants as agents of development   104
Conclusions   110
Key terms in this chapter   112
Further reading   112

5 REFUGEES   **118**

Introduction   118
Refugees in historical perspective   120
Defining refugees in the Cold War era   123
Refugee crises and the politics of asylum since the Cold War   125
Refugee politics in the Global South   137
Refugee experiences   140
Conclusions   143
Key terms in this chapter   145
Further reading   145

6 IMMIGRATION CONTROL AND BORDER POLITICS   **151**

Introduction   151
Entry policies and border control in historical perspective   153
Theorizing immigration control in contemporary liberal democracies   156
Migration management and the proliferation of migrant categories   159
The securitization of migration   161
Rethinking the geography of borders: interior surveillance and the off-shoring
    of immigration control   166

Conclusions   170
Key terms in this chapter   172
Further reading   172

7   THE POLITICS OF CITIZENSHIP AND INTEGRATION   178

Introduction   178
Conceptualizing citizenship and integration   179
Citizenship and integration in national contexts   183
The opening up of societal membership   188
Citizenship closure   191
Uneven landscapes of citizenship and integration   195
Conclusions   198
Key terms in this chapter   199
Further reading   199

8   MIGRANT IDENTITIES, MOBILIZATIONS, AND PLACE-MAKING PRACTICES   205

Introduction   205
Immigrant experiences through the lens of Assimilation Theory   206
Immigrant lives through the lens of 'difference'   209
Migrant transnationalism and the formation of diasporas   218
Conclusions   223
Key terms in this chapter   224
Further reading   224

Index   230

Figures

1.1 Top destination countries by number of immigrants (in millions), 2010   9
1.2 Top sending countries by number of emigrants (in millions), 2010   10
1.3 Top destination countries by percent of population, 2010   11
1.4 Top sending countries by percent of population, 2010   12
1.5 Net migration (in millions) in select countries by five-year intervals, 1950–2010   14
2.1 Urbanization ratios in Europe, population in cities 10,000 and over, 1500–1890   31
2.2 Estimated population (in millions) in select European countries, 1800–1910   36
4.1 The migration hump model   95
4.2 Value of remittances (in US$ millions) in select countries, 1990–2014   100

Tables

2.1 Estimated population in select European cities, 1800, 1850, 1900   37
4.1 Value of remittances (in US$ millions) in select countries, 1990, 2000, 2005, 2010, 2014 (estimated)   99
5.1 First-time asylum applications in select European countries, 1985–2000   126
5.2 Total asylum applications submitted in selected industrialized countries, 2005–14, with percent change from previous five years   133
5.3 Initial decisions on asylum applications (with percentages), select EU countries, 2008, 2010, 2012, 2014   134
5.4 Top ten refugee hosting countries, 2005, 2010, 2014   138
6.1 Immigrant removals from the US, 1983–2013   168

Plates

1.1 African asylum seekers sleeping rough in Tel Aviv's Levinsky Park, close to the city's bus terminal, Israel, 2010   2

1.2 Asian migrant workers prepare concrete at a construction site in front of the Jumeira Beach Residence towers in Dubai, United Arab Emirates, 2005   3

1.3 Two refugees asleep on a beach in Kos, Greece   6

2.1 Chinese labourers helping to build the railroads in the USA   35

2.2 Landing at Ellis Island, 1902   39

2.3 Greek immigrants in Germany   44

3.1 Moroccan vegetable pickers working in the fields beside the half-completed Polaris World La Torre Golf Resort, 2006   60

3.2 Kitchen at a curry house, Birmingham, UK   64

3.3 A typical contract for domestic workers due to work abroad, Manila, Phillippines   68

3.4 Polish supermarket, Hammersmith, London, UK   80

4.1 Women queue for jobs in Manila, Philippines, as domestic workers in mainly Middle Eastern countries   101

4.2 A billboard advertisement for a money transfer service Dahabshiil in Eastleigh, Kenya   102

5.1 Syrian boy on a truck   118

5.2 A sign, in Calais, France, produced by Eurotunnel, which warns about the dangers of trying to illegally travel through the Channel Tunnel, 2015   127

5.3 General view of a mostly Eritrean sector of the main so-called 'Jungle Camp' on the northern outskirts of Calais, 2015   128

5.4 A man enters through the gates of the Refugee Processing Centre at Lombrum, Manus Island   130

5.5 Refugees waiting to get on the ferry to Athens from Kos   131

5.6 Words on a wall at Shatila Refugee Camp, Lebanon   136

5.7 Young Syrian refugees play in a dry riverbed at the Fayda informal settlement in the Bekaa Valley, Zahle, Lebanon   137

5.8 Palestinian holding symbolic key   140

5.9 Mural in a school at Shatila refugee camp, Lebanon   141

6.1 Mexican migrants on the border with the USA at Tijuana   152

6.2 A French customs officer discovers four Romanian immigrants stowed away in a truck heading for the UK, Calais, France   160

6.3 A US border patrol agent fingerprints a recently arrested immigrant at a detention
     facility, Nogales, Arizona, USA   162
6.4 Memorial crosses in Nogales, left for people who perished in the Arizona Desert near
     the Mexican–USA border, 2010   165
7.1 A welcome sign and an Israeli flag hang at Ulpan Etzion in Jerusalem   183
7.2 Immigrants on subway with citizenship poster in background, Toronto, Canada   190
7.3 Numerous Jamaicans disembarking the MV Empire Windrush in 1948   193
8.1 Muslim man praying next to his hot dog stand, US   212
8.2 Religious book stall outside Birmingham central mosque, UK   213
8.3 Greek–Australian festival at Mornington Park, near Melbourne, January 2012   214
8.4 A plea for racial tolerance and strength in diversity, Cape Town, South Africa, 2008 216

Boxes

1.1 Net migration   13
1.2 A note on geographical terminology   16
2.1 Polish workers in the German Empire (1871–1918)   38
2.2 Japanese imperialism and Korean immigration   50
3.1 A note on terminology: 'native worker'   59
3.2 Middleman minorities   63
3.3 Trafficking   72
4.1 Migrant remittances   104
4.2 The Transfer of Knowledge through Expatriate Nationals (TOKTEN) Programme   106
5.1 The Uighurs, Saudi Arabia, and post-Cold War geopolitics   125
5.2 Contemporary resettlement politics   132
6.1 A note on terminology: visas and passports   154
6.2 Frontex: Europe's border agency   163
6.3 Secure Communities   167
7.1 The ghetto   180
7.2 A note on terminology: race versus ethnicity   187
7.3 British multiculturalism and the 'race relations' paradigm   192
8.1 Robert Parks' 'The Marginal Man'   208
8.2 Historical perspectives on transnationalism and diaspora   222

Acknowledgements

This book has its roots in the classroom. We had been teaching courses on global migration for several years at our respective universities when Routledge asked if we might be interested in producing an introductory text on migration. Being familiar with each other's research and teaching, we had spoken now and again about writing a book together. Now the opportunity had presented itself to us. We set out to write a book that would explain human migration clearly and concisely to undergraduate students and others new to the field. We have generally followed the order of topics in our course syllabi, and many of the sources cited in the book have been assigned as readings at one time or another to our students. Because this book is so closely tied to our teaching, it seems fitting that we begin by acknowledging the hundreds of students whom we have taught—and who have taught us—through the years. Our students have typically come to us with no formal background in migration studies, but with a recognition that there is more to migration than what they hear in public discourse. Our students have challenged us when our explanations are unclear and our arguments unconvincing; and they have told us when we have assumed too much or too little about what they know. They have also shared their own migration stories with us. In these ways, our students have made us better teachers and scholars. We hope that our years of student feedback will be apparent in the comprehensiveness and accessibility of this book.

There are many others to whom we owe a debt of gratitude, including those who mentored us in our academic careers and who introduced us to many of the themes and topics addressed in this book. It is not possible for us to provide an exhaustive list here of the scholars who gave us advice, training, and guidance early in our careers, but we would like to recognize Lynn Staeheli and Cheryl McEwan. We would also like to thank our academic colleagues at Loughborough University, the University of South Carolina, and other institutions who have given us feedback on our work over the years and who have developed a good deal of the scholarship that we cite in this book. We give special thanks to Heike Jöns, Marco Antonsich, Jon Beaverstock, Tracey Skelton, Anastasia Christou, and Patricia Ehrkamp. Thanks are owed, as well, to the graduate assistants at the University of South Carolina—Catherine Cottrell, Amelia Ayoob, Alysha Baratta, and Beth Nelson—who assisted with data collection, editing, and the production of tables and graphs, and to Aga Szewczyk, who provided Plate 7.2. Caroline would be remiss if she did not thank Sean McCrossin, the owner of Drip Coffee in Columbia, South Carolina, for providing a much-needed refuge from the office and an ideal space for writing.

Special thanks go to Routledge both for inviting us to write this book and for helping to make it a reality. Egle Zigaite and her predecessor, Sarah Gilkes, demonstrated immense patience with us and were always responsive to our queries. We appreciate the faith they placed in us to complete this project.

While we approach migration as scholars, migration is an important part of our own biographies and the biographies of our parents and grandparents. Migration experiences—the crossing of borders, the maintenance of ties with places of origin, the negotiation of membership in places of settlement—are not abstractions to us. Rather, they are woven into the memories and identities of our families. We give thanks to our family members who have shared their stories with us over the years about starting new lives in faraway places.

Finally, we give thanks to our spouses and children for providing happy homes where we could decompress after long days of research and writing. They provided endless encouragement to finish this project, and we appreciate their love and support.

1

Making sense of global migration

Introduction

In May 2012, around one thousand demonstrators marched through the streets of Tel Aviv, Israel, to protest the presence of tens of thousands of unauthorized African migrants in the country. According to media accounts, the protestors who gathered in Tel Aviv chanted 'Blacks out' and held signs calling for the expulsion of African migrants; some looted African-owned businesses and physically assaulted African people. Addressing the protestors were politicians who described African immigrants as a 'cancer in our body' and who vowed to 'bring them back to where they belong' (*Guardian*, 2012). This outburst of hostility towards migrants shocked some Israelis, but the protest was not an isolated event. Shortly before the protests, the Israeli Prime Minister Benjamin Netanyahu had stated publicly that the surge of 'illegal infiltrators' was threatening Israel's identity as a Jewish state. Two years earlier, the Netanyahu government had begun construction on a steel barrier near the Egyptian border to block the flow of African migrants. The government had also consistently demonstrated a hardnosed approach to African asylum seekers, granting refugee status to only one claimant out of 4,600 in 2011. In the wake of the 2012 protests, Israel's parliament approved legislation allowing authorities to detain unauthorized immigrants from Africa for up to a year without a trial (earlier legislation permitting detention for up to three years

was overturned by Israel's Supreme Court). This legislation enabled authorities to send migrants to Holot, a new detention facility where, in the summer of 2014, detainees held protests and hunger strikes to draw attention to Israel's refusal to act on their asylum applications (*Guardian*, 2014; *Al Jazeera*, 2013a).

The situation in Israel is far from unique. In November 2013, for instance, the Saudi Arabian government embarked on a sweep of construction sites and businesses with the aim of rounding up and deporting the tens of thousands of unauthorized workers residing in the kingdom. This sweep had been preceded by a seven-month period in which the Saudi government had warned foreign workers to regularize their status or to face detention and deportation. Authorities claimed that over 17 million foreign workers had, in fact, complied with the government's order, but the state police managed to identify and to detain approximately 16,000 workers in the first two days of the crackdown (*Al Jazeera*, 2013b). By March 2014, the Saudi government claimed to have detained more than a quarter million unauthorized migrants (the majority of them Ethiopians, Sudanese, and Somalis), and perhaps two million migrant workers had left the country (*Al Jazeera*, 2014; Black, 2013). Across the Mediterranean, Italian authorities were also responding harshly to the presence of migrants from Africa and the Middle East. Facing a growing number of unauthorized arrivals, including many seeking political asylum during the Arab Spring uprisings, Italian legislators in 2011 had passed one of Europe's most repressive laws on unauthorized immigration, allowing migrants to be detained for up to 18 months. Today, approximately 8,000 migrants—including many who have been living in Italy for years but whose immigration status has lapsed—have been detained in one of several prison-like detention facilities scattered around the country. As in Israel and Saudi Arabia, Italy's detention practices have been roundly criticized by international organizations for violating the human rights of migrants (Povoledo, 2013).

These cases—and there are many more like them—speak to the prevalence of human movement in the world today and the seemingly unstoppable tide of impoverished immigrants washing up (sometimes literally) on the shores of wealthy countries. These cases speak, as well, to the deep anxiety that receiving societies harbour towards 'uninvited guests' and the hostility that awaits migrants when they reach their destinations. Yet these rather sensational cases of global migration—featuring clandestine journeys across deserts and seas, violent police crackdowns, and long-term detention in dismal living conditions—can obscure what are often very complicated and ambivalent attitudes and practices towards migrants in most destination societies. Israel's recent crackdown on unauthorized immigrants, for instance, can be contrasted with its liberal policy towards Jewish immi-

Plate 1.1 African asylum seekers sleeping rough in Tel Aviv's Levinsky Park, close to the city's bus terminal, Israel, 2010

Source: Robin Hammond/Panos

Plate 1.2 Asian migrant workers prepare concrete at a construction site in front of the Jumeira Beach Residence towers in Dubai, United Arab Emirates, 2005

Source: © Andrew Holbrooke/Corbis

grants. Since its creation in 1948, the state of Israel has treated immigration as a cornerstone of its nation-building project and has settled over three million Jews from Eastern Europe, the former Soviet Union, Ethiopia, and the Middle East. Since the 1990s, the Israeli state has also sanctioned the importation of thousands of non-Jewish workers, many from The Philippines, Sri Lanka, and Eastern Europe, to fill low-waged jobs once held by Palestinians from the Israeli-Occupied Territories (Yacobi, 2008). In Saudi Arabia, skilled and unskilled migrants have had a major presence in the country's labour force since the oil boom of the 1970s. With over half of its labour force coming from outside the kingdom, Saudi Arabia has been aptly described as being 'addicted' to foreign labour (Walker, 2013). The current crackdown on unauthorized workers is part of a longer-term strategy

of 'Saudization', whereby the state has sought to reduce high levels of unemployment among Saudi citizens by replacing migrant workers with Saudi workers. But Saudization, which was initiated in 1994, has until recently been almost entirely ignored, especially in the private sector, and the state has typically turned a blind eye towards migrant workers who overstay their visas (ibid.). While the reliance on foreign workers is perhaps less pronounced in Italy than in Saudi Arabia, Italian employers have similarly relied on a steady flow of both documented and undocumented migrants since the 1980s. Until recently, regulation of migrant flows has been haphazard, and the Italian state has dealt with the growth of the migrant population in an ad hoc manner, mainly by offering migrants periodic opportunities to regularize their status (Schuster, 2005). Attitudes towards migrants in Italy have certainly hardened in recent years, but migrants continue to find work in the light manufacturing sector and in low-end service sectors. In these and other contexts, one is perhaps as likely to hear migrants described as desirable workers as to hear them described as a societal threat.

These cases, and the many contradictions that arise from them, raise a number of issues that require further investigation. We might begin by asking a series of empirical questions about the nature of migration processes: What drives people to leave their homes and to go to unfamiliar places where they may be subject to harsh treatment or even detention and expulsion? What kinds of people are most likely to move? How do migrants choose their destinations? How do they become incorporated into the economic, political, and social systems in the places where they settle? Digging a bit deeper, we might ask: Who determines the conditions and circumstances under which people can leave one place and go to another? How do borders work, and what purpose do borders serve? Why do states welcome certain migrants at certain times and restrict migration at other times? What impact do migrants have on the economies and political systems of sending and receiving societies? And at what point do 'foreigners' cease to be foreign?

This book is intended to help readers make sense of these complex and often thorny questions. While we have written this as an introductory-level text, we have aimed to provide a comprehensive understanding of migration processes and to convey the many ambiguities that surround migration whether we look at the issue from the perspective of sending societies, receiving societies, or migrants themselves. We are concerned, first, with *patterns* of migration: what migration flows look like today and what they looked like in the past; where migrants are going and why; who is migrating and who is not migrating; what circumstances they are leaving and what circumstances they are entering.

Second, we are concerned with *processes* relating to migration—that is, the political, economic, and social dynamics that shape migrants' mobility, their experiences in the labour force, their relationships with homelands, their identities, and their everyday interactions with members of receiving societies. Third, we are concerned with the *politics* of migration—that is, the practices, policies, and discourses through which sending and receiving societies attempt to manage and control migrants, as well as the practices through which migrants resist, accommodate, and negotiate these attempts at control and management. Before providing a more detailed overview of the content of this book, we wish to address some basic questions and to define some key terms that provide the basis for deeper inquiry into global migration. These questions include: What 'counts' as migration? Why does migration matter? In what sense is migration 'global'? And, finally, how do we study migration?

What counts as migration?

We want to begin by explaining what we mean by 'migration' and who counts as a 'migrant'. This may seem pedantic, but the terminology surrounding migration is more complex and confounding than one might expect. Social scientists often define migration simply as movement from one geographical location to another. This can include movement from one region to another in the same country—usually called **internal migration**—and movement from one country to another—usually termed **international migration**. Scholars also distinguish migration from other forms of movement, like commuting and residential relocation, that are largely confined to metropolitan areas. Migration, in this sense, can be identified by the relatively long timescale and relatively long distances involved. With this said, there are many kinds of migrations that complicate distinctions based on timescale and distance. One example is rural-to-urban migration, a phenomenon common in industrializing societies, which can take place over short distances and can involve everything from permanent moves to frequent relocations between urban areas and villages. Another example is sojourning, which is usually understood as a form of short-term, seasonal or circular migration that can take place over great distances.

International organizations and national governments have their own, more-or-less precise definitions of migration and migrants. The United Nations Statistics Division (2014) defines a migrant as someone 'who moves to a country other than that of his or her usual residence for a period of at least a year, so that the country of destination effectively becomes his or her new country of usual residence'. The International Organization for Migration (IOM) has a broader definition of migration as 'the movement of a person or group of persons from one geographical unit to another across an administrative or political border, wishing to settle definitely or temporarily in a place other than their place of origin' (IOM, 2003, 8).

If 'migration' speaks broadly and abstractly to relatively permanent and relatively long-distance movements of people, the terms **emigration** and **immigration** speak more specifically to movement and settlement across nation-state borders—emigration signifying movement *from* one's national 'homeland' and immigration signifying movement *to* a destination country (readers should note that emigrants are often referred to using the French term **émigré**). Emigration and immigration, in other words, make specific reference to migration and settlement that takes place in a nation-state system.

The individual who emigrates from one country and settles in another becomes the object of the receiving state's policies towards 'aliens' and 'foreigners'. States can use the term 'immigrant' in rather specific ways within their systems of population management. For instance, the British government, like the UN, regards anyone who stays or intends to stay for at least one year, whether as a student, a businessperson, or a labourer, to be an immigrant. In the United States, in contrast, the term 'immigrant' is usually reserved for those granted permanent residency upon entry and who are eligible for US citizenship. There is thus a distinction made between immigrants and those who enter on temporary, 'non-immigrant visas'.

These definitional differences can make it challenging for migration scholars to compare migration patterns and processes across national contexts. Compounding these definitional differences are the peculiarities of migration data collection within nation-states. In the United States, most migration data come either from the decennial census, which counts all foreign-born, regardless of legal status, or the Department of Homeland Security, which distinguishes more clearly between different types of visa holders. When reviewing US immigration data, scholars need to be aware of the source of the data and what any given statistic might include or not include. Those working with British data must be equally wary, though for different reasons. Many analyses of immigration to and emigration from the United Kingdom are based on the International Passenger Survey (IPS), which gathers data from a sample of about 250,000 passengers out of millions who pass through British ports every year. Survey respondents are asked about their intentions to stay in the UK, and adjustments are then made to account for those who initially come to, or leave from, the UK for a short period but subsequently stay for a year or longer ('visitor switchers'), and those who intend to be migrants, but who actually stay in the UK or abroad for less than a year ('migrant switchers'). Critics charge that the data set on migrants generated by the IPS—typically 2–3 percent of the sample total—is too small to be valid: as Cangiano (2010, 5) states, 'subsets of the sample are subject to high uncertainty' and 'sampling errors are too large to measure with a reasonable degree of accuracy the number of migrants to a single region within the UK, from a single country of origin . . . or from a single age group'. Moreover, the IPS does not allow for an accurate measure of people's movement in and out of different immigrant categories. Some scholars find it more useful to look at numbers of work permits issued by the Home Office; but one then must look elsewhere to find the number of dependents who arrive with work-permit holders, as well as the substantial number of workers in Britain who originate within the European Union (EU).

Thus, defining migration and determining its scale and scope is seldom straightforward or easy. Migration scholars are often working with multiple definitions and data sources even within a single national context. They are also dealing with numerous categories and types of migrants—minor or spousal dependents, humanitarian migrants, retirees, students, and returnees, among others—who are recognized in varying ways and to varying degrees by state authorities. Any single data category can hide a multitude of circumstances that exist within and between national contexts and migrant groups. For instance, the concept of **asylum seeker** is rooted in international law and refers to a person who migrates to another country to seek official refugee status. All countries that are signatories to the 1951 UN Convention relating to the Status of Refugees abide by the UN definition of asylum seeker and have procedures in place to handle asylum claims in accordance with international law. Nevertheless, as alluded to above in the case of Israel, each national government

Plate 1.3 Two refugees asleep on a beach in Kos, Greece

Source: Francois Razon

deals with asylum seekers in its own way, applying criteria more or less stringently to different groups and extending rights and privileges to varying degrees. Being an asylum seeker in Israel, therefore, can be a very different experience from being an asylum seeker in Sweden or South Africa. Likewise, entering the asylum system of any country as a child or a woman is likely to be a very different experience from entering as an adult or a man.

The concept of **illegal immigrant**, as well, obfuscates a multitude of circumstances (Anderson and Ruhs, 2010). In the United States, the term 'illegal immigrant' conjures up images of throngs of impoverished Mexicans streaming over the US–Mexico border in defiance of US law and the US Border Patrol. Yet an estimated 40 percent of 'illegal immigrants' have entered the US legally and have overstayed their entry visas. The very notion of 'illegality' is highly problematic in the US context insofar as US immigration law is concerned: while 'improper entry by an alien' is considered a criminal act and is punishable by a fine or a prison term, 'unauthorized presence' is a civil violation that results in deportation, not prison time. In other words, migrants do not actually break any criminal laws or do anything 'illegal' simply by being present in the US without legal documents. In most national contexts, the term 'illegal immigrant' glosses over the role of disjointed government policies in keeping migrants in a precarious legal situation (Calavita, 2005). Some scholars (like ourselves) thus prefer to use less politically loaded terms like '**undocumented immigrant**' or '**unauthorized immigrant**' to refer to those who cross borders without documents or overstay visas. As we argue elsewhere in the book, however, the term 'illegal' can be used in a critical fashion to highlight the power of the state to withhold and to withdraw legal rights from foreigners.

In recent years some scholars, in an effort to create an alternative to nation-state centric definitions of migration, have begun to speak in general terms about **mobility** rather than immigration or emigration (Cresswell, 2006). The concept of mobility is an attractive one that brings together multiple forms of human movement and circulation within a single analytical framework. Mobility encourages us to move past the concepts, categories, and terminology imposed by governments and to consider how the movement of goods, people, and capital operates simultaneously through cities, within neighbourhoods, and across political boundaries. It encourages us to think about the ways societies understand and evaluate movement, whether in terms of freedom and progress or in terms of deviance and danger. Finally, the concept of mobility draws our attention to ways that impediments to mobility operate across geographical scales (think, for instance, of racism, which can block residential mobility in a city and also mobility across national borders).

In this book, we recognize that the boundary between migration and mobility is not a clear one (King, 2012), and we continuously emphasize the relationships between different forms of circulation (labour, capital, commodities) and different geographies of circulation (e.g. intra-urban, interregional, international). We hesitate, however, to abandon nation-state-centred perspectives on migration, as some scholars have tried to do (including some who have advocated replacing the terms 'immigrant' and 'emigrant' with 'transmigrant'—see, for instance, Wimmer and Glick Schiller, 2002). Certainly, we must view state practices through a critical lens; but approaching state power critically requires that we make state practices—and the assumptions about belonging and membership that underpin them—more visible rather than less visible. As much as state-produced categories obscure the causes and consequences of migration, these categories and the policies that flow from them have a crucial role in shaping migrants' realities and experiences.

Why does migration matter?

According to 2010 UN population statistics, there were approximately 214 million people living in a country other than their country of birth, up from 155 million in 1990 and 178 million in 2000 (UN Department of Economic and Social Affairs, 2014). Two-hundred fourteen million certainly sounds like a substantial number—it is, for instance, more than two-fifths the population of the European Union, seven-tenths the population of the United States, and three times the combined population of Australia and Canada. But, in fact, these 214 million people constitute a mere 3 percent of the world's population. One can easily ask why, in a supposed era of globalization, 97 percent of the world's population seems to be staying put.

On the one hand, the rather limited scale of migration in the world today lays bare the rampant hyperbole that characterizes many discussions and debates about migration, especially in wealthy countries. The fears articulated in many immigrant-receiving societies about being overwhelmed by foreign invaders and flooded by unwanted aliens is seldom borne out by evidence and statistics (however imperfect these may be). But on the other hand, the relatively small proportion of the world's population living across national borders belies both the high levels of human mobility that exist within and between national borders and the concentrated effects of migration on localities, both in sending and receiving contexts. Inflated perceptions aside, migration does matter.

International migrations, as we alluded to above, take place in a wider context of mobility. While numbers of international migrants may be small, the number of people who cross international borders for various reasons and various periods of time is massive. For instance, almost 100 million people from outside the European Union pass through British ports-of-entry each year. In 2012 more than 67 million foreign visitors entered the United States, while 60 million US citizens travelled overseas; in addition, tens of millions of trucks, rail containers, buses, and personal vehicles crossed US land borders with Mexico and Canada (US Office of Travel and Tourism Industries, 2014; US Bureau of Transportation Statistics, 2014). Worldwide, over a billion people visited another country as tourists in 2011. The vast majority of the many hundreds of millions of people who cross international borders every year are doing so on a temporary basis—as visitors, businesspeople, tourists, exchange students, and the like. The point, though, is that we live in a world that is increasingly on the move—a world in which different places are bound together by dense networks of commercial activity (including tourism) and relatively inexpensive modes of transport. International migration is but one piece of this wider picture of international mobility.

International migration figures also obscure the enormous scale of human movement *within* national boundaries. For every ten people who sought refuge across borders from civil conflict, there were 26 displaced within their own countries (UNHCR, 2015). For every Chinese-born person living outside of China's borders in 2010, there were 18 living and working outside their province of birth (Chan, 2013). Internal and international movements are often linked to each other, rather than discrete phenomena. Individuals and families, for instance, may undertake multiple internal migrations before crossing an international border, and international migrations typically take place in circumstances marked by significant internal mobility.

While situating international migration in a wider context of mobility, we must also recognize the geographically concentrated effects of international migration flows and the profound social, economic, and political impacts on cities, regions, and countries that send and receive migrants. Migration flows are not evenly distributed across the globe. Most of the world's migrants originate from a small number of countries. Indeed, over a third of the world's migrant population comes, in descending order, from Mexico, India, the Russian Federation, China, Ukraine, Bangladesh, Pakistan, the United Kingdom, the Philippines, and Turkey (World Bank, 2011b). Likewise, most of the world's migrants are destined for a handful of relatively wealthy countries. The US alone hosts around 20 percent of the world's international migrants (a total of 40 million in 2012); the top ten immigrant-receiving countries (the US, the Russian Federation, Germany, Saudi Arabia, Canada, the UK, Spain, France, Australia, and India) together host over half of the world's international migrant population (see Figures 1.1 and 1.2). A significant portion of the world's

migration, moreover, takes place within well-established 'migration corridors', including the Mexico–US corridor (the world's largest, encompassing almost 12 million migrants in 2010), the Russia–Ukraine corridor, the India–Bangladesh corridor, and the Germany–Turkey corridor.

In many countries, migrants' proportion of the total population has increased markedly in recent decades. This is the case in historical settler countries such as the US, where the foreign-born population was under 5 percent in 1970, but is today over 13 percent of the population—similar to what it was in the last great wave of migration in the late 19th and early 20th centuries. Many Americans, if not immigrants themselves, are the children of immigrants: about a quarter of

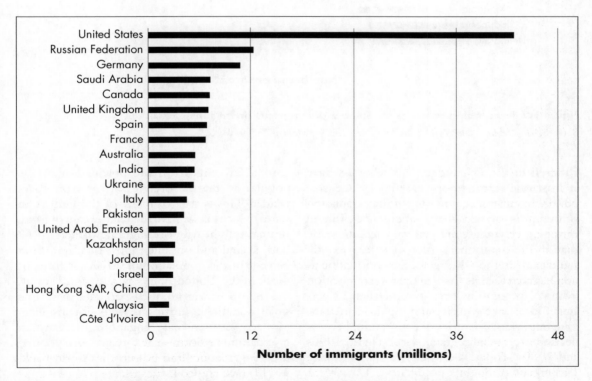

Figure 1.1 Top destination countries by number of immigrants (in millions), 2010

Source: Adapted from the World Bank Migration and Remittances Factbook 2011

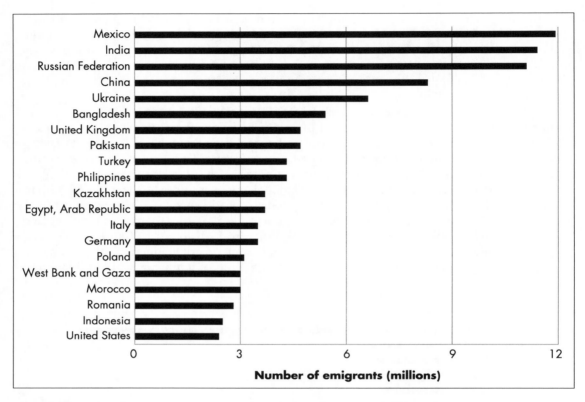

Figure 1.2 Top sending countries by number of emigrants (in millions), 2010

Source: Adapted from the World Bank Migration and Remittances Factbook 2011

children in the US under the age of 18 have at least one foreign-born parent (US Census, 2010). In Australia, a quarter of the population is foreign-born; in Canada, about one-fifth. In Europe, percentages are generally less dramatic than in the traditional settler societies, but still significant. In the UK, the foreign-born population has increased its share of the total population from 4.2 percent in 1951 to more than 12 percent today. Likewise, Ireland, Spain, and Italy, long important countries of emigration, became net importers of immigrants starting in the 1990s and 2000s. Today, the foreign-born constitute 14 percent of Spain's population, 12 percent of Ireland's, and 9 percent of Italy's (Eurostat, 2012; Rienzo and Vargas-Silva, 2012).

In a few countries, the proportion of the population that is foreign-born is truly spectacular. This is true of many of the Gulf Arab states, which, as we have seen in the case of Saudi Arabia, rely heavily on migrant workers to fill both skilled and unskilled jobs. In Qatar, 86.5 percent of the population in 2010 was foreign-born; in the United Arab Emirates and Kuwait, this figure was around 70 percent. In several small, wealthy countries as well—for instance, Monaco, Lichtenstein, Singapore, the Cayman Islands, and Andorra—the foreign-born population ranges from 40 to 60 percent (World Bank, 2011a) (see Figure 1.3).

Within the major receiving countries, immigrants tend to cluster in particular **gateway**

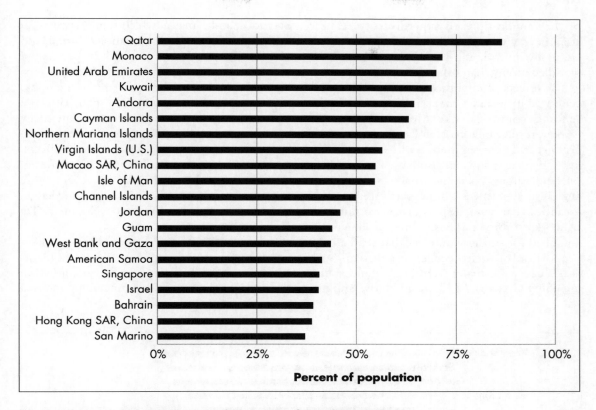

Figure 1.3 Top destination countries by percent of population, 2010
Source: Adapted from the World Bank Migration and Remittances Factbook 2011

cities and regions. In Britain, over a third of Britain's foreign-born population resides in Greater London, and over 40 percent of Inner London's population in 2011 was foreign-born (Rienzo and Vargas-Silva, 2012). In the United States, the foreign-born in 2011 constituted 13 percent of the population; but 27 percent of California's population in this year was foreign-born, and almost two-thirds of foreign-born people in the United States were living in just six states: California, New York, Florida, New Jersey, Texas, and Illinois. Within these states, the foreign-born are heavily represented in major metropolitan areas like New York City (31 percent foreign-born), Los Angeles (34 percent foreign-born), Chicago (19 percent foreign-born), and Miami (38 percent foreign-born) (US Census, 2010). In Sydney, Australia, around a third of the population is foreign-born, and in several of Sydney's inner districts over half the population is foreign-born. The presence of the foreign-born is thus felt very strongly in a few, key economic centres. Within these destinations, one often finds a multitude of languages spoken and cultural traditions practised. Vertovec (2007) has described immigration as producing a condition of 'superdiversity' in cities like London, Sydney, and New York, and he suggests that this condition has significant impacts on local economies, identities, and cultural and political outlooks (see Matejskova and Antonsich (2015) and Wilson (2014) for further discussion of the ramifications of superdiversity). These are, in every way, 'global cities'—cosmopolitan, culturally diverse, and more 'plugged into' the world economy than other cities.

The effects of migration are also highly concentrated in societies that send migrants. Major sending countries, like Mexico, India, and Turkey, receive billions of dollars in **remittances** every year. These remittances often sustain families and villages and can also have a major effect on land values, consumer markets and tastes, and cultural practices within specific regions and localities that send disproportionate numbers of workers abroad. These kinds of effects are amplified for smaller countries that send a large proportion of their populations abroad. Such is the case with many Caribbean island states, including Grenada, St Kitts and Nevis, Antigua,

Barbados, and Jamaica, which send between 35 and 65 percent of their populations abroad, and El Salvador, which in 2010 had 20 percent of its national population residing overseas (see Figure 1.4). As we will discuss later in the book, important questions arise when many of those leaving are the highest educated and potentially most productive. For sending countries, the outflow of workers can have major societal effects. Emigration can drain a country of its young, better educated population; however, these émigrés can also return with skills, knowledge, and capital to boost economic development (De Haas, 2005).

In sum, global migration statistics—which are perhaps not very impressive in and of themselves—need to be considered in conjunction with a wider set of mobilities, including internal

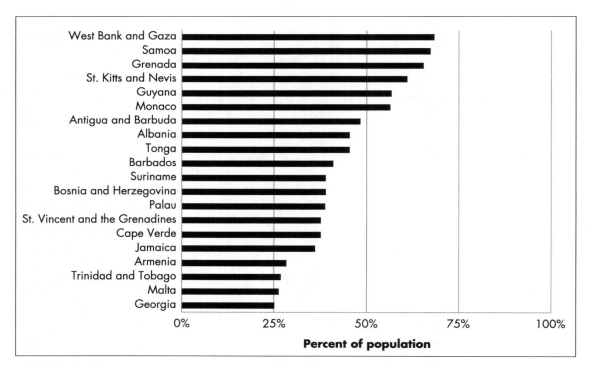

Figure 1.4 Top sending countries by percent of population, 2010

Source: Adapted from the World Bank Migration and Remittances Factbook 2011

migration, internal displacement, and the massive flows of people who cross international boundaries every year as tourists, business people, students, and the like. At the same time, we need to be cognizant of the specific regional patterns and the amplified effects of migration in certain places. Migration matters in historical settler societies, where foreign-born populations have increased significantly in the past several decades and have brought new diversity to what had been overwhelmingly white, European-origin dominated places. It matters in cities like London, Los Angeles, and Sydney, where school systems must contend with children who come from homes where English is not the first language. It matters in Dubai, where the vast majority of workers do not enjoy the rights and privileges of Emirati citizens. It matters in Lebanon, which is both one of the world's top sources of remittances (from the hundreds of thousands of foreign domestic servants and construction workers resident in the country) and one of the world's largest recipients of remittances (from the estimated 400,000 Lebanese professionals who work in the Gulf, West Africa, and the United States and elsewhere). Migration, in short, matters.

BOX 1.1 NET MIGRATION

Net migration measures the difference between in-migration and out-migration in a given time period. Politicians, journalists, and scholars in the Global North tend to focus on numbers of migrants *entering* a country without taking into account those *leaving*, leading in some cases to an inflated or inaccurate understanding of the demographic changes caused by migration. Net migration figures can help to counter the hyperbole that characterizes public discourse on migration while also providing insights into long-term relationships between sending and destination societies and short-term events that affect population flows. Looking at Figure 1.5, Mexico clearly has been a major country of emigration for several decades. The net outflow of population from Mexico tracks the phenomenal increase in positive net migration in the United States. And indeed, the Mexico–US migration corridor is the world's largest in terms of the volume of migrants crossing the border. The graph also indicates, however, that Mexican migration cannot fully account for the surge of positive net migration in the US in the late 1990s and early 2000s. While Mexican migration continues to be the focus of political debate in the US, positive net migration in the US has many sources and causes beyond Mexico. Another interesting case is the rise in net immigration to the Russian Federation in the 1990s, which reflects, in part, the movement of many ethnic Russians from former Soviet republics to Russia after the fall of the Soviet Union. There continues to be positive net immigration to the Russian Federation, but this net immigration seems quite modest given that the Russian Federation is one of the world's top destination countries. One can surmise from net migration statistics (and from the fact that the Russian Federation is also one of the world's top sending countries) that there is significant two-way mobility between Russia and the former Soviet republics. Finally, one can clearly visualize the shift in Spain's status from a country of net emigration in the 1950s and 1960s to a country of net immigration in the 2000s. The timing of this shift corresponds with Spain's incorporation into the Eurozone, which opened up access to cheap credit and led to a major construction boom. Construction, as we discuss elsewhere in this book, is a sector that heavily relies on migrant workers, so it is not surprising to see a rather sudden increase in net immigration in the 2000s. We encourage you to look at net migration figures in conjunction with gross immigration and emigration statistics. What do net migration figures signify in different contexts and at different historical moments?

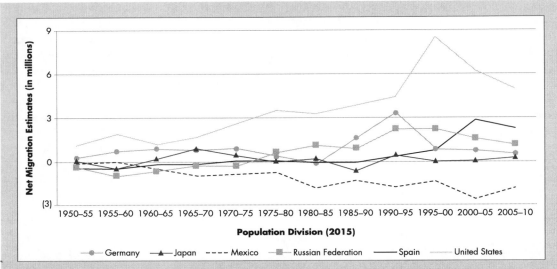

Figure 1.5 Net migration (in millions) in select countries by five-year intervals, 1950–2010

*Source: United Nations Department of Economic and Social Affairs, Population Division (2015)
World Population Prospects*

In what sense is migration global?

Our introductory discussion thus far has focused on the idea of inter*national* flows and inter*national* migrants; throughout the book, we focus on national-level policies, national ideologies, national labour markets, and so on. With the nation-state so much at the centre of the analysis, why have we titled the book *Global Migration*? What is it about migration that is global, and how do we understand the relationship between the international and the global?

Globalization often refers to the complex economic, social, political, and technological processes that link together many, if not all, parts of the world. Globalization brings together disparate, far-flung parts of the globe through trade, complex production networks, common frameworks of governance (e.g. the UN and the World Trade Organization), unbounded currency and commodity markets, and through the relatively free flow of information via the internet, satellite, and other technologies. Migration

is a key element of globalization and can be seen both as a cause and effect of global integration. The expanding volume of migratory flows signifies the globalization of labour markets and the ability for firms to draw on sources of labour that extend well beyond national borders. At the same time, migration generates global flows of money (through remittances), culture, and information. Migration creates connections between sending and receiving countries and generates complex, multidirectional relationships and networks between particular regions, cities, towns, villages, households, and people.

As we have seen, however, migration is not evenly distributed across the globe; there are very specific geographical patterns—certain countries that send a large proportion of the world's immigrants, certain countries that receive a large proportion of the world's immigrants, and certain corridors that capture most of the world's major flows. Much the same can be said of globalization overall: globalization is highly uneven and affects many places, but not to the same degree and not in the same way. There are winners and losers of globalization, places that are plugged in and places that are largely left out. People and places all experience globalization in different ways and to different degrees of intensity.

The unevenness of globalization has many causes. It is partly a legacy of colonialism and imperialism, which has left some parts of the world in debt, dependent on the export of natural resources, and subject to unfair trading and investment practices. Uneven globalization can also be tied to the particular ways states engage with integrated labour and commodity markets and position themselves in global flows of capital and investment. Some, like the Philippines, have fashioned themselves as suppliers of workers worldwide, while also attempting to attract inward investment. The United Arab Emirates, flush with petrodollars, has fashioned itself as a new global centre of finance, energy, transit, and tourism. Others have been more circumspect and have attempted to shelter national labour markets and industries from global competition. The key point is that nation-states shape and mediate globalization. Flows of people, commodities, money, and information cross boundaries, muddling these boundaries or even, at times, subverting them, but they do not erase boundaries. Perhaps more than any other field of border-crossing activity, migration demonstrates the power of the state to monitor, control, and manage global flows. Today more than ever, nation-states have the will, the desire, and the technological capacity to control population flows. Certainly there are many instances when states seem to lack control over migrants: images of impoverished migrants from Africa clandestinely entering Israel, Saudi Arabia, and Italy, for instance, indicate the limitations of nation-state sovereignty. But for wealthy countries, in particular, increasing rates of migration have more often been the result of choices made by states to invite migrants or to tolerate their presence than of the lack of technological and bureau-

cratic capacity to control flows of people crossing borders (Andreas, 2000).

This book, then, is about global migration in the sense that it understands migration as taking shape in a world characterized by increasing economic, political, and social integration. It also understands all dimensions of globalization to be shaped and mediated by nation-state boundaries and the uneven landscape of rights, privileges, and opportunities for a better life.

Theoretical perspectives on migration

By acknowledging the integrative forces of globalization *and* the enduring power of the state to shape migration flows, we raise a more basic set of questions about how we *explain* migration. How do scholars theorize why migrants leave certain places and why do they choose particular destinations? What are the main forces and processes that generate the myriad migration patterns that we observe today?

Much of our discussion thus far has connected migration to economic processes. Most migrants today are in some way responding to labour market signals—typically low wages in one place and higher wages in another. While there are important migration corridors between wealthy, developed countries, and from wealthy countries to poor countries, most migrations in the world flow from relatively poor countries and regions to relatively rich countries and regions. According to the UN (2012), to illustrate, only 6 percent of international migrants in 2010 moved from the Global North (the wealthy countries of North America and Europe, plus Australia and New Zealand) to the Global South, while 35 percent moved from the Global South to the Global North. A further 34 percent moved *between* countries in the Global South, but many of these migrants moved from relatively poor regions in South Asia and Southeast Asia to wealthier Gulf Arab countries. Most migrants—whether internal or international— are on the move to improve their livelihoods in one way or another and to help sustain not only themselves but their family members back home. Understandably, the dynamics of economies, labour markets, and wages are central to most theoretical understandings of why migrants move and where they move.

One of the earliest efforts to theorize migration flows was Ernst Georg Ravenstein's 'laws of migration', which were published in a series of academic articles between 1876 and 1885 (see,

BOX 1.2 A NOTE ON GEOGRAPHICAL TERMINOLOGY

Discussions of global processes like migration often make use of geographical terminology to distinguish between different kinds of places and to describe relationships between these places. In the 1950s and 1960s, in the midst of the Cold War, the terms 'First World', 'Second World', and 'Third World' were widely used to describe key political, ideological, and geographical divisions between capitalist liberal democracies, communist states, and newly independent post-colonial societies, respectively. The term 'Third World' was initially associated with the Non-Aligned Movement, led by a group of charismatic post-colonial leaders who sought to steer an independent course during the Cold War. Over time, however, the term 'Third World' came to be applied more broadly to poor, aid-dependent, post-colonial societies. While the Second World designation has faded into obscurity with the demise of the Cold War, the terms 'First World' and 'Third World' continue to be widely used, and some scholars and activists added the term 'Fourth World' to describe populations—mainly indigenous groups and nomadic people—who have been excluded from the modern national institutions. But 'World' terminology has had many competitors. Development professionals have often employed seemingly more neutral and objective terms like 'less developed countries' and 'more developed countries' to denote relative levels of industrial development and wealth in different parts of the world. Those with more radical philosophical leanings have used the geographical terms of 'core', 'periphery', and 'semiperiphery'. These terms suggest that uneven development does not emerge randomly, but rather is actively constituted through unequal relationships between wealthier and poorer societies (e.g. colonialism). In recent decades, scholars, activists, and development practitioners have relied more on Global North/Global South terminology when distinguishing between relatively rich and relatively poor parts of the world. This terminology comes from the observation that many of the world's wealthiest countries are located in northern latitudes of the globe while many of the world's poorest countries are in more southerly latitudes. There are, of course, many exceptions to this general observation (two of the world's wealthiest countries, New Zealand and Australia, are in southern latitudes). A more serious criticism of the North/ South terminology is that it glosses over enormous differences within these broad latitudinal divisions. The Global South category, for instance, lumps together the emerging economies of Brazil and Indonesia with extremely poor countries like Burkina Faso, Mali, and Yemen. Likewise, the Global North category contains regions and populations whose poverty would not be out of place in the Global South. The tendency to gloss over differences within and between places is a shortcoming of all categorizations, so it is important to remember why we employ categories in the first place. Categories like Global North/Global South and core/periphery are problematic, but they are a kind of shorthand for significant global disparities and the geographical concentration of wealth and economic productivity. In this book, we use Global North/Global South terminology along with core/periphery, while also recognizing more complicated geographies of inequality that contribute to migration flows.

for instance, Ravenstein, 1885). Ravenstein's 'laws' were really empirical generalizations based on his observations of migration patterns in late-19th-century England—a time of rapid, heavy industrialization and urbanization. Ravenstein noted that migrants tended to move over relatively short distances (reflecting what scholars today call the 'distance-decay effect') and in a stepwise pattern, and that migration flows tended to flow from agriculture areas to areas of industry and commerce. He suggested, as well, that every current of migration has a counter-current and that migration increases in volume as industrialization increases and as transportation improves. Ravenstein also noted that women are more migratory than men, but that men are more likely than women to go farther afield. Above all, Ravenstein suggested, migration is an economic process related to the search for higher wages and jobs. While Ravenstein's use of the term 'law' to describe his observations may have been overly ambitious, many scholars have noted that the patterns he identified broadly hold true today (Tobler, 1995; Samers, 2010).

Ravenstein's work formed the basis of migration theory well into the 20th century. Geographers, economists, and others devised various macro-level models—many of them borrowing concepts from Newtonian physics—to represent Ravenstein's observations. Of particular importance starting in the early 20th century were gravity models, based on the Newtonian principle that the gravitational force between two objects is proportional to their masses and inversely proportional to the distance between them. Applied to population flows, this meant that the volume of flows between two points in space could be reasonably predicted by the relative sizes of their populations (mass) and the distance between them. In the 1970s and 1980s, entropy models, based on the principles of thermodynamics, became increasingly popular. Entropy refers to disorder and uncertainty present in a given system. The aim of entropy

models, as applied to human societies, was to identify the most likely spatial configuration within a system characterized by disorder and uncertainty. This was usually accomplished through 'flow matrices' with mathematical equations representing all of the possible pairwise interactions that might take place between places (for an overview, see Willekens, 1980; Willekens, Pór, and Raquillet, 1981).

Throughout this period, from the 1950s through the 1970s and even beyond, the application of physical principles to social phenomena was regarded as the height of scientific rigour. Yet writing in 1966, Everett Lee expressed his dissatisfaction with the state of migration theorization, arguing that little progress had been made in understanding migration flows since Ravenstein. Lee (1966) laid out a new theoretical framework that had a profound impact on subsequent generations of migration scholars. Lee conceived of migration flows as the aggregate of individual decision-making processes. He identified four main sets of factors determining the shape and volume of these flows: factors associated with area of origin, factors associated with the area of destination, intervening obstacles, and personal factors. In every place, Lee suggested, there are countless economic and non-economic factors holding people in place or repelling them. The influence of different factors vary significantly by individual, reflecting income levels, sex, stages in the lifecycle, and the like. These factors could be represented by pluses and minuses at the point of destination and Lee argued, however, that the simple calculus of pluses and minuses was not enough to understand migration flows. One also needed to consider the many obstacles facing potential migrants—including costs of moving, lack of information, and inertia. Lee emphasized that migration decisions were not purely rational. Rather, they could be based on individuals' personal sensitivities, perceptions, and access to information about destinations. Lee also emphasized that migration is a selective, rather than random, process: those who are responding to pull factors in a destination are usually those who, by virtue of higher education and greater access to resources, are in a position to weigh advantages of moving; those who respond to push factors in places of origin, in contrast, are often those who have failed economically and who are less able to cope with war, famine, or a lack of economic opportunity. Lee's thoughts on migration factors led him to propose a set of hypotheses: the volume of migration varies with the diversity of people; unless checks are imposed, the volume and rate of migration tend to increase with time; migration will continue along well-worn paths; and where costs and barriers are high, counter-streams are low.

Lee's push-and-pull model sparked a great deal of theoretical work among geographers, economists, demographers, and others. Especially popular were mathematical models expressing the role of particular push-and-pull factors in generating migrant flows. In contrast to gravity and entropy models, these were micro-scale models concerned with individual migration decision-making processes. Many of these models incorporated concepts and principles from neoclassical economics, describing migration decisions in terms of individuals' efforts to maximize utility—usually understood as income or wages—and to achieve the highest return on their skills and education. While emphasizing economic rationales, many of those working in this framework also highlighted that migrants often act on *expectations* of employment and/or higher wages rather than on perfect knowledge about the labour market (Todaro, 1971). They also emphasized the importance of economic and non-economic factors in overcoming the so-called 'poverty constraint'—that is, the barrier to migration posed by lack of resources needed to leave one place and migrate to another. Scholars thus incorporated a host of factors—transportation costs, risk of deportation, and the presence of kin at the destination, as well as relative wage levels—into their migration models.

These economic models underwent various permutations through the 1970s and 1980s. Some scholars, for instance, attempted to situate individuals within a wider social context, using the household rather than the individual as the main unit of analysis. This body of literature, known as the 'new economics of migration', described the household as both an income-maximizing and risk-minimizing unit, and focused on household strategies to diversify income streams in the face of possible crop failures, unemployment, and other catastrophes (for an overview, see Stark and Bloom, 1985). Other scholars highlighted non-economic reasons for migration, emphasizing individuals' desire for a higher quality of life and amenities. These 'behavioural' theories of migration modelled people's destination choices, focusing on their perceptions of destinations and their search for satisfaction rather than the drive to maximize some economic utility (e.g. Roseman, 1983).

Whether looking at neoclassical economic models, 'new economic' models centred on households, or behavioural approaches, these kinds of models represented a shift away from the very deterministic macro-level models based on principles from the physical sciences. Yet they did not represent a definitive break. With their neat, elegant mathematical formulae, these models, while offering a degree of explanatory power, were (and continue to be) quite abstract and sterile, providing little understanding of the historical and geographical contexts in which migration dynamics take shape. They were soon challenged by a very different set of theories focusing on the structures of the capitalist political economy.

Political-economy perspectives

Structuralist theories emerged in the 1970s to challenge the conventional and largely apolitical approaches that dominated the social sciences in the post-World War II period, and that were typified by entropy and gravity models, as well as by neoclassical economics and behaviourialism. Structural theorists—many of them Marxist or neo-Marxist in orientation—sought to explain social phenomena like migration in terms of well-established relationships and inequalities in the capitalist political economy. While not a strict Marxist, economist Michael Piore (1979) offered one of the earliest and most powerful structuralist critiques of conventional models of migration. Starting in the late 1960s, Piore began to theorize the concept of the **dual labour market**, which referred to the division of industrial economies into a primary labour market, dominated by relatively high-waged, stable, and often unionized jobs, and a secondary labour market, dominated by marginalized immigrant workers (and including, as well, women and minorities). In his 1979 book, *Birds of Passage*, Piore argued that migration flows were generated not by wage differentials but by the actions and motivations of employers in industrialized economies. These employers, he suggested, actively recruited migrants for particular low-waged, low-status, and unstable jobs. Migrants, Piore suggested, were willing to tolerate menial work and job uncertainty because they were mainly interested in earning wages and returning home, not in becoming permanent members of the receiving society. (Piore also suggested, however, that their amenability to exploitation would diminish if and when they came to view themselves as permanent settlers.) Employers used status differentials to maintain control over labour forces and to reduce pressure on wages—that is, migrants and other marginalized workers could simply be 'let go' when no longer needed and re-hired at the same low wage rates when economic conditions improved. Migration, from this perspective, is not determined by the invisible hand of the market, but by the actions of industrial employers, who control labour supply and demand by recruiting from a readily available secondary labour market. Far from correcting wage imbalances and creating equilibrium in labour markets, as neo-

classical economic theories suppose, migration perpetuates wage inequalities (see also Piore, 1986).

If Piore's work emphasized fundamental and persistent inequalities in the labour markets of industrialized societies, neo-Marxist accounts offered a more global perspective, tying migration flows to uneven power relations in the global capitalist economy. These structural accounts viewed migration as symptomatic of, and central to, a host of interrelated historical-geographical processes: colonialism, imperialism, and neo-imperialism; the concentration of wealth and financial power in a small number of states and global cities; and the ongoing exploitation of the 'periphery' by the 'core' (Zolberg, 1989; Portes, 1978; Morawska, 1989; Sassen-Koob, 1984). Accounts written in this vein explored the transformative power of capitalism in rural hinterlands, the role of post-colonial development agendas in disrupting subsistence economies, and the discrimination against and exploitation of non-white workers in receiving contexts. In their broad view of large-scale processes, these accounts mirrored the macro-level perspective of gravity theories; the difference, however, was that neo-Marxist theories very clearly attributed uneven pressures to a particular causal force—namely, capitalism. Like Piore, neo-Marxist accounts rejected the idea that equilibrium between labour supply and demand would be achieved through migration. Indeed, they viewed uneven development as an endemic feature of capitalism: as capital constantly seeks new sources of labour, new resources, and new investments, it creates new demands for labour mobility. Meanwhile, the boundaries of the nation-state system, and the parsing of rights between citizens and non-citizens, ensure that migrant workers are placed in a highly marginalized position in destination countries.

Integrating perspectives: structure and agency

By the early 1980s, scholars were lamenting the increasing polarization of migration theory between neoclassical economic models and neo-Marxist political-economy approaches and were seeking common ground between individualistic and structuralist accounts (Bach and Schrami, 1982). While dissatisfied with the economistic and atomistic perspectives that had dominated mainstream migration theory, scholars were also tiring of the overly deterministic thinking of structuralists and the tendency to view migrants as simply 'carrying the necessary attributes of labour to satisfy the abstract requirements of the "general law of capitalist accumulation"' (ibid., p. 324). Some found a way around this theoretical impasse through a 'migration systems' approach, with scholars like James Fawcett (1989) bringing a wide array of social institutions and networks—including international aid programmes, state regulations, trade flows, family obligations, and mass media—into a single heuristic framework for analysing migration. Feminist migration scholars also sought to capture the multi-layered complexity of migration, but they gave more explicit attention to the workings of power relations—and especially gender relations—within and between societies. Migration theorists of all stripes, feminists charged, had failed to account for the highly differential impacts of migration on men and women and had largely ignored the dynamics of gender ideologies in capitalist economies as well as in households. Understanding migration, they argued, required an understanding of the ways in which relations of domination and subordination operate at multiple geographical scales—households, local communities, sending and receiving societies, the global economy—and the ways individuals and communities respond to and interact with these relations (Kofman, 1999; Kofman, Phizacklea, Raghuram, and Sales, 2000; Lawson, 1998; Fernandez-Kelly, 1983).

A growing sensitivity to power relationships situated in households, workplaces, state institutions, and the global economy has informed many accounts of migration in a variety of social science disciplines. It can be seen, for instance, in Victoria Lawson's (1998, 1999) work, which examines how household divisions of labour are reworked in the context of major political-economic shifts in Latin America, influencing who migrates and the reasons for migration. In Ecuador, neoliberal economic policies, imposed by global institutions like the International Monetary Fund as a condition for loans in the 1980s and 1990s, have led to intensified cross-border movements of capital, the deregulation of work, an intensification of export-oriented production, and a significant reduction of social spending. These processes, in turn, have led to the dislocation of thousands of workers and the growing reliance on employment in informalized sectors of the economy, including garment work. Many migrants leaving rural areas for the city are women; but their access to work is shaped by their domestic roles and responsibilities, and especially by patriarchal ideologies and the expectation that women's work will support male aspirations. Needing to balance multiple roles as wives, daughters, and mothers, women are typically confined to unstable and poorly paid jobs. Rachel Silvey's work on female migrant workers in Indonesia similarly illustrates how women's labour and their ability to migrate is tied simultaneously to processes of neoliberal economic restructuring, state-led development, patriarchal household relations, and gender norms (Silvey, 2000).

Feminist approaches demonstrate that the nature of migration flows—who migrates, where they migrate, why they migrate—can only be understood in light of gender, age, class, racial, and legal/political hierarchies. The recognition that migrants (and non-migrants) are positioned in complex, multi-layered power relations has prompted scholars to pay careful attention to differences within and between migrant groups and to account for the specific experiences of those who migrate, whether as children or adults, workers or retirees, refugees or 'lifestyle migrants', skilled professionals or unskilled labourers (for instance, Chatty and Hundt, 2005; Tyrrell et al., 2013; O'Reilly, 2007; King and Christou, 2014). Literature in this vein emphasizes the myriad circumstances situated in families and households, in nation-states, and in a globally integrated economy, that open up or close off options and opportunities for people, encouraging (or compelling) individuals to move or to stay put. This literature also highlights the **agency**—or individual capacity—to negotiate options, opportunities, and constraints. Discussions of migrant agency, in turn, draw attention to the embeddedness of individuals in social networks that span nation-state borders and that can provide a variety of resources for those on the move (Levitt and Glick Schiller, 2004). These networks are often discussed under the rubric of **transnationalism**, a topic we discuss in detail later in the book.

Migration, in sum, is not a discrete, isolated process, but one that is intimately bound up with a multitude of societal processes operating within and across territorial boundaries. Migration relies on and produces connections between people and places, working through and altering the inequalities and disparities that exist between them. Migration is both an outcome of social, political, and economic transformations and a driver of new transformations that may spur further migrations or may cause flows to diminish or cease. Like feminist researchers, we urge our readers to resist the temptation, all too common in the social sciences, to define complex social phenomena in abstract terms, to isolate causes and effects, and to focus attention on one or two measurable variables. Migration must be embraced and appreciated in all of its complexity, fluidity, and messiness.

Overview of the book

This is intended to give as comprehensive a survey of migration as is possible in a reasonably sized book. We introduce our readers to key themes and topics in migration studies, and we familiarize readers with the various debates that have shaped scholarly inquiry on migration-related processes. Our approach is multidisciplinary and brings together different theoretical perspectives from the social sciences. As we have indicated above, migration is not an isolated or discrete phenomenon. In 'real life', labour-force participation, border-control policy, integration, citizenship, and migrant identities are inextricably connected to each other, and the boundaries between different types of migrants—e.g. forced migrants, voluntary migrants, labour migrants, refugees—are typically muddled. For pedagogical purposes, however, we do parse out specific themes in each chapter. You will notice, however, that we frequently cross-reference between chapters and encourage our readers to make connections between themes and arguments presented at various points in the book.

We begin the book with an historical overview of migration that traces the contours of global migration since the emergence of a European-centred world economy in the 16th century. This chapter is intended to familiarize readers with major migration flows and to serve as a basis for more detailed, thematic discussions in later chapters. It is broad in scope, covering the gamut from intra-European migrations of the early modern period and the transatlantic slave trade to the great migrations of the late 19th century to newer flows within Asia and between Asia and the Middle East. In surveying key migration patterns, this chapter introduces readers to some of the intersections between large-scale political-economic transformations (e.g. colonialism, imperialism, industrialization) and historically and geographically specific configurations of race, class, and gender. By the end of this chapter, readers will have a sound basis from which to consider questions of labour market participation, border control policy, economic development, and settlement processes in greater depth.

Chapter 3 elaborates on a key theme that emerges very clearly in the historical overview (and that we have touched upon already in our brief discussion of migration theory): the role of migrants in the global economy and in national labour markets. This chapter is organized around the concept of labour-market segmentation, and it examines a number of different theoretical explanations as to why migrants tend to occupy certain niches within labour markets. We consider how a combination of migrant characteristics, state regulation, social ideologies, and discriminatory practices positions migrants in particular ways within labour markets. Our account emphasizes the exploitation that both skilled and unskilled migrants face while also highlighting the ways that migrants exercise agency in finding and creating opportunities for economic gain.

Chapter 4 shifts the focus of discussion from receiving societies to sending societies and attempts to disentangle the relationship between migration and 'development'—a term that signifies 'modernization' and economic growth in post-colonial contexts. This chapter recognizes that migration affects not only places of destination but also places of origin. Whether migration's effects on places of origin are positive or negative, of course, is a matter of some debate. While some scholars, development professionals, and government leaders have raised concerns about the loss of skills and labour power, others have touted migration as a key source of capital investment and skills transfers. As with many themes in migration studies, the realities of migration and development are complex and defy simple answers and explanations. Migration, it seems, is a mixed bag for sending societies, boosting household consumption, and providing a crucial source of foreign exchange but altering household relationships, local econ-

omies, and political systems in ways that are not always empowering to ordinary people.

From this economics-heavy discussion, we turn our attention to migration politics (while recognizing that politics and economics are not completely separable). Chapter 5 focuses on refugee flows and the particular political issues that have surrounded the movement of people in response to civil conflict and political persecution. After providing an overview of politically motivated migrations and the formation of an international human rights regime designed to protect refugees, we examine the way in which wealthy countries of the Global North have responded to those seeking asylum on their shores. While only a minute fraction of the world's refugees find their way to the Global North, wealthy countries have viewed the presence of asylum seekers as a major problem that must be repelled at all costs. This chapter highlights the geographical strategies that wealthy states have pursued in order to curb asylum applications and asks whether the current formulations of 'refugees' in international law provide a just and effective means of dealing with forced migrations.

Our focus on state-level asylum policies leads into a wider discussion of the modern state's regulation of migration in Chapter 6. This chapter examines the historical development of the state's capacity to regulate population flows both internally and across borders and its motivations for doing so. The state, we show, has always sought to balance the conflicting impulses that emanate from the interstate system and the world economy. While states, on the one hand, are often eager to promote economic development and trade, they are equally concerned with controlling the presence of foreigners on their soil and maintaining the boundaries of national citizenship. Migration policy (or more accurately, immigration policy), in this sense, is often fraught with contradictions, as states open up borders to certain kinds of workers under specific conditions, while closing themselves off to others. Again, it is crucial here to understand the intertwining of political and economic processes: economic interests play an important role in pressing for the lowering of migration barriers, while the state's capacity to monitor, manage, and classify immigrants serves to position migrants in the labour force.

Having examined the ways in which states regulate and manage the movement of foreign populations across their borders, we turn to the issue of how states incorporate newcomers into national societies—what policies and procedures they put in place to include immigrants in the body politic or to preserve distinctions between immigrants and citizens. This chapter examines the national models that scholars have commonly used to analyse state approaches to integration and citizenship. We suggest, though, that a national-model approach tends to gloss over the enormous shifts that take place within national contexts and the many patterns and trends that cut across national contexts. We examine some of these shifts and trends, paying attention to the significant openness towards immigrants that has occurred as countries have de-coupled formal citizenship from ethnocultural markers. Yet we also point out that states have (among other policies) raised the bar of naturalization in recent years, making it increasingly difficult for migrants to exercise rights of membership. Yet again, we emphasize the ambiguity of this situation, demonstrating that states often enact policies that in some respects enhance societal inclusiveness towards immigrants and in other respects reinforce exclusion. There is, we demonstrate, a pronounced geographical component to immigrant incorporation insofar as localities—municipalities, provinces, and states—can provide a more-or-less welcoming environment for immigrant groups and can enhance or restrict access to rights.

Chapter 8 adopts a more migrant-centred perspective and explores the ways that immigrants navigate the complex social and political landscapes of destination societies and produce and perform community identities. This chapter begins with a critical discussion of 'assimilation theory', which is the most well-established framework that scholars have used to understand immigrant identities and experiences. We also explore an alternative framework for interpreting immigrant experiences that has been offered by critical race scholarship. This race-centred approach, which highlights the ways in which immigrants negotiate, resist, and accommodate themselves to dominant social hierarchies, discourses, and categories, provides a useful lens through which to explore immigrant identities, immigrant space, and immigrant politics. We then turn our attention to the concepts of transnationalism and diaspora, which have had a profound impact on migration studies in the past two decades. A new generation of scholars has challenged the host-society bias of most scholarship on immigrant experiences and has brought into focus the ways in which migrants remain deeply engaged with their countries of origin at the same time that they participate in countries of settlement. Migrants' lives, according to this perspective, span borders and combine 'here' and 'there' in everyday cultural and political practices. In exploring the transnational perspective, we ask whether host-society-centred concepts like assimilation have a place anymore in migration studies and whether the idea of the permanent settler cut off from his or her former life and identity has any meaning in an increasingly interconnected world.

Finally, we conclude the book with some final thoughts on migration and globalization and on the ways that we, as students and scholars, can understand and appreciate the complex, multifaceted nature of migration. Contemporary societies are constantly wrangling with questions of whether migrants are harmful or beneficial to national economies, whether they integrate or 'self-segregate', whether their requests for humanitarian assistance are valid or 'bogus'. We hope that it will be abundantly clear by the end of this book that such debates typically rest on highly simplistic understandings of migration processes and of relationships between economic flows, regulatory regimes, and sociocultural practices. Our aim is to give our readers the wherewithal to engage critically with public discourses and to participate meaningfully and constructively in political debates on immigration.

Key terms in this chapter

agency

asylum seeker

dual labour market

emigration

émigré

gateway cities

illegal immigrant

immigration

internal migration

international migration

mobility

remittances

transnationalism

unauthorized immigrant

undocumented immigrant

Further reading

Bakewell, O. (2010) Some reflections on structure and agency in migration theory, *Journal of Ethnic and Migration Studies*, 36(10): 1689–1708.

Blunt, A. (2007) Cultural geographies of migration: mobility, transnationality, and diaspora, *Progress in Human Geography*, 31(5): 684–694.

Brettell, C. B. and Hollifield, J. (Eds.) (2000) *Migration Theory: Talking Across Disciplines*. London: Routledge.

Lawson, V. A. (2000) Arguments within geographies of movement: the theoretical potential of migrants' stories, *Progress in Human Geography*, 24(2): 173–189.

Massey, D. S., Arango, J., Hugo, G., Kouaouci, A., Pellegrino, A., and Taylor, J. E. (1993) Theories of international migration: a review and appraisal, *Population and Development Review*, 19(3): 431–466.

Smith, D. Finney, N., Halfacree, K., and Walford, N. (2015) *Internal Migration*. Farnham, UK: Ashgate.

Vaiou, D. (2012) Gendered mobilities and border-crossings: from Elbasan to Athens, *Gender, Place, and Culture*, 19: 249–262.

White, P. and Jackson, P. (1995) (Re)theorising population geography, *International Journal of Population Geography*, 1(2): 111–123.

References

Al Jazeera (2013a) Israel approves detention without charges for African migrants (10 December 2013). Retrieved from http://america.aljazeera.com/articles/2013/12/10/israel-approves-detentionwithoutchargesforafricanmigrants.html (accessed 9 September 2014).

Al Jazeera (2013b) Ethiopian migrant killed in Saudi crackdown (6 November 2013). Retrieved from http://www.aljazeera.com/news/middleeast/2013/11/ethiopian-migrant-killed-saudi-crackdown-2013116182628828345.html (accessed 9 September 2014).

Al Jazeera (2014) Migrant dies in Saudi detention centre riot (3 March 2014). Retrieved from http://www.aljazeera.com/news/middleeast/2014/03/migrant-dies-saudi-detention-centre-riot-201433135930166393.html (accessed 9 September 2014).

Anderson, B. and Ruhs, M. (2010) Guest editorial: researching illegality and labour migration, *Population, Space and Place*, 16(3): 175–179.

Andreas, P. (2000) *Border Games: Policing the US–Mexico Divide*. Ithaca, NY: Cornell University Press.

Bach, R. L. and Schrami, L. A. (1982) Migration,

www.rita.dot.gov/bts/data_and_statistics/by_subject/passenger.html (accessed 1 September 2014).

United States Census (2010) American fact finder (online database). Retrieved from http://factfinder2.census.gov/faces/nav/jsf/pages/index.xhtml (accessed 1 September 2014).

United States Office of Travel and Tourism Industries (2014) 2014 U.S. Travel and Tourism statistics. Retrieved from at http://travel.trade.gov/ (accessed 9 September 2014).

Vertovec, S. (2007) Super-diversity and its implications, *Ethnic and Racial Studies*, 30(6): 1024–1054.

Walker, I. (2013) Saudi Arabia and its immigrants, The COMPAS Blog (1 August 2013). Retrieved from http://compasoxfordblog.co.uk/2013/08/saudi-arabia-and-its-immigrants/ (accessed 9 September 2014).

Willekens, F. (1980) Entropy, multiproportional adjustment, and the analysis of contingency tables, *Sistemi Urbani*, 2: 171–201.

Willekens, F., Pór, A., and Raquillet, R. (1981) Entropy, multiproportional, and quadratic techniques for inferring detailed migration patterns from aggregate data. Mathematical theories, algorithms, applications, and computer programs, *IIASA Reports*, 4: 83–124.

Wilson, H. F. (2014) Multicultural learning: parent encounters with difference in a Birmingham primary school, *Transactions of the Institute of British Geographers*, 39(1): 102–114.

Wimmer, A. and Glick Schiller, N. (2002) Methodological nationalism and beyond: nation-state building, migration, and the social sciences, *Global Networks*, 2(4): 301–334.

World Bank (2011a) *Migration and Remittances Factbook* (2nd edition). Washington, DC: The International Bank for Reconstruction and Development/World Bank (p. 1). Retrieved from http://www.worldbank.org/prospects/migrationandremittances (accessed 10 September 2014).

World Bank (2011b) *Migration and Remittances Factbook* (summary). Retrieved from http://siteresources.worldbank.org/INTPROSPECTS/Resources/334934-1199807908806/Top10.pdf (accessed 10 September 2014).

Yacobi, H. (2008) Irregular migration to Israel: the sociopolitical perspective, European University Institute, CARIM analytic and synthetic notes (2008/63), Irregular Migration Series. Retrieved from http://cadmus.eui.eu/bitstream/handle/1814/10108/CARIM_AS%26N_2008_63.pdf?sequence=1 (accessed 14 September 2014).

Zolberg, A. (1989) The next waves: migration theory for a changing world, *International Migration Review*, 23(3): 403–430.

2

Global migration in historical perspective

Introduction

This chapter presents a broad overview of major historical migrations and provides context for later thematic chapters on immigrant labour markets, immigration policy, and integration. Migrations have been part of the human experience for millennia, but we focus here on migrations connected to the formation of a European-centred world economy and the modern interstate system starting in the 16th century. We pay particular attention to the transformation to capitalist modes of production—a transformation that unfolded over centuries and that involved the commodification of rural production, industrialization, urbanization, and imperial expansion. These processes had profound effects both on European societies and on the non-European societies that were incorporated in a subordinate position within the capitalist world economy. The emergence of a European-centred world economy set into motion massive interregional and transoceanic migrations that varied significantly in terms of the level of coercion involved. These historical migration patterns—where and why they started and how they shifted over time and space—provide a point of comparison and contrast with contemporary migration flows in our increasingly interdependent global economy.

This account highlights macro-level processes of labour supply and demand in driving migration flows. Yet it also emphasizes that such processes operate in complex social and political contexts marked by profound disparities in the power that individuals and groups exercise over their own lives and the terms of their labour. Understanding the specificities of migration flows—who moves and who doesn't move, where they go and why—requires that we consider the ways in which racialized and gendered social ideologies and power relationships permeate everything from labour recruitment to industrial divisions of labour to individual migrants' decisions to migrate. This account also highlights the interconnected nature of migrations. Scholars have long commented on **stepwise** patterns of migration—that is, the tendency for many migrants to engage in more localized migrations and rural-to-urban migrations before embarking on longer-distance and international migrations (Ravenstein, 1885; Thomas, 1972; Keown, 1971). As we will see, not all migrations follow a neat stepwise trajectory. But the idea of stepwise migration draws our attention to the close relationship between internal and international migrations and the simultaneity of different kinds of migration.

Migration and the emergence of a European-centred world economy

While it is difficult to put an exact date on the emergence of 'modernity', many scholars see the 16th and 17th centuries as a time of major transformations associated with the development of capitalist economies, urbanized societies, and the interstate system (Wallerstein, 1979). Prior to the modern period, the political geography of Europe was highly fragmented, with thousands of realms controlled by feudal lords in a complex system of overlapping allegiances and territorial sovereignty. Feudal Europe was overwhelmingly rural, with a large peasantry tied to relatively self-sufficient landed estates controlled by the landed elite. Important transformations, however, would gradually undermine the feudal system. Of primary importance was the expansion of Mediterranean trade and the development of new trade networks in Northern Europe, which encouraged both territorial consolidation (necessary for the movement of goods) and the growth of cities, most of them chartered by feudal rulers eager for new revenues (Pounds, 2005). The growing importance of trade and cities, in turn, encouraged the expansion of commercialized agriculture as landholders sought to supply new urban markets with food and non-food crops, including flax (for linen), wool, and dyes. This mediaeval commercial economy spurred inter-regional migration flows of seasonal workers, who were increasingly reliant on wages for survival. Many scholars have noted the surprising levels of labour mobility during the mediaeval period—most of it over relatively short distances—that run contrary to assumptions of static pre-industrial societies (Whyte, 2000).

While it took centuries for feudalistic relationships to disappear in Europe, the fragmented feudal political geography gradually gave way, through warfare and conquest, to a more consolidated territorial system of kingdoms, seen especially in Spain, Portugal, England, France, Sweden, Denmark, and Poland. An array of European power rivalries, religious conflicts, and crises of royal succession led to almost non-stop continental warfare for much of the late 16th and early 17th centuries. Exhausted from decades of conflict, Europe's major powers sought to define the terms of state sovereignty with

the Peace of Westphalia in 1648. The Peace of Westphalia did not put an end to warfare and instability in Europe; nor did it spell the demise of existing political-territorial concepts and systems (Croxton, 1999). But the peace negotiations that took place in Westphalia were instrumental in the creation, over the long term, of a new political order in which individual territorial states had the authority (in theory, if not in practice) to conduct their own internal and external affairs free from interference. As we discuss in Chapter 6, the interstate system forged with the Peace of Westphalia would become central to the regulation of populations and to the production of sharp distinctions between 'citizens' and 'foreigners'.

The competition between territorial states was intense, and it spurred European powers to seek new sources of wealth overseas (especially precious metals) and control over lucrative trade routes for spices and other luxury goods. Portugal was one of the first European powers to begin transoceanic exploration, making its way down the coast of West Africa in the late 15th century and eventually to the Arabian Peninsula, the west coast of India, and Southeast Asia. Spain, meanwhile, sailed westward in the hope of finding an easier route to China, but instead 'discovered' the Western Hemisphere. The Spanish Crown's territorial ambitions in the Americas were soon checked by Portugal, which gained control over Brazil; the Netherlands, which set up imperial outposts in the Caribbean and the northern coast of South America; and England and France, which established colonies in North America and the Caribbean.

European migrations from Europe to the 'New World' were initially quite small. Among the European settlers in Spanish America were imperial administrators, soldiers, missionaries, hidalgos (members of the gentry and lower nobility), as well as artisans, craftsmen, traders, and entrepreneurs (Sánchez-Albornoz, 1984). Through the middle of the 17th century, fewer than 500,000 Spaniards had made the voyage and settled in the Americas (Gibson, 1966). Likewise, a mere 70,000 Portuguese had settled in Brazil by 1700 (Burns, 1980). Emigration to the English and French colonies in the Americas was similarly small in scale in the early centuries of European exploration and empire-building. In 1700, the total British population in the Americas was only 257,000 (Hofstadter, 1973). The small numbers of European settlers reflected the high cost and danger of the passage over the Atlantic, not to mention the tribulations that settlers faced when they arrived in the Americas (including rampant malaria and yellow fever). There was, as well, some reluctance among European rulers to release labour to the colonies stemming from the mercantilist mindset, which viewed population as a form of wealth to be retained for the benefit of the crown. Eventually, though, colonial administrators used various incentives to increase settlement, which was deemed necessary to maintain control over territory and to exploit resources. The colonial bureaucracy in Lisbon, for instance, urged greater immigration to Brazil of married Portuguese couples, giving small land grants and supplies to settlers. Slowly, European settlement gained momentum in the context of important transformations taking place in Europe itself.

Migration and socioeconomic change in early modern Europe

While imperial armies were wresting control over far-flung territories, major social, political, and economic changes were taking place in Europe itself. The development of a commercial economy, which had begun in Europe during the Middle Ages, continued apace in the 16th and 17th centuries. The ongoing consolidation of landholdings, the expansion of commercial agriculture to meet demands both for foodstuffs and non-food crops, and the conversion of more land to sheep pasturage caused many peasants to face an increasingly marginal existence. From the

17th century onward, landowners were increasingly inclined to enclose their properties, thus eliminating access to what had traditionally been commons, while squeezing tenants with high rents (Moch, 1992). The breakdown of feudalistic relationships and economic pressures in the countryside were aggravated by continued population growth, especially after 1700, when the European population climbed from 81 million to 123 million in one century. Scholars cite a number of interrelated reasons for European population growth in this period, including the introduction of New World crops, relative peace, the lower prevalence of plague and disease, and younger marriage (Langer, 1975; Livi-Bacchi, 1991).

Facing immense economic insecurity and the inability to subsist on the land, rural families engaged in multiple income- and wage-generating strategies—a process called **proletarianization**. Such strategies often required one or more family members to migrate. Some participated in seasonal agricultural migration flows, which included work digging ditches, logging, and building and improving canals; others (both young men and women) moved to neighbouring villages to work as servants in the homes and farms of wealthy landowners. Other country folk sent their sons into towns and cities to take up apprenticeships, or, more commonly, to work as labourers or, in the case of girls, as servants. Port cities and capitals like London and Paris, which had attracted many migrants in the mediaeval period, grew rapidly, as did many smaller provincial cities, though rural areas continued to support the vast majority of Europeans into the 19th century (see Figure 2.1) (Moch, 1992).

Many of the rural poor also found employment in **cottage industries** (also called 'proto-industries'), including spinning and dying yarns, weaving and garment production, metalworking, and uniforms and armaments for standing armies (see Ogilvie and Cerman, 1996). These cottage industries were, as the name suggests,

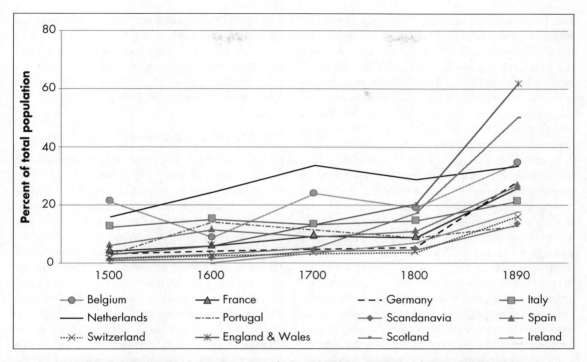

Figure 2.1 Urbanization ratios in Europe, population in cities 10,000 and over, 1500–1890

Source: (a) de Vries, J. (1984) European Urbanization, 1500–1800. London: Methuen (pp. 30, 36, 46). (b) United Nations Department of Economic and Social Affairs, Population Division (2004) World Urbanization Prospects, The 2003 Revision. New York: United Nations (pp. 111–128)

situated in the cottages of landless peasants and tenant farmers. Small-scale industrial production, along with larger, water-powered textile mills, which were introduced in the late 18th century, employed hundreds of thousands of workers—including many young women—across Europe and caused some rural areas to become quite thickly populated by in-migrants. It is important here to appreciate the complexity of migrations in this context. While migration scholars commonly speak of urban-to-rural migration, many households at this time were engaged in multiple forms of income generation that required frequent movement of household members between rural and urban economies.

Migration and the colonial economy

The American colonies, as well, began to absorb growing numbers of Europeans after about 1700, reflecting lower costs of transportation and efforts by colonial bureaucracies to attract settlers in order to boost the production of key agricultural commodities. The Portuguese, for instance, encouraged the migration of Italian-speaking migrants from the Madeira Islands, renowned for their expertise in sugar cultivation, which had become Brazil's primary commodity (Burns, 1980). The discovery of gold in the Brazilian interior in the late 1600s brought even more Europeans, and the European population of Brazil increased tenfold in the 18th century. Even more substantial growth of European populations took place in Britain's North American and Caribbean colonies, which were booming with the production of tobacco, rice, indigo, and sugar. The population in the American colonies reached over 1.2 million by 1750 and doubled again 20 years later. Much of the population growth in the British colonies was fuelled by migration of Ulster Scots, Irish, Germans, Swiss, and Dutch, as well as English men and women, eager for land and opportunity.

Many of the migrants to the British colonies—probably more than half—arrived not as independent workers but as bonded, or indentured, servants. **Indentured servitude** grew out of existing systems of fixed-term contract labour, including apprenticeships, that were widely used in England in the 1500s. The system of indentured servitude involved the combined workings of merchants, ship captains, and labour recruiters, who fanned out through Europe—especially the German principalities and Holland—to entice workers. The trans-Atlantic passages of indentured servants would be paid by an agent or a potential employer; the indentured worker would then repay the cost through his or her labour for a fixed number of years, usually four to seven. Alternatively, the contract of indenture would be held by the ship's captain, who would then sell or auction the indentured worker to employers upon arrival in the Americas (Hofstadter, 1973; Whyte, 2000).

Indentured workers were predominantly men who laboured on plantations. But there were also many women working primarily as domestic servants. Terms of service for both men and women could be harsh, and indentured workers could be penalized with lashings and lengthened periods of service for withholding labour or running away from an employer. Indentured servants could also be sold on to other employers for the duration of their terms. At the end of their service, indentured workers would receive a parting payment—or 'freedom dues'—which varied from colony to colony. This might include a small piece of land, some cash, or a new suit of clothes. But there is little evidence that indentured servants enjoyed a great deal of mobility

at the end of their contract period (for a detailed discussion, see Bade, 2003, 82–92). Still, indentured servants did enjoy some legal protections and traditional freedoms, which set them apart from the slave labour that came to dominate the colonial economy in the 18th century.

Slavery and plantation agriculture

While numbers of European migrants increased steadily through the 18th century, they could never satisfy the immense demand for labour in colonial economies based on plantation agriculture and resource extraction. Increasingly, therefore, Europeans turned to involuntary forms of labour. In Spanish and Portuguese America, colonists had instituted various means of coercing labour from native populations, including the semi-feudal *encomienda* and *mita* systems in the Spanish colonies and widespread practices of capture and enslavement in Brazil (Burns, 1980). English colonists in North America also enslaved Indians (see Mann, 2011). Native populations, however, plummeted due to a combination of diseases brought by European settlers and the social and physical effects of conquest and labour coercion (Sánchez-Albornoz, 1984). In the Spanish colonies, in particular, the scale of population decline was staggering: from a population of perhaps 50 million *indios* just prior to European contact, the native population declined to about four million by the 1600s (Hofstadter, 1973). In Central Mexico alone, the native population plummeted from about 25 million to scarcely 750,000 by 1630. Native populations in the Caribbean were all but eradicated. With the diminishment of native populations, the Spanish and Portuguese soon turned to the African slave trade, and the British, French, and Dutch colonies followed suit.

The Portuguese had established the European slave trade in the 1400s and continued to dominate the trade into the 1600s. Thereafter, other European powers—the Dutch, the French, and especially the British—displaced the Portuguese.

Merchant vessels engaged in a highly lucrative trade involving the exchange of European manufactured goods, American agricultural commodities, and African human cargo across the Atlantic. While colonial administrators and Christian missionaries, especially in Latin America, had offered a degree of 'protection', at least on paper, to Indians (especially as their numbers began to plummet), there appeared to be no such compunction towards Africans. Seemingly cursed with black skin, Africans were deemed by virtually all European colonizers to be created for permanent bondage (Jordan, 1968). The slave trade was sanctioned, and even encouraged, by European states eager for a share of the massive revenues. Usefully for Europeans, Africans had higher immunity to many of the tropical diseases that ravaged the colonies, and were thus more economical than white indentured servants. By the mid-1700s, African slaves were the largest group of migrants in many colonies.

Most sources estimate that 10–20 million people were forcibly removed from Africa during the colonial period. One of the biggest recipients of slaves was Brazil, which received an estimated 3.5 million Africans from 1550 to 1850. Throughout this period, slaves were the primary workforce on sugar, tobacco, cotton, and coffee plantations, as well as in the mines. Blacks significantly outnumbered whites in Brazil, and of the 3.5 million inhabitants of Brazil in 1818, only slightly more than a million could be classified as white, while two million were black and about half a million of mixed race (Burns, 1980). The Caribbean islands belonging to the Spanish, Dutch, French, and British were the other major recipient of slaves, receiving about 40 percent of slaves imported into the Americas. According to the renowned German geographer Alexander von Humboldt, 375,000 slaves entered the port of Havana in Cuba in a span of just thirty years, from 1790 to 1820 (Meagher, 2008, 41). As in Brazil, whites on many Caribbean sugar-producing islands by the mid-1700s were vastly outnumbered by black slaves, creating substantial anxiety about slave revolts. In relative terms, Britain's 13 North American colonies were on the fringes of the slave trade, receiving less than 5 percent of all slaves brought to the Western Hemisphere during the colonial period (Hofstadter, 1973). Still, African slaves constituted the largest stream of immigration into the American colonies in the mid-1700s, and between 1700 and 1770, the black portion of the colonial population, concentrated in the South, doubled to almost 22 percent (ibid.).

A smaller but still important source of involuntary labour were convicts—spared the death sentence but then forced to go overseas and to work in virtual slave-like conditions. Whyte (2000) suggests that while some of these were violent offenders, many of them were petty criminals, guilty of little more than stealing food. These were brought to work in the American colonies, as well as to Australia, which Britain began to settle in the 18th century.

The end of the slave trade and the re-emergence of indentured servitude

The European colonial project, then, hinged on commodity production, and this commodity production relied heavily on slave labour. Slavery endured well into the 19th century—not ending in the United States until 1865 (following a devastating Civil War largely fought over the right for Southern planters to own slaves) and in Brazil until 1888. But the slave trade, and eventually slavery itself, did come to an end, forcing planters to find new sources of labour. In many contexts, plantation owners kept freed slaves under virtual slave-like conditions (as in the American South), and thus needed to look no further to find workers; others found ways of impressing indigenous people, whose numbers had recovered through the 19th century, into labour, as seen with 'debt peonage' systems that emerged on the henequen plantations of Mexico (Alston, Mattiace, and Nonnenmacher, 2009).

Still others found more distant sources of 'free labour', creating new transoceanic labour flows. Such was the case of planters in the vast British Empire.

With the abolition of slavery in the British Empire in 1833, British planters began to look for potential sources of labour within the Empire. India, which had a large and increasingly landless population of peasants, soon became a major supplier of indentured workers, usually referred to as **coolies** (a derogatory term believed to derive from the Hindi word for hired labour). The coolie system began with the transport of workers from the Indian region of Bengal to the island of Mauritius, a British possession in the Indian Ocean that had become an important sugar producer. Shortly thereafter, a shipload of Bengali workers was transported to British Guiana to replace manumitted slaves (Kale, 1998). It is important to note that planters viewed Indian workers as an alternative to former slaves, reasoning that freed black workers would no longer feel compulsion to toil under white masters (and, in fact, many former slaves balked at working on plantations under the conditions offered by plantation owners, and, where land was available, they cultivated their own plots of land—see Meagher, 2008). Certainly the presence of Indian coolies served to discipline black workers and to diminish any power they might exercise over the terms of labour. The coolie system from the start was highly controversial, with many arguing that the recruitment of poor, illiterate peasants—many of whom could not understand the terms of labour contracts or the nature of the work they had agreed to perform—was no better than slavery. Such workers, it seemed, occupied an uneasy position between slave and wage labourer, bound to plantations by severe penal sanctions and indebtedness and unable to seek better wages and working conditions elsewhere (Kelly, 1992). Proponents of coolie labour, however, responded that the system gave otherwise impoverished Indians the opportunity for wages, housing, and medical care (Kale, 1998).

In spite of the debates that raged for decades about the morality of indentured labour, the system took hold in British possessions throughout the Caribbean and the Indian Ocean, as well as in East and South Africa and Fiji. Between 1837 and 1917, approximately 1.5 million Indians migrated as indentured servants within the British Empire. While indentured servants had fixed-term (usually five-year) contracts, many of them—perhaps two-thirds—stayed on in the colonies at the end of their contracts, creating sizable Indian communities in places like Uganda, Kenya, South Africa, and Trinidad and Tobago. The majority of those recruited into indentured servitude were men, but labour recruiters made a concerted effort through the 19th century to increase the proportion of women, with the understanding that labourers would be more willing to stay on if they could establish a family in the colonies. A further seven million Indians participated in short-term and seasonal contract labour flows to plantations in Burma, Ceylon, and Malaya; most of these returned to India (Clarke, Peach, and Vertovec, 1990).

Coolie labour was not limited to the British Empire or to workers from India. The increasing pressure placed on the transatlantic slave trade by the British navy in the 1840s encouraged the development of a brisk trade in Chinese indentured workers. Chinese workers—overwhelmingly young men—were escaping severe economic pressures and political strife in China caused partly by high population growth and famines, the latter a result of changing agricultural practices (Mann, 2011). Despite a long history of Chinese settlement in Southeast Asia, the Chinese government was reluctant to sanction emigration. But growing labour demands in South America, North America, the Caribbean, and Australia, along with a well-established pattern of smuggling in which local officials were usually complicit, ensured that emigration would take place, with or without official sanction (the Chinese government did eventually lift restrictions). The emigration industry was led by

Chinese 'crimpers', who recruited workers—usually through various forms of deceit—for Western labour brokers operating in Western-dominated ports like Macau and Hong Kong; workers were then transported by Peruvian, British, French, and American vessels to various destinations. Between 1847 and 1874, upwards of 250,000 Chinese workers were brought to South America, where they toiled in very difficult conditions on sugar plantations in Cuba and Brazil and in the guano mines off the coast of Peru. At least 550,000 went to California, British Columbia, and Australia, where they worked building railroads and in mines (Meagher, 2008). As we will see in Chapter 6, their presence in North America and Australia sparked a strong reaction among white workers, who accused the Chinese of undercutting wages, and led to some of the earliest formal restrictions on immigration.

nies contributed to the phenomenal expansion of industrialization. Britain led industrialization in Europe—both in manufacturing and in steel production—but was soon joined by France, Belgium, Switzerland, and its main 19th-century rival, Germany, which became a unified state in 1871. While rural industry persisted in many parts of Europe through the 19th century, manufacturing was an increasingly urban-based process that gave rise to major urban-industrial clusters in the British Midlands, northwest France, the Rhine-Ruhr region in western Germany, Upper Silesia (an historically Polish region that was controlled by Prussia and then Germany from the mid-1700s onward), and the Po River Valley in northern Italy. By the early 20th century, industrialization and urbanization had affected all parts of Europe to a greater or lesser degree.

The dwindling of cottage industries and the intensification of commercial agriculture in the

Migration and the Industrial Revolution

By the 19th century a complex and geographically extensive system of labour mobility—encompassing Europe, the Americas, Asia, and Africa—had emerged, closely tied to the development of a modern, European-centred, globally integrated commercial economy. We turn back now to Europe to highlight the mass migration flows that were taking shape in the latter half of the 19th century as industrialization gained momentum. Manufacturing, as we described earlier, had been an important part of European economies even during the Middle Ages. During the early modern period, the expansion of rural and semi-rural cottage industries and water-powered textile mills generated important intraregional and rural–urban migration flows. In the late 18th and 19th centuries, technological innovations, improved transportation via canals and later by railways, and growing markets for inexpensive manufactured goods in cities and in the colo-

Plate 2.1 Chinese labourers helping to build the railroads in the USA

Source: © Underwood & Underwood/Underwood & Underwood/Corbis

countryside induced further proletarianization and labour mobility within Europe—first in western Europe and then in eastern and southern Europe. So, too, did continued population growth (see Figure 2.2). Relatively short-distance rural–urban migrations and local seasonal agricultural migrations remained common well into the 19th century, but workers were increasingly drawn farther afield in the search for wage income. Their movement was facilitated by railways, which drastically reduced the costs of travel. Indeed, the railways, as Bade (2003) notes, generated a remarkable set of symbiotic relationships: railroad construction both transported workers and created numerous jobs for migrant workers; moreover, by expanding and integrating markets across Europe, the railways spurred industrial production, which led to additional demands for workers. In general, workers flowed between more peripheral, low-waged areas into areas with labour shortages and higher wages. Importantly, many of these mobile workers were crossing what were now

modern nation-state boundaries, monitored and controlled by bureaucrats, albeit minimally for most of the 19th century.

There were several notable migration flows taking place during this period. One was the migration of Poles to the industrial cities of eastern Germany, which experienced labour shortages as Germans moved farther west to the heavily industrialized Ruhrgebiet (see Box 2.1). Italy, which became a unified nation-state in the 1850s, was also a major source of immigrants. Between 1876 and 1920, there were around a million Italians migrating within Europe, most of them involved in construction and road building. France was the main destination for Italian workers in Europe, and their numbers more than quintupled between 1881 to 1911, from 77,000 to 419,000 (Bade, 2003, 54). In France, immigrant workers (Italians, Poles, and others) were heavily represented not only in construction, but also in metalworking, chemical manufacturing, beet-sugar factories, and textiles. Switzerland also became an important recipient of immigrant

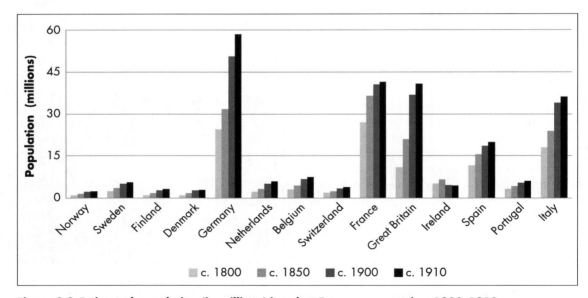

Figure 2.2 Estimated population (in millions) in select European countries, 1800–1910

Source: Moch, L. P. (1992) Moving Europeans: Migration in Western Europe since 1650. Indianapolis: Indiana University Press, (p. 109)

Table 2.1 Estimated population in select European cities, 1800, 1850, 1900

City	1800	1850	1900	% change 1800–1900
Amsterdam	201,000	224,000	515,000	156%
Barcelona	115,000	175,000	533,000	363%
Berlin	172,000	419,000	1,889,000	998%
Copenhagen	101,000	127,000	401,000	297%
Glasgow	77,000	357,000	1,052,000	1266%
London	1,117,000	2,685,000	7,488,000	570%
Stockholm	76,000	131,000	301,000	296%
Turin	247,000	444,000	1,675,000	578%
Vienna	247,000	444,000	1,675,000	578%
Warsaw	60,000	114,000	423,000	605%

Source: Pearson, R. (1994) *The Longman Companion to European Nationalism, 1780–1920*. London; New York: Longman (p. 240).

workers in the late 19th century. With a small existing population, Switzerland soon came to rely on migrant workers more than any other country in Europe. In 1910, 15 percent of the Swiss population was foreign (compared with only 2.7 percent in France and 1.7 percent in Germany), and almost 17 percent of the Swiss labour force came from abroad, mostly from southern Germany and Northern Italy (Bade, 2003; Gabaccia, 2000). A final notable flow took place between Ireland and Britain. Ireland at this time was essentially a British colony with a small English elite owning approximately 80 percent of the land and stifling local markets and production. The impoverished Irish population became an important source of inexpensive surplus labour, and numbers of Irish workers in British industrial cities swelled with the Irish potato famine of the 1840s. By the mid-19th century, over 700,000 Irish men and women were living in Britain (Williamson, 1986). In all cases, urban and industrial migrants, along with coal miners, were overwhelmingly male, but there were important streams of female workers, as well, who found work as domestic servants or as textile workers. Cities grew expo-

nentially through the 19th century partly as a result of these migrations, and Europe increasingly became a collection of urbanized societies (see Table 2.1).

During this period of urbanization and industrialization, agriculture continued to be an important economic sector. New commodity crops—especially root vegetables like potatoes and sugar beets—intensified the demand for seasonal workers, and over time, more localized seasonal labour markets were replaced by newer, long-distance and often international seasonal migration streams. As with industrial and construction sectors, agricultural work in northwestern Europe drew workers from Europe's periphery, particularly Polish-speaking regions and Italy. Importantly, around half of these workers were women and girls, and some sectors were dominated by women. These workers were often paid **piece rates**, a highly exploitative practice that compensated workers for the quantity of items picked rather than by time worked. The availability of these workers in many cases substituted for labour-saving but costly machinery, making agricultural production profitable, if only minimally (Bade, 2003).

BOX 2.1 POLISH WORKERS IN THE GERMAN EMPIRE (1871–1918)

The case of German labour recruitment in the late 19th and early 20th centuries illustrates well a number of themes that we will encounter throughout this book: the tension between economic interests and state interests in the recruitment of labour; the role of the state in producing distinctions between 'foreign' and 'native' workers; and the use of border controls and immigration policies to maintain and to enforce such distinctions. While Germany was primarily a sender of immigrants well into the 1890s, eastern parts of the German Empire (notably eastern Prussia) began to import Polish workers from Russia and Austria in the 1870s to work primarily in the agricultural sector. Poland did not exist as an independent state at this time; rather, historically, Polish lands had been partitioned and annexed by regional powers (an independent Poland would be reconstituted after World War I). As Esser and Korte (1985) describe, Germany's recruitment of Poles from Austria and Russia soon came into conflict with its policies of Germanization in its own Polish territories. Fearing that 'foreign' Poles would stoke nationalist sentiment among German Poles, the German state decided to close its borders and to expel foreign Polish workers. This move was adamantly opposed by German landowners and industrialists, who forced a compromise with the German state. This compromise reopened the country to Polish migration, but it created the *karenzzeit*, or waiting period, in which foreign Poles were required to leave Germany to prevent them from taking up permanent residence within Germany's borders. It also barred foreign Poles from working in the industrialized Ruhr region of western Germany. Restrictions on foreign Poles in the west worked to the advantage of German Poles, who eventually constituted a third of the labour force in the Ruhr region. German Poles, however, continued to be subject to aggressive Germanization efforts, including restrictions on the hiring of non-German-speaking citizens.

It is important to recognize that migration patterns in Europe were not necessarily stable, either at a collective level or an individual level. Among individuals, migration practices could change from year to year as work options disappeared and new ones emerged. At a collective level, migrant workers moved in and out of sectors and geographical regions. Agricultural workers, in particular, formed a large itinerant workforce, with many of them taking off-season jobs in industry or in construction. One thing that was relatively constant was the inferior treatment of unskilled migrant workers. Whether in agriculture, industry, or construction work, foreign workers generally took jobs (or were given jobs) that were less desirable for native workers. The stratification of workers allowed employers to maintain a degree of flexibility at a time when native workers were agitating for higher pay and workplace rights, allowing employers to shed some workers easily when circumstances required. The theme of a two-tiered labour market of native and foreign workers has been an enduring theme in migration studies (e.g. Piore, 1979), and one we examine further in Chapter 3.

Mass migration to the industrializing New World

Growing income insecurity in rural economies encouraged many migrants to leave Europe altogether. Just as innovations in transportation facilitated mass flows of labour migrants *within* Europe, so too did they facilitate mass flows of labour across the oceans. Prior to about 1840, ocean travel was dangerous and expensive, discouraging free labour migration and encouraging practices of indentured servitude and slavery. Indeed, for the first 350 years of European colonization of the New World, the

Plate 2.2 Landing at Ellis Island, 1902

Source: Library of Congress (LC-USZ62-12595)

forced migration of Africans far outpaced the voluntary migration of Europeans. It was not until the 1840s that annual migration of white Europeans to the Americas exceeded African forced migration, and it was not until the 1880s that cumulative European migration exceeded that of African forced migration (which had reached about eight million by 1820) (O'Rourke and Williamson, 1999). The advent of the steamship did not cause the shift to European labour, but it enabled the shift to take place by greatly diminishing the cost of travel and reducing the travel time between major European ports and New York from six weeks in the age of sailing to one week after 1900. As overseas labour demands increased, a greater percentage of European workers made the ocean passage. From around 1850 to 1880, the annual migration of Europeans to the Americas averaged about 300,000. This figure more than doubled between 1880 and 1900, and approached or exceeded one million per year thereafter. According to most estimates, around 50 million Europeans arrived in the Americas between 1820 and 1920, and most of these after 1860 (ibid.).

Over half of these European migrants were destined for the United States, which had emerged in the late 19th century as a major industrial power. Chronic labour shortages in the US had generated high wages relative to what was available in Europe, attracting young Europeans. Some of these migrants came to acquire land for farming, but the vast majority entered the industrial sector. The majority (about 64 percent) of migrants between 1851 and 1913 were men, but sex ratios varied from group to group, and many migrants arrived as families. Most migrant workers were unskilled, and migrant cohorts became less and less skilled as the 19th century progressed, reflecting the increasingly rural origins of migrants and the shift in migrant origins from north-western Europe (Britain, Germany, and Sweden) to the European periphery, namely, Poland and southern Italy (Ireland was also a major source from the 1840s onward) (O'Rourke and Williamson, 1999). Overall, about 14 percent of the population in the United States was foreign-born on the eve of World War I.

As the 19th century drew to a close, a growing proportion of European émigrés chose destinations other than the United States. After 1900, for instance, the majority of British migrants went to Canada, Australia, and New Zealand rather than to the United States. Many British migrants, as well, settled in Britain's white-settler colonies in Africa, most notably South Africa and Southern Rhodesia (present-day Zimbabwe). Approximately 75,000 whites had settled in Southern Rhodesia by the 1920s—a number that would swell to more than a quarter million after World War II. The white population of South Africa was even larger, owing to a long history of Dutch and British colonization, surpassing one million by the turn of the century (Tinker, 1995). As in Southern Rhodesia, the white European population in South Africa would continue to grow well into the 20th century. White settlement was also a salient feature of French colonization of North Africa, which began with the seizure of Algiers in 1830. About 170,000 Europeans (including not only French but also Spanish, Italian, Maltese, and Swiss settlers) were residing in Algeria by the mid-19th century. These numbers increased rapidly in the late 19th century, with the European population— including immigrants and those of European origin born in Algeria—reaching 412,000 in 1882, 630,000 in 1900, and close to a million by 1936. Additionally, hundreds of thousands of European settlers—French, Spanish, and Italian, among others—resided in the French protectorates of Tunisia and Morocco by the early 20th century (Heffernan, 1995). With the collapse of European empires in the three decades after World War II, millions of European colonists would abandon, flee, or be expelled from newly independent states in Africa and Asia. Among these 'returnees' would be almost the entirety of Algeria's European settler population, who came to be known as *pieds noirs*. Widely blamed for instigating and prolonging Algeria's war for independence, the *pieds noirs* faced a difficult 'reintegration' into the metropole (Shepard, 2008).

During this same period, large numbers of Italian, Spanish, and Portuguese migrants were destined for Brazil and Argentina. South American economies had experienced rapid growth in the late 19th century with the expansion of labour-intensive export commodities, particularly Brazilian coffee and Argentinean beef and wool. Commodity revenues spurred industrial growth, which, in turn, raised wages and attracted even more immigrants. For a time, real wages in Argentina exceeded those of Britain, and the 'Southern Cone' of Latin America had a large wage advantage over many parts of Southern Europe. Liberal elites in Argentina and Brazil were eager to entice these European immigrants who would settle their vast territories and bring a measure of 'European civilization' to them, though they failed to attract much-coveted Northern Europeans (Moya, 1998). Between 1840 and 1932, Argentina admitted around 6.5 million European migrants, while Brazil admitted around four million. In addition, about 1.4 million European migrants went to Cuba between 1880 and 1932 (ibid.; Bade, 2003).

The declining cost of travel allowed many migrants in the 19th and early 20th centuries to return to homelands from overseas. While some groups, like the Irish, Russians, and Scandinavians, rarely returned to places of origin, Italians did in great numbers. Some estimate that 40–50 percent of those who left Italy eventually returned, and many sojourned between Italy and the Americas, earning them the name *golondrinas*, or swallows (Gabaccia, 2000). Whether or not they eventually returned, migrants sustained important links with homelands in the form of monetary remittances and in the form of letters that conveyed information about destination countries. Migrants commonly financed the ocean passages of family members and friends in Europe, contributing to patterns of **chain migration** that sustained migration flows even during times of economic hardship. Chain migration was abetted by shipping lines, which sent agents to rural villages to encourage emigration. These kinship connections and patterns of chain migration created very specific regional flows and contributed to the tendency for migrants to occupy particular economic niches, which we discuss in more detail in Chapter 3.

The beginning of the 20th century, in sum, featured a global migration system that encompassed Europe, the Americas, India, Africa, and the Asia-Pacific region. This migration system grew out of, and made possible, a globally integrated capitalist economy marked by liberal economic policies and the relatively free trade of commodities and manufactured goods. The migration of tens of millions of people, and the political and economic transformations that accompanied it, left an indelible mark on sending and receiving societies. Consider Ireland, which experienced the loss of millions of people to emigration during the 19th century. At a time when Europe's population was growing rapidly through natural increase, the population of Ireland declined from eight million in 1846 to only 4.5 million in 1901 (Bade, 2003, 105). By 1890, 40 percent of those born in Ireland were living elsewhere, mainly in the United States. Likewise, between 1860 and 1914, more than a third of the Polish population had migrated within Europe or had settled overseas, with more than two million emigrating permanently. Human mobility on this scale had enormous impacts on local, regional, and national politics, on rural and urban life, and on household and family relationships. Migration affected not only migrants themselves, but everyone in towns, cities, and countries that sent or received migrants. It contributed both to urban transformations and to rural transformations, including the depopulation of the European countryside and the re-ruralization of many villages that had once been centres of cottage industry (Moch, 1992). In receiving contexts—and especially in settler societies—migrations were central to national mythologies. But almost everywhere, as we will see in Chapter 7, migrations set into motion intense anxieties about societal change— the ability to cope with fewer people or to absorb newcomers, and the willingness of newcomers to change their foreign ways and to become more like 'us'. Such anxieties, combined with severe economic recession and looming wars, contributed to the dramatic contraction of global migration in the early 20th century.

Migration and the upheavals of the 20th century

The mass migrations of the mid- to late-19th century are remarkable for the absence of the state in directing, restricting, or controlling population movements across nation-state borders. The relative openness of labour migration systems came to an abrupt halt early in the 20th century, though there had been some important precedents to state control of immigration in the US, Canada, Germany, and Britain. The outbreak of war in 1914 meant the conscription of millions of young men into militaries, which caused migrant workers to retreat behind national lines. The economic depression between the First and Second World Wars brought out a strong impulse towards autarky, protectionism, and state intervention in the economies of the industrial core. Governments began to restrict and to manage flows of commodities, capital, and people, and they sought to cultivate national labour forces and 'national economies'. This impulse was punctuated by heightened concerns about ethno-national homogeneity and the racial composition of national societies. Yet warfare, economic policies, and racial ideologies, while disrupting labour flows, did not spell the end of population mobility; on the contrary, they precipitated massive population flows, some more voluntary than others.

In Europe, the war economy generated significant demands for workers in munitions factories, mining, and agriculture, and some countries— notably France—continued to turn to foreign workers to fill labour needs. During World War I France recruited labour largely from Southern Europe—Spain, Italy, Portugal, and Greece—

but, presaging post-war trends, also imported, on a temporary basis, tens of thousands of workers from its colonies in North Africa and Indochina. For its part, Germany relied on more forcible methods of securing an adequate labour force during World War I, forbidding Polish workers to leave Germany at the start of the war and making extensive use of prisoners of war (POWs) and occupied populations during the war to harvest crops and to perform other difficult and undesirable jobs. According to Bade (2003), two-thirds of the 2.5–3 million foreign workers in Germany at the end of World War I were POWs.

After World War I, France opened its borders to millions of foreign workers, though it required foreigners to hold a work permit and work contract, and it made increasing use of bilateral labour recruitment agreements with migrant-sending countries. It also excluded certain groups as 'unsuitable', including colonial workers, who had received a tepid reception during World War I (tens of thousands of Algerians nevertheless continued to enter the French labour force during the interwar period). Foreign labour, as in the past, tended to be confined to heavy and difficult work, which, in the post-war context, included clearing away war debris and filling in trenches, as well as mining, manufacturing, and construction. Overall, the immigrant population in France increased from around 1.5 million in 1921 to 2.7 million in 1931. Few countries, however, continued to import labour to the same degree as France (Verbunt, 1985). Certainly, the extensive migrant labour systems that had characterized pre-war Germany were significantly diminished (Esser and Korte, 1985).

Pre-war migration patterns were also disrupted by growing restrictions on immigration in the settler societies. In the US, the 1920s were a time of relative prosperity; nonetheless, the native-born American population was increasingly wary of immigrants, especially Jews and Catholics from Eastern and Southern Europe (tight restrictions on Chinese immigration were already in force in the US at this point). We

examine immigration restriction in greater detail in Chapter 6; suffice it to say here that a series of US laws in the early 1920s imposed severe, racially motivated, restrictive quotas on immigration from the Eastern Hemisphere that would not be lifted until the 1960s (King, 2000). After five decades in which immigration had averaged between 370,000 and 880,000 people *per year*, immigration declined to approximately 530,000 in the *entire decade* between 1931 and 1940; between 1941 and 1950, an average of only 100,000 immigrants per year entered the United States (ibid.). Similar patterns of racially motivated restrictions presented themselves in other settler societies. Both Canada and Australia, for instance, instituted 'white only' immigration policies in the early 1900s, restricting settlement to migrants from the British Isles and northwest Europe. As in the US, these policies were preceded by bars on Chinese immigration in the late 19th century (Ongley and Pearson, 1995).

In the case of the US, strong restrictionist measures did not put a complete stop to sizable labour migrations. Most notable was the movement of Mexicans across the US border to the rich agricultural valleys of the American West (Mexican migration, and other migrations from the Western Hemisphere, were exempted from national origins quotas). The US Border Patrol, formed in 1924 to enforce immigration restrictions, generally bowed to growers' demands for Mexican seasonal migrants, though periodic crackdowns and, indeed, the deportation of thousands of Mexicans and Mexican-Americans during the Great Depression indicated that Mexican workers would remain a vulnerable and exploitable group (Andreas, 2000; King, 2000). As well, tens of thousands of black immigrants from the Caribbean entered the United States through the mid-1930s, despite legislative efforts to impose restrictions on them.

If labour migration was relatively subdued after 1914, massive population movements relating to ethno-national conflict and ethnic 'unmixing' became disturbingly commonplace. The reorganization of Europe's map after World War I, and the power of nationalist ideologies that insisted on cultural unity and homogeneity, meant the expulsion of hundreds of thousands of people deemed unassimilable within new nation-state boundaries (Brubaker, 1995). These dynamics could be seen in the out-migration of hundreds of thousands of Germans from the newly reconstituted Polish state after World War I and from the provinces of Alsace and Lorraine, which had been ceded to France. Even larger were the compulsory population transfers between Greece and the new Turkish Republic, negotiated in 1923 in the wake of a successful Turkish counter-offensive against occupying Greek forces. Overall, an estimated 1.5 million Greeks and Turks were affected by these transfers (ibid.). The Russian Revolution, and later the civil war in Spain, generated millions of refugees, while German expansion into neighbouring European countries in the lead-up to the Second World War resulted in large-scale deportations and expulsions. Jews were an especially vulnerable group in the context of German expansionism. Some Jews in the interwar period managed to flee Europe, finding refuge in British-mandate Palestine and in the United States. But restrictions of immigration in the US and in Palestine meant that millions of Jews were doomed to perish.

The mass displacements of the 20th century reached their apogee with the Second World War, which displaced an estimated 40 million people and which created a refugee crisis in Europe that took years to solve. Among those displaced were 14 million ethnic Germans who were driven out of Czechoslovakia, Poland, Russia, and elsewhere following Germany's defeat (Bade, 2003). There were also millions of POWs and forced labourers all over Europe who required repatriation, and millions of others who, having fled Nazi invasions at the start of the war, refused to return to their home countries in the face of the Soviet advance into Eastern Europe. Some of these, as we will see in the following section, became important sources of labour for the booming post-war economies of Western Europe.

Exhausted by decades of war, European powers began a long, often violent, process of decolonization that produced a number of significant migrations shortly after World War II. Most notable was the partition of India following the demise of the British Raj in 1947. The partition, which created the Islamic Republic of Pakistan, was an episode of 'unmixing' surpassing that seen in Turkey and Greece in the 1920s. Scholars estimate that 10–15 million people were displaced by the partition and forced to flee across borders in the midst of violence and chaos. This model of partition was replicated in Palestine, which, like India, had seen deepening social rifts under British colonial rule. In the case of Palestine, irreconcilable differences between European Jewish settlers and the indigenous Arab population, who had been promised political independence during World War I, led the newly created United Nations to propose a partition plan that would have created separate Jewish and Arab states. This plan was promptly rejected by Arab representatives, leading to open warfare between the two parties. Jewish forces eventually defeated the Arabs, leading to the creation of an independent state of Israel. The approximately 750,000 Arabs who had fled the conflict were refused re-entry by the new Israeli state, leading to a refugee crisis that continues to this day. (We discuss events in Turkey and Israel/Palestine again in Chapter 5.) Meanwhile, the newly created Jewish state welcomed in tens of thousands of European Jews who had managed to survive the Holocaust; in following decades, Israel experienced large inflows of Jewish immigrants from the Soviet Union, Ethiopia, and surrounding Arab countries, all of whom have had access to Israeli citizenship under Israel's 'Law of Return' (Willen, 2007).

Migrations in the post-World War II era

Europe lay devastated after World War II, its urban and industrial infrastructure in ruins. Fearing the further spread of communism in the midst of such despair, the American government stepped in with billions of dollars of aid for Europe, beginning a process of economic recovery and European economic integration. The reconstruction effort required significant quantities of labour, which was in short supply both because of millions of war casualties and

decades of declining birth rates. Britain found a ready source of workers in Europe's POW and refugee camps, as well as among the thousands of Polish resistance fighters who had fought with the British military during the war. Britain's Foreign Labour Committee looked favourably upon these European labour recruits, who were viewed as eminently assimilable into British society and thus as ideal permanent settlers. Paul (1997) notes the irony that while the British government was actively recruiting European workers, it was also supporting the emigration of hundreds of thousands of its citizens to Canada,

Plate 2.3 Greek immigrants in Germany
Source: © Ducklau/dpa/Corbis

Australia, New Zealand, and Rhodesia in order to shore up its influence in the Commonwealth. Through a variety of organized labour recruitment schemes, as well as a generous work permit system, the British state funnelled these European workers—a significant proportion of whom were single women—into industries that were generally unattractive to native workers (McDowell, 2003). In total, about 345,000 Europeans came to Britain as part of this postwar recruitment. Britain during this time also welcomed Irish workers, who, owing to colonial ties, had free entry and settlement rights in Britain. By 1961, there were approximately 700,000 Irish-born people living in Britain, and Britain had replaced the US as the primary destination for Irish immigrants (Office of National Statistics, 2013; Paul, 1997).

Like Britain, many other Western European states sought workers, as they had in the past, in Europe's more economically peripheral states, including Italy, Spain, Portugal, Greece, and Yugoslavia. In several instances, European governments negotiated bilateral agreements with sending countries and instituted formal labour recruitment agencies to screen and to facilitate migrant flows. The French government, for instance, instituted the Office National d'Immigration (ONI) shortly after World War II to meet labour needs. Germany, likewise, created the Bundesanstalt fur Arbeit (BfA, Federal Labour Office) to recruit *gastarbeiter*, or **guest workers**. Switzerland, Belgium, and the Netherlands also had important guest worker recruitment programmes. In all cases, though, many workers arrived outside of formal channels and later regularized their work and residency status (Hammar, 1985). Over time, labour recruitment in Western Europe came to rely more heavily on workers from beyond the European periphery, especially North Africa and Turkey. These migrant workers, like their forebears, were generally destined for low- or semi-skilled work in factories, mines, agriculture, and construction; and while overwhelmingly male, there were significant percentages of female workers among them—in Germany, for instance, approximately one-quarter to one-third of guest workers were women, many of them employed in manufacturing, hotel, catering, and hospital sectors (Erdem and Mattes, 2003). Both men and women were subject to various limitations and forms of discrimination to keep them in a subordinate position vis-à-vis native workers. They also faced restrictions on bringing in family members, intended to discourage them from settling permanently (pregnant women and women with children were barred from recruitment as guest workers). As we will see, however, such restrictions did not prevent the eventual settlement of permanent Turkish and North African communities in Europe.

Labour needs in some European countries were also met by spontaneous migrations from colonies and former colonies, whose residents had, to varying degrees, legal rights of settlement. Over 600,000 workers from Pakistan, India, the Caribbean, and Africa, for instance, settled in Britain in the 1950s and 1960s, filling labour demands in textile factories, steel plants, and, especially for Caribbean migrants, in the National Health Service and in London Transport (Layton-Henry, 1992). In France, hundreds of thousands of workers from Algeria, Morocco, and Tunisia laboured in automobile factories and in the construction sector. The Algerian population alone grew from 350,000 in 1961 to 884,000 in 1975 (Bade, 2003, 248). As with guest workers, colonial settlers were slotted into racialized and gendered divisions of labour and were subject to significant discrimination despite their status as 'subjects', citizens, and/ or legal residents. The permanent settlement of formerly colonized peoples was viewed from the very start with a significant degree of alarm by governing elites and soon led to a flurry of legislative activity to curtail settlement rights. As we will see in Chapter 7, the growth of non-white communities—both through colonial settlement and guest worker programmes—has been a continual source of societal debate about national identity, integration, and minority rights.

The renewal of mass migration in the settler societies

The post-war period also saw the renewal of mass migration in the settler societies, both through labour recruitment and through the gradual dismantling of race-based restrictions. In the United States, for instance, persistent demands for inexpensive seasonal labour in the agricultural sector were fulfilled by the Bracero Program, a cooperative venture between the Mexican and American governments that operated from 1942 to 1964 (the term *bracero*, from the Spanish word for 'arm', makes reference to physical labour). During the decades of its existence, the Bracero Program provided more than 4.5 million individual contracts for temporary employment (Andreas, 2000, 33); it also encouraged hundreds of thousands of Mexicans to migrate outside of legally sanctioned channels—a pattern that continued long after the programme ended.

The Bracero Program and other legal labour recruitment programmes were soon overshadowed by the expansion of settlement-oriented immigration starting in the mid-1960s. Opposition to racially discriminatory immigration laws mounted during the 1950s and 1960s, in the midst of the American Civil Rights movement. The movement to reform immigration laws culminated in the passage of the Immigration and Nationality Act of 1965 (also known as the Hart-Celler Act), which abolished national-origins quotas and excluded race and ancestry as a basis for the selection of immigrants. Instead, it gave priority for admission to family members of US citizens or legal residents, and also extended favourable treatment to highly skilled immigrants (King, 2000). The largely unintended result of this legislation and subsequent reforms (including the elimination of ceilings on immigration by hemisphere in

1978) was a dramatic upsurge of immigration from Asia and Latin America. Between 1970 and 1990, for instance, the Asian-American population nearly quintupled, growing from 1.5 to 7.3 million, and Mexicans became the largest immigrant group in the United States. Overall, immigration increased rapidly after 1965, with immigrant admissions reaching 4.5 million in the decade 1971–80. Between 1966 and 1991, more than 15 million immigrants were legally admitted into the United States. At the same time, irregular and often temporary migration from continued apace.

Discriminatory restrictions were also lifted in Canada and Australia, leading, as in the United States, to the rapid expansion of immigration. In Australia, for instance, the state looked to immigration after World War II as a means to stimulate economic growth and to expand markets. Australia recruited some settlers from the many Europeans displaced by the war; the country also accepted a significant number of Cold War refugees from Eastern Europe. These post-war immigrations from Europe peaked at around 185,000 settler arrivals in 1970 (Ongley and Pearson, 1995). The acceptance of thousands of Eastern Europeans in the post-war period was accompanied by the dismantling of racially discriminatory policies. The last vestiges of the White Australia policy were removed in 1973, paving the way for the growth of ethnically diverse immigration flows in the 1980s.

Economic restructuring and a shifting migration system at the end of the 20th century

Major changes were afoot in the global economy during the post-World War II period, and the era of post-war expansion and prosperity in the old industrial core came to a halt by the early 1970s. Industrial economies of Western Europe and North America were facing growing competition from Asian export-oriented economies, and a major recession brought on in part by high oil prices led to high levels of unemployment and the collapse of many older industrial sectors. At the same time, many large corporations began to shift production to lower-waged economies—mostly in Asia, but also in Latin America and the Middle East and, after 1991, Eastern Europe—and to practise more flexible and geographically dispersed forms of production. These profound shifts in the global economy, including the emergence of new centres of banking and finance, brought with them changing patterns of migration.

Continuity and change in the old industrial core

In Europe, economic recession meant the termination of post-war labour migration programmes, as well as continuous efforts to restrict post-colonial migrations in France, Britain, and the Netherlands. Inflows of migrants, however, continued in the 1980s and 1990s due largely to family reunification, which European governments found difficult to control. (We discuss the effectiveness of contemporary immigration control measures in Chapter 6.) Also significant in sustaining migration to Europe was the development of flows of asylum seekers—individuals entering a country specifically to claim official refugee status. At the height of the Cold War in the 1950s and 1960s, Western European countries had welcomed hundreds of thousands of Eastern Europeans fleeing political repression by communist governments. By the end of the Cold War, however, Western governments were expressing growing scepticism towards asylum seekers. The first major conflict of the post-Cold War era—the dissolution of Yugoslavia—generated enormous flows of asylum seekers, most of them bound for Germany. Many of these were given at least temporary refuge, but the German state's wariness towards asylum seekers was very much in evidence as the Yugoslav conflict wore on, and the German state soon took measures

to restrict its liberal asylum provisions. Through the 1990s and 2000s, hundreds of thousands of people escaping conflicts and political repression in Sri Lanka, Turkey, Ethiopia, Eritrea, Somalia, Sudan, Iraq, Afghanistan, and elsewhere streamed into Europe but faced growing hostility from European governments. Indeed, the presence of asylum seekers became one of the most contentious political issues in Europe during this time and spurred the harmonization of asylum policies in the European Union (Leitner, 1997). We discuss these themes further in Chapters 5 and 6.

The increasing salience of family reunification and asylum in Europe did not spell the end of economic migration. Indeed, economic restructuring generated significant new demands for workers in Europe. The rapid expansion of banking, finance, and high-technology sectors after the 1980s, in particular, has relied heavily on highly educated foreign workers, as well as labour mobility within the EU. Today hundreds of thousands of **knowledge workers** from Asia, North America, and the Middle East and across Europe can be found in cities like London, Paris, Amsterdam, and Frankfurt. Europe's healthcare systems have also produced a steady demand for skilled foreign workers from across the globe. There continue to be, as well, demands for low-skilled workers in burgeoning tourism, hotel, and catering sectors, and in more traditional migrant-labour sectors like construction, agriculture, and manufacturing. Many European countries have formal visa programmes for certain categories of temporary and seasonal workers, especially in agriculture and hospitality industries; and since the expansion of the European Union in 2004 and 2007, wealthier countries of the EU have had access to a large supply of relatively low-waged labour from Eastern Europe. Britain, for instance, attracted an estimated 600,000 Polish workers following the 2004 accessions; while many of these Polish workers have left Britain in recent years due to an economic slump, they can still be found in cleaning jobs and domestic work, construction, plumbing, and other trades (Datta and Brickell, 2009).

Many other low-skilled workers participate in Europe's labour market as undocumented immigrants. In many cases these migrants start out with visas or various forms of legal status; in other cases, they undertake the often harrowing journey to Europe as clandestine migrants. The phenomenon of undocumented migration has been especially pronounced in Southern Europe. Starting in the 1980s, Spain, Greece, Portugal, and Italy shifted from being net exporters to net importers of immigrants, hastily creating new immigration laws and regulations to contend with growing numbers of foreign workers. Demand for labour in these countries was encouraged partly by the inflow of structural funds and cheap credit from the European Union, which prompted a construction boom, and partly by the expansion of tourism, commercial agriculture, and, especially in Italy, small- and medium-sized industries. By 2003, an estimated 2.4 million foreigners—more than 700,000 without legal documents—were living in Italy; in Spain, 1.6 million foreigners had legal residency, and at least 300,000 were living without legal documentation (Calavita, 2005, 51). Most migrants to Southern Europe originate in North Africa, Latin America, Albania, and some sub-Saharan African countries and are employed in agriculture, low-end manufacturing and textile/garment production, construction, and domestic work—sectors that are deeply informalized and that have long resisted government oversight. Policies towards undocumented immigration in Southern European countries have lurched between hardline efforts to curtail the rights of documented and undocumented immigrants and relatively liberal efforts to encourage legalization and integration. Overall, the impacts of regularization policies in Southern Europe have been very mixed, with relatively few immigrants able to avail themselves of residency permits because of their inability to provide evidence of continuous legal employment (ibid.).

In the settler societies, the expansionary immigration policies of the 1960s and early 1970s have continued to the present. In the United States, annual legal immigration since 1990 has ranged between 650,000 and 1.8 million, averaging around one million per year, and the percentage of the population that is foreign-born has grown to approximately 13 percent—close to where it was at the highpoint of late 19th- and early 20th-century migrations. The main sending countries of legal permanent residents since the 1980s have included Mexico, the Philippines, South Korea, India, China, Vietnam, Cuba, El Salvador, and the Dominican Republic. Sustained levels of immigration have led some to call for reductions in immigration and for more selective immigration criteria that emphasize skills rather than family ties (Borjas, 1999). But these arguments have not led to substantive changes in actual immigration policy. A far more hotly contested issue has been undocumented immigration. With an estimated 10–12 million undocumented immigrants living in the United States today—around half of them from Mexico and many of them with US-citizen children—immigration reform has become a topic of heated political debate. The 'problem' of undocumented immigration, however, may be solving itself to some extent, as more active immigration enforcement combined with employment growth in Mexico has led for the first time in decades to the net out-migration of Mexicans from the United States (Pew Hispanic Center, 2012).

Canada and Australia have also pursued expansionary immigration policies that have produced increasingly diverse populations. Having eliminated racial barriers in the 1960s and 1970s, both Australia and Canada established selective immigration systems that gave preference to those with capital and skills; these systems have become more selective over time. In Canada, annual immigrant intake has exceeded 175,000 every year since 1990, reaching over 280,000 in 2010. Since the 1990s, more than half of these have entered Canada under the economic/ skill category, and a shrinking percentage have come under family or humanitarian categories (Citizenship and Immigration Canada, 2010). Around 80 percent of Canada's immigrants since 2001 have come from Asia, Africa, the Middle East, and Latin America. Australian immigration has grown steadily since the 1990s, reaching over 170,000 per year since 2008–9. The Asia-Pacific and the Middle East regions provide the bulk of Australia's immigrants (India and China were the top two source countries in 2012–13), though Britain has consistently been among the top sources of immigrants to Australia (Australian Department of Immigration and Citizenship, 2013).

Migration and emerging economies in Asia and the Arab world

The phenomenal growth of Asian immigrant populations in Australia, Canada, and the United States hints at the profound economic transformations that have taken place in Asia since the 1970s. Asia's rapid economic development was centred initially in Japan, which recovered its premier economic position in East Asia after World War II with the development of its export-oriented manufacturing sector. This export-oriented manufacturing model was soon emulated by other Asian countries—South Korea, Taiwan, Malaysia, Thailand, Indonesia, China, and, more recently, Vietnam. These profound economic transformations have generated extensive internal and international migration systems.

With a rapidly aging population and a highly skilled labour force unwilling to perform menial work, Japan has long sought sources of inexpensive foreign labour for unskilled occupations, especially in the service sector and in small- and medium-sized manufacturing firms. Japan has generally shunned permanent immigration as a solution to its demographic situation, turn-ing instead to temporary and irregular forms of migration mostly from other Asian countries (it has also off-shored production to less expensive labour markets in Asia). Japan has for decades hosted large Korean and Filipino populations, both of whom have had only tenuous access to formal rights and who have often suffered from discriminatory treatment (see Box 2.2). Filipinos, in particular, have been confined to low-level and demeaning work, with a significant number of Filipina women employed in the 'entertainment' industry and the sex trade, though a growing number of Filipinas are being recruited into the nursing sector. In its eagerness to limit the size of the foreign population and to maintain ethnic homogeneity, the Japanese state in the 1980s began to recruit Japanese-origin people from Brazil and other South American countries to work in Japanese factories (as described earlier, hundreds of thousands of contract workers from China and Japan went to South America in the late 19th and early 20th centuries to work in mines and fields). The programme attracted more than 200,000 South American migrants, who, unlike other immigrants, were granted long-term work visas. Many of these workers found employment with automobile and electronics subcontracting firms (Douglass and Roberts, 2003). By the mid-1990s, there were approximately 1.4 million registered foreigners in Japan; today there are believed to be more than two million, most of them Koreans, Chinese, Filipinos, and Brazilians (ibid.).

Even more substantial are migrations taking place between Southeast Asian countries. Rapid export-oriented economic development in Thailand, Malaysia, and Singapore since the 1970s has transformed these countries into important labour importers. There are, according to Kaur (2010), two major migration corridors in Southeast Asia: from Indonesia and the Philippines to Singapore and Malaysia, and from Vietnam, Cambodia, and Laos to Thailand. Significant complexity exists within these general

BOX 2.2 JAPANESE IMPERIALISM AND KOREAN IMMIGRATION

Much of this chapter focuses on the formation of a European-centred global economy and the relationship between European imperialism and global migration flows. It is important to recall, however, that Japan was a major imperial power in East Asia in the early 20th century and that its imperial ambitions were highly influential in shaping migration flows in Asia. Japan's annexation of Korea in 1910, and the subsequent settlement of hundreds of thousands of Japanese colonists, transformed Korea's agricultural sector, introducing large-scale, intensive, export-oriented farming. These transformations put enormous pressures on peasant producers, causing many to leave Korea. Some settled in relatively ungoverned and rural areas of southern Manchuria. Others sought waged employment in Japan's growing industrial and mining sectors, some of them enticed by Japanese labour recruiters (Weiner, 1994). Chain migration meant that workers from the same region or village could often be found in the same factory. Korean workers were joined by Japanese rural migrants, though Japanese employers employed a racialized division of labour, which ensured that Korean workers would be paid less and subjected to worse conditions than their Japanese counterparts. The use of Korean labour intensified as Japan mobilized for war in the late 1930s, and by 1938, there were 800,000 Koreans in Japan. During the war, Koreans were also forced through conscription to work in Japanese industries. By the end of the war, more than two million Koreans were residing in Japan. Many of these were repatriated after the war, but at the end of the 20th century, around 600,000 permanent residents of Korean origin were living in Japan (Douglass and Roberts, 2003).

patterns; Malaysia, for instance, is a net importer of foreign workers, yet it also sends a significant number of skilled and unskilled migrants to other Asian countries. More broadly, outflows of migration from one country are typically complemented by inflows of migrants from another. Immigration policy in labour-importing countries has been dominated by the desire for a steady flow of inexpensive, temporary, and highly flexible labour—labour that is crucial to these countries' economic competitiveness in the global economy. They have thus implemented a combination of guest worker programmes, temporary contract employment systems, and bilateral labour agreements to secure workers in the domestic sector, plantation agriculture, manufacturing, and construction. In 2010, a third of Singapore's labour force was foreign (a total of around one million workers), and about a quarter of Malaysia's labour force (approximately three million out of a total of 12 million) was foreign. Despite—or perhaps

because of—measures to control and to regulate migration, however, unauthorized migration is the norm in the region, especially in Malaysia and Thailand. In Malaysia, for instance, workers who come through authorized channels easily lapse into undocumented status due to the temporary nature of work contracts and the lack of workplace rights; if caught, migrant workers face punitive treatment from the state, reflected in the alarmingly high levels of incarceration in Malaysia for immigration-related offenses. Thailand, like Southern Europe, has relied on periodic regularizations and registrations to manage its foreign labour force; however, the registration process is burdensome both for workers and for employers, and many choose to circumvent the state. In both Malaysia and Thailand, the extensive use of labour contractors who demand extortionate fees from low-skilled migrant workers and who collude in the exploitation of foreign workers provides further incentives for migrants to seek extra-legal channels for migration. The result overall is that the vast majority of workers in Malaysia and Thailand are undocumented. Of the 1.8 million foreign workers in Thailand in 2008, for instance, only about half a million were registered (Kaur, 2010). We return to these issues in Chapter 3.

The development of extensive migration systems within Southeast Asia has been accompanied by large-scale migration flows between Southeast Asia and the Gulf Arab states—Saudi Arabia, Kuwait, Qatar, Bahrain, Oman, and the United Arab Emirates (UAE). The Gulf Arab states (along with oil-rich countries of Iraq and Libya) began labour importation programmes in the 1970s, as high oil prices prompted a flurry of development projects. Initially, Arab states drew primarily on Palestinian, Jordanian, Egyptian, and Yemeni workers, both skilled and unskilled and overwhelmingly male, to fill labour needs in the oil industry and in construction and engineering. Widespread support for Saddam Hussein by many Arabs during the first Gulf War (1991), however, led to the expulsion of hundreds of thousands of Arab workers from Kuwait and Saudi Arabia. Approximately 750,000 Yemeni workers, 300,000 Jordanians, and at least 150,000 Palestinians were expelled (in addition, many Egyptians lost their jobs in Iraq as a result of the war). Egyptians remained an important source of workers in the Gulf (as well as in Libya) after 1991, but Palestinians and others have never recovered their position in the region (Richards and Waterbury, 1996; Galbraith, 2003). They were replaced by Asian workers—Bangladeshis, Pakistanis, Indians, Indonesians, Filipinos, and others—who were cheaper and, from the perspective of conservative Gulf leaders, less of a political liability. Among these newer waves of Asian workers have been numerous women, most of them finding employment in the domestic and healthcare sectors; the Indonesian government has been particularly active in promoting the migration of women to Saudi Arabia and other Gulf states (Silvey, 2005). Today, there are at least 400,000

foreign-born domestic workers—most of them women—in the UAE alone. At the same time, ambitious programmes by the emirs of Abu Dhabi and Dubai (both part of the United Arab Emirates) to transform themselves into global centres of finance, media, tourism, and transport since the 1990s have led to the migration of many Western professionals to the region (Malecki and Ewers, 2007). The demographic impacts of these various migrations have been staggering. In the Gulf region today, the proportion of the population that is foreign-born ranges from approximately 30 percent in Oman to 74 percent in Qatar and nearly 85 percent in the UAE (UN Department of Economic and Social Affairs, 2014; see also Malit and Al Youha, 2013).

Conclusions

We have in this chapter sketched out the broad contours of global migrations, past and present. This broad overview by necessity glosses over numerous migration systems that are significant at a regional level, including those operating within sub-Saharan Africa and Latin America. Some of these are seasonal or circular migrations that shift from year to year; others are more persistent and may be connected to longer-distance migrations to Europe, North America, and elsewhere. Adepoju (2008) notes that in Africa as a whole, the percentage of international migrants in the population steadily declined from the 1960s onward; likewise, the region's share of the world's migrants declined from the 1980s until the mid-2000s. But migration has increased in recent years, and today, approximately 13 percent of the world's international migrants are Africans (United Nations, 2012). West Africa stands out for its growing population of international migrants, with the migration corridor between Burkina Faso and Cote d'Ivoire among the highest volume corridors in the world today (ibid). South Africa, as well, has been an important destination for undocumented migrants and asylum seekers, especially from neighbouring Zimbabwe and Mozambique (Jacobsen, 2007). In recent years, migrants from sub-Saharan Africa have had a growing presence in North African countries. Many of these migrants intend to transit through Morocco or Libya on their way to Southern Europe but may be unable to gather the funds necessary to pay the smugglers who control the passage across the Mediterranean. In 2005, there were an estimated half-million migrants from Chad, most of them unauthorized, residing in Libya (Adepoju, 2008). Within Latin America, Argentina and Venezuela are important destinations for migrants, and significant migration corridors have formed between Guatemala and Mexico, Nicaragua and Costa Rica, Bolivia and Argentina, and Peru and Chile (Mazza and Sohnen, 2011). We will touch on some of these regional migrations in subsequent chapters, especially in our discussions of development (Chapter 4), refugees (Chapter 5), and immigration control and border politics (Chapter 6). As well, we encourage our readers to consult the recommended readings at the end of this chapter, which will fill in the details of the many migrations that we have discussed only briefly.

In summarizing some of the key migrations that have taken place over the past 400 years or so, we have tried to indicate some of the social and political processes that have consistently shaped migration flows. It should be evident at this point that labour supply and demand—the dynamics of which take shape within a geographically integrated, yet highly unequal and often unstable capitalist economy—drive a great deal of human mobility. But it should be equally evident that migrations are not a straightforward reflection of neutral market forces. Employers, as we will explore further in the next chapter, demand certain kinds of workers for certain kinds of jobs. The foreignness of workers in and of itself denotes a particular level of exploitability that allows capitalist enterprise to thrive

even under highly competitive conditions. Typically, migrant workers have occupied jobs marked by dangerous working conditions, vulnerability, and low social prestige; these are jobs that are unlikely to be filled by 'native' workers under the terms and conditions granted by employers. When a sufficient supply of 'voluntary' workers is not available to fill such jobs, then employers—often with the assistance of states—will make use of more coercive forms of labour.

To be sure, not all migrations are purely economic in nature. We have seen multiple instances in this chapter of population transfers and expulsions in a context of nation-state formation and ethno-national conflict. Migration, in this sense, can be understood simultaneously as a function of global capitalism and of a modern interstate system built around the logic of ethno-national exclusivity. In many cases it is difficult to attribute causation solely to economic or political forces. So often in the modern capitalist world system, such forces are intimately connected, with political transformations setting the stage for economic transformations, and vice versa.

Having said very little about migrants themselves in this chapter, we emphasize in closing that migrants are not automatons who respond in a straightforward manner to economic stimuli. Migrants at an individual level have many reasons for migrating—reasons that are seldom exclusively economic—and their migratory trajectories can be tortuous and convoluted. We should not lose sight of the complex and often heroic biographies of even the most 'ordinary' of migrants. Nor should we lose sight of the ways in which migrants, through their more-or-less willful decisions to leave one place and go to another, set into motion often profound societal transformations in points of origin and destination. In the first instance, the crossing of borders that modern migrants undertake requires national societies to grapple continuously with the question of who they are as national societies and the terms by which they allow foreign others to participate in their societies. Such dynamics will be addressed in the remainder of this book.

Key terms in this chapter

chain migration	indentured servitude
coolies	knowledge workers
cottage industries	piece rates
	proletarianization
guest workers	stepwise migration

Further reading

Amrith, S. S. (2011) *Migration and Diaspora in Modern Asia*. Cambridge: Cambridge University Press.

Burrell, K. and Panayi, P. (Eds.) (2006) *Histories and Memories: Migrants and Their History in Britain*. Boulder, CO: IB Taurus.

Chee-Beng, T. and Lai, W. L. (2010) *The Chinese in Latin America and the Caribbean*. Leiden: Koninklijke Brill NV.

Cordell, D. D., Gregory, J. W., and Piche, V. (1998) *Hoe and Wage: A Social History of a Circular Migration System in West Africa*. Boulder, CO: Westview Press.

Falola, T. and Usman, A. (Eds.) (2009) *Movements, Borders, and Identities in Africa*. Rochester, NY: University of Rochester Press.

Fisher, M. (2014) *Migration: A World History*. Oxford: Oxford University Press.

Manning, P. (2012) *Migration in World History*. London: Routledge.

Sassen, S. (1999) *Guests and Aliens*. New York: The New Press.

Sharpe, P. (Ed.) (2011) *Women, Gender, and Labour Migration: Historical and Cultural Perspectives*. London: Routledge.

References

Adepoju, A. (2008) Migration in Sub-Saharan Africa, Current African Issues Series, number 23. Uppsala, Sweden: Nordiska Afrikainstitutet. Retrieved from http://www.diva-portal.org/smash/get/diva2:241148/FULLTEXT01.pdf (accessed 14 September 2014).

Alston, L. J., Mattiace, S., and Nonnenmacher, T. (2009) Coercion, culture, and contracts: labor and debt on henequen haciendas in Yucatan, Mexico, 1870–1915, *The Journal of Economic History*, 69(1): 104–134.

Andreas, P. (2000) *Border Games: Policing the US–Mexico Divide*. Ithaca, NY: Cornell University Press.

Australian Department of Immigration and Citizenship (2013) 2012–2013 Migration program report (program year to 30 June 2013). Retrieved from http://www.immi.gov.au/media/statistics/pdf/report-on-migration-program-2012-13.pdf (accessed 30 October 2014).

Bade, K. J. (2003) *Migration in European History* (translated by Allison Brown). Malden, Oxford: Blackwell.

Borjas, G. (1999) *Heaven's Door: Immigration Policy and the American Economy*. Princeton, NJ: Princeton University Press.

Brubaker, R. (1995) Aftermaths of empire and the unmixing of people: historical and comparative perspectives, *Ethnic and Racial Studies*, 18(2): 189–218.

Burns, E. B. (1980) *A History of Brazil* (second edition). New York: Columbia University Press.

Calavita, K. (2005) *Immigrants at the Margins: Law, Race, and Exclusion in Southern Europe*. Cambridge: Cambridge University Press.

Citizenship and Immigration Canada (2010) Canada Facts and Figures: immigration overview, permanent and temporary residents. Retrieved from http://www.cic.gc.ca/english/pdf/research-stats/facts2010.pdf (accessed 30 October 2014).

Clarke, C., Peach, C., and Vertovec, S. (1990) *South Asians Overseas: Migration and Ethnicity.* Cambridge: Cambridge University Press.

Croxton, D. (1999) The Peace of Westphalia of 1648 and the origins of sovereignty, *The International History Review,* 21(3): 569–591.

Datta, A. and Brickell, K. (2009) 'We have a little bit more finesse, as a nation': constructing the Polish worker in London's building sites, *Antipode,* 41(3): 439–464.

De Vries, J. (1984) *European Urbanization, 1500–1800.* London: Methuen.

Douglass, M. and Roberts, G. S. (2003) Japan in a global age of migration. In M. Douglass and G. S. Roberts (Eds.), *Japan and Global Migration: Foreign Workers and the Advent of Multicultural Society.* Honolulu: University of Hawaii Press (pp. 3–28).

Erdem, E. and Mattes, M. (2003) Gendered policies–gendered patterns: female labour migration from Turkey to Germany from the 1960s to the 1990s. In R. Ohlinger, K. Schonwalder, and T. Triadafilopoulos (Eds.), *European Encounters: Migrants, Migration, and European Societies since 1945.* Aldershot: Ashgate (pp. 186–210).

Esser, H. and Korte, H. (1985) Federal Republic of Germany. In T. Hammar (Ed.), *European Immigration Policy: A Comparative Study.* Cambridge: Cambridge University Press (pp. 165–205).

Gabaccia, D. (2000) *Italy's Many Diasporas.* London: UCL Press.

Galbraith, P. (2003) Refugees from war in Iraq: what happened in 1991 and what may happen in 2003, Migration Policy Institute Policy Brief. Retrieved from http://www.migrationpolicy.org/pubs/MPIPolicyBriefIraq.pdf (accessed 30 October 2014).

Gibson, C. (1966) *Spain in America.* New York: Harper and Row.

Hammar, T. (Ed.) (1985) *European Immigration Policy: A Comparative Study,* Cambridge: Cambridge University Press.

Heffernan, M. (1995) French colonial migration. In R. Cohen (Ed.), *The Cambridge Survey of World Migration.* Cambridge: Cambridge University Press (pp. 33–38).

Hofstadter, R. (1973) *America at 1750: A Social Portrait.* New York: Vintage Books.

Jacobsen, K. (2007) Migration within Africa: the view from South Africa, *The Fletcher Forum of World Affairs,* 31(1): 203–214.

Jordan, W. (1968) *White over Black: American Attitudes toward the Negro, 1550–1812.* Chapel Hill, NC: University of North Carolina Press.

Kale, M. (1998) *Fragments of Empire: Capital, Slavery, and Indian Indentured Labor Migration in the British Caribbean.* Philadelphia, PA: University of Pennsylvania Press.

Kaur, A. (2010) Labour migration trends and policy challenges in Southeast Asia, *Policy and Society,* 29(4): 385–397.

Kelly, J. D. (1992) 'Coolie' as a labour commodity: race, sex, and European dignity in colonial Fiji. In E. V. Daniel, H. Bernstein, and T. Brass (Eds.), *Plantations, Proletarians, and Peasants in Colonial Asia.* London: Frank Cass & Co. (pp. 246–267).

Keown, P. A. (1971) The career cycle and the stepwise migration process, *New Zealand Geographer,* 27(2): 175–184.

King, D. (2000) *Making Americans: Immigration, Race, and the Origins of the Diverse Democracy.* Cambridge, MA: Harvard University Press.

Langer, W. L. (1975) American foods and Europe's population growth, 1750–1850, *Journal of Social History,* 8(2): 51–66.

Layton-Henry, Z. (1992) *The Politics of Immigration: Immigration, 'Race', and 'Race' Relations in Post-War Britain.* Cambridge, MA; Oxford, UK: Blackwell.

Leitner, H. (1997) Reconfiguring the spatiality of power: the construction of a supranational framework for the European Union, *Political Geography,* 16(2): 123–143.

Livi-Bacci, M. (1991) *Population and Nutrition:*

An Essay on European Demographic History. Cambridge: Cambridge University Press Archive.

Malecki, E. J. and Ewers, M. C. (2007) Labor migration to world cities: with a research agenda for the Arab Gulf, *Progress in Human Geography,* 31(4): 467–484.

Malit, F. T. Jr. and Al Youha, A. (2013) Labor migration in the United Arab Emirates: challenges and responses, Migration Policy Institute. Retrieved from http://www.migrationin-formation.org/Feature/display.cfm?ID=965 (accessed 30 October 2014).

Mann, C. (2011) *1493: Uncovering the New World Columbus Created.* New York: Alfred A. Knopf.

Mazza, J. and Sohnen, E. (2011) Labor migration in Latin America and the Caribbean: a look at new trends and policies, Inter-American Development Bank, Labor Markets and Social Security Unit (Technical Notes number IDB-TN-205). Retrieved from http://idbdocs.iadb.org/wsdocs/getdocument.aspx?docnum=36764 (accessed 10 September 2014).

McDowell, L. (2003) Workers, migrants, aliens or citizens? State constructions and discourses of identity among post-war European labour migrants in Britain, *Political Geography,* 22(8): 863–886.

Meagher, A. J. (2008) *The Coolie Trade: The Traffic in Chinese Laborers to Latin America, 1847–1874.* Bloomington, IL: XLibris Press.

Moch, L. P. (1992) *Moving Europeans: Migration in Western Europe since 1650.* Indianapolis: University of Indiana Press.

Moya, J. (1998) *Cousins and Strangers: Spanish Immigrants in Buenos Aires.* Berkeley; Los Angeles: University of California Press.

Office of National Statistics (2013) Immigration patterns of non-UK-born populations in England and Wales in 2011. Retrieved from www.ons.gov.uk/ons/rel/census/2011-census-analysis/immigration-patterns-of-non-uk-born-populations-in-england-and-wales-in-2011.html?format=print (accessed 15 January 2015).

Ogilvie, S. C. and Cerman, M. (Eds.) (1996) *European Proto-Industrialization.* Cambridge: Cambridge University Press.

Ongley, P. and Pearson, D. (1995) Post-1945 international migration: New Zealand, Australia, and Canada compared, *International Migration Review,* 29(3): 765–793.

O'Rourke, K. H. and Williamson, J. G. (1999) *Globalization and History: The Evolution of a Nineteenth-Century Atlantic Economy.* Cambridge, MA; London: MIT Press.

Paul, K. (1997) *Whitewashing Britain: Race and Citizenship in the Postwar Era.* Ithaca, NY: Cornell University Press.

Pearson, R. (1994) *The Longman Companion to European Nationalism, 1780–1920.* London; New York: Longman (p. 240).

Pew Hispanic Center (2012) Net migration from Mexico falls to zero—and perhaps less, Washington, DC: Pew Trust. Retrieved from http://www.pewhispanic.org/files/2012/04/Mexican-migrants-report_final.pdf (accessed 30 October 2014).

Piore, M. (1979) *Birds of Passage.* Cambridge, UK; New York: Cambridge University Press.

Pounds, N. (2005) *The Medieval City.* Westport, CT: Greenwood Press.

Ravenstein, E. G. (1885) The laws of migration, *Journal of the Statistical Society of London,* 48(2): 167–235.

Richards, A. and Waterbury, J. (1996) *A Political Economy of the Middle East.* Boulder, CO: Westview Press.

Sánchez-Albornoz, N. (1984) The population of colonial Spanish-America. In N. Bethell (Ed.), *The Cambridge History of Latin America.* Cambridge: Cambridge University Press (pp. 3–35).

Shepard, T. (2008) *The Invention of Decolonization: The Algerian War and the Rmaking of France.* Ithaca, NY: Cornell University Press.

Silvey, R. (2005) Transnational Islam: Indonesian migrant domestic workers in Saudi Arabia.

In G. W. Falah and C. R. Nagel (Eds.), *Geographies of Muslim Women: Gender, Religion, and Space*. New York: Guilford Press (pp. 127–246).

Thomas, R. N. (1972) The migration system of Guatemala City: spatial inputs, *The Professional Geographer*, 24(2): 105–112.

Tinker, H. (1995) The British colonies of settlement. In R. Cohen (Ed.), *The Cambridge Survey of World Migration*. Cambridge: Cambridge University Press (pp. 14–20).

United Nations (2012) Migrants by origin and destination: the role of South-South migration, population facts (Department of Economic and Social Affairs, Population Division), No. 2012/3, June 2012. Retrieved from http://www.un.org/en/development/desa/population/publications/pdf/popfacts/popfacts_2012-3_South-South_migration.pdf (accessed 1 September 2014).

United Nations Department of Economic and Social Affairs, Population Division (2004) *World Urbanization Prospects: The 2003 Revision*. New York: United Nations.

United Nations Department of Economic and Social Affairs, Population Division (2014) International migration stock interactive database. Retrieved from http://esa.un.org/migration/ (accessed 1 September 2014).

Verbunt, G. (1985) France. In T. Hammar (Ed.), *European Immigration Policy: A Comparative Study*. Cambridge: Cambridge University Press (pp. 127–164).

Wallerstein, I. (1979) *The Capitalist World-Economy: Essays by Immanuel Wallerstein*. Cambridge, UK: Cambridge University Press.

Weiner, M. (1994) *Race and Migration in Imperial Japan*. Abingdon, UK; New York: Routledge.

Whyte, I. D. (2000) *Migration and Society in Britain, 1550–1830*. Basingstoke and London: Macmillan Press.

Willen, S. (Ed.) (2007) *Transnational Migration to Israel in Global Comparative Context*. Lanham, MD: Lexington Books.

Williamson, J. J. (1986) The impact of the Irish on British labor markets during the Industrial Revolution, *The Journal of Economic History*, 46(3): 693–720.

3

Migrant labour in the economy

Introduction

Both our discussion of migration theories and our overview of historical migration flows highlight the economic basis of migration. We cannot reduce all migration-related phenomena to economic processes. Many migrations, as we will see in Chapter 5, are outcomes of non-economic pressures, such as civil conflict. By the same token, not all migrants act purely out of economic interests or make migration decisions solely on the basis of economic calculations. Yet it is hard to miss that most migrants move from relatively poorer places to relatively wealthier or more economically dynamic places and that many, if not most, of the world's migrants are seeking jobs, higher wages, and better opportunities. Most migrations—including many refugee flows—have some economic component, and so it is not surprising that most theoretical explanations of migration refer in one way or another to labour market dynamics, whether in terms of wage disparities, labour supply and demand, uneven economic development, or exploitation.

Insofar as we observe some general patterns of migrant labour market participation that transcend historical-geographical context—e.g. migrants from relatively poor societies tend to cluster in low-waged, low-skilled occupations in relatively wealthy societies—our aim should be to interrogate, rather than take for granted, the diverse processes that generate these patterns. What particular purpose do migrant workers serve in labour markets? On what terms do migrants participate in the workforce of destination societies? What kinds of jobs are, or are not, available to them? And what are the mechanisms through which they are included and excluded in particular occupations and sectors? In addressing these questions, we try to strike a balance between recognizing migrants' individual and collective agency in the labour market and the constraints on migrant agency posed by occupational hierarchies and racial and gender stereotypes that operate both in sending and receiving societies. On the one hand, we account for migrants' ability to weigh the costs and benefits of seeking employment abroad, their efforts to secure work that is commensurate with their skill levels and training, and their ability to mobilize social networks to ease their integration into labour markets. On the other hand, we consider the role of employers' expectations, state practices, and societal norms in structuring migrant participation in economies. Migrants, we emphasize, are not homogenous but rather are differently positioned in hierarchies of class, race, gender, nationality, and legal status; moreover, they enter labour markets that are highly segmented in terms of sector, skills, and social status. It is therefore imperative to explain the generally subordinate position of migrant workers in destination societies while considering the diversity of migrant work experiences in destination societies.

Matching workers to jobs: skills, education, and qualifications

An understanding of the role and position of migrant workers in the economies of receiving societies begins with an understanding of the complexities of occupational categories and hierarchies and the diverse social processes that match workers to jobs. All economies consist of multiple sectors of economic activity, including manufacturing, resource extraction, agriculture and forestry, medicine and healthcare, banking and finance, hotels and entertainment, and the like. Within each of these sectors are multiple occupational categories that require different levels of education, skill, and experience. These occupational categories (e.g. administrative staff, accountant, manager, machinist, technician) operate within and across industrial sectors and individual firms. When workers enter the labour market, they choose, and are chosen by, employers for positions based on their qualifications, skills, training, and educational level. One generally does not find unskilled labourers in the upper echelons of investment banking firms, just as one would not expect to find a highly trained surgeon working behind the counter at a fast food restaurant. We therefore start our discussion of migrant participation in labour markets by considering the matching up of individuals' **human capital** to occupations.

Economists in the early 1960s advocated the term 'human capital' as a means of recognizing the differentiation of workers by skill and educational levels. Such differentiation had rarely been recognized—at least explicitly—by traditional economic theories. Human capital refers to an individual's 'stock of marketable skills and abilities' (Borjas, 1999, 34). Patterns of human capital are seen to reflect investments in human resources through training and education that are made by individual workers, by firms, and by society as a whole. The idea here is that workers become more valuable in terms of productivity by acquiring knowledge and skill and

therefore command higher salaries and incomes. Investments in human capabilities, at the same time, offer the prospect of economic growth for firms and for society at large.

Writing in 1961, Theodore Schultz—one of the original proponents of the human capital concept—argued that many of the disparities we see in labour markets are a result of differential levels of investment in human capital. 'When farm people take nonfarm jobs', Schultz (1961, 4) observed, 'they earn substantially less than industrial workers of the same race, age, and sex. Similarly non-white urban males earn much less than white males even after allowance is made for the effects of differences in unemployment, age, city size and region'. These differentials, he argued, corresponded closely with, and could be explained by, different levels of education. Schultz also suggested that lower earnings among black farmers compared with white farmers in the American South could be attributed to different levels of schooling and health, and that even lower earnings among migratory farmworkers could be explained by the fact that 'many of them have virtually no schooling, are in poor health, are unskilled, and have little ability to do useful work' (ibid).

To contemporary readers, this explanation might seem naive and simplistic: surely, centuries of discrimination and inequality (not to mention slavery) had something to do with unequal income among blacks and whites in the South in 1961. Yet the concept of human capital remains very relevant (though hotly contested) in explanations of labour market disparities. Human capital arguments have been very prominent, for instance, in discussions of African-American workers, who suffer a significantly higher unemployment rate than white workers in the US. The argument here is that the restructuring of the American economy in the 1970s and 1980s, which led to the demise of thousands of well-paying manufacturing jobs, disproportionately affected African Americans, who had flocked to northern cities in the early 20th century to work in the manufacturing sector.

BOX 3.1 A NOTE ON TERMINOLOGY: 'NATIVE WORKER'

The term 'native worker' is widely used to refer to non-immigrant workers and to distinguish between citizens and non-citizens in the labour market. The term 'native', which hints at the relationship between societal membership and place of birth, naturalizes differences between workers and hides the processes by which states and societies politically construct 'natives' and 'immigrants'. The term native also has connections to European colonial history. While recognizing the problematic elements of this term, we do use it in this and other chapters to reflect the meaningful social and political distinctions that exist between workers based on citizenship status, nationality, and place of birth. We urge our readers to be cognizant of the ways such distinctions are actively produced in national societies.

While educational disparities have been diminishing for decades, African Americans continue to have lower educational attainment than whites, and have thus had more limited access to decent jobs in the growing service-based economy, which require 'soft skills' and higher levels of education (e.g. O'Neill, 1990; Kasarda, 1990). Those emphasizing the role of human capital do not necessarily dismiss the effects of discrimination on workers' earnings and opportunities: educational attainment reflects, in part, access to better schools and teachers, which are more commonly found in wealthier, whiter neighbourhoods. But the emphasis is on the role of disparities in skills and education in producing labour market outcomes (for a discussion of human-capital 'deficits' among Mexican immigrants in the US, see Trejo, 1997).

The concept of human capital has commonly been deployed in debates about the impacts of migrants on national economies—that is, whether migrants contribute to economic growth or whether they put a drag on economic productivity by consuming more societal resources than they produce. Those who are sceptical of the value of expansionary immigration policies often point to the relatively low levels of education and skill among contemporary immigrants. Writing in the US context, economist George Borjas (1999) has argued that a decline in the level of skills and education among immigrants

to the US since the mid-20th century means that these immigrants are unable to meet demands for workers in key growth sectors. Moreover, these immigrants, lacking desired skills, are unable to advance economically or to close the wage gap with 'native' workers, making them more likely to consume government services (see Box 3.1 for an explanation of the term 'native'). Borjas thus advocates a more selective immigration policy for the US that prioritizes skill and education over family ties (we review these debates in more detail at the end of this chapter).

Immigrant social capital in the labour market

The sorting of particular types of workers into particular types of jobs, therefore, relates in some way to the complementarity (or lack thereof) between the occupational structure of the labour market and workers' skills. Yet human capital alone does not fully explain the many peculiar patterns that we see within labour markets. Why, for instance, does there seem to be a preponderance of women in nursing, human resources, and secretarial work, and a disproportionate presence of migrant men in construction trades and seasonal agriculture? What explains the concentration of Chinese workers in Australia's high-tech industry, the ubiquity of Vietnamese women in nail salons in California, the clustering of Albanians in Greece's agricultural sector, and the disproportionate presence of Filipinas in domestic service, nursing, and personal care in many parts of the world? This clustering of certain kinds of workers in certain professions and jobs may have something to do with human capital, but such patterns encourage us to think, as well, about social relationships and networks that can increase access to employment in particular sectors. These relationships and networks are often referred to as **social capital**.

Social capital suggests that job options and choices are shaped not only by an individual's skill levels, but also by the social networks through which individuals and groups acquire information about jobs, learn about prospective employers, and engage in market-based exchange. Economic relationships, in this sense, must be understood as embedded within broader sets of social relationships (Granovetter, 1985). The concept of social capital has been applied to a wide variety of labour market phenomena. In the 1980s and 1990s, for instance, a number of studies explored the role of women's social networks in producing pronounced occupational segregation on the basis of sex. These studies suggest that gender 'homophily'—the tendency to associate with people of the same sex and to acquire information within gender-specific social networks—plays a role in channelling men and women into certain types of jobs and in

Plate 3.1 Moroccan vegetable pickers working in the fields beside the half-completed Polaris World La Torre Golf Resort, 2006

Source: Steve Forrest/Panos

producing labour-market outcomes (e.g. Ibarra, 1992). In the migration literature, social capital has referred more specifically to relationships of obligation, reciprocity, mutuality, and trust based on kinship, co-ethnicity, and place of birth. Typically, migrants utilize ties with family, friends, and compatriots who are already established in the receiving context to find work and a place to live. Such relationships greatly reduce the uncertainties and costs associated with migration and can give streams of newly arriving migrants a foothold in the place of settlement. The iteration of this process within a given group can lead eventually to self-sustaining patterns of chain migration and to the creation of ethnic occupational niches and residential enclaves.

Grasmuck and Grosfoguel's (1997) discussion of Caribbean immigrants in New York City illustrates how social capital contributes to varying levels of economic success for different groups. Grasmuck and Grosfoguel note the wide discrepancies among Dominicans, Puerto Ricans, Jamaicans, Cubans, and Haitians in terms of income, poverty rates, education, and home-ownership. They attribute these discrepancies partly to human capital differences—that is, the varying levels of skills and education brought by different groups to the United States. But these variations are amplified by differential access to employment networks in a context of broader economic restructuring. Dominicans and Puerto Ricans, for instance, clustered early on in manufacturing employment, in part because of co-ethnic patterns of hiring in Dominican and Puerto Rican-owned garment plants. As the garment industry declined, these immigrants not only suffered from their relatively low educational levels, but also from a lack of access to other employment networks, connected partly to their tendency to reside in residential clusters. Jamaicans, in contrast, came to New York with higher educational levels and English-language skills than either Puerto Ricans or Dominicans, allowing them much earlier access to jobs outside of the manufacturing sector and outside of declining neighbourhoods. As New York's economy shifted, they had far more diversified employment networks, which allowed them to maintain relatively low levels of unemployment.

Wright and Ellis (2000) also discuss the importance of social capital to the positioning of immigrant workers in the Los Angeles labour market, arguing that ethnic networks go further than human capital in explaining the 'sorting' of immigrants into different sectors in the regional economy. Importantly, though, the authors also consider that gender-based networks may act independently of ethnic-based networks to shape labour market outcomes. Their data, for instance, reveal that among some groups—notably Mexicans and Central Americans—occupational distributions are highly segregated by gender, suggesting that distinctive social networks provide information about different jobs to women and men of the same immigrant cohort and nationality. By the same token, there appear to be gender networks that operate independently of nationality; thus, Wright and Ellis note that immigrant women are more likely to funnel into occupations where other immigrant women work, regardless of nativity, than into jobs with co-ethnic men. The authors note that patterns of occupational segregation are likely to vary across geographical contexts, as immigrant social networks interact with regionally specific labour markets; indeed, they speculate that in buoyant, growing economies, immigrants 'may rely less on ethnic networks because of the numerous employment opportunities' compared with places that are experiencing slower job growth (Wright and Ellis, 2000, 597).

The concept of social capital has been especially influential in discussions of **immigrant entrepreneurialism** and the clustering of immigrant-owned small business in certain economic sectors. Beginning in the 1980s, scholars began to take note of the increase in self-employment and small-business formation in industrialized societies after decades of industrial consolidation. Scholars noted, as well, that a disproportionate share of new small-business owners and the self-employed were immigrants. Entrepreneurial tendencies, however, were not evenly distributed across foreign-born populations; rather, certain groups—Chinese, Indians, Koreans, Turks—displayed more entrepreneurialism than others. Many scholars have explained this variability in terms of social capital, arguing that even in the absence of human capital, immigrants are able to mobilize strong kinship and ethnic solidarities and networks to generate income. In particular, cooperative familial relationships provide access to unpaid familial labour, which allows immigrant-owned firms to survive in what is often a competitive environment (Sanders and Nee, 1996). Beyond the immediate and extended family, immigrants have access to other 'ethnic resources', including rotating credit funds through which immigrants secure starting capital for their businesses. The social capital rooted in families and in ethnic communities gives immigrants comparative advantages in particular economic niches—most notably in small retail establishments (such as convenience stores and small groceries) and in manufacturing industries that are being abandoned by native capital (such as the garment industry). Scholars often refer to the sum total of group-specific economic relationships, networks, and niches as an **ethnic economy** (Bonacich and Modell, 1980).

A notable example of immigrant entrepreneurialism and ethnic economy formation is the Korean community in Los Angeles, whose members started thousands of businesses in the 1970s and 1980s (Light and Bonacich, 1988). Many of these were small retail establishments, clustered in what became known as Koreatown, serving Korean and non-Korean clientele. Koreans found other niches, as well, investing (along with Chinese and other immigrant groups) in garment manufacturing, which was booming in LA in the 1980s due to the availability of inexpensive immigrant workers. Koreans were also noted for opening small grocery stores in

predominantly black inner-city neighbourhoods, which had been abandoned by large supermarket chains. While less than 1 percent of the city's population, Koreans owned 2.6 percent of all businesses and 5 percent of all retail establishments. The 1980 census showed that over one-fifth of Koreans in Los Angeles were business owners or worked in family businesses; in this sense, they were nearly three times more likely than members of the population at large to own or to work in a family-owned business. Including the co-ethnic employees of Korean firms, over 60 percent of working Koreans were either self-employed or employed in Korean-owned firms in the 1980s (ibid.). This high level of entrepreneurialism bore witness to the extraordinary social capital and solidarity present within the Korean community. (Box 3.2 explains the use of the term 'middleman minority' to describe Koreans and other entrepreneurial groups.)

Another notable example of social capital, immigrant entrepreneurialism, and the formation of an ethnic economy is the Greek Cypriot community in Britain, which settled mainly in London in the 1950s and 1960s. Greek Cypriots by the 1980s had established a dominant presence in the garment industry, which was in steep decline due to global competition but which nonetheless offered niches of opportunity, especially in the production of women's outerwear and casual wear for large retail chains like Marks and Spencer. By the mid-1990s, there were an estimated 30,000 workers, mostly women, employed in 2,500 small, hypercompetitive firms. While Greek Cypriots dominated the garment industry, there was a complex system of specialization in the industry involving different ethnic groups, each with its own networks (Panayiotopoulos and Dreef, 2002). Turkish Cypriots, for instance, established themselves in heavy outerwear production in Northeast London, while Bengalis cornered East London's leather production. Labour recruitment in garment factories relied heavily on social networks

BOX 3.2 MIDDLEMAN MINORITIES

An important concept that appears in discussions of immigrant entrepreneurialism is **middleman minority**. This term, popularized by Edna Bonacich and associates in the 1970s and 1980s (e.g. Bonacich, 1973; Bonacich and Modell, 1980), refers to migrant groups who occupy an intermediate position between elites and subordinated groups, often in colonial or post-colonial contexts. Middleman minorities tend to form a 'petty bourgeoisie' of shopkeepers, merchants, brokers, and small-business owners, typically fulfilling economic roles that are shunned by others. Examples of middleman minorities include Indian communities who settled initially as indentured workers in East Africa and the Caribbean. Lebanese communities, likewise, have often formed middleman minorities wherever they have settled and are perhaps most visible in this role today in West Africa. Other groups who have historically formed middleman minorities are Armenians, Chinese, and Jews. As with ethnic entrepreneurs more generally, middleman minorities leverage familial and co-ethnic bonds to gain a competitive edge in their business sector. These groups tend to intermarry and to maintain strong diasporic relationships with their country of origin, nurturing in some cases a **myth of return**. Their tendency towards social insularity and their uneasy social position make middleman minorities vulnerable to attack in times of political transition. Well-established Indian communities in Uganda, for instance, were expelled in 1972 by the regime of Idi Amin, which viewed Indians as a vestige of British colonialism and an unwanted foreign presence.

based on kinship, town of origin, and membership in political or social organizations. As Panayiotopoulos and Dreef (ibid.) describe, large community gatherings like weddings and baptisms became opportunities for networking and labour recruitment. By the 1990s, however, Greek Cypriot factory owners faced both increasing competition from outsourcing and increased difficulty in recruiting British Cypriot women to work in the garment trade. This situation led some of the larger and more successful Cypriot enterprises to subcontract to Asian-owned enterprises in the British Midlands or to build off-shoring networks in Cyprus (ibid.). The latter strategy points to the ways that immigrant enterprises are connected to the wider global economy through transnational social networks—social networks, that is, that stretch between places of origin and destination. Recent literature has highlighted the important role of these transnational networks in providing resources, opportunities, and markets for many immigrant businesses (see, for instance,

McEwan et al., 2005; Portes, Guarnizo, and Haller, 2002; Poros, 2001; Bagwell, 2008). We return to the theme of **transnationalism** in Chapter 8.

The literature on social capital has tended to look at immigrant social networks and ethnic resources in a relatively positive light, suggesting that these networks and resources provide immigrants a foothold in local economies and a degree of social and economic mobility despite low human capital and host-society discrimination (Sanders and Nee, 1996; see also Ramirez and Hondagneu-Sotelo (2009) for a positive, yet nuanced, take on Mexican self-employment in the highly competitive landscaping services sector). Portes and Sensenbrenner (1993, 1322), however, suggest that there are also costs associated with group solidarity that can 'constrain or derail economic goal seeking'. Tight intergroup relationships, they argue, can give rise to the problem of 'free riding', whereby 'less diligent group members can enforce on successful members all types of demands backed by the same

Plate 3.2 Kitchen at a curry house, Birmingham, UK
Source: Steve Forrest/Panos

normative structure that makes the existence of trust possible' (ibid., 1338). The enforcement of group norms within a given community can compel individuals to make business decisions that are not necessarily in their best economic interest, or discourage individuals from seeking or pursuing opportunities that might take them out of the group's orbit. In other instances, the control over ethnic resources by a small number of families can be used to sanction or to exclude those who do not conform to group norms.

Others have highlighted the ways that social capital operates through, and reinforces, gender disparities. Anthias and Mehta (2003), for instance, have argued that immigrant men use sexist rules and norms to exploit women in ethnic economies, and they caution that the family

unit should not be understood as a place of collective interests. Their interviews with female and male ethnic entrepreneurs in Britain suggest that social capital is often male-dominated and that women seldom have access to ethnic resources. By the same token, while married men typically count on the unpaid labour of their wives to ensure the profitability of their businesses, it does not appear that female entrepreneurs can similarly count on their husbands.

More broadly, it is not clear that social capital provides a great deal of economic security or mobility for immigrants. Social networks tend to funnel immigrant workers into highly exploitative sectors, both inside and outside the ethnic economy, closing off other work options and often putting migrants at the mercy of unscrupulous labour brokers. While entrepreneurialism may provide a better option for many migrants than the waged-labour market, migrant businesses are usually marginal enterprises that only succeed, as we have seen, because of the availability of cheap or unpaid labour. So while ethnic resources may help newcomers to generate income in the absence of valued human capital, they may do little to help immigrants to overcome structural disadvantages and discrimination.

Employer expectations, stereotyping, and segmented labour markets

These critical reflections on social capital hint at deeper critiques of the social-capital perspective. A number of scholars have criticized social-capital approaches for their tendency to view immigrants' position in the labour force as a sociocultural phenomenon connected to migrants' ethnic traits and behaviours. Kloosterman and Rath (2001), for instance, have argued that the focus on social capital has cast immigrants as unchanging ethnic subjects whose participation in labour markets can be explained in terms of static cultural traditions and loyalties. This focus deflects attention from the vagaries of national and urban economies and institutional and regulatory contexts (see also Rath and Kloosterman, 2003; Pang and Rath, 2007). Kloosterman and Rath suggest that the rapid growth of migrant small businesses in the Netherlands in the 1980s was more immediately attributable to high levels of unemployment among Turkish and Moroccan guest workers and their children than to the existence of social networks. Deindustrialization, they show, disproportionately affected immigrant workers, who had always been slotted into low-level employment; that these workers turned to self-employment was symptomatic of the lack of other options in the Dutch labour market. At the same time, the regulatory context in Dutch cities fostered small-scale manufacturing operations and looked favourably upon business formation

as an answer to chronic unemployment among immigrants; this both enabled and reinforced immigrant entrepreneurialism. In fairness, many of the key works on social capital (including those cited above) *do* acknowledge the changing political-economic contexts in which migrants are situated. But by focusing on the *supply* side of the labour market (i.e. the traits and characteristics of workers), social capital approaches tell us relatively little about the *demand* side—that is, the role of employers, economic regulators, and policymakers—in creating economic opportunities and constraints for migrant workers.

To explain demand-side approaches to immigrant participation in labour markets, we turn once again to Dual Labour Market Theory, which we encountered in Chapter 1. Dual Labour Market Theory highlights the role of employers in driving migration flows and in creating a polarized employment and wage structure in industrial economies. This body of theory contends that industrial employers have a strong motivation to control workers, to ensure a flexible labour force, and to reduce wage inflation in the economy overall. They achieve these aims by creating a segmented labour market consisting of a primary sector (in which jobs are well-paid, secure, often unionized, and typically filled by native workers) and a secondary sector (in which jobs are relatively low-paid, insecure, and filled by immigrants and minorities). Because immigrant workers, from this perspective, are mainly interested in remitting wages and generally intend to return to places of origin, they are usually willing to tolerate poor working conditions, minimal job progression, and wage disparities vis-à-vis native workers. Native workers, meanwhile, are eager to preserve their privileges and therefore tend not to advocate on behalf of migrant workers. A key point here concerns the *social coding* of jobs allotted to native and immigrant workers. As might be expected, dangerous, difficult, and dirty jobs are often coded as immigrant (or minority) jobs, while more skilled and less degrading jobs are reserved for native workers. Because native workers tend not to compete for immigrant jobs, remuneration levels in the immigrant sector remain low, reducing wage pressures in the economy overall (see Piore, 1979; also Bonacich, 1972; Reich, Gordon, and Edwards, 1973).

Dual Labour Market Theory was developed in the early 1970s, when heavy industry still dominated Western economies and when many immigrants, especially in Europe, were employed in the manufacturing sector. Since then, increased competition from Asian manufacturers has brought about a transition to post-industrial, service-based economies in the old industrial core. Along with the expansion of services—ranging from advanced financial services to low-end personal services, like restaurant and domestic work—have come ever-more complex patterns of **labour market segmentation** (Waldinger and Lichter, 2003). While it has become increasingly difficult in this contemporary context to speak of a 'dual' labour market, many of the themes identified by Dual Labour Market Theory remain relevant, including the social coding of jobs, the structural demand for low-skilled workers, and the tendency for immigrant and minority workers to be locked into low-end jobs.

In discussing segmented labour markets, scholars today have become increasingly attuned to the intersections of legal/immigrant status, race, and gender within occupational hierarchies. From this perspective, the fact that labour markets are remarkably differentiated on the basis of race, gender, nativity, and legal status speaks less to human capital or social networks than to social ideologies and discriminatory practices (Samers, 1998; Bauder, 2006). When wielded by employers, these ideologies and practices have a significant role in shaping who does what in society. Employers' attitudes towards and expectations about workers based on gender, race, national origins, and the like circulate within particular industries and firms and produce a particular structure of opportunities and constraints for immigrants and non-immigrants alike. The sorting of specific groups into particular occupations takes place even before an individual applies for a job: job types and job titles are pre-defined on the basis of race, gender, and migrant status and on the basis of employers' perceptions of who will make a good worker. The particular coding of jobs is then used to justify wage levels. The labour market, in this sense, simultaneously reflects, produces, and reinforces social differences and stereotypes within society (Waldinger and Lichter, 2003; Bauder, 2006).

We can see these processes at work both in the present and in the past, as employers have sought out workers they perceive to be especially suited to particular types of work in terms of physical size, temperament, and other 'natural' endowments. These perceptions usually seem reasonable and objective at the time, but are shot through with racist and sexist assumptions. In Chapter 2, for instance, we discussed the growing reliance on Indian workers on plantations throughout the British Empire following the abolition of slavery. Slavery, of course, had originally been justified through an elaborate ideology of race, which posited black Africans as somehow destined—by virtue of their supposed moral and intellectual inferiority—for hard, coerced labour on white-owned plantations. With abolition, plantation owners looked to Indian workers, whom they viewed as more pliable and docile than freed African slaves. Employers revived systems of indenture, which had been common in the early colonial period, committing Indian workers to what were often highly exploitative labour contracts (Kale, 1998).

Both historically and in the present day, the workings of racialized and gendered stereotypes have been especially evident in domestic work (Anderson, 2001). Whether or not they participate in the paid labour force, women are usually associated with what Anderson calls the three c's of cooking, caring, and cleaning. Women are funnelled into these occupations both through society's expectations of what is appropriate work for them, and through employers' expectations of what kind of workers are desirable for domestic and caring roles. In the late 19th and early 20th centuries, hundreds of thousands of migrant women were destined for domestic service in affluent households—Irish women in British and American homes, Polish women in German homes, and Italian women in French homes. After a sharp decline in the mid-20th century, the use of domestic workers—nannies, cooks, housekeepers—began to rise again as growing numbers of educated women in the Global North entered the paid labour force and found themselves in need of a 'replacement' in the domestic sphere (Lutz, 2008; Hondagneu-Sotelo, 2001). Increasing affluence in Asia and the Middle East further fuelled the global demand for domestic workers. As in the past, worker recruitment has been shaped by gendered and racialized expectations and stereotypes. Lazaridis (2000) demonstrates how such stereotypes operate in the Greek context, where the employment of Albanian and Filipina domestic workers became commonplace in the 1990s. Greek families, Lazaridis suggests, often entrust their children to Filipinas, whom they view as especially bright and patient. In contrast, Greek employers tend to view Albanian women as more specifically suited to physical drudgery; Albanian women are therefore given heavier domestic chores than their Filipina counterparts. Scholars note that high levels of racial and gender stereotyping, combined with the hidden, unregulated nature of domestic work, render domestic workers extremely vulnerable to employer abuse. This is especially well documented in the Middle East, where perceptions of Asian domestic workers as racially inferior are pronounced. Jureidini and Moukarbel (2004), for instance, examine the dire position of Sri Lankan women in Lebanon, who are often subject to physical and verbal abuse, degrading work, and the confiscations of passports to prevent escape. (For further discussion of the racialization and gendering of domestic labour, as well as the ways in which migrant women navigate the challenges of domestic work, see Parreñas, 2001; Hondagneu-Sotelo, 2001; Momsen, 1999.)

We can observe the way that employer expectations and stereotypes produce racialized and gendered divisions of labour not only between sectors (e.g. domestic labour, nursing, agricultural labour), but also *within* a single workplace or firm. Manufacturers have commonly assigned particular jobs within factories to particular groups on the basis of national origin, race, and gender, differentiating wages and other privileges accordingly. Agricultural employers, as well, make use of gendered and racialized hierarchies, assigning different tasks to different groups. (Several works illustrate the workings of such hierarchies in the Greek agricultural sector—see Kasimis, 2008; Kasimis et al., 2010.) Especially influential in creating a differentiated wage structure in both industrial and agricultural workplaces—and undermining worker solidarity—has been the ideology of the male breadwinner and the idea that women's wages are merely a supplement to men's earnings (Parr, 1990). This norm has justified lower wages for women and has often been used to close off certain skilled occupations to women.

We can also see employer stereotypes and societal norms at work in contemporary service industries, in which face-to-face contact between firms and customers is of the utmost importance. McDowell, Batnitsky, and Dyer's (2007) research on international hotels in London, for instance, uncovers the ways that employer expectations and preferences produce complicated gendered and racialized divisions of labour. Interviews with hotel managers reveal the importance of subjective evaluations of workers—based on gender, nationality, personal style, skin colour, weight, and language abilities—in deciding whether to hire certain individuals. Managerial positions, McDowell and her associates show, are dominated by migrants from Western Europe, southern Africa, and North America, who are

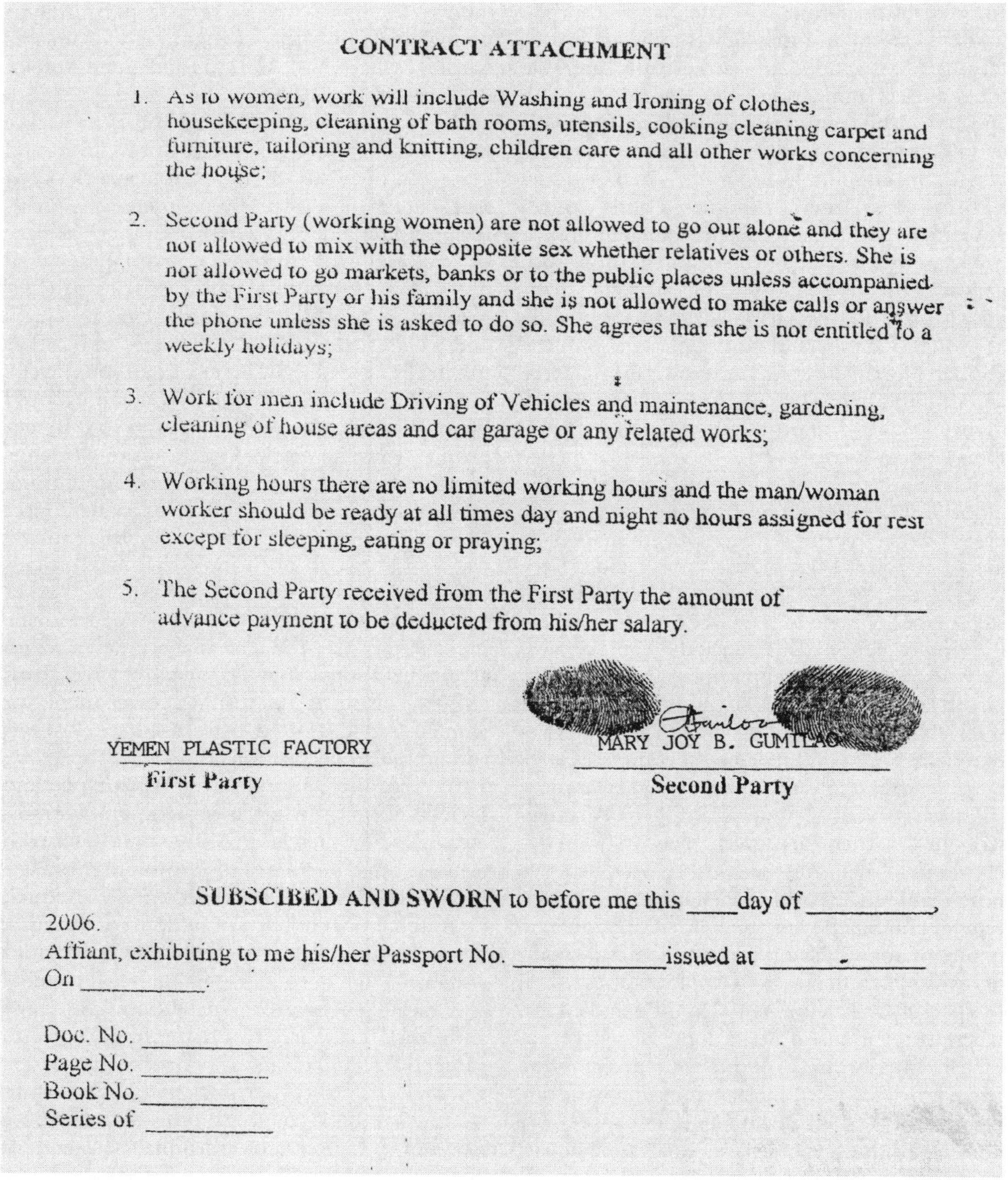

CONTRACT ATTACHMENT

1. As to women, work will include Washing and Ironing of clothes, housekeeping, cleaning of bath rooms, utensils, cooking cleaning carpet and furniture, tailoring and knitting, children care and all other works concerning the house;

2. Second Party (working women) are not allowed to go out alone and they are not allowed to mix with the opposite sex whether relatives or others. She is not allowed to go markets, banks or to the public places unless accompanied by the First Party or his family and she is not allowed to make calls or answer the phone unless she is asked to do so. She agrees that she is not entitled to a weekly holidays;

3. Work for men include Driving of Vehicles and maintenance, gardening, cleaning of house areas and car garage or any related works;

4. Working hours there are no limited working hours and the man/woman worker should be ready at all times day and night no hours assigned for rest except for sleeping, eating or praying;

5. The Second Party received from the First Party the amount of _____ advance payment to be deducted from his/her salary.

YEMEN PLASTIC FACTORY
_____
First Party

MARY JOY B. GUMILAO
_____
Second Party

SUBSCIBED AND SWORN to before me this ____ day of _____, 2006.

Affiant, exhibiting to me his/her Passport No. _____ issued at _____

On _____.

Doc. No. _____
Page No. _____
Book No. _____
Series of _____

Plate 3.3 A typical contract for domestic workers due to work abroad, Manila, Phillippines

Source: Robin Hammond/Panos

almost entirely white; at lower levels, the proportion of staff from lower-income countries (e.g. Poland) increases. That the vast majority of front-desk staff are women speaks to common associations 'between femininity and the presentation of self as available, willing, and pleasant that have been identified so many times in different service sector occupations, from flight attendants to selling banking services' (ibid., 12). The authors also note the management's growing reliance on foreign workers in the catering arm of the hotel. The most popular source of kitchen and restaurant staff in recent years has been India, with managers making twice-yearly trips to select trainees. While these immigrants, in some respects, are filling technical skills gaps, their popularity among employers reflects an assumption that foreign workers are more appropriate for the hospitality sector than British-born workers, whom employers view as lacking 'soft' interpersonal skills.

Social networks, McDowell and her associates recognize, are an important factor in explaining the segmentation of workers in the hotel industry. Transnational social networks, for instance, are crucial in channelling young Eastern European women into housekeeping jobs. Yet the agencies subcontracted to supply housekeeping staff invariably select young women whom they view as quick, reliable, and unencumbered by dependents. Immigrant networks, from this perspective, are effective because they serve employers' ends. As Waldinger and Lichter (2003, 38) remark, employers are loath to invest in worker training and are thus apt 'to prefer workers who resemble the incumbents who will teach them'. In the case of London's international hotels, descriptions of preferred workers by recruitment agencies are replete with references to the work ethic of different national groups and the ability of certain groups to be modest in appearance, to maintain a degree of invisibility, and to comport themselves in a manner that is commensurate with the low status of their work. The literature on the healthcare sector in the Global North is replete with similar analyses of employer stereotyping and the formation of gendered and racialized divisions of labour—see Batnitzky and McDowell's (2011) account of institutional discrimination within the UK's National Health Service (NHS), and Oikelome and Healy's (2013) discussion of the experiences of female international medical graduates in the NHS.

The role of the state in shaping an 'unskilled' immigrant labour force

In turning towards a more demand-side analysis of labour market segmentation, we have thus far focused on the ways employers draw upon and enact stereotypes based on gender, race, national origins, and the like. We must, in addition, consider the role of the state in producing occupational segmentation. Both sending and receiving states shape labour markets in a variety of ways. Sending states, for their part, can actively market their nationals overseas and facilitate the recruitment of their citizens in certain sectors both by negotiating bilateral labour agreements with receiving states and by subsidizing and promoting worker training in certain fields. A notable example is the Philippines, where the state has famously (or infamously, depending on one's perspective) made a business of promoting Filipino workers as diligent, compliant, and intelligent (Tyner, 2000; McKay, 2007). McKay (2007) reveals, for instance, how the National Seaman's Board, a state institution created in the 1970s to facilitate overseas employment for Filipino mariners, worked to differentiate Filipinos from their competitors. The state, working in conjunction with labour agents, constructed an image of Filipinos as 'natural' seafarers with the 'innate' qualities of pliability and passivity essential for low-rung jobs aboard cruise ships and merchant vessels. One brochure from the early 1980s boasted:

[W]hat truly makes a Filipino the most dependable shipmate are certain inherent traits. He is adaptable and hard-working. The Filipino's charm and friendliness makes for a harmonious relationship essential to the working situation on board. He is neat and disciplined. Reflective of household breeding, the Filipino is particularly observant of clean surroundings and good grooming. Moreover, he keeps within set rules and regulations.

(cited in McKay, 2007, 70)

Another example of a sending state's involvement in the production of segmented labour markets is Indonesia's encouragement of young women to work as domestic servants in Saudi Arabia. Rachel Silvey (2007) describes how the Indonesian state has drawn upon the moral authority of Islam to encourage young women to seek employment in Saudi Arabia, even as these young women encounter a barrage of news reports about the abuse of Asian workers at the hands of Saudi employers. The Indonesian state in this case has recast feminine ideals to include not only wife and mother, but also migrant worker whose earnings will contribute to Indonesia's national development. (We return to the role of post-colonial states in encouraging migration for the purpose of national development in Chapter 4.)

Meanwhile, receiving states contribute to the segmentation of labour forces by regulating flows of migrants across borders and by encouraging (or discouraging) the flow of migrant workers into particular sectors of the economy. Receiving states are more-or-less responsive to employer demands for particular kinds of workers—demands that are usually framed in terms of 'labour shortages', but which do not always reflect an actual lack of able-bodied native workers capable of performing certain jobs. As we have seen, employers want certain workers whom they view as hard-working and compliant and who can be paid less than native workers. They thus work with (or pressure) states to encourage specific flows of desired workers. In some cases, states respond to employer demands by implementing bilateral labour recruitment schemes, such as the German guest worker programme, which recruited thousands of Turkish, North African, and Southern and Eastern European manufacturing workers in the 1950s and 1960s, and the Bracero Program, which supplied farms in the American Southwest with Mexican seasonal workers between 1942 and 1964. In other cases, states respond to employer pressure through the non-enforcement of border- and immigration-control measures. This can be seen in the case of agribusiness interests in the United States who have, until recently, ensured weak enforcement of laws against the hiring of undocumented immigrants on commercial farms and in meat-packing plants (Andreas, 2000). (We return to the issue of undocumented immigrants shortly.)

States also participate in the segmentation of labour forces by constructing a multitude of legal categories with varying levels of rights and privileges attached to each. By withholding certain rights from foreign workers—such as the right to change jobs or to leave a sponsoring employer, which is a common condition of temporary work visas worldwide—states can increase the vulnerability of workers and can ensure that they remain confined to lower-end jobs. The discriminatory practices of employers, in this sense, are reinforced or exacerbated by the regulatory and policing power of the state. Conversely, by extending rights and protections to certain classes of workers—those deemed more desirable by virtue of particular skills or perceived racial similarity to the dominant population—states can ensure some degree of economic mobility within segmented labour markets.

Linda McDowell's (2003) account of the British government's recruitment of refugees from the Soviet-occupied Baltic republics after World War II—euphemistically called European Volunteer Workers (EVWs)—illustrates well the ways in which receiving states participate in the construction of labour markets along the lines of gender, race, and legal status. Following the war, the British state initiated labour recruitment schemes to funnel Eastern European workers into key sectors facing labour shortages, including hospitals and factories. That native women were not available for these jobs reflected the state's pronatalist policies that encouraged British women to view themselves first and foremost as wives and mothers. There were other options for the British state to fill these jobs, including women from Britain's Caribbean colonies, who were British citizens and who were streaming into Britain in the 1950s (not least because of active recruitment efforts by British employers). Many Afro-Caribbean women did indeed enter the lower echelons of the National Health Service, but the British state viewed Eastern European women as having superior work habits and attitudes and as being more racially assimilable into British society (Irish women, a traditional source of domestic labour, were likewise seen as a step up from non-white post-colonial migrants). Despite its favourable opinion of EVWs, the British state imposed strict, explicit conditions on their entry into Britain: female workers were required to be single, to have no dependents, and to be in good health; and male and female workers were compelled to stay in the low-level jobs assigned to them by the Ministry of Labour usually for two years. These restrictions on EVW employment mobility were necessary for the state to gain the support of British trade unions, which were wary of competition from foreign workers.

A present-day example of state participation in labour market segmentation is the Live-In Caregiver programme in Canada, which was instituted in the early 1990s, replacing an earlier programme of overseas domestic-worker recruitment. The decision to recruit foreign workers to serve as live-in domestic help, in the first instance, reflects the state's sanctioning of gendered ideologies that place the work of caring for children within private homes, rather than in publicly supported childcare centres (see Dillaway and Paré, 2008). The Canadian government has described the programme as responding to shortages of care workers, but it is clear that this is a shortage created by the poor remuneration and conditions of childcare and domestic work and the subsequent coding of these jobs as 'immigrant work'. For several years, live-in caregivers were excluded from regulations governing overtime pay and standard work hours for Canadian workers. Even with the extension of formal labour protections to live-in caregivers, the fact that these workers, by definition, work in private homes means that they are often treated as family members rather than as wage earners or professionals with certain workplace rights. Despite the fact that many programme participants have university degrees in nursing or other professions, Filipinas have become one of the most occupationally segregated groups in Canada, with a disproportionate number employed as nannies and housekeepers. It seems that the two years in which programme participants are not permitted to pursue other employment opportunities or to receive professional training or education has the effect of closing off employment options to them when they have finished their time as live-in caregivers (Pratt, 1999; Brickner and Straehle, 2010).

The state and undocumented workers

The role of the state in generating cleavages in labour markets is nowhere more evident than in the case of undocumented workers. In Malaysia, Saudi Arabia, Israel, Greece, the US, and many other contexts, undocumented migrants serve as an inexpensive, compliant labour force that accepts difficult and degrading work conditions that would be unacceptable to native workers or even to authorized immigrants. Their presence has become crucial in highly competitive industries with large seasonal labour requirements (like agriculture and construction) and in declining industries where cheap labour compensates for the lack of capital investment in productivity (as with garment manufacturing

BOX 3.3 TRAFFICKING

Trafficking refers to the recruitment and transportation of a person by means of force, abduction, fraud, and deception for the purpose of controlling and exploiting that person for economic gain. Trafficking is commonly associated with sexual exploitation, prostitution, and forced labour. International organizations and advocacy groups describe trafficking as a growing phenomenon that affects hundreds of thousands of people—especially girls and women—every year. Consequently, it has become a *cause célèbre* in some policymaking and academic circles in the Global North. There are, however, critics of anti-trafficking organizations. Some argue, for instance, that anti-trafficking groups have revived the 'white slave panic' that swept Europe and the United States in the early 20th century and that thrived on lurid accounts of young white women being lured into prostitution by corrupt older men. Critics charge that such narratives past and present have not only exaggerated the extent of the trafficking phenomenon but have also enforced rigid conceptions of women's sexual purity and innocence while demonizing foreign men. Current discussions of trafficking, these critics argue, deny the possibility that migrant women might knowingly and purposefully engage in undocumented migration and sex work (Doezema, 1999). Others, while critical of the sensationalism and assumptions of women's passivity found in many current discussions of trafficking, emphasize that the participation of migrant women in the sex trade must be understood both as a matter of individual agency and of marginalization created by anti-immigrant measures in the Global North (Agustín, 2005).

in the Global North). We also find high levels of undocumented immigration in feminized sectors like childcare and domestic service, where, as we have seen, levels of state oversight tend to be low because this work is performed inside private homes. Another feminized sector that utilizes undocumented (and sometimes trafficked) labour is sex work and the 'entertainment' industry in Europe, East Asia, the Gulf Arab states, and elsewhere (Box 3.3 provides a detailed discussion of **trafficking**).

While we might think of undocumented immigrants as defying state authority—as overwhelming the state's capacity to control migration flows—we must consider how state authority and legal systems *produce* the category of 'undocumented' or 'illegal' immigrants as a subset of migrants and, indeed, as a particular kind of member of society (Chauvin and Garcés-Mascareñas, 2012; Garcés-Mascareñas, 2010; De Genova, 2002). 'Illegal immigrant', as mentioned in Chapter 1 of this book, is a rather pejorative term that obscures the ways that migrants can

move in and out of legal status. Yet the term can be used critically to highlight the capacity of sovereign, territorial nation-states to control the movement of workers across borders and to place certain migrants outside the bounds of formal membership (Ngai, 2003; Willen, 2007). Illegal immigration results when states close off legal paths of migration and restrict legal means of crossing into national territory. The state, in a sense, *illegalizes* certain migrations. In the US context, to illustrate, the category of 'illegal immigrant' emerged in the 1920s shortly after the creation of national-origins quotas, which greatly curtailed what had been virtually unrestricted flows of immigrants. Prior to numerical restrictions, as Ngai (2003) explains, the idea of unlawful entry and the possibility of summary deportation applied only to very specific groups: Chinese immigrants, the insane and mentally ill, prostitutes, and criminals. However, with the implementation of national-origins quotas, and with the subsequent creation of the US Border Patrol, 'illegal immigration achieved mass proportions' and 'deportation assumed a central place in immigration policy' (Ngai, 2003, 70).

The increasing salience of 'illegal immigrant' as a category, then, goes hand in hand with state's prioritization of border control, usually in response to domestic political pressures. Being illegal, however, is not so much about being excluded from national societies as it is about being incorporated within societies in a subordinate fashion (Chauvin and Garcés-Mascareñas, 2012). In some instances, the undocumented *do* achieve some measure of legal rights as workers and residents (Bosniak, 1994) and are offered paths to **regularization** (Calavita, 2005). Nonetheless, the position of undocumented immigrants in economies and national societies is most often marked by precariousness and vulnerability owing to periodic crackdowns by immigration authorities (De Genova, 2002). Of particular importance in configuring the vulnerability of these workers is the threat of **deportation**, which, as Garcés-Mascareña (2010, 85) notes, serves 'not so much to reduce illegal migration as to delimit a symbolic precinct of illegality'. Put another way, as De Genova (2002, 438) suggests, 'It is deportability, and not deportation per se, that has historically rendered undocumented migrant labour a distinctly disposable commodity'. In this respect, while border patrol and immigration-policing activities can make life very difficult for undocumented workers, employers are seldom penalized for hiring them, ensuring a steady demand for their labour and providing a strong incentive for unauthorized border crossings and the overstaying of visas.

The case of Malaysia illustrates these dynamics well. Large-scale migration to Malaysia began in the 1970s, at a time when the Malaysian state was embarking on an ambitious post-colonial development agenda that relied heavily on cheap foreign labour. In the 1970s, Malaysia had no formal, legal mechanisms for the recruitment of low-skilled foreign workers, and so many arrived without documents mainly from Indonesia, the Philippines, and Thailand. Initially, many of these were employed on plantations in rural areas, but they began to find work in cities in construction and the service sector and as small-scale entrepreneurs. Eventually, they became an important presence in the manufacturing sector. In order to wrest control over the growing numbers of undocumented migrant workers—whom Malaysians have episodically blamed for disease, drug trafficking, terrorism, and other ills—the Malaysian state sought in the early 1990s to implement a legal recruitment programme for foreign workers. While the number of legal foreign workers increased due to regularization efforts, so, too, did that of irregular migrants, reaching perhaps two million by 2011 (Kassim and Zin, 2011). Subsequent efforts by the Malaysian state to control undocumented immigration through detention centres, deportations, and employer sanctions have been ineffective because of weak enforcement. Employers have had an important role in reducing the effectiveness of these measures, which they have viewed as disruptive to productivity. As Kassim and Zin (2011) remark, employers violate rules on foreign-worker employment with impunity, recruiting workers through informal agents and ignoring amnesty and legalization directives. The lack of compliance is especially rampant on rural plantations, where employment practices are largely hidden from regulators. (The issue of state control over migration comes up again in Chapter 6.)

Labour market segmentation and skilled migration

Much of our discussion thus far has centred on the lower echelons of the labour market—on the masses of 'unskilled' migrant workers who fill positions in construction, manufacturing, domestic service, and the like. But migrants also fulfil labour market demands in the higher echelons of the labour market—in positions that require high levels of education and professional training. We give special attention here to **skilled migration**, weaving together human capital, social capital, and demand-side perspectives. The following discussion highlights both the differences and disparities between skilled and unskilled migrants—especially in terms of mobility within and access to the labour markets of the Global North—and the similarities between them in terms of their subjection to various forms of exploitation and precariousness.

The very concept of skilled migration suggests that there are some migrants endowed with particular forms of human capital that are especially valued and rewarded by employers. In today's technology-, information-, and service-driven economy, the most highly prized workers are those with specialized technical and management skills. Scholars have paid increasing attention to skilled migration in recent decades as part of a more general effort to understand the workings of global economic integration (Koser and Salt, 1997; Favell and Smith, 2007). Some of this research has explored the role of migration in the globalization of advanced producer services (e.g. high-level accountancy and investment banking) and corporate management. Beaverstock (2005), for instance, has documented the phenomenon of short-term inter- and intra-company transfers of business professionals that link together corporate offices in global cities like London, New York, and Singapore. Complementing Beaverstock's analysis is Ley's (2011) discussion of footloose Chinese elites who manage business interests in East Asia and Canada (see also Ryan and Mulholland's (2014a) research on French skilled migrants in London). Others have commented on the ways in which the rapid expansion of the healthcare industry in the Global North has required the recruitment of medical professionals from the Global South (Ray et al., 2006; Raghuram, 2009). The British National Health Service, as we have seen, has relied heavily on the recruitment of foreign doctors and nurses since its formation in the late 1940s. Today, around 30 percent of doctors and 40 percent of nurses in the NHS are foreign-born (Snow and Jones, 2011; also Young et al., 2010). The recruitment of foreign doctors and nurses is a similarly common phenomenon in the United States, especially in less desirable parts of the country that have difficulty attracting native medical professionals.

Scholars have also given attention to the recruitment of academics and scientists (Jöns, 2009; Ackers, 2005; Harvey, 2008) and information technology (IT) workers by the Global North. These immigrant knowledge workers have been viewed as crucial to the development of high-technology sectors in wealthy economies. Saxenian (2002), for instance, credits highly skilled Chinese and Indian immigrants with reviving Silicon Valley's flagging high-tech industries in the early 1990s. By the early 2000s, she notes, Chinese and Indian immigrants constituted nearly a quarter of company heads in this premier high-tech cluster. Prominent examples of entrepreneurialism and business formation among immigrant knowledge workers remind us of the role of social capital in shaping migrant participation in receiving economies. Earlier, we described entrepreneurialism mainly as a strategy of lower-income migrants to generate income under difficult economic circumstances. But entrepreneurialism is also common among relatively privileged skilled migrants who, by virtue of their educational and class backgrounds, have extensive business connections with tech firms and entrepreneurs in countries of origin. As Wong (2004) illustrates in his account of Taiwanese entrepreneurs in Canada, skilled workers in some instances make use of business and social connections with places of origin to build successful transnational enterprises.

If the growth of skilled migrant flows in the Global North is a reflection of profound economic shifts that have increased demands for highly educated workers, it is also a reflection of state policies that grant favourable treatment to those with valued human capital. In sharp contrast to mass, unskilled migration, which is often framed as a societal problem (regardless of actual labour demands), skilled migration has typically been understood as essential to economic growth and the global competitiveness of national economies (Walsh, 2008). Thus, as they have raised barriers to unskilled workers, many countries especially in the Global North have lowered barriers to those with desired skills. Some have made available special work permits and visas that in some cases can be converted to permanent residency (if not full citizenship) after a given period of time. In the early 2000s, for instance, Britain decoupled work permits from pre-arranged employment with British firms, making it possible for skilled foreigners to enter the country to search for employment or to start a business. Prospective migrants were assigned points depending upon their level of education and field of expertise and were granted access to the British labour market accordingly. Other European states, including Germany, France, and Sweden, followed suit with various incentives for skilled workers. Sensing fierce competition among European states for migrant professionals, the European Union proposed the so-called 'blue card' to encourage EU members to work together to attract skilled workers (Collett and Zuleeg, 2008). The Blue Card was enacted in 2009, allowing holders to seek employment in any member state without going through any further immigration hurdles.

In seeking to make themselves more attractive to skilled workers through liberal work-permit provisions, the EU and individual European countries have been emulating (and competing against) traditional settler societies, who for several decades have had expansive immigration programmes that favour the highly skilled. Australia and Canada, to illustrate, reformed their immigration system in the 1960s and 1970s, dropping white-only provisions and giving priority through a points system to immigrants with high levels of education, skill, and capital (Walsh, 2008). In Canada, the Immigration Act of 1976 made employment skills, education, and language abilities important pillars of immigrant admission. These preferences were reinforced by the 2001 Immigration and Refugee Protection Act, which emphasized education, language, and adaptability, rewarding those with tertiary degrees and significant work experience with more admission points. In 2010, economic immigrants, most of whom are highly educated, constituted more than 60 percent of all immigrants admitted to Canada, double the figure in the mid-1980s (Challinor, 2011). Australia likewise has placed greater emphasis on skilled migration in recent decades as it has sought to build its banking and finance sector and its knowledge-based industries. Since the 1990s, skilled migration has outstripped other forms of immigration, including family and humanitarian migration; in addition, Australia has facilitated the entry of temporary skilled workers, placing no limits on the numbers admitted through its 'subclass 457' visa program (Inglis, 2004).

Throughout the Global North, an important, and less visible, mode of entry for skilled migrants has been through university systems, and especially through postgraduate programmes in the sciences and engineering. Higher education has become a major growth industry, especially in English-speaking countries like Britain, Canada, the United States, and Australia, and universities are keen to attract foreign students, many of whom will pay full fees—a boon to cash-strapped public universities (Brooks and Waters, 2011). In the United States alone, the number of international undergraduate and postgraduate students increased from 34,000 in 1954–5 to 565,000 in 2005–6, jumping to almost 820,000 in 2013. Foreign students today account for almost 4 percent of the US university student population (up from 1.4 percent in 1954–5) (Batalova, 2007; Porter and Belkin, 2013). A disproportionate number of foreign students enter technical programmes that are rapidly being abandoned by native students, and during their course of study they provide valuable labour as research assistants (often to foreign-born academics) and as graduate instructors. Many of these students stay on after they receive their advanced degrees, taking advantage of liberal skilled-migrant visa programmes to find employment in biotechnology, engineering, and software firms. Indeed, the Australian government in the early 2000s explicitly incorporated foreign students into its skilled migration programme, allowing foreign graduates of Australian universities to apply for permanent resident status without leaving Australia first (Hawthorne, 2005; also Ziguras and Law, 2006; for a discussion of state policies towards student migration in other Global North contexts, see Alberts, 2007; Gribble, 2008; Baas, 2006; Mavroudi and Warren, 2013).

The deskilling of skilled migrants

As wealthy, developed countries have rushed to attract skilled workers and to lower barriers to entry in the name of global competitiveness and economic growth, they have produced what is, in many ways, a global market for skills. Those with the 'right' skills have relatively easy access to multiple labour markets in the Global North and can move between them in search of the highest return on their skills. Yet we cannot assume that all skilled migrants are the privileged members of a hyper-mobile, elite labour force. Skilled migrants face multiple forms of discrimination, deeply embedded in immigration policies and workplace practices, that limit their mobility within and between labour markets and that prevent them from capitalizing on their skills and education (Colic-Peisker and Tilbury, 2007; Kofman, 2014).

While in high demand in the Global North, highly educated immigrants in some cases suffer from surprisingly high rates of unemployment. For instance, Kogan (2011) demonstrates that immigrants to Germany since 1990—most of them from Eastern Europe, Africa, and the Middle East—have struggled to integrate into the German labour market, despite their high levels of formal education relative to the German population overall. Kogan explains this discrepancy in terms of an 'ethnic penalty', showing that education and human capital alone cannot account for labour market performance. Likewise, analyses of Canadian employment data in the 2000s revealed that over a quarter of university-educated immigrant men and around 40 percent of similarly educated immigrant women were employed in positions that normally required at most a secondary-school education; the comparable statistic for native-born Canadians, male and female, was around 10 percent. Such disparities appeared to persist even among immigrants who had resided in Canada for a decade or more (Galarneau and Morissette, 2008). Writing in the Canadian context, Harald Bauder (2003) attributes the gap in earnings between the Canadian-born population and immigrants to the workings of professional associations that regulate entry to various professions by setting standards for licensing and certification. These associations, Bauder contends, often refuse to recognize education and experience gained overseas, effectively barring immigrants from practising their professions in Canada while giving native workers easier access by lowering competition. Government bodies become complicit in these practices by imposing their own requirements on various professional fields, most notably in medicine. (See Iredale (2005) and Hawthorne (2005) for further discussion of professional gatekeepers and the non-recognition of immigrant credentials in the Australian context.)

The process by which immigrants lose access to the occupations and status they held in their countries of origin and are compelled to take lower-level work is called **deskilling**. Scholars have recognized deskilling to be a particularly severe problem for female migrants with professional qualifications (Iredale, 2005; Kofman and Raghuram, 2005; Man, 2004; Jöns, 2011; Lazaridis, 2007). While women have benefitted from the expansion of skilled migration opportunities, especially in traditionally feminine sectors like nursing and education, they have also experienced significant downward mobility—though the fact that many women migrate as 'dependents' means that this downward mobility is not always recognized by policymakers (Kofman and Raghuram, 2005; Man, 2004). As with all women, migrant women are disadvantaged in the professional labour force by career breaks and the need to balance household and childcare responsibilities with paid employment. But migrant women are especially disadvantaged by the lack of social and family networks in countries of settlement that are so crucial to managing domestic responsibilities. As well, prior to migrating, women may have had fewer years of host-language training or work experience in a host-language-speaking workplace than their male counterparts. For women faced with the burden of establishing domestic life in a country of settlement, the time and expense involved in updating qualifications or receiving language training may be daunting and may cause highly educated women to give up entirely on careers. When faced with economic hardships, these women will accept jobs in low-wage, flexible forms of employment, especially in service and sales (Man, 2004). Regardless of the type of employment they accept, there is evidence that migrant women of colour are hampered in their career progression by racism, sexism, and xenophobia among employers (Man, 2004; Purkayastha, 2005)—a pattern that has been widely discussed in the context of nursing and healthcare (Batnitzky and McDowell, 2011; Oikelome and Healy, 2013; for a related discussion of deskilling among refugees and asylum seekers, see Colic-Peisker and Tilbury, 2007).

Women migrants can also be deskilled by policies in some receiving countries that bar spousal employment, especially in the case of temporary visa holders. This phenomenon has been commented on in relation to the so-called **trailing spouses** of mobile business professionals and intra-company transferees. Intra-company transfers and overseas secondments are heavily dominated by men, for whom short-term assignments overseas serve as an important means of career advancement. The wives of these 'skilled transients' experience a lengthy break in their own career trajectories and are confined to domestic roles for the duration of their husbands' overseas assignments. Beaverstock (2002) comments on the important role of corporate wives in building the social networks that grease the wheels of corporate capitalism in global financial centres (also Yeoh, Huang, and Willis, 2000). Others, however, have noted the social isolation experienced by trailing spouses and the obstacles they face in building social connections during their husbands' overseas assignments (Ryan and Mulholland, 2014b).

Skilled workers as an exploited labour force?

The deskilling experienced by many highly educated migrant workers speaks to a broader issue of worker exploitation. While we tend to associate exploitation with low-skilled and undocumented workers, we must also ask whether skilled migration programmes create a pool of cheap, flexible, foreign labour for corporations and contribute to the neglect of training and education for the local workforce. The exploitation of educated migrants is very evident in academia, where foreign postgraduate students and postdoctoral fellows provide crucial support on research projects and in the classroom for very little pay (Cantwell, 2011). The abuse of foreign students has been especially egregious in Japan, where highly restrictive immigration policies have been circumvented by various 'trainee' and Japanese-language programmes that provide employers with access to inexpensive, flexible workers. Every year thousands of Chinese university students enrol in (mostly profit-driven) language schools in Japan and take up low-waged part-time jobs in restaurants, factories, supermarkets, or construction sites, using their earnings to finance their studies in Japan or to support families back home (Liu-Farrer, 2009). The situation seems to improve for students who manage to enrol in proper undergraduate or postgraduate degree programmes, and some do go on to successful careers in Japanese corporations that do business in China. However, many others find themselves trapped in low-waged, insecure, and irregular jobs.

Charges of exploitation have also entered into discussions of temporary skilled-worker programmes in the US, and especially the H-1B programme. The **H-1B visa** allows employers to hire foreign workers with specialized skills in engineering and other technical fields on a short-term basis. These visas are especially prevalent in Silicon Valley and in other high-tech clusters, where workers from India and China are reputed to toil long hours for relatively little pay in the hope of converting their status to permanent residency. Chakravartty (2006) emphasizes that many Indian H-1B workers come from privileged backgrounds and successfully leverage their US experience in the Indian high-tech industry. But for many others, the experience of being an H-1B worker is one of difficult transitions, discrimination, and segregation at work and outside of work. Chakravartty is especially critical of 'bodyshops', or temporary placement agencies—most of them run by Indians—that place young, mostly male computer programmers from India in short-term jobs in the US. These bodyshops have been known to trap workers in unfair contracts and to withhold immigration papers as a means of managing potential complaints against employers.

While skilled migration is generally less politically problematic than mass migration, it can become quite contentious in contexts of fiscal austerity and high unemployment. Indeed, some wealthy countries have scaled back the recruitment of skilled migrants, placing caps on educated workers and raising entry barriers as a means of guaranteeing that only the most desirable and most highly qualified migrants in specific fields can enter. In response to the 2008–9 global economic recession, for instance, Britain has made it more difficult for skilled, educated workers from outside the European Economic Area to migrate without employer sponsorship (Mavroudi and Warren, 2013; for an overview of the recent retooling of points systems and the renewed emphasis on employer sponsorship in Britain, Australia, Canada, and other wealthy countries, see Sumption, 2014). The European Union, as well, has been slow to implement the EU Blue Card, which was intended to attract the world's skilled workers to Europe. With European institutions weakened by the EU financial crisis of 2009, member states, it seems, have been increasingly reluctant to relinquish their sovereignty. Van Riemsdijk (2012, 353) notes that the final version of the Blue Card plan that was implemented in 2009 'granted member states considerable power and authority in the admission of skilled migrants . . . and reduced the rights of applicants'. Likewise, 'the application requirements vary considerably among member states in terms of job offer requirements, minimum salary levels, and recognition of qualifications', thereby defeating the purpose of a common EU policy to attract skilled workers.

Opposition to skilled temporary worker programmes has been especially strong among labour interests in the United States, who accuse technology firms of undercutting wages of native-born engineers, software developers, and technicians by creating a class of high-tech indentured servants. Pressures from labour interests have been successful in limiting the H-1B programme, dropping the number of visas granted from 195,000 in 2000 to 65,000 in 2013 (with an additional 20,000 visas granted for those with advanced degrees). Employers have vociferously opposed caps on temporary visas, arguing that these caps have created debilitating worker shortages. As we have seen earlier, however, scholars and labour activists alike express some scepticism about the notion of 'labour shortages', suggesting that these are fabricated by employers in order to suit their particular interests. Writing in the Irish context, for instance, Wickham and Bruff (2008) argue that the apparent shortage of skilled workers in the Irish software industry in the 1990s and 2000s was largely the product of the Irish state's lack of investment in the country's technical education system and the ease with which employers could simply 'buy' skills from overseas rather than produce them at home. Firms realized quickly that they could slash training costs of existing workers by continuously importing necessary skills, and they were enabled in doing so by generous work permit provisions.

Recovering migrant agency

Much of the preceding discussion has explored the role of employers and the state in shaping the participation of migrants in the labour force, often in ways that disadvantage both skilled and unskilled migrants. Our focus on employer and state practices, we must concede, can obscure the ways in which migrants themselves produce and shape labour market outcomes. In this final section, we wish to reiterate the capacity of migrants (and workers more generally) to negotiate, manipulate, and/or subvert state policies and workplace norms to suit their own livelihood strategies, personal ambitions, and interests (Carswell and De Neve, 2013).

Migration, we should remind ourselves, is an important strategy through which workers pursue a variety of aims, ranging from the provision of support for children and family members to the achievement of personal independence and financial security. Reynolds (2006), for instance, describes how highly educated Nigerian women treat migration to Britain, the US, and other wealthy countries as a means of fulfilling what

they feel to be their responsibilities to their families' economic well-being. Migration for these women is a conscious choice, albeit one made in a context of diminishing economic opportunities in Nigeria, and professional employment abroad provides them with the opportunity to enhance their status in their families and communities. Even low-status jobs provide opportunities for personal advancement and empowerment. Szewczyk (2014), for instance, suggests that some educated Polish migrants in Britain view low-status jobs as a 'stepping stone' on the path to economic success and personal fulfilment, and they understand such jobs to be one of a suite of strategies that can help them advance in the labour market. Writing in a very different context, Rogaly (2009) describes the informal, individualistic actions through which seasonal agricultural workers in India improve the circumstances of their paid labour and create new opportunities for income generation. Migrant workers, Rogaly shows, exercise a degree of leverage over employers, who rely on the cooperation of workers to harvest perishable crops. Workers negotiate better wages and work conditions and may press employers to improve the quality and quantity of food provided to them. Such improvements may be short-lived, Rogaly suggests, but they are significant to migrants' subjective experience of work. At the same time, the wages earned through seasonal labour can be invested in small enterprises. These enterprises are usually quite marginal, yet they mean freedom from employer supervision.

We also see evidence of migrant agency in the manipulation of employer stereotypes. While implicated in discriminatory practices, stereotypes can provide desired opportunities, and workers can willingly and actively participate in the stereotyping of themselves (partly by cultivating particular behaviours and demeanours) in order to gain an advantage in a given sector or firm (Waldinger and Lichter, 2003). Datta and Brickell's (2009) interviews with Polish construction workers in Britain show how foreign

Plate 3.4 Polish supermarket, Hammersmith, London, UK
Source: Ian Teh/Panos

workers can reproduce stereotypes for their own benefit. Following the accession of post-socialist Eastern European states to the European Union in 2004, over 600,000 workers—mostly young, single people from Poland—came to Britain to work. As we have seen, many young women entered the hotel sector as cleaning staff. Many young men, meanwhile, entered the building trades despite having few skills. These workers were eagerly hired nonetheless by English employers, who viewed them as hard workers and quick learners. Young Polish men, in turn, successfully marketed themselves as having more desirable, refined qualities than young British men, whom they described as drunk, football-obsessed, and unmotivated. As they have acquired training in the building trades, Poles have constructed themselves as artisans committed to high-quality work and as flexible workers whose presence in Britain is deserved.

Focusing on migrant agency and intentionality is especially pertinent in the case of undocumented migrants. Undocumented status renders migrants highly vulnerable to exploitation by employers. Yet we might consider the ways in which undocumented status serves particular ends for migrants, such that they are willing to accept the risk involved in migrating clandestinely or overstaying a visa. Illegality provides certain options for workers when state policies to regularize the migrant labour force prove too costly and onerous. To illustrate, the Malaysian state's efforts to increase oversight of migration flows has made legal entry very difficult and expensive and has involved the creation of labour contracts that come close to indenture (Killias, 2010). For many migrants, then, illegal entry or overstaying a tourist visa is a far more rational option than migrating legally (Garcés-Mascareñas, 2010). Illegality is preferred not only because it is inexpensive and relatively hassle-free, but also because it gives workers some freedom to choose jobs and employers, which is not the case if they migrate through legal recruitment channels (ibid). Helma Lutz (2004) makes a similar observation with respect to undocumented domestic workers in Germany, who are seemingly attracted to insecure, precarious jobs precisely because of the lack of regulation and state surveillance. These observations prompt us to look beyond the workings of states and employers and to recognize the ingenuity of migrants in circumventing state power and responding to opportunities abroad.

Of course, while undocumented migration is, for many, a conscious strategy to improve earning potential, unauthorized migrants may seek to regularize their situation in order to reduce their vulnerability to state authorities and employers. There have been a number of examples in recent years of political mobilization among undocumented immigrants and the articulation of demands for political inclusion. An example of such mobilization is United We Dream, a national organization of immigrant youth in the US—many of them the children of undocumented Latino immigrants—that has lobbied for the rights of undocumented families and that has assisted undocumented immigrants in applying for various amnesty and regularization programmes. Another example of migrant political mobilization is the United Workers Association, a London-based organization that campaigned in the 1990s for labour rights for domestic workers, who, as we have seen, often lack workplace protections (Anderson, 2001). In more recent years, the Filipino Domestic Workers Association and Justice for Domestic Workers have played a similar role in advocating

for migrant rights in Britain. Such cases of collective action point further to the active role of migrant workers in shaping and transforming the circumstances in which they live and work. (For a more detailed discussion of the mobilization of undocumented immigrants, see Nicholls, 2014.)

Conclusions

This chapter has explored the varying ways that migrants participate in the economies of destination societies. Labour migration at one level is a matter of labour supply and demand and the unevenness of wages levels across space. But it is much more than that. Migration and labour-market formation are social processes that involve a range of actors and interests and that operate through social relationships and networks. Employers, states, and migrants themselves are all implicated in the construction of labour markets and particular modes of working. Migration is not incidental to the functioning of labour markets, but rather is part and parcel of the way participants in market economies differentiate between workers, types of work, and levels of compensation for that work (Bauder, 2006). It is for this reason that migrant participation in the labour markets of industrial and post-industrial societies tends to be contentious: migrant workers are not just any workers; they are outsiders who fulfil specific roles in economies that, in spite of globalization, continue to be defined in national terms. Their presence makes possible certain labour practices and inequalities that filter through their entire employment structure. Their advantages *and* their exploitability are interpreted equally as threats to native workers.

Understanding the roles and functions that migrant workers serve in economies gives us a critical perspective on debates about whether migrants are 'good' or 'bad' for the economy. Such debates have become prevalent in the past two or three decades in many wealthier, immigrant-receiving societies, with each side presenting evidence about the relative costs and benefits of immigration to the economy overall. On one side of the debate are those who support immigration, ranging from business interests and free-market advocates to those who support the right of workers to cross borders as a matter of social justice. These pro-immigration interests draw on a multitude of studies showing that migrants provide goods and services that might otherwise not be available, that they keep inflation in check, that they boost economic productivity, and that their contributions to economies far outweigh any costs they impose on welfare states (see, for instance, the *Economist*, 2014; Lemos and Portes, 2008; Lucchino et al., 2012). On the other side of the debate are labour interests who see competition and declining wages, business groups who fear declining skill levels among migrants, and social conservatives who fear the presence of cultural and racial 'Others'. These interest groups are able to draw on equally copious data demonstrating that migrants use a disproportionate amount of public services, that they depress wages, and that they do not contribute significantly to economic growth.

The truth, of course, is much messier than either side is willing to admit. Dustmann et al. (2005) highlight the difficulties of assessing the impacts of immigration on labour market outcomes for local workers, not least because of the shortcomings of data gathering within and between national contexts. While they have found little evidence that migration has either negative or positive impacts on local workers in the UK in aggregate, they also concede that consequences are likely to vary according to the skills and qualifications of the workers being studied. Whether one views migration in positive or negative terms, it seems, hinges on the position one occupies in the labour market and in social hierarchies. As George Borjas (1999) has argued, the expansion of migration in the United States after 1965 has been a boon for the American middle class, which has benefitted

from the plenitude of inexpensive service workers (e.g. cleaners, nannies, restaurant workers). But renewed mass immigration has been more problematic for the lowest echelon of native workers, who have faced stagnant or declining wages—though some economists would dispute that immigration is the main cause of growing wage inequality (Card, 2005). Borjas, as we mentioned earlier, argues that the United States should do more to increase the 'quality' of its immigrants by adopting a more selective immigration system, akin to that which exists in Australia and Canada. Yet selective immigration offers its own set of quandaries. To what extent do skilled migration programmes allow governments and businesses to ignore the training and education of national labour forces? To what extent does the emphasis on skilled migration shut out those who fulfil labour-market demands in low-end sectors and force them into the ranks of the undocumented?

The case of the American poultry industry illustrates well the difficulties involved in assessing whether migration is 'good' or 'bad'. In the mid-20th century, meatpacking was a highly unionized industry concentrated in metropolitan areas in the American Midwest. Starting in the 1970s, however, there was strong price competition from foreign producers and from a rapidly growing low-cost poultry processing industry based in the rural, non-unionized South. Along with a move to more rural locations, the meatpacking industry experienced advances in mechanization that downgraded skill requirements. Wages in the industry overall declined, and poultry producers and packagers increasingly turned to immigrant workers, predominantly Latino, both documented and undocumented, who were willing to work for the wages on offer (Champlin and Hake, 2006). Unionization rates in the industry overall have plummeted since the 1980s, and meatpacking today is marked by high levels of both worker turnover and workplace injuries and deaths (Kandel and Parrado, 2005).

Who has benefitted from the transformation of the meatpacking industry? Have migrants helped or hurt the economy in this instance? It depends entirely on your perspective and your position in society. Those in agriculture and food processing industries argue that without migrants, they could not survive growing competition from foreign producers; nor could they be competitive in foreign markets. The presence of immigrant workers, in other words, has preserved the US meatpacking industry, much as it kept the US garment industry afloat in the 1980s. The declining cost of producing poultry, at the same time, has provided Americans with a plentiful supply of extremely cheap, conveniently packaged food (given their continued responsibility for domestic reproduction, American women, in particular, appreciate the availability of skinned, cut-up, ready-to-cook poultry). These jobs, of course, also provide a wage for many low-skilled immigrant workers—a source of livelihood for families in the US and abroad. It is important to note that many of those working in rural packing plants in the South started out in California and other western states and moved east due to diminishing wages and employment opportunities in those areas. Working in a poultry plant, while not very pleasant, is a choice and a strategy for household survival (Marrow, 2011).

Equally, we can look at the transformations of the poultry industry—and the role of immigrants in it—as part of a wider process of industrial restructuring in the face of intensified global competition. This process has seen the decline of compensation and of work conditions, the deskilling of many industrial jobs, and the increasing precariousness of work. It has also contributed significantly to widening wage disparities in the US. American consumers' access to cheap and convenient products (whether chicken or clothing or electronics), in large part, has come at the expense both of the American working class, which no longer enjoys high wages or stable employment, *and* immigrant workers, who labour in very poor working conditions. Clearly over the past 40 years the relationship between labour and capital has become increasingly unbalanced and one-sided, with corporations exercising far more control over the terms of work and demanding increasing flexibility among workers with less compensation (Sparke, 2012). In evaluating whether immigration is good or bad—whether we should promote or discourage the mobility of workers across borders—we must think very carefully about the place of migrant workers in wider systems of production and our complicity as consumers of goods and services in the creation of segmented and highly unequal labour markets.

Key terms in this chapter

deportation	middleman minority
deskilling	myth of return
ethnic economy	regularization
H-1B visa	skilled migration
human capital	social capital
immigrant entrepreneurism	trafficking
	trailing spouses
labour market segmentation	transnationalism

Further reading

Bloch, A. (2013) The labour market experiences and strategies of young undocumented migrants, *Work, Employment, and Society*, 27(2): 272–287.

Castles, S. (2011) Migration, crisis, and the global labour market, *Globalizations*, 8(3): 311–324.

Jeeves, A. (1985) *Migrant Labour in South Africa's Mining Economy: The Struggle for* the Gold Mines' Labour Supply, 1890–1920. Montreal: McGill-Queen's University Press.

Kaur, A. (2010) Labour migration in Southeast Asia: migration policies, labour exploitation and regulation, *Journal of the Asia Pacific Economy*, 15(1): 6–19.

Lewis, H., Dwyer, P., Hodkinson, S., and Waite, L. (2015) Hyper-precarious lives: migrants, work, and forced labour in the Global North, *Progress in Human Geography*, 39(5): 580–600.

Lutz, H. (Ed.) (2008) *Migration and Domestic Work: A European Perspective on a Global Theme*. Aldershot, UK; Burlington, VT: Ashgate.

Wills, J., May, J. Datta, K., Evans, Y., Herbert, J., and McIlwaine, C. (2009) London's migrant division of labour, *European Urban and Regional Studies*, 16: 257–271.

References

Ackers, L. (2005) Moving people and knowledge: scientific mobility in the European Union, *International Migration*, 4(5): 99–131.

Agustín, L. (2005) Migrants in the mistress's house: other voices in the 'trafficking' debate, *Social Politics: International Studies in Gender, State and Society*, 12(1): 96–117.

Alberts, H. C. (2007) Beyond the headlines: changing patterns in international student enrollment in the United States, *GeoJournal*, 68(2–3): 141–153.

Anderson, B. (2001) Different roots in common ground: transnationalism and migrant domestic workers in London, *Journal of Ethnic and Migration Studies*, 27(4): 673–683.

Andreas, P. (2000) *Border Games: Policing the US–Mexico Divide*. Ithaca, NY: Cornell University Press.

Anthias, F. A. and Mehta, N. (2003) The intersection between gender, the family, and self-employment: the family as a resource, *International Review of Sociology*, 13(1): 105–116.

Baas, M. (2006) Students of migration: Indian overseas students and the question of permanent residency, *People and Place*, 14(1): 8–23.

Bagwell, S. (2008) Transnational family networks and ethnic minority business development: the case of Vietnamese nail shops in the UK, *Journal of Entrepreneurial Behaviour and Research*, 14(6): 377–394.

Batalova, J. (2007) The 'Brain Gain' race begins with foreign students, Migration Information Source. Retrieved from www.migration information.org/Feature/display.cfm?ID=571 (accessed 18 November 2014).

Batnitzky, A. and McDowell, L. (2011) Migration, nursing, institutional discrimination and emotional/affective labour: ethnicity and labour stratification in the UK National Health Service, *Social & Cultural Geography*, 12(2): 181–201.

Bauder, H. (2003) 'Brain abuse', or the devaluation of immigrant labour in Canada, *Antipode*, 35(4): 699–717.

Bauder, H. (2006) *Labor Movement: How Migration Regulates Labor Markets*. Oxford; New York: Oxford University Press.

Beaverstock, J. (2002) Transnational elites in global cities: British expatriates in Singapore's financial district, *Geoforum*, 33(4): 525–538.

Beaverstock, J. (2005) Transnational elites in the city: British highly-skilled intercompany transferees in New York City's financial district, *Journal of Ethnic and Migration Studies*, 31(2): 245–268.

Bohmer, C. and Shuman, A. (2007) *Rejecting Refugees: Political Asylum in the 21st Century*. London: Routledge.

Bonacich, E. (1972) A theory of ethnic antagonism: the split labor market, *American Sociological Review*, 37(5): 547–559.

Bonacich, E. (1973) A theory of middleman minorities, *American Sociological Review*, 38(5): 583–594.

Bonacich, E. and Modell, J. (1980) *The Economic Bases of Ethnic Solidarity: Small Business in the Japanese-American Community*. Berkeley; Los Angeles: University of California Press.

Borjas, G. (1999) *Heaven's Door: Immigration Policy and the American Economy*. Princeton, NJ: Princeton University Press.

Bosniak, L. (1994) Membership, equality, and the difference that alienage makes, *New York University Law Review*, 69(6): 1047–1149.

Brickner, R. and Straehle, C. (2010) The missing link: gender, immigration policy and the Live-in Caregiver Program in Canada, *Policy and Society*, 29(4): 309–320.

Brooks, R. and Waters, J. (2011) *Student Mobilities, Migration, and the Internationalization of Higher Education*. Basingstoke: Palgrave Macmillan.

Calavita, K. (2005) *Immigrants at the Margins: Law, Race, and Exclusion in Southern Europe*. Cambridge, UK; New York: Cambridge University Press.

Cantwell, B. (2011) Academic in-sourcing: international postdoctoral employment and new modes of academic production, *Journal of Higher Education Policy and Management*, 33(2): 101–114.

Card, D. (2005) Is the new immigration really so bad? *The Economic Journal*, 115(507): 300–323.

Carswell, G. and De Neve, G. (2013) Labouring for global markets: conceptualising labour agency in global production networks, *Geoforum*, 44: 62–70.

Chakravartty, P. (2006) Symbolic analysts or indentured servants? Indian high-tech migrants in America's information economy, *Knowledge, Technology, and Policy*, 19(3): 27–43.

Challinor, A. E. (2011) Canada's immigration policy: a focus on human capital, Migration Information Source. Retrieved from http://www.migrationinformation.org/feature/display.cfm?ID=853 (accessed 18 November 2014).

Champlin, D. and Hake, E. (2006) Immigration as industrial strategy in American meatpack-ing, *Review of Political Economy*, 18(1): 49–69.

Chauvin, S. and Garcés-Mascareñas, B. (2012) Beyond informal citizenship: the new moral economy of migrant illegality, *International Political Sociology*, 6(3): 241–259.

Colic-Peisker, V. and Tilbury, F. (2007) Integration into the Australian labour market: the experiences of three 'visibly different' groups of recently arrived refugees, *International Migration*, 4(1): 59–85.

Collett, E. and Zuleeg, F. (2008) Soft, scarce, and super skills: sourcing the next generation of migrant workers in Europe, Migration Policy Institute. Retrieved from http://www.migrationpolicy.org/transatlantic/scarc-eskills.pdf (accessed 18 November 2014).

Datta, A. and Brickell, K. (2009) 'We have a little bit more finesse, as a nation': constructing the Polish worker in London's building sites, *Antipode*, 41(3): 439–464.

De Genova, N. P. (2002) Migrant 'illegality' and deportability in everyday life, *Annual Review of Anthropology*, 31: 419–447.

Dillaway, H. and Paré, E. (2008) Locating mothers: how cultural debates about stay-at-home versus working mothers define women and home, *Journal of Family Issues*, 29(4): 437–464.

Doezema, J. (1999) Loose women or lost women? The re-emergence of the myth of white slavery in contemporary discourses of trafficking in women, *Gender Issues*, 18(1): 23–50.

Dustmann, C., Fabbri, F., and Preston, I. (2005) The impact of immigration on the British labour market, *The Economic Journal*, 115(507): 324–341.

Economist (2014) What have the immigrants ever done for us? Rather a lot, according to a new piece of research (8 November 2014). Retrieved from http://www.economist.com/news/britain/21631076-rather-lot-according-new-piece-research-what-have-immigrants-ever-done-us (accessed 15 May 2015).

Favell, A. and Smith M. P. (2007) The human face of global mobility: a research agenda, *Society*, 44(2): 15–25.

Galarneau, D. and Morissette, R. (2008) Immigrants' education and required job skills, *Perspectives* (a publication of Statistics Canada), catalogue number 75-001-X. Retrieved from http://www.statcan.gc.ca/pub/75-001-x/2008112/pdf/10766-eng.pdf (accessed 15 May 2015).

Garcés-Mascareñas, B. (2010) Legal production of illegality in a comparative perspective: the cases of Malaysia and Spain, *Asia Europe Journal*, 8(1): 77–89.

Granovetter, M. (1985) Economic action and social structure: the problem of embeddedness, *American Journal of Sociology*, 91(3): 481–510.

Grasmuck, S. and Grosfoguel, R. (1997) Geopolitics, economic niches, and gendered social capital among recent Caribbean immigrants in New York City, *Sociological Perspectives*, 40(3): 339–363.

Gribble, C. (2008) Policy options for managing international student migration: the sending country's perspective, *Journal of Higher Education Policy and Management*, 30(1): 25–39.

Harvey, W. S. (2008) Strong or weak ties? British and Indian expatriate scientists finding jobs in Boston, *Global Networks*, 8(4): 453–473.

Hawthorne, L. (2005) 'Picking winners': the recent transformation of Australia's skilled migration policy, *International Migration Review*, 39(3): 663–696.

Hondagneu-Sotelo, P. (2001) *Doméstica: Immigrant Workers Cleaning and Caring in the Shadow of Affluence*, Berkeley; Los Angeles: University of California Press.

Ibarra, H. (1992) Homophily and differential returns: sex differences in network structure and access in an advertising firm, *Administrative Science Quarterly*, 37(3): 422–447.

Inglis, C. (2004) Australia's continuing transformation, Migration Information Source. Retrieved from http://www.migrationinformation.org/Profiles/display.cfm?ID=242 (accessed 18 November 2014).

Iredale, R. (2005) Gender, immigration policies and accreditation: valuing the skills of professional women migrants, *Geoforum*, 36(2): 155–166.

Jöns, H. (2009) 'Brain circulation' and transnational knowledge networks: studying long-term effects of academic mobility to Germany 1954–2000, *Global Networks*, 9(3): 315–338.

Jöns, H. (2011) Transnational academic mobility and gender, *Globalisation, Societies and Education*, 9(2): 183–209.

Jureidini, R. and Moukarbel, N. (2004) Female Sri Lankan domestic workers in Lebanon: a case of 'contract slavery'?, *Journal of Ethnic and Migration Studies*, 30(4): 581–607.

Kale, M. (1998) *Fragments of Empire: Capital, Slavery, and Indian Indentured Labor Migration in the British Caribbean*. Philadelphia, PA: University of Pennsylvania Press.

Kandel, W. and Parrado, E. (2005) Restructuring of the US meat processing industry and new Hispanic migrant destinations, *Population and Development Review*, 31(3): 447–471.

Kasarda, J. (1990) Structural factors affecting the location and timing of urban underclass growth, *Urban Geography*, 11(3): 234–264.

Kasimis, C. (2008) Survival and expansion: migrants in rural Greek regions, *Population, Space and Place*, 14(6): 511–524.

Kasimis, C., Papadopoulos, A. G., and Pappas, C. (2010) Gaining from rural migrants: migrant employment strategies and socioeconomic implications for rural labour markets. *Sociologia Ruralis*, 50: 258–276

Kassim, A. and Zin, R. H. M. (2011) Policy on irregular migrants in Malaysia: an analysis of its implementation and effectiveness, Philippines Institute for Development Studies, Discussion Paper Series 2011–34. Retrieved from http://dirp3.pids.gov.ph/ris/dps/pidsdps1134.pdf (accessed 18 November 2014).

Killias, O. (2010) 'Illegal' migration as resistance: legality, morality, and coercion in Indonesian domestic worker migration to Malaysia, *Asian Journal of Social Science*, 38(6): 897–914.

Kloosterman, R. and Rath, J. (2001) Immigrant entrepreneurs in advanced economies: mixed embeddedness further explored, *Journal of Ethnic and Migration Studies*, 27(2): 189–201.

Kofman, E. (2014) Towards a gendered evaluation of (highly) skilled immigration policies in Europe, *International Migration*, 52(3): 116–128.

Kofman, E. and Raghuram, P. (2005) Editorial—gender and skilled migrants: into and beyond the work place, *Geoforum*, 36(2): 149–154.

Kogan, I. (2011) New immigrants—old disadvantage patterns? Labour market integration of recent immigrants into Germany, *International Migration*, 49(1): 91–117.

Koser, K. and Salt, J. (1997) The geography of highly skilled international migration, *International Journal of Population Geography*, 3(4): 285–303.

Lazaridis, G. (2000) Filipino and Albanian women migrant workers in Greece: multiple layers of oppression. In F. Anthias and G. Lazaridis (Eds.), *Gender and Migration in Southern Europe: Women on the Move*. London: Bloomsbury Academic (pp. 49–89).

Lazaridis, G. (2007) Les infirmières exclusives and migrant quasi-nurses in Greece, *European Journal of Women's Studies*, 14(3): 227–245.

Lemos, S. and Portes, J. (2008) New labour? The impact of migration from Central and Eastern European countries on the UK labour market, IZA Discussion Papers, No. 3756. Bonn, Germany: IZA (Institute for the Study of Labour).

Ley, D. (2011) *Millionaire Migrants: Trans-Pacific Life Lines*. Malden, MA; Oxford, UK: Wiley-Blackwell.

Light, I. and Bonacich, E. (1988) *Immigrant Entrepreneurs: Koreans in Los Angeles, 1965–1982*. Berkeley; Los Angeles: University of California Press.

Liu-Farrer, G. (2009) Educationally channeled international labor mobility: contemporary student migration from China to Japan, *International Migration Review*, 43(1): 178–204.

Lucchino, P., Portes, J., and Rosazza-Bondibene, C. (2012) Examining the relationship between immigration and unemployment using National Insurance Number registration data. NIESR Discussion Paper No. 386. London: National Institute of Economic and Social Research.

Lutz, H. (2004) Life in the twilight zone: migration, transnationality and gender in the private household, *Journal of Contemporary European Studies*, 12(1): 47–55.

Lutz, H. (2008) Introduction: migrant domestic workers in Europe. In H. Lutz (Ed.) *Migration and Domestic Work: A European Perspective on a Global Theme*. Aldershot, UK; Burlington, VT: Ashgate (pp. 1–11).

Man, G. (2004) Gender, work and migration: deskilling Chinese immigrant women in Canada, *Women's Studies International Forum*, 27(2): 135–148.

Marrow, H. (2011) *New Destination Dreaming: Immigration, Race, and Legal Status in the Rural American South*. Stanford, CA: Stanford University Press.

Mavroudi, E. and Warren, A. (2013) Highly skilled migration and the negotiation of immigration policy: non-EEA postgraduate students and academic staff at English universities, *Geoforum*, 44: 261–270.

McDowell, L. (2003) Workers, migrants, aliens or citizens? State constructions and discourses of identity among post-war European labour migrants in Britain, *Political Geography*, 22(8): 863–886.

McDowell, L., Batnitzky, A., and Dyer, S. (2007) Division, segmentation, and interpellation: the embodied labours of migrant workers in a Greater London hotel, *Economic Geography*, 83(1): 1–25.

McEwan, C., Pollard, J. S., and Henry, N. D.
(2005) The 'global' in the city economy:
multicultural economic development in
Birmingham, *International Journal of Urban
and Regional Research*, 29(4): 916–933.

McKay, S. C. (2007) Filipino sea men: identity
and masculinity in a global labor niche. In
R. Parreñas and L. C. D. Siu (Eds.), *Asian
Diasporas: New Formations, New Conceptions*.
Stanford, CA: Stanford University Press (pp.
63–84).

Momsen, J. (Ed.) (1999) *Gender, Migration,
and Domestic Service*. London; New York:
Routledge.

Ngai, M. (2003) The strange career of the illegal
alien: immigration restriction and deportation
policy in the United States, 1921–1965, *Law
and History Review*, 21(1): 69–108.

Nicholls, W. J. (2014) From political opportunities to niche-openings: the dilemmas of
mobilizing for immigrant rights in inhospita-
ble environments, *Theory and Society*, 43(1):
23–49.

Oikelome, O. and Healy, G. (2013) Gender,
migration and place of qualification of doctors
in the UK: Perceptions of inequality, morale
and career aspiration, *Journal of Ethnic and
Migration Studies*, 39(4): 557–577.

O'Neill, J. (1990) The role of human capital in
earning differences between black and white
men, *The Journal of Economic Perspectives*,
4(4): 24–45.

Panayiotopoulos, P. and Dreef, M. (2002)
London: economic differentiation and policy-
making. In J. Rath (Ed.), *Unravelling the Rag
Trade: Immigrant Entrepreneurship in Seven
World Cities*. Oxford; New York: Berg (pp.
49–72).

Pang, C. L. and Rath, J. (2007) The force of
regulation in the land of the free: the per-
sistence of Chinatown, Washington, DC, as
a symbolic ethnic enclave, *Research in the
Sociology of Organizations*, 25: 191–216.

Parr, J. (1990) *The Gender of Breadwinners:
Women, Men, and Change in Two Industrial
Communities, 1880–1950*. Toronto: University
of Toronto Press.

Parreñas, R. S. (2001) *Servants of Globalization:
Women, Migration, and Domestic Work*.
Stanford, CA: Stanford University Press.

Piore, M. J. (1979) *Birds of Passage: Migrant
Labor and Industrial Societies*. New York:
Cambridge University Press.

Poros, M. V. (2001) The role of migrant networks in linking local labor markets: the case
of Asian Indian migration to New York and
London, *Global Networks*, 1(3): 243–260.

Porter, C. and Belkin, D. (2013) Record number of foreign students flocking to U.S.
Wall Street Journal (11 November 2013).
Retrieved from http://www.wsj.com/arti-
cles/SB100014240527023048684045791
90062164404756 (accessed 21 June 2015).

Portes, A. and Sensenbrenner, J. (1993)
Embeddedness and immigration: notes
on the social determinants of economic
action, *American Journal of Sociology*, 98(6):
1320–1350.

Portes, A., Guarnizo, L. E., and Haller, W. J.
(2002) Transnational entrepreneurs: an
alternative form of immigrant economic
adaptation, *American Sociological Review*,
67(2): 278–298.

Pratt, G. (1999) From registered nurse to reg-
istered nanny: discursive geographies of
Filipina domestic workers in Vancouver, BC,
Economic Geography, 75(3): 215–236.

Purkayastha, B. (2005) Skilled migration and
cumulative disadvantage: the case of highly
qualified Asian Indian immigrant women in
the US, *Geoforum*, 36(2): 181–196.

Raghuram, P. (2009) Caring about 'brain drain'
migration in a post-colonial world, *Geoforum*,
40(1): 25–33.

Ramirez, H. and Hondagneu-Sotelo, P. (2009)
Mexican immigrant gardeners: entrepreneurs
or exploited workers? *Social Problems*, 56(1):
70–88.

Rath, J. and Kloosterman, R. (2003) The
Netherlands: a Dutch treat. In R. Kloosterman

and J. Rath (Eds.), *Immigrant Entrepreneurs: Venturing Abroad in the Age of Globalization.* Oxford, UK; New York: Berg (pp. 123–146).

Ray, K. M., B., Lowell, L., and Spencer, S. (2006) International health worker mobility: causes, consequences, and best practices, *International Migration*, 44(2): 181–203.

Reich, M., Gordon, D. M., and Edwards, R. C. (1973) A theory of labor market segmentation, *American Economics Review*, 63(2): 359–363.

Reynolds, R. R. (2006) Professional Nigerian women, household economy, and immigration decisions, *International Migration*, 44(5): 167–188.

Rogaly, B. (2009) Spaces of work and everyday life: Labour geographies and the agency of unorganised temporary migrant workers, *Geography Compass*, 3(6): 1975–1987.

Ryan, L. and Mulholland, J. (2014a) Trading places: French highly skilled migrants negotiating mobility and emplacement in London, *Journal of Ethnic and Migration Studies*, 40(4): 584–600.

Ryan, L. and Mulholland, J. (2014b) 'Wives are the route to social life': an analysis of family life and networking amongst highly skilled migrants in London, *Sociology*, 48(2): 251–267.

Samers, M. (1998) 'Structured coherence': immigration, racism, and production in the Paris car industry, *European Planning Studies*, 6(1): 49–72.

Sanders, J. and Nee, V. (1996) Immigrant self-employment: the family as social capital and the value of human capital, *American Sociological Review*, 61(2): 231–249.

Saxenian, A. (2002) *Local and Global Networks of Immigrant Professionals in Silicon Valley* (with Y. Motoyama and X. Quan). San Francisco, CA: Public Policy Institute of California.

Schultz, T. W. (1961) Investment in human capital, *The American Economic Review*, 51(1): 1–17.

Silvey, R. (2007) Mobilizing piety: gendered morality and Indonesian–Saudi transnational migration, *Mobilities*, 2(2): 219–229.

Snow, S. and Jones, E. (2011) Immigration and the National Health Service: putting history to the forefront, *History and Policy* (online journal) March. Retrieved from www.history-andpolicy.org/papers/policy-paper-118.html (accessed 18 November 2014).

Sparke, M. (2012). *Introducing Globalization: Ties, Tensions, and Uneven Integration.* Hoboken, NJ: Wiley-Blackwell.

Sumption, M. (2014) The points system is dead, long live the points system. Migration Information Source (10 December). Retrieved from http://www.migrationpolicy.org/article/top-10-2014-issue-9-points-system-dead-long-live-points-system (accessed 21 March 2015).

Szewczyk, A. (2014) Continuation or switching? Career patterns of Polish graduate migrants in England, *Journal of Ethnic and Migration Studies*, 40(5): 847–864.

Trejo, S. (1997) Why do Mexican Americans earn low wages?, *Journal of Political Economy*, 105(6): 1235–1268.

Tyner, J. A. (2000) Global cities and circuits of global labor: the case of Manila, Philippines, *The Professional Geographer*, 52(1): 61–74.

Van Riemsdijk, M. (2012) (Re)scaling governance of skilled migration in Europe: divergence, harmonization, and contestation, *Population, Space and Place*, 18(3): 344–358.

Waldinger, R. and Lichter, M. I. (2003) *How the Other Half Works: Immigration and the Social Organization of Labor.* Berkeley; Los Angeles: University of California Press.

Walsh, J. (2008) Navigating globalization: immigration policy in Canada and Australia, 1945–2007, *Sociological Forum*, 23(4): 786–813.

Wickham, J. and Bruff, I. (2008) Skills shortages are not always what they seem: migration and the Irish software industry, *New Technology, Work and Employment*, 23(1–2): 30–43.

Willen, S. S. (2007) Toward a critical phenomenology of 'illegality': state power, criminalization, and abjectivity among undocumented migrant workers in Tel Aviv, Israel, *International Migration*, 45(3): 8–36.

Wong, L. L. (2004) Taiwanese immigrant entrepreneurs in Canada and transnational social space, *International Migration*, 42(2): 113–150.

Wright, R. and Ellis, M. (2000) The ethnic and gender division of labor compared among immigrants to Los Angeles, *International Journal of Urban and Regional Research*, 24(3): 583–600.

Yeoh, B., Huang, S., and Willis, K. (2000) Global cities, transnational flows, and gender dimensions: the view from Singapore, *Tijdschrift voor Economische en Sociale Geografie*, 91(2): 147–158.

Young, R., Weir, H., and Buchan, J. (2010) Health professional mobility in Europe and the UK: a scoping study of issues and evidence (research report produced for the National Institute of Health Research Service Delivery and Organisation Programme). London: National Institute for Health. Retrieved from www.netscc.ac.uk (accessed 18 November 2014).

Ziguras, C. and Law, S. F. (2006) Recruiting international students as skilled migrants: the global 'skills race' as viewed from Australia and Malaysia, *Globalization, Societies, and Education*, 4(1): 59–76.

4

Migration and development

Introduction

Most of our discussion thus far has centred on immigrant-receiving societies and the ways migrants are positioned within immigrant-receiving contexts. Yet migration is very much an interaction between sending and receiving societies, and migration has profound effects not only on migrant destinations but also on migrant origins. As we have seen, the bulk of migrations flow from relatively poorer places to relatively wealthier places, whether internally or internationally. Neoclassical economic approaches suggest that these flows will lead eventually to a degree of equilibrium as labour supply and demand, and hence wages, even out. But while there are cases in which migration produces a degree of labour market equilibrium, the evening out of conditions in sending and receiving societies cannot be assumed to take place as a matter of course, much less in any straightforward, predictable fashion. Observations of the effects of migration on sending societies vary widely and speak to a complicated relationship between mobility and regional economic prosperity. Some suggest that migrants, by funnelling much needed capital, skills, and expertise to the towns and cities they have left, boost economic growth and prosperity, thereby reducing pressures to migrate. Conversely, others argue that the departure of large numbers of young, able-bodied workers—many of them more educated and skilled than the population at large—hinders a country's ability to grow and prosper economically, thereby pushing more and more people to migrate.

The relationship between migration and economic conditions in sending societies is a topic of heated debate among policymakers and development professionals in both sending and receiving societies. Sending societies have at times treated emigration as a problem for national development and at other times as an opportunity; currently, opinion has settled on viewing migration as beneficial to national societies and as a means of generating economic growth. Receiving societies, for their part, are wary of migration pressures from poorer sending countries, even as they benefit from a large supply of flexible, inexpensive foreign labour. Thus, while sending societies increasingly promote migration as a means of development, receiving societies are inclined to promote development in sending states as a means of *controlling* and reducing unwanted migration. Whether development policies actually prevent migration (and whether that migration is, in fact, 'unwanted'), as we will see, remains a matter of debate.

This chapter focuses on these complex relationships between sending and receiving societies, placing sending contexts at the centre of analysis. We refer to these complex relationships collectively as the **migration-development nexus** (Faist, 2008; Skeldon, 2011)—a term that highlights the linkage between human movements and socioeconomic change in the Global South. We emphasize in this discussion that there is rarely a single way of interpreting the effects of migration on development, or vice versa. Indeed, how we interpret the migration-development nexus depends a great deal on how we choose to define 'development' (Castles, 2009; Skeldon, 2011). Policymakers and international institutions typically regard development in positive terms as economic modernization, growth, and progress; yet the changes associated with development typically are fraught with ambiguities (Hermele, 1997). As Skeldon (2011, 105) notes, 'Development typically involves the undermining, even destruction of certain ways of life as well as the improvement or promotion of others'.

We begin by explaining in greater detail how scholars and policymakers use the concept of development and how they have assessed the relationship between migration and development. In exploring the migration-development nexus, we focus first on the ways development (or the lack thereof) fosters emigration, and second, on the ways that emigration may contribute to development. Throughout this discussion, we remind our readers to think critically about the meaning of development being advocated by national and international institutions.

What is development?

'Development' may seem like an objective, measurable concept, but it carries a great deal of ideological baggage from the Cold War era, when Western scholars first began to discuss development in a systematic manner (while we generally prefer the term 'Global North' when referring to wealthier, core regions of the world, we use the terms 'West' and 'Western' here in recognition of the Cold War context in which development concepts emerged). The concept of development emerged at a time when the United States was solidifying its post-World

War II political and economic hegemony through the creation of institutions designed to spur reconstruction and economic recovery in post-war Europe. Among these institutions were the International Monetary Fund (IMF) and the International Bank of Development and Reconstruction, which would later become the World Bank. With decolonization, the development agenda shifted to the post-colonial world, with the aim of integrating newly independent states into the international system and the global capitalist economy. Western development institutions were, of course, eager that post-colonial states join the capitalist fold rather than falling under the influence of the Soviet Union.

Post-war development theory worked with the assumption that that poorer parts of the world would eventually achieve standards of economic growth and prosperity seen in the West—that they would transition, in a linear fashion, from being 'backward' societies to advanced, modern, industrial societies like the United States. One of the most influential development thinkers at the time was W. W. Rostow, an economic historian who devised a model of development based on his interpretations of industrialization in the West. Rostow (1950) posited that 'traditional' societies would need to undergo a multi-step process of change in order to achieve the status of industrialized, democratic, mass-consumer society. His ideas were not merely descriptive but prescriptive. Traditional, post-colonial societies, he suggested, needed investment in order to establish high-growth manufacturing sectors, as well as an institutional, political and social framework capable of fostering democracy and economic growth. It was the role of Western 'experts' to set post-colonial societies on a scientific, rational path towards development and to remove obstacles to modernization (for more detailed accounts of Cold War-era development theory, see Haefele (2003) and Gilman (2003)). This mode of thinking provided the intellectual foundation for Western development practice in the post-World War II period, justifying significant investments by Western aid agencies in large-scale infrastructure projects and in the modernization of agricultural production.

Western development theory and practice came under heavy criticism starting in the 1960s, especially by adherents of neo-Marxist 'Dependency' and world-systems theories (described briefly in Chapter 1). These critics disputed the characterization of post-colonial societies as 'backward' and 'traditional' and questioned that Western assistance would lead such societies into a future of modernity and prosperity. They argued that post-colonial patterns of development had largely followed colonial-era patterns of resource extraction that had long served the interests of powerful local elites and foreign capitalists. The post-colonial world, from this perspective, was not 'traditional' but 'underdeveloped'—politically dominated by the imperialist, capitalist core and relegated to the role of resource periphery in the global economy. The condition of underdevelopment was not a temporary phase to be overcome by Western aid, but rather a structural condition borne of neo-colonial relationships between core and periphery (Frank, 1967).

Mainstream development scholars and practitioners, as well, began to criticize Western development models in the 1980s, arguing that billions of dollars of aid had been squandered on large, environmentally destructive infrastructure projects that did little to benefit impoverished populations. Caught up with the ideological struggles of the Cold War, development aid had become politicized and had been used to support dictatorial regimes. Critics of the post-war development paradigm devised new concepts like 'sustainable development', which sought to place people's basic needs and the protection of the environment at the centre of the development agenda. Advocates of sustainable development argued, moreover, that development should no longer be measured purely in terms of economic growth, but must also take into consideration people's access to education, welfare, clean water, and economic opportunities (Brundtland, 1987).

Concepts relating to sustainable development have become ubiquitous in the activities of the World Bank and governmental and non-governmental aid organizations, seen in the proliferation of participatory- and community-based development projects, women's empowerment initiatives, and fair trade certification programmes. Today, many aid organizations make use of the UN's Human Development Index, which measures literacy, life expectancy, and the like, when assessing the success of a given development project, rather than relying on measures of national economic output. Yet the post-war emphasis on economic growth and modernization has not disappeared from the agenda of development professionals and policymakers. If anything, the drive to increase economic output has increased as countries in the Global South have found themselves mired in debt.

Certainly when discussing the migration-development nexus, policymakers in both sending and receiving countries remain focused on questions of economic growth: Will migration boost or hinder economic development? Will industrialization, agricultural modernization, and economic reforms diminish pressures to emigrate? Do outflows of young, skilled workers slow the growth of key economic sectors? Are the funds sent home by migrants spent in a 'productive' manner? We explore the ways that scholars and development professionals address these questions while bearing in mind the more radical critiques of development offered by neo-Marxist theorists. To what extent do discussions of the migration-development nexus ignore the inequalities and geographical disparities produced by the global capitalist economy? How do concerns with economic development and growth obscure broader questions of global justice?

Migration and development: the view from the Global North

Our first step in examining the migration-development nexus is to consider how scholars and policymakers understand the ways that development processes affect migration flows—that is, the ways these processes might instigate migration or curtail it. As we have seen, neoclassical economic theories and neo-Marxist theories alike link imbalances of labour supply and demand to geographically uneven levels of economic development: poorer, less developed (or 'underdeveloped') economies are unable to absorb growing populations of workers. At least some of this surplus labour will seek work in wealthier, industrialized regions where employment (especially in low-status segments of the labour market) is more readily available and where wages are higher. This is a pattern we have seen over and over again throughout migration history, whether we are looking at Chinese 'coolies' seeking economic opportunities in North and South America in the 1870s, Italians streaming over their northern frontier into France in the 1880s, or Mexicans making their way into the United States from the early 1900s until the present day.

From the perspective of wealthy countries and regions, the growing populations of the Global South provide an important source of inexpensive, flexible labour, but they also pose numerous political problems for governments, who must police the boundaries of nationhood and citizenship (Hollifield, 2004). To anxious politicians in the Global North, the hundreds of millions of impoverished people in the world today appear to be a uniform mass of *potential* migrants who are eager for higher wages and better job opportunities in wealthier countries. For many policymakers, the answer to these mounting migration pressures has been to promote 'development' in the traditional, Western-centric, economic sense of industrialization, economic reform and modernization, and

export production. The logic here—which stems from neoclassical economic thinking—is that the growth of manufacturing and export sectors in sending regions will absorb excess labour supply and will make migration a less attractive option.

This logic, in fact, has guided US economic policies towards Mexico for decades. Starting in the 1960s, the American government supported the Border Industrialization Program (BIP), which was initiated by the Mexican government to help alleviate unemployment in northern Mexico following the demise of the Bracero Program (Rivera-Batiz, 1986). (The Bracero Program, described in Chapter 2, provided for the legal importation of Mexican seasonal workers to meet labour demands in the US agricultural sector.) The BIP offered numerous incentives to foreign (mainly US-based) corporations to establish assembly plants, known as *maquiladoras*, along the US–Mexico border. More specifically, the US negotiated a 'twin plant' agreement with the Mexican government, allowing raw materials to be imported duty-free into Mexico for assembly by (mostly female) Mexican workers, and then exported back to the US, with duty paid only on value added by the assembly process.

US trade negotiators were primarily interested in securing a source of inexpensive labour for US manufacturers, who had been hard hit in the 1970s by competition from Asia. But both Mexican and US officials also touted border industrialization as a means of reducing the unauthorized migration of Mexicans to the US. The aim of reducing migration by generating development and job growth in Mexico was even more explicit in the negotiation of the North American Free Trade Agreement (NAFTA) in the 1990s.

As we will see in a moment, neither the Border Industrialization Program nor NAFTA diminished migration flows between Mexico and the United States. If anything, migration flows increased in volume, leading to a growing emphasis on border control measures (Cornelius,

2005; Andreas, 2000). Still, many policymakers in the United States persist in viewing development—i.e. investment in manufacturing and export sectors—as the solution to the 'problem' of migration. Similarly, the European Union's aid agency states as its main priority to address the 'root causes' of emigration by targeting employment opportunities in countries of origin (see European Commission, 2014). Towards this end, the EU has been forming 'partnerships' with North African and Middle Eastern countries in which development aid is linked explicitly to migration control measures. The idea is that North African and Middle Eastern governments will crack down on undocumented migration into Europe; meanwhile, development aid will provide the economic growth necessary to absorb the surplus labour force (Del Sarto, 2010; Faist, 2008; Adepoju et al., 2010; Sørensen, 2012).

Many scholars have taken a sceptical view of state policies that aim to control migration flows through development. It has been widely observed that most migration flows originate not in the poorest countries, but those of intermediate levels of economic development and that are undergoing rapid transformations in their rural-agricultural and industrial sectors. The top migrant-sending countries today—India, China, Mexico, the Philippines, Turkey, and Morocco—all have vibrant and growing industrial sectors and are experiencing profound economic changes, mostly in the direction of growing foreign investment and integration into the global economy. Major migration patterns are also found in Southeast Asia, a region that has seen dramatic transformation in terms of industrial development, urbanization, and global integration in recent decades.

The concept of the 'poverty constraint', mentioned in Chapter 1, is central to understanding this pattern. Migration theorists have long argued that a lack of economic resources poses a major barrier to migration. Migration, in this sense, is an expensive and risky process that requires money: those living in the poorest

and most isolated economies will have fewer economic resources to migrate. In contrast, those in rapidly developing economies are likely to have some access to wages in industrial and export commodity sectors. There are, of course, many additional, non-economic barriers to potential migrants, but access to cash in the form of wages earned in modern, industrial sectors allows potential migrants, in the first instance, to overcome the poverty constraint.

Scholars have used the 'migration hump' model to visualize this relationship between migration and development (see Figure 4.1). As development increases, so does the level of migration, and migration increases until the point when the income differential between sending and receiving countries starts to even out, i.e. when wage equilibrium is reached. After this point, rates of out-migration drop rapidly, and the migrant-sending country may become a migrant-receiving country (Martin, 1993). The migration hump illustrates well the transitions experienced by many European countries over the course of the 20th century. Italy, for instance, experienced high levels of out-migration to the US and South America in the late 19th and early 20th centuries, just as its

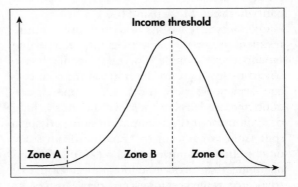

Figure 4.1 The migration hump model

Source: House of Commons International Development Committee (2004) Migration and Development: How to Make Migration Work for Poverty Reduction. Sixth Report of Session 2003–2004. (I). London (p. 20)

industrial sector began to develop in earnest and as rural transformations gained momentum. Net out-migration continued well into the 20th century, but levelled out with economic growth and industrialization in the post-World War II era. A similar pattern can be seen in Ireland, where heavy, sustained outflows of migrants to Britain and the United States took place from the mid-19th century through the mid-20th century, but slowed and eventually reversed as Ireland developed a robust export-oriented economy. Both Italy and Ireland became net recipients of migrants by century's end.

In the short and medium term, then, development, far from discouraging migration, seems to promote it (De Haas, 2005). The development process disrupts rural livelihoods, produces a mobile wage labour force, and encourages migration to cities and abroad. Thus, the Border Industrialization Program and subsequent efforts to boost industrialization and economic development in Mexico, if anything, corresponded with higher rates of undocumented border crossings and the rapid expansion of the Mexican-origin population resident in the United States. Recent declines in unauthorized border crossings speak more to highly restrictive border control policies (described in Chapter 6) and to the severe 2008–9 recession in the US than to economic parity between Mexico and the US.

Of course, if we assume that other countries will follow the same trajectory as Italy and Ireland, then we might expect the income threshold to be just beyond the horizon for countries like Turkey, Mexico, India, and China. It certainly seems plausible there will be, in the long run, diminishing out-migration and perhaps a shift from emigration to immigration in some or all of these countries. Martin (2003, 17) thus maintains that 'economic integration should be advocated as the best long-run policy to promote "stay-at-home" development'. (Martin also suggests that the observed decline of fertility rates in many emerging economies will help these countries to move along the migration hump

trajectory.) At a *systemic* level, however, the equilibrium predicted by the migration hump model seems more elusive than inevitable. Capitalism requires geographical inequalities in wages and labour conditions in order to derive profits: as capitalists invest and disinvest in different locales, they set into motion continuous cycles of boom and bust, ascent and decline, expansion and contraction. Capitalism, in other words, rarely tends towards stasis or balance. **Neoliberal** development policies, which prioritize free trade, privatization, deregulation, flexible labour markets, and capital mobility, seem to intensify the dynamic and disruptive qualities of capitalism (Phillips, 2011; Hermele, 1997). 'Sustainable development' discourse aside, most contemporary development projects are designed to boost export earnings, to encourage foreign investment, to take advantage of 'comparative advantages', and to open up new markets—*not* necessarily to create equality within or between nation-states. Critics charge that these neoliberal modes of development tend to serve the narrow interests of economic and political elites rather than the interests of ordinary people (Fernández-Kelly and Massey, 2007).

At the same time that we can look dubiously at development as a means of achieving economic equilibrium and diminishing migration pressures at a systemic level, we can also wonder whether diminishing labour mobility is actually what wealthy countries want. Measures to control migration, whether through development projects or through border control, appear to be at odds with actual demands for labour in the Global North, as discussed in Chapter 3. Immigration control measures have rendered labour migrants more vulnerable but have done little to diminish demands for migrant workers. Development policies seem particularly disingenuous in light of wealthy states' unwillingness to penalize employers in certain sectors, like agriculture, who make heavy use of undocumented immigrants (Cornelius, 2005). We will explore in greater detail these deep contradictions in immigration and border control policy in Chapter 6.

Migration and development: the view from the Global South

While wealthy countries advocate development, paradoxically, as a means of restricting migration flows, poorer countries have increasingly looked to those very migration flows as a means of achieving economic development. Over the past few decades, many countries of the Global South have come to view their workers as a key export commodity—a valuable good that will generate foreign exchange earnings and that will, in turn, fuel economic development and prosperity. The conventional wisdom, in this respect, is that migration not only absorbs surplus labour and reduces poverty, but also fosters investment in education and productive activities (Faist, 2008). In recent years, this conventional wisdom has been espoused not only by sending governments but also by international institutions like the Organization for Economic Cooperation and Development (OECD), the International Organization for Migration (IOM), and the United Nations. The UN, for instance, suggests that 'international migration is usually positive both for countries of origin and of destination', and that migration's 'potential benefits are larger than potential gains from freer international trade, particularly for developing countries' (United Nations, 2006, 13). Why has migration become the new 'mantra' in development circles (Kapur, 2003)? And what is the evidence that migration is more beneficial to sending societies than conventional development programmes?

The 'problem' of emigration in the Global South

Many sending states historically have viewed the loss of workers through emigration as weakening national economies, and they have therefore sought to control or to limit out-migration. In some instances, sending states have also been politically suspicious of émigré communities and have accused them of betraying their homelands. Through the first half of the 20th century, for instance, the Mexican government attempted to control the migration of its nationals to the United States, arguing that the US farmers were siphoning Mexico's chief economic asset—plentiful, cheap labour—away from Mexican industry and agriculture. The Mexican government, as well, viewed the steady northward flow of workers as a sign that its citizens' dedication to the Mexican nation had been weakened and compromised by the pull of higher wages (Phillips, 2011; Fitzgerald, 2009). As alluded to earlier, Mexico's promotion of border industrialization was intended, in part, to stanch the flow of workers northward; as we will discuss in Chapter 6, the Mexican government also participated in the early militarization of the US–Mexico border in the 1940s and 1950s in order to prevent its nationals from emigrating (Hernández, 2006). Not all countries were so averse to emigration during this period. Turkey, Morocco, and Tunisia, for instance, eagerly negotiated bilateral guest worker agreements with West Germany and other Western European governments in the 1950s and 1960s as a means of expanding employment opportunities for their working-age populations. But while they embraced the guest worker programmes, these governments displayed a notable lack of trust in their émigré populations and exercised tight control over them through their consulates and so-called 'friendship societies' (or *amicales*) that were closely tied to home regimes (Brand, 2010).

Just as many governments were initially reluctant to embrace emigration as a solution to development problems, scholars, too, were ambivalent about emigration. Scholars were especially alarmed by the emigration of tens of thousands of skilled professionals—doctors, nurses, teachers, engineers, and architects—from the Global South in search of higher salaries and better working conditions in the Global North. Scholars interpreted this phenomenon—referred to as the **brain drain**—as an outcome of fundamental economic deficiencies in poor countries. As Portes (1976, 498–499) argued, poor countries had created educational systems that, in a sense, had 'run ahead of the rest of society', and they were 'training professionals for a level of development [they had] not yet reached'. In other words, poor countries had invested in advanced education to boost development, only to find themselves with a surfeit of highly educated people (Pernia, 1976). Some economists maintained that the emigration of professionals—like all forms of emigration—was a natural, and even desirable, outcome of labour market imbalances in countries like the Philippines, India, and South Korea. Indeed, some scholars suggested that it was better, from the standpoint of political stability, to have underemployed professionals emigrate overseas, where they would not be agitating for revolution. Yet most had a more pessimistic view of the brain drain, treating it as a direct transfer of wealth from poor countries to rich countries and yet another way in which core economies warped internal markets and labour systems in the Global South. As Bhagwati (1976, 35) put it,

> The oft-made remark that a doctor driving taxicabs in Manila is no loss to the Philippines when he migrates to New York misses the point that the ability to migrate to New York prevents him from giving up driving taxicabs at some stage and migrating to the hinterland to start up a practice there. . . . The 'brain drain' cuts into the 'internal diffusion' process that carries the doctors gradually to the countryside where they are needed.

Some economists sought ways of compensating poor countries for the loss of their best and brightest. Some proposed that developing countries grant scholarships only under the condition that recipients limit their time abroad and commit to returning home (Kwok and Leland, 1982). Others, including Bhagwati, argued in favour of a system of taxation, coordinated by the UN, on the earnings of expatriate workers in order to compensate sending countries. Such a plan, Bhagwati remarked, would most likely be embraced by skilled émigrés, many of whom continued to identify emotionally with their places of origin and to feel a moral imperative to contribute to their country's development (Bhagwati, 1976). This idea was never formally implemented, but the notion that development could best be served by maintaining ties between émigrés and their countries of origin, as we will see, proved prescient.

Re-thinking the 'problem' of emigration: labour export as development strategy

While some scholars and politicians continue to raise concerns about the outflow of skilled workers—and especially medical professionals—to the Global North (e.g. Ahmad, 2005; Dovlo, 2004; Raghuram, 2009a; 2009b), such concerns have been largely superseded since the 1990s by the idea that both skilled and unskilled migrations are far more beneficial than detrimental to the Global South (Taylor, 1999). In other words, migration has been construed as a development strategy—a means of achieving goals of economic growth and of boosting employment. Of particular importance in altering perceptions of emigration was the dramatic increase through the 1990s in remittance flows—that is, transfers of wages and earnings from migrant destinations to places of origin. Economists in the 1970s and 1980s had paid scant attention to remittances, but took note in the mid-1990s as many countries in the Global South found themselves heavily in debt after decades of spending on economic modernization programmes. Declining prices of export commodities on the world market added to the economic woes of indebted countries. Facing financial collapse, many indebted countries in the Global South submitted to harsh **structural adjustment policies** that required them to slash social spending and to privatize state industries as a condition for further loans. These policies, implemented by the IMF and other international financial institutions, created significant hardships for ordinary people and tended to widen economic inequalities. In this context, migration and the sending home of earnings became a crucial means of household survival for millions of people (Victoria Lawson's research on Ecuador, described in Chapter 1, provides an excellent illustration of migration under conditions of structural adjustment—see Lawson, 1999).

Remittances from international migrants began growing rapidly after 2000, outpacing both foreign aid and foreign direct investment in many countries in the Global South (see Table 4.1 and Figure 4.2). Consequently, development professionals and policymakers in sending countries became more inclined to think of émigrés not as squandered human capital, but as a resource to be fostered and harnessed for the benefit of developing economies (Page and Mercer, 2012).

These shifting understandings of the migration-development nexus have led policymakers in the Global South to incorporate emigration

Table 4.1 Value of remittances (in US$ millions) in select countries, 1990, 2000, 2005, 2010, 2014 (estimated)

Country	1990	2000	2005	2010	2014 (estimated)	% of GDP, 2010
India	2,384	12,883	22,125	54,035	70,389	3.0%
China	196	4,822	23,478	53,038	64,140	0.8%
Philippines	1,465	6,961	13,566	21,423	28,403	10.7%
Mexico	3,098	7,525	22,742	22,048	24,866	2.1%
Nigeria	10	1,392	3,329	10,045	20,921	4.5%
Egypt	4,284	2,852	5,017	12,453	19,612	3.0%
Pakistan	2,006	1,075	4,280	9,690	17,060	4.8%
Bangladesh	779	1,968	4,315	10,850	14,969	9.6%
Vietnam	no data	1,340	3,150	8,260	12,000	5.1%
Lebanon	no data	no data	4,924	7,558	8,899	19.6%
Indonesia	166	1,190	5,420	6,916	8,551	1.0%
Poland	no data	1,496	6,482	7,575	7,466	1.7%
Morocco	2,006	2,161	4,590	6,423	6,962	6.8%
Nepal	no data	111	1,212	3,469	5,875	20.0%
El Salvador	366	1,765	3,030	3,449	4,236	15.7%
Moldova	no data	179	920	1,392	1,981	23.2%

Source: World Bank (2011a) *Migration and Remittances Factbook* (2nd edition). Washington, DC: The International Bank for Reconstruction and Development/World Bank (p. 13). Retrieved from http://www.worldbank.org/prospects/migrationandremittances (accessed 1 September 2014)

World Bank (2015) Bilateral Remittance Data Matrix. Migration and Remittances Data. Retrieved from http://econ.worldbank.org/WBSITE/EXTERNAL/EXTDEC/EXTDECPROSPECTS/0,,contentMDK:22759429~pagePK:64165401~piPK:64165026~theSitePK:476883,00.html

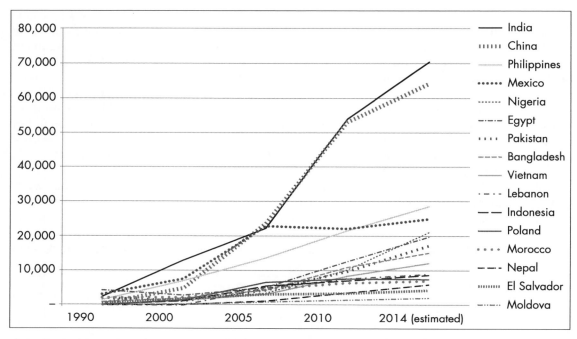

Figure 4.2 Value of remittances (in US\$ millions) in select countries, 1990–2014

World Bank (2011) Migration and Remittances Factbook *(2nd edition), p. 13. Retrieved from http://www.worldbank. org/prospects/migrationandremittances*

World Bank (2015) Bilateral Remittance Data Matrix. Retrieved from http://econ.worldbank.org/WBSITE/EXTERNAL/ EXTDEC/EXTDECPROSPECTS/0,,contentMDK:22759429~pagePK:64165401~piPK:64165026~theSitePK:476883,00.html

explicitly into development plans and, as described in Chapter 3, to take a proactive role in promoting the export of labour—both skilled and unskilled. Asian states have been leaders in encouraging and facilitating **labour export** as a development strategy, in parallel with broader export-oriented industrialization policies. Asian states, for instance, have been instrumental in seeking new markets for overseas workers, negotiating bilateral agreements with destination states, placing labour attachés in destination countries, setting standards for labour contracts, and, more generally, providing an environment in which labour export flourishes. The Philippines has perhaps the most well developed labour export bureaucracy in the form of the Philippine Overseas Employment Agency, which was created in the 1970s to facilitate the training and emigration of millions of Filipino workers to

the Arab Gulf States, the United States, and elsewhere in Asia (Tyner, 1999). By the late 1990s, over six million Filipino migrants were working in over 130 countries (Hugo and Stahl, 2004). Other Asian states—Bangladesh, India, Indonesia, Thailand, and more recently Vietnam and China—have followed suit. In most cases, states have made ample use of private sector recruiters and employment agencies. The result has been a burgeoning and highly lucrative migration industry throughout Asia (Yeates, 2009; Piper, 2004; Castles, 2002; Sørensen, 2012).

The role of states in facilitating labour export as a means of achieving economic development is illustrated well in the case of the export of nurses and heathcare workers—most of them female—from the Philippines, Indonesia, India, Sri Lanka, Bangladesh, Pakistan, and China.

Plate 4.1 Women queue for jobs in Manila, Philippines, as domestic workers in mainly Middle Eastern countries

Source: Robin Hammond/Panos

Women overall have been an important component of labour export strategies, with millions emigrating to work in the Gulf Arab states and highly developed Asian economies (Silvey, 2007; Piper, 2004). Many of these are placed as domestic workers, but Asian states have sought to increase the human capital of overseas workers in order to enhance their earnings. These states have thus expanded their nursing institutions and have raised educational standards to make their graduates more competitive in the growing global healthcare market. Today, the vast majority of nurses trained in the Philippines and other Asian countries are working overseas. It is important to reiterate that this process is explicitly gendered: those recruited into these global labour circuits of healthcare workers are women,

both because most societies view women as ideal care workers, and also because sending countries view them as a 'better bet than men' in terms of long-term employment and the remittance of earnings (Yeates, 2009).

In creating a regulatory and policy framework that encourages labour export, states in the Global South have also portrayed their overseas citizens as national heroes and have attempted to instill in émigrés a sense that they belong to a **diaspora**—that is, that they form a culturally cohesive social unit that is deeply connected to its 'homeland' despite living outside of its borders (Rodriguez, 2002). At a practical level, this has involved the creation of governmental agencies and institutions that are devoted to fostering personal and business networks between émigrés

Plate 4.2 A billboard advertisement for a money transfer service Dahabshiil in Eastleigh, Kenya
Source: Sven Torfinn/Panos

and homelands. One notable example has been the Dominican Republic, which in the 1990s tellingly changed the terminology used to describe Dominican émigré communities from *dominicanos ausentes* (absent Dominicans) to *dominicanos en el exterior* (Dominicans abroad) (Itzigsohn, 2000). The Dominican state has maintained relationships with 'Dominicans abroad' (most of them living in the United States) through consulates and political organizations, and has courted émigrés' investments in Dominican enterprises. The sending state's active cultivation of diasporic identities and practices is also evident in China, where the state celebrates emigration as an act of patriotism and modernization (Nyíri, 2001). China's 'new migrants'—those who have gone abroad since 1978, when China began its trans-

formation to a market-based economy—have been regarded by the Chinese state as a key resource for economic development, and they are routinely exhorted to 'serve the country' by repatriating earnings, by attracting foreign investors and business partners, and by regaining the loyalties of earlier migrant cohorts who have supposedly lost touch with Chinese culture. An important component of China's connections with the Chinese diaspora has been the creation of globalized Chinese media networks, consisting of periodicals, newspapers, television stations, websites, and so on, that reproduce the idea of a global Chinese identity and migrants' unbreakable connection with the Chinese polity. Also significant has been the Chinese state's encouragement of migrant organizations, whose meetings—sometimes involving thousands of participants—serve as a 'transnational social space' where official discourses can circulate and gain traction (Nyíri, 2001).

Facilitating the creation of diasporic connections has been the growing acceptance of dual citizenship by both sending and receiving states. Sending states in the past typically viewed their émigrés' naturalization in the destination society as a renunciation of their homelands. Until recently, few sending countries had provisions for dual citizenship that would allow émigrés to naturalize in the destination country while maintaining their existing citizenship. State attitudes towards dual citizenship, however, have changed significantly, and sending states are more inclined not only to tolerate naturalization but to encourage it (Faist and Gerdes, 2008; Jones-Correa, 2001). In cases where émigrés had been reluctant to renounce their birth citizenship, sending states have adopted or liberalized dual citizenship laws in order to promote naturalization in the destination country, thus ensuring émigrés' security, stability, and, most importantly, economic productivity. Instructive in this regard has been the Dominican Republic, which adopted dual citizenship provisions in 1994 specifically to encourage their nationals to secure legal and political rights in the United States and to improve their social and economic circumstances (Itzigsohn, 2000). Mexico, likewise, liberalized citizenship laws in the 1990s to encourage its nationals to adopt US citizenship, and Turkey in the same period encouraged the descendants of Turkish guest workers to take up German citizenship (this as Germany was liberalizing its own citizenship laws in recognition of the permanence of guest worker populations) (Kadırbeyoğlu, 2007).

In cases where émigrés had been more readily inclined to relinquish their birth citizenship in favour of receiving-society nationality (as had been the case with Egyptian professionals in Europe and North America in the 1970s and 1980s), dual citizenship has been a means of maintaining migrants' emotional and financial attachments to homelands. No longer regarded as 'absent' from the nation-state, émigrés remain an integral part of sending societies both symbolically and in more substantive ways. Many states, for instance, have extended voting rights and elements of political representation to émigrés. This has been especially notable in Latin America and the Caribbean (Itzigsohn, 2000; Escobar, 2007) and can also be found in India, the Philippines, Egypt, Morocco, Tunisia, and elsewhere (Brand, 2010; Castles, 2007). That migrants are simultaneously incorporated into two national polities raises important questions about the nature of contemporary citizenship, which no longer seems predicated on the exclusive relationship between citizens and the territorial state (Fitzgerald, 2009; Faist and Gerdes, 2008; Brubaker, 2010). We return to these issues later in the book.

As we have emphasized throughout this discussion, the promotion of labour export, the fostering of diasporic consciousness, and the encouragement of dual citizenship are ultimately about encouraging and facilitating the flow of remittances, which states aim to channel into productive investments. Many states have reformed their banking systems to make it easier and cheaper for migrants to channel remittances into the formal banking sector, and have also created investment accounts for remittance senders that offer currency conversion and tax advantages (Hadj Nacer and Almeras, 2008). In Mexico, the state has gone a step further in soliciting development funds from migrants by offering matching funds for remittances. The Mexican state of Zacatecas in the 1990s, for instance, initiated a **tres-por-uno** (three-for-one) programme, which matches each 'migradollar' with three dollars from the state and federal governments; this programme has since been copied by other Mexican states and by other countries to fund local infrastructure improvement, education, medical clinics, and business development (Rivera-Salgado and Rabadán, 2008). Such programmes often work through

BOX 4.1 MIGRANT REMITTANCES

According to a recent World Bank Migration and Development Brief, remittance flows to developing countries have more than quadrupled since 2000 (World Bank, 2014). Officially recorded remittance flows to 'developing countries' (a category that includes emerging economies like China as well as very poor countries) were expected to reach $435 billion in 2014, an increase of 5 percent over the previous year. Growth rates were expected to moderate slightly in 2015, reflecting slowing GDP growth in major remittance-sending countries. Remittance flows in 2013 were three times larger than official development assistance and were significantly higher than foreign direct investment in all developing countries with the exception of China. The report links rising remittances in part to the sharp decline in the cost of sending money overseas, due mainly to mobile- and internet-based technologies. The reduction of money transfer costs has been most dramatic in Sub-Saharan Africa, where there has been an explosion of mobile services in the past few years. These have allowed African migrants working within Africa or farther afield to send even small sums of money to households. According to 2014 IMF estimates, the top recipients of *officially* recorded remittances were India ($71 billion), China ($64 billion), the Philippines ($28 billion), and Mexico ($24 billion). If we consider remittances as a percentage of GDP, the top recipients in 2013 were Tajikistan (42 percent of GDP), the Kyrgyz Republic (32 percent), Nepal (29 percent), Moldova (25 percent), and Lesotho (25 percent). These figures likely underestimate the actual scale of remittances, as they do not account for the value of non-monetary remittances or remittances that flow through informal channels (Pieke et al., 2007; Glytsos, 1997).

hometown associations (HTAs)—voluntary organizations of emigrants that pool money for specific projects in towns and regions of origin. Funds pooled through HTAs and other migrant organizations are sometimes referred to as 'collective remittances' and can be distinguished from more individualistic modes of remitting income to family members and households. In 2009, there were over 1,000 HTAs registered with the Mexican state; these organizations have raised tens of millions of dollars—matched by the Mexican federal, state, and local governments—for thousands of projects aimed at social development (e.g. education and healthcare) and public works (e.g. water and road infrastructure) (Burgess and Tinajero, 2012). In some contexts, HTAs work more independently of the national state, as in El Salvador where HTAs collaborate more closely with local 'counterpart organizations' and public-works committees (see Box 4.1 for an overview of current trends in global remittances).

Evaluating migrants as agents of development

States in the Global South, then, have come to view migrants as key agents of development whose channelling of overseas earnings to towns and regions of origin stimulates local markets, boosts local production of consumer goods, encourages entrepreneurialism, and makes possible the modernization of societies and economies. Empirical studies seem to bear out these arguments in favour of emigration and remittances as a development strategy with positive material effects on sending societies (Adams and Page, 2005). One example is De Haas's (2006) detailed study of migration and development in the Todgha region of Morocco, where a third of households rely on remittances from international migrants. De Haas demonstrates that the average incomes of households with at least one international migrant are more than double those of households without migrant members. Some of this income has been invested in the agricultural sector, and particularly in diesel water pumps that have allowed for the cultivation of marginal lands. Migrant households have also invested in home construction and in various small enterprises, including cafes, shops, and taxi services. These investments create greater income security for households while also generating employment opportunities. De Haas concedes that the inflow of money from international migrants has created some problems. In the agricultural sector, for instance, the boom in diesel water pumps has disrupted traditional agricultural institutions and water management systems, leading to the abuse and neglect of communal irrigation systems. But overall, the inflow of remittance income from migrants has meant a significant reduction of poverty in the region and better living conditions for many people, whether in migrant or non-migrant households.

In addition to their monetary remittances, migrants are viewed as transmitting new and potentially beneficial ideas, information, and expertise through their communications with friends and family members and visits home— what scholars call **social remittances** (Levitt, 1998). Levitt and Lamba-Nieves (2011), for instance, describe how participants in Dominican HTAs in the United States have become increasingly attuned to American organizational practices based around well-defined rules and procedural fairness. Such practices are then conveyed back to the Dominican Republic, where they influence local civic life. Levitt and Lamba-Nieves also show that, along with new management skills, HTAs develop new aspirations, which then inform the investments they make in their hometowns. Social remittances, they suggest, may eventually be 'scaled up', as recipients of new skills and attitudes begin to demand greater transparency and more accountability of municipal and national officials. And indeed, recent studies show that Eritrean and Afghan émigrés have become agents of broader

political change by putting pressure on regimes (partly through online activism) to democratize themselves and to be more responsive to local development needs (Brinkerhoff, 2004; Bernal, 2006).

Advocates of migration as a development strategy, moreover, have replaced the concept of brain drain with the idea of **brain circulation**, emphasizing the ability of highly skilled migrants to participate in economic and human-capital development without permanently returning to countries of origin (Jöns, 2009; Saxenian, 2002). The idea of brain circulation (and the related concept of 'brain exchange') suggests that the growth of sizable expatriate populations of scientists and engineers does not necessarily mean the hollowing out of these countries' scientific and research institutions, but rather the energizing of these institutions through the traffic of personnel, resources, and ideas (see Box 4.2).

The case of India is often held up as the exemplar of brain circulation and its positive role in fostering national development. The Indian state has long cultivated relationships with its highly skilled émigré communities in the United States, Australia, and other wealthy countries, offering them, among other benefits, high-interest accounts in the State Bank of India that are subject to little or no taxation. In turn, 'non-resident Indians' (NRIs) have established important linkages between high-tech business sectors in countries of settlement and India's thriving software industry. We are reminded here of the immigrant entrepreneurs in California's Silicon Valley mentioned in Chapter 3. In the 1990s and early 2000s, Indian software engineers in Silicon Valley—many of them flush with cash from the sale of early internet-based companies—formed venture capital and private equity firms, seeking to invest in newer high-tech start-ups. With ties to both Silicon Valley and India, these Indian entrepreneurs were ideally positioned 'to identify appropriate market niches, mobilize domestic skill and knowledge, connect to international markets, and work with domestic policymakers

BOX 4.2 THE TRANSFER OF KNOWLEDGE THROUGH EXPATRIATE NATIONALS (TOKTEN) PROGRAMME

In recent decades, international institutions like the United Nations and the International Organization for Migration have had an important role in promoting brain circulation. Of particular note has been the Transfer of Knowledge through Expatriate Nationals (TOKTEN) programme, created in 1977 by the United Nations Development Programme (UNDP). TOKTEN connects migrant professionals to specific programmes in their countries of origin and maintains databases of expatriates who can be called upon to volunteer their services on a short-term basis when various needs arise in the fields of healthcare, engineering, education, and economic development (Mahroum, Eldridge, and Daar, 2006). From the start, the UNDP envisioned TOKTEN as a means of providing low-cost technical services to the developing world and of giving countries of the Global South more power over, and responsibility for, their own development (Murphy, 2006). TOKTEN was also viewed as a means of circumventing problems commonly associated with traditional development assistance, including foreign aid workers' lack of knowledge of local circumstances. Since its creation, TOKTEN has operated in around 50 countries and has recruited 5,000. TOKTEN's presence has been especially notable in Afghanistan, Rwanda, Vietnam, Sudan, Lebanon, Bosnia and Herzegovina, Turkey, the occupied Palestinian territories, and Pakistan. Evaluations of TOKTEN programmes are generally positive. One report on TOKTEN activities in Rwanda, for instance, notes that the programme attracted 47 Rwandan expatriates with high levels of education and training in science, technology, agricultural, and health fields. The report describes the TOKTEN volunteers as highly motivated by their connections to Rwanda, and it remarks that nine of the volunteers ended up returning permanently to Rwanda. The report, however, also comments on several challenges faced by TOKTEN volunteers, including inadequate staffing, transportation constraints, and insufficient funding (Touray, 2008). In evaluating the overall effectiveness of TOKTEN in alleviating poverty in the Global South, it is important to note the lack of systematic, comprehensive research on TOKTEN programmes. The same can be said for research on brain circulation more generally. This lack of evidence has led some scholars to express scepticism about the effectiveness of brain gain in countering brain drain. Despite such scepticism, development agencies in the Global North increasingly look to diasporas as important agents of development in the Global South.

to identify and devise strategies to overcome obstacles to further growth' (Saxenian, 2005, 40; see also Upadhya, 2004; Hunger, 2004). As the Indian state loosened restrictions on investments by overseas investment funds, hundreds of millions of NRI dollars flowed into Indian IT enterprises. India has since experienced significant growth in its middle class, and many of its corporations today have a global presence. India's experiences with émigré investment have been mirrored in other contexts, most notably China and Taiwan, albeit with significant variations in the dynamics between the state, local

businesses, and émigré communities (Saxenian, 2005; Tseng, 2000).

Of course, not all migrant-sending countries have seen the stellar economic growth experienced by India, China, or Taiwan. Still, many scholars maintain that emigration has been, on balance, beneficial to sending countries. At the very least, remittances play a direct role in alleviating poverty by giving households the wherewithal to purchase necessities (De Haas, 2005; Adams and Page, 2005). The emerging consensus on the benefits of emigration has led to a shift in the policies of international development agencies in the Global North, which have begun to view migrant-led development as an alternative to traditional development assistance. The notion of migrants as agents of development fits well within a broader neoliberal framework that regards top-down state spending as inefficient, ineffective, and prone to corruption and waste. From a neoliberal perspective, remittances put spending directly into the hands of ordinary people while circumventing corrupt officials and bloated bureaucracies. This is seen as a more individualized form of development that works from the ground up rather than from the top down.

The positive view of migrants as development agents is reflected in growing support for **co-development** programmes, through which international aid institutions in the Global North support migrants' investments in productive activities in their homelands (Ratha, 2007). Such programmes favour small-scale projects that work through non-governmental organizations (NGOs) and other civil-society organizations, and they often make use of HTAs as partners in local projects and micro-financing initiatives (Orozco and Rouse, 2012; Portes and Zhou, 2012). A Malian regional association in France known as Association Gidimaxa Jikké is often cited as a model of co-development. This association emerged in the 1980s as Malian families became increasingly dependent on remittances from France in a context of failed state agricultural policies compounded by a severe drought. Gidimaxa Jikké brought together thousands of Malian migrants to channel investments in irrigation and communications infrastructure, health centres, literacy programmes, and micro-enterprises. Later, the municipal government of the Paris suburb where most Malian migrants live embarked in a partnership with the organization, supporting its projects in Mali while also assisting young Malians in France (Grillo and Riccio, 2004). Advocates of co-development often describe these kinds of partnerships involving small-scale, migrant-led projects as far

more empowering to migrants than traditional development programmes and as more effective in generating the economic growth that many policymakers in the Global North believe will stem migration flows from the Global South.

Questioning the benefits of emigration

Not all scholars, however, offer such positive assessments of emigration as a development strategy. For every piece of research that extols the virtues of emigration and remittances, there is another that cautions strongly against the optimistic migration-as-development model that has been embraced by development professionals and sending governments. Scholars have long noted that in most sending contexts, it is typically not the poorest or most vulnerable who emigrate for economic opportunities abroad, but those who are relatively better off; likewise, it is often relatively well-off regions that send larger numbers of emigrants, not the poorest ones (Kapur, 2003). The benefits of emigration and remittances, in this sense, are not evenly distributed socially or geographically, and emigration tends to exacerbate, rather than to alleviate, uneven patterns of development.

Fitzgerald's (2009) account of emigration from the state of Jalisco in Mexico illustrates the uneven patterns of development generated by emigration and remittances. The municipality of Arandas in Jalisco, with its thriving tequila distilleries funded partly through migrant remittances, has been viewed as a remittance success story. However, while this town thrives, others in Jalisco have suffered from abandonment. At the same time, Mexican states like Chiapas, which have seen comparatively few of the benefits of international remittances, have become labour reservoirs for better-off regions within Mexico, including Jalisco, where migrants increasingly perform the low-paid and difficult work of agave cultivation related to tequila production. A similar situation can be found in the state of Punjab in India, which has been an important migrant-sending region since the late 19th century. Scholars note that NRI associations have made significant investments in improving infrastructure and social services in Punjab. But scholars also note that the flow of remittances has, in a sense, given the local and national state an excuse to neglect infrastructure and basic services in rural areas. While migrant-sending villages thrive through remittances, those without large numbers of migrants are left to founder (Walton-Roberts, 2004). Remittances, furthermore, have reinforced class and caste divisions within migrant-sending districts of Punjab because they tend to flow to what is already a relatively privileged segment of the population. In the early 20th century, remittances were used by upper-caste groups to purchase land, the traditional basis of wealth and prestige in the region. More recently, a significant proportion of spending has been directed towards personal consumption, most visible in the construction of palatial homes. Not surprisingly, those excluded from NRI kinship and social networks are deeply hostile to these displays of wealth. Their resentment is not just a matter of jealousy. NRI spending increases the cost of land and can be highly disruptive to local markets, rendering livelihoods increasingly precarious for those who do not have access to remittances.

The tendency for remittances to flow into status and prestige items and to widen regional and social disparities has also been evident in Central America. Klaufus' (2010) study of mid-sized Central American cities suggests that remittance-driven housing construction, most notably in the form of suburban gated communities, has skewed local housing markets, leaving strong demands for lower-income housing unmet because of a lack of credit structures to finance the purchase of older housing stock. Klaufus adds that housing construction has accelerated urban sprawl, contributed to disinvestment in traditional urban cores, and led to deforestation and the depletion of groundwater supplies.

In addition to questioning the benefits of remittance flows, scholars have questioned the capacity of migrants to generate the employment opportunities and economic growth that governments expect of them. Several studies, for instance, suggest that the benefits of brain circulation may be exaggerated and that the willingness and ability of highly skilled migrants to participate substantively in the transfer of skills and expertise to countries of origin is highly uneven and contingent on many circumstances (Pellegrino, 2001; Harvey, 2008). This scholarship emphasizes that the brain drain continues to be a pressing problem in many parts of the world, notably in Africa, where the emigration of healthcare professionals has limited the ability of public health officials to contend with epidemic diseases and high rates of maternal and infant mortality (Gerein, et al., 2006; Kuehn, 2007; Sako, 2002).

Scholars have also been critical of co-development initiatives, which, we have seen, have been promoted by many international development agencies in the Global North as a means of generating job opportunities in the Global South. Grillo and Riccio's (2004) account of Italian co-development projects involving Senegalese migrants highlights the marginality and precariousness of many migrant enterprises. Grillo and Riccio describe a joint venture between a group of Senegalese migrants and an Italian NGO that provided training and technical assistance in the fishing sector. The venture, funded by regional and municipal governments in Italy as well as the European Social Fund, was intended to train Senegalese migrants in the fishing industry so these migrants could return to Senegal and set up their own fishing businesses. The project from the start was fraught with problems. There were tensions among the Senegalese involved in the project, especially between those who intended to use project funds to push their own individual business interests and those who favoured collective efforts. When trainees in the programme in Italy went to Senegal to initiate fishing enterprises, they faced bureaucratic obstacles and problems with Senegalese fishers' organizations. There were also problems with a key institutional partner in Italy, which reneged on its original agreement with the Senegalese migrants; this partner eventually withdrew from the project. The Senegalese participants struggled to maintain the flow of funds from European agencies. In the end, the project failed to fulfil one of the key conditions that European funders had imposed on the project: that it would lead to trainees' return to Senegal.

Critical scholarship, furthermore, has painted a rather ambivalent picture of the social dynamics within hometown associations and diasporic networks. HTAs, as we have seen, are important institutional mechanisms for the channelling of migrant resources to community-based development projects. But while they are important expressions of migrant collective agency, HTAs can reinforce patriarchal relationships and gender hierarchies in households, communities, and national societies. HTAs, Goldring (2001) asserts, represent a privileged arena for men's transnational political and economic activity. In her discussion of HTAs from Zacatecas, Goldring notes that few women served in leadership positions in HTAs or were involved in negotiations with the Mexican and Zacatecan governments over project financing. Women, she suggests, were almost entirely relegated to passive, supporting roles—as icons of femininity, as mothers and bearers of Zacatecan culture, and as the beneficiaries of HTA 'charity'. Goldring cautions that women's marginality in HTAs does not signify their actual passivity; she notes, for instance, that Zacatecan women are very much involved in civic activism in the US context. But her research, and that of other feminist scholars, suggests that development strategies based on labour export may reinforce gender-based inequalities.

Finally, critics of the migration-as-development model question the reliability of remittances. Setting aside the question of whether migrant earnings are used productively, remittances are not always a stable source of income. In some cases, political events can disrupt remittance flows. After the 1991 Gulf War, for instance, Saudi Arabia and Kuwait expelled hundreds of thousands of Palestinian, Yemeni, and Egyptian workers suspected of supporting Iraq's leader, Saddam Hussein. As described in Chapter 2, employment of these groups in the Gulf declined significantly, with serious financial ramifications for their home countries. Another case is that of Somalia, which became heavily dependent on migrant remittances in the 1990s in a context of unrelenting war, poverty, and political chaos. When the US shut down the sole company in Somalia that handled migrant remittances, accusing it of financing terrorism, the consequences for ordinary Somalis were devastating (Kapur, 2003). Border control regimes in the Global North may be equally disruptive to the flow of remittances. Cornelius (2005), Massey and Riosmena (2010), and others, for instance, have noted the tendency for stricter border enforcement along the US–Mexico border to 'bottle up' undocumented migrant workers in the US; that is, over time, many of these workers settle permanently in the US because of the danger and cost of movement across the border. These migrants may continue to send remittances, but their relationship with Mexico may lose strength. For their US-born children, who have American citizenship, connections with Mexico can become even more tenuous. This situation, Escobar Latapí (2008) suggests, has contributed to Mexico's low remittances-to-per capita GDP ratios relative to other countries in Latin America and the Caribbean (see also Yarnall and Price, 2010).

The case of permanent settlement of Mexican workers in the US raises a broader set of questions about the permanency of the diasporic condition and of being in diaspora. The migration-as-development model hinges on the idea that migrants will be forever willing and eager to support their countries and cities of origin, and that their children, likewise, will continue to feel the pull of their homeland. As we have seen, sending states expend significant resources and energy to ensure that their émigrés do indeed maintain this close identification. But the reality of diasporic identities and linkages may be more complex than this model assumes (Larner, 2007; Ho, 2011; Page and Mercer, 2012; Jöns, Mavroudi, and Heffernan, 2015). Taylor, et al. (2007), for instance, observe in the case of Punjabi migrants that a sense of material obligation to families may be present in the early years of settlement in a destination country, but this can quickly subside once sufficient money has been earned to bring family members to the place of settlement. Mavroudi's (2015) research on the Greek diaspora in Australia also speaks to the vagaries of diasporic connections. Mavroudi shows that while many first- and second-generation Greek-Australians were emotionally distraught by the Greek economic crisis that began in 2008, they were not necessarily willing to contribute monetarily to the country's recovery. Some have sent money to relatives and have invested in property, but they have been reluctant to invest in business ventures partly because of their lack of trust and confidence in the Greek government. (In his work on Mexican HTAs, Fitzgerald (2009) makes the related point that émigré organizations are not always willing to cooperate with the state on particular development initiatives.) Tellingly, Mavroudi's research subjects describe themselves as outsiders in Greece even though most have close sociocultural connections to the country. For second-generation Greek-Australians, in particular, a lack of fluency in Greek language and lack of knowledge about localities seems to discourage investment. In short, we cannot make easy assumptions either about the permanency of diasporas or about the nature of relationships between diasporas and homelands—a theme to which we return in Chapter 8.

Underlying some of these critical assessments is a deeper objection to the placement of the burden of development on the shoulders of migrant workers, who, with some notable exceptions, occupy marginal positions in rich economies. Casting migrants as 'heroes' of development, Delgado Wise and Márquez Covarrubias (2009, 96) argue, is 'an utterly cynical move that renders them responsible for the promotion of said development, while the state, opting for the conservative stance of minimal participation, is no longer held accountable'. As with other neoliberal political strategies, the promotion of emigration offloads responsibility for national well-being onto individuals, families, and communities, while serving the interests of global capital by creating a flexible, mobile, and expendable labour force (Phillips, 2011; Rodriguez, 2002). Nicola Yeates' (2009) analysis of the migrant workers in the global healthcare industry is indicative of this pessimistic view of labour-export strategies. Yeates emphasizes the abuse and vulnerability that migrant workers experience at every point in the emigration process—from their dealings with unscrupulous labour recruiters and inefficient government bureaucracies to the deskilling that takes place in destination countries (described in Chapter 3). While emigration may be an important income-generating strategy for poor households and a form of human agency, Yeates suggests it does not offer a definitive solution to the structural constraints experienced by the world's poor (Skeldon, 2011; Phillips, 2011).

Conclusions

We seem to arrive at an impasse. The complex relationships between emigration and economic growth, prosperity, and well-being, as we have seen, lend themselves to widely divergent interpretations. We can view the sending of remittances, for instance, as a massive transfer of wealth from the Global North to the Global South, or we can view these remittances as a relatively paltry return on the vast human resources that the Global South exports to the Global North. Empirical evidence of the impacts of emigration on the development of sending societies speaks to both positions, pointing equally to the great benefits of emigration for sending societies and to great harms (Kapur, 2003). In some ways, debates about the relationship between migration and development reflect profound differences in our interpretations of migration more generally: Is migration a means of alleviating labour-market imbalances and the geographical unevenness of wages and employment? Or is migration an inherent feature of a global economy that is predicated on imbalances, inequalities, and underdevelopment?

Even if we settle on a single definition of development as, say, human well-being or as economic growth and modernization, we can surmise that relationships between migration and development are highly contingent on innumerable, highly localized, circumstances: the motivations and resources of émigré communities; the nature of connections between migrants and their home and destination communities; the capacity of the sending state to secure the loyalty of émigrés; the sociopolitical position of migrants in both sending and destination contexts; and the ability of men and women, young and old, migrants and non-migrants, to leverage financial and social remittances in particular places (Bailey, 2010; De Haas, 2005; Carling, 2007). Determining how localized transformations might then affect migratory pressures at a global level is a daunting task, to say the least.

Regardless of these complexities, seemingly simple 'solutions' to the 'problem' of migration and development abound. As we have seen, most governments in the Global North view unskilled migration from the Global South through the lens of state sovereignty. Thus, even as employers rely on migrant workers, policymakers are inclined to promote a combination of development assistance, free-trade policies, and border-control measures that will reduce (at least in theory) migration pressures on a

medium- and long-term basis. In contrast, some scholars have argued that if the Global North wishes to stem migration flows and to reduce the settlement of undocumented workers in their borders, they should ease restrictions on circular migration flows, which allow workers to return home and to use their earnings to boost economic growth in their places of origin (De Haas, 2005). Some go further, arguing that migration should be viewed as a normal part of people's lives, rather than some kind of crisis that requires intensive state management (e.g. Bakewell, 2008). Yet others continue to suggest that skilled and unskilled migration is a drain on economies of poor countries, that remittances are insufficient compensation for the value of lost labour, and that temporary-worker programmes simply perpetuate the exploitation of migrant workers (Castles, 2006). Escobar Latapí (2008), commenting on the Mexican case, thus advocates the use of monetary incentives for people in poor communities to stay put and for migrants to return and resettle.

There are in these viewpoints fundamental differences not only about empirical evidence—whether emigration actually contributes measurably to economic growth or social well-being, and whether development assistance reduces migration pressures—but also about the prerogatives and interests of states, the inherent rights of people, the properties of capitalist markets, and the very nature of human agency. We find ourselves wandering into a rather philosophical realm where the migration-development nexus proves difficult to disentangle—where we struggle to define what the central 'problem' of migration and development is and what the 'solution' to that problem should be. The main point we wish to convey here is that all policies—whether designed to promote migration or to hinder it, to secure national borders or to open them, to encourage industrialization or to ease poverty—carry promises and pitfalls, opening up opportunities for some people while closing off opportunities for others. Any accounting of the migration-development nexus must avoid simple 'either/or' formulations and recognize that migration processes present us with contradictions and ambiguities far more often than they present us with definitive outcomes.

Key terms in this chapter

brain circulation

brain drain

co-development

diaspora

hometown associations (HTAs)

labour export

migration-development nexus

neoliberal

social remittances

structural adjustment policies

tres-por-uno

Further reading

De Haas, H. (2012) The migration and development pendulum: a critical view on research and policy, *International Migration*, 50(3): 8–25.

Délano, A. and Gamlen, A. (2014) Comparing and theorizing state–diaspora relations, *Political Geography*, 41: 43–53.

Ho, E. (2011) 'Claiming' the diaspora: elite mobility, sending state strategies and the spatialities of citizenship, *Progress in Human Geography*, 35(6): 757–772.

Page, B. and Mercer, C. (2012) Why do people do stuff? Reconceptualising remittance behaviour in diaspora-development research and policy, *Progress in Development Studies*, 12(1): 1–18.

Population, Space and Place (2009) Special Issue: Rethinking the Migration-Development Nexus —Bringing marginalized visions and actors to the fore, 15(2).

Portes, A. (2009) Migration and development: reconciling opposite views, *Ethnic and Racial Studies*, 32(1): 5–22.

References

Adams Jr., R. H. and Page, J. (2005) Do international migration and remittances reduce poverty in developing countries? *World Development*, 33(10): 1645–1669.

Adepoju, A., Van Noorloos, F., and Zoomers, A. (2010) Europe's migration agreements with migrant-sending countries in the Global South: a critical review, *International Migration*, 48(3): 42–75.

Ahmad, O. B. (2005) Managing medical migration from poor countries, *British Medical Journal*, 331(7507): 43–45.

Andreas, P. (2000) *Border Games: Policing the US–Mexico Divide*. Ithaca, NY: Cornell University Press.

Bailey, A. (2010) Population geographies, gender, and the migration-development nexus, *Progress in Human Geography*, 34(3): 375–386.

Bakewell, O. (2008) 'Keeping them in their place': the ambivalent relationship between development and migration in Africa, *Third World Quarterly*, 29(7): 1341–1358.

Bernal, V. (2006) Diaspora, cyberspace, and political imagination: the Eritrean diaspora online, *Global Networks*, 6(2): 161–179.

Bhagwati, J. N. (1976) Taxing the brain drain, *Challenge*, 19(3): 34–38.

Brand, L. (2010) Authoritarian states and voting from abroad: North African experiences, *Comparative Politics*, 43(1): 81–99.

Brinkerhoff, J. M. (2004). Digital diasporas and international development: Afghan-Americans and the reconstruction of Afghanistan, *Public Administration and Development*, 24(5), 397–413.

Brubaker, R. (2010) Migration, membership, and the modern nation-state: internal and external dimensions of the politics of belonging, *Journal of Interdisciplinary History*, 41(1): 61–78.

Brundtland, G. H. (1987) *Our Common Future* (Report of the World Commission on

Environment and Development). New York: United Nations General Assembly.

Burgess, K. and Tinajero, B. (2012) Collective remittances as non-state transfers: patterns of transnationalism in Mexico and El Salvador. In S. Brown (Ed.), *Transnational Transfers and Social Development*. Basingstoke; New York: Palgrave Macmillan (pp. 29–54).

Carling, J. (2007) Interrogating remittances: core questions for deeper insight and better policy. In S. Castles and R. Delgado Wise (Eds.), *Migration and Development: Perspectives from the Global South*. Geneva: International Organization for Migration (pp. 43–64).

Castles, S. (2002) International migration at the beginning of the twenty-first century: global trends and issues, *International Social Science Journal*, 52(165): 269–281.

Castles, S. (2006) Guestworkers in Europe: a resurrection? *International Migration Review*, 40: 741–766.

Castles, S. (2007) Comparing the experience of five major emigration countries. In S. Castles and R. Delgado Wise (Eds.), *Migration and Development: Perspectives from the Global South*. Geneva: International Organization for Migration (pp. 255–284).

Castles, S. (2009) Development and migration—migration and development: What comes first? Global perspective and African experiences, *Theoria: A Journal of Social and Political Theory*, 56(121): 1–31.

Cornelius, W. (2005) Controlling 'unwanted' immigration: lessons from the United States, 1993–2004, *Journal of Ethnic and Migration Studies*, 31(4): 775–794.

De Haas, H. (2005) International migration, remittances, and development: facts and myths, *Third World Quarterly*, 26(8): 1269–1284.

De Haas, H. (2006) Migration, remittances, and regional development in Southern Morocco, *Geoforum*, 37(4): 565–580.

Delgado Wise, R. and Márquez Covarrubias, H. (2009) Understanding the relationship between migration and development, *Social Analysis*, 53(3): 85–105.

Del Sarto, R. (2010) Borderlands: the Middle East and North Africa as the EU's southern buffer zone. In D. Bechev and K. Nicolaidis (Eds.), *Mediterranean Frontiers: Borders, Conflicts and Memory in a Transnational World*. London: I. B. Tauris (pp. 149–167).

Dovlo, D. (2004) The brain drain in Africa: an emerging challenge to health professionals' education, *Journal of Higher Education in Africa*, 2(3): 1–18.

Escobar, C. (2007) Extraterritorial political rights and dual citizenship in Latin America, *Latin American Research Review*, 42(3): 43–75.

European Commission (2014) Technical assistance for study on concrete results obtained through projects on migration and development financed under AENEAS and the Thematic Programme for migration and asylum—FINAL REPORT. Directorate General for International Cooperation and Development. Retrieved from http://ec.europa.eu/europeaid/technical-assistance-study-concrete-results-obtained-through-projects-migration-and-development_en (accessed 24 March 2015).

Faist, T. (2008) Migrants as transnational development agents: an inquiry into the newest round of the migration-development nexus, *Population, Space and Place*, 14(1): 21–42.

Faist, T. and Gerdes, J. (2008) *Dual citizenship in an age of mobility*. Transatlantic Council on Migration. Washington, DC: Migration Policy Institute.

Fernández-Kelly, P. and Massey, D. (2007) Borders for whom? The role of NAFTA in Mexico–US migration, *The Annals of the American Academy of Political and Social Science*, 610(1): 98–118.

Fitzgerald, D. (2009) *A Nation of Emigrants: How Mexico Manages its Migration*. Berkeley; Los Angeles: University of California Press.

Frank, A. G. (1967) *Capitalism and Underdevelopment in Latin America: Historical Studies of Chile and Brazil*. New York: Monthly Review Press.

Gerein, N., Green, A., and Pearson, S. (2006) The implications of shortages of health professionals for maternal health in sub-Saharan Africa, *Reproductive Health Matters*, 14(27): 40–50.

Gilman, N. (2003) *Mandarins of the Future: Modernization Theory in Cold War America*. Baltimore, MD: Johns Hopkins University Press.

Glytsos, N. P. (1997) Remitting behaviour of 'temporary' and 'permanent' migrants: the case of Greeks in Germany and Australia, *Labour*, 11(3): 409–435.

Goldring, L. (2001) The gender and geography of citizenship in Mexico–U.S. transnational spaces, *Identities*, 7(4): 501–537.

Grillo, R. and Riccio, B. (2004) Translocal development: Italy–Senegal, *Population, Space and Place*, 10(2): 99–111.

Hadj Nacer, A. and Alméras, G. (2008) Maghreb banks and financial markets. In G. C. Hufbauer and C. Brunel (Eds.), *Maghreb Regional and Global Integration: A Dream to Be Fulfilled*. Washington, DC: Peterson Institute for International Economics (pp. 125–138).

Haefele, M. H. (2003) Walt Rostow's stages of economic growth: ideas and actions. In D. C. Engerman, N. Gilman, M. H. Haefele, and M. E. Latham (Eds.), *Staging Growth: Modernization and the Cold War*. Amherst, MA: University of Massachusetts Press (pp. 81–103).

Harvey, W. S. (2008) Brain circulation? British and Indian scientists in Boston, Massachusetts, USA, *Asian Population Studies*, 4(3): 293–309.

Hermele, K. (1997) The discourse on migration and development. In T. Faist (Ed.), *International Migration, Immobility, and Development: Multidisciplinary Perspectives*. Oxford; New York: Berg (pp. 133–158).

Hernández, K. L. (2006) The crimes and consequences of illegal immigration: a cross-border examination of Operation Wetback, 1943 to 1954, *Western Historical Quarterly*, 37(4): 421–444.

Ho, E. (2011) 'Claiming' the diaspora: elite mobility, sending state strategies and the spatialities of citizenship, *Progress in Human Geography*, 35(6): 757–772.

Hollifield, J. (2004) The emerging migration state, *International Migration Review*, 38(3): 885–912.

House of Commons International Development Committee (2004) *Migration and Development: How to Make Migration Work for Poverty Reduction*. Sixth Report of Session 2003–2004 (Volume I/HC 79-1). London: The Stationery Office Ltd. (p. 20).

Hugo, G. and Stahl, C. (2004) Labor export strategies in Asia. In D. S. Massey and E. J. Taylor (Eds.), *International Migration: Prospects and Policies in a Global Market*. Oxford: Oxford University Press (pp. 174–200).

Hunger, E. (2004) Indian IT entrepreneurs in the US and India: an illustration of the 'brain gain' hypothesis, *Journal of Comparative Policy Analysis: Research and Practice*, 6(2): 99–109.

Itzigsohn, J. (2000) Immigration and the boundaries of citizenship: the institutions of immigrants' political transnationalism, *International Migration Review*, 34(4): 1126–1154.

Jones-Correa, M. (2001) Under two flags: dual nationality in Latin America and its consequences for naturalization in the United States, *International Migration Review*, 35(4): 997–1029.

Jöns, H. (2009) 'Brain circulation' and transnational knowledge networks: studying long-term effects of academic mobility to Germany, 1954–2000, *Global Networks*, 9(3): 315–338.

Jöns, H., Mavroudi, E. and Heffernan, M. (2015) Mobilising the elective diaspora: US–German academic exchanges since 1945, *Transactions of the Institute of British Geographers*, 40: 113–127.

Kadırbeyoğlu, Z. (2007) National transnationalism: Dual citizenship in Turkey. In T. Faist (Ed.), *Dual Citizenship in Europe: From National to Societal Integration*. Aldershot: Ashgate (pp. 127–145).

Kapur, D. (2003) Remittances: the new development mantra? Harvard University and the Center for Global Development, Report presented at G-24 Technical Group Meeting. Retrieved from http://dspace.cigilibrary.org/jspui/bitstream/123456789/13268/1/Remittances%20The%20New%20Development%20Mantra.pdf?1 (accessed 21 June 2015).

Klaufus, C. (2010) Watching the city grow: remittances and sprawl in intermediate Central American cities, *Environment and Urbanization*, 22(1): 125–137.

Kuehn, B. M. (2007) Global shortage of health workers, brain drain stress developing countries, *JAMA*, 298(16): 1853–1855.

Kwok, V. and Leland, H. (1982) An economic model of the brain drain, *The American Economic Review*, 72(1): 91–100.

Larner, W. (2007) Expatriate experts and globalising governmentalities: the New Zealand diaspora strategy, *Transactions of the Institute of British Geographers*, 32(3): 331–45.

Latapí, A. E. (2008) Mexican policy and Mexico–US migration. In A. E. Lapatí and S. Martin (Eds.), *Mexico–US Migration Management: A Binational Approach*. Plymouth, MA: Lexington Books (pp. 179–216).

Levitt, P. (1998) Social remittances: migration-driven local-level forms of cultural diffusion, *International Migration Review*, 32(4): 926–948.

Levitt, P. and Lamba-Nieves, D. (2011) Social remittances revisited, *Ethnic and Migration Studies*, 37(1): 1–22.

Mahroum, S., Eldridge, C., and Daar, A. (2006) Transnational diaspora options: how developing countries could benefit from their emigrant populations, *International Journal on Multicultural Societies*, 8(1): 25–42.

Martin, P. L. (1993) Trade and migration: the case of NAFTA, *Asian and Pacific Migration Journal*, 2(3): 329–367.

Martin, P. L. (2003) Economic integration and migration: the Mexico–US case, WIDER Discussion Papers, World Institute for Development Economics (UNU-WIDER), No. 2003/35. Retrieved from http://hdl.handle.net/10419/52907 (accessed 15 July 2014).

Massey, D. and Riosmena, F. (2010) Undocumented migration from Latin America in an era of rising U.S. enforcement, *The Annals of the American Academy of Political and Social Science*, 630(1): 294–321.

Mavroudi, E. (2015) Helping the homeland? Diasporic Greeks in Australia and the potential for homeland-oriented development at a time of economic crisis. In A. Christou and E. Mavroudi (Eds.), *Dismantling Diasporas: Rethinking the Geographies of Diasporic Identity, Connection and Development*. Farnham, UK; Burlington, VT: Ashgate (pp. 175–188).

Murphy, C. (2006) *The United Nations Development Programme: A Better Way?* Cambridge: Cambridge University Press.

Nyíri, P. (2001) Expatriating is patriotic? The discourse on 'new migrants' in the People's Republic of China and identity construction among recent migrants from the PRC, *Ethnic and Racial Studies*, 24(4): 635–653.

Orozco, M. and Rouse, R. (2012) Migrant hometown associations and opportunities for development. In J. DeFilippis and S. Saegert (Eds.), *Community Development Reader* (2nd Edition). New York; Abingdon: Routledge (pp. 280–285).

Page, B. and Mercer, C. (2012) Why do people do stuff? Reconceptualising remittance behaviour in diaspora-development research and policy, *Progress in Development Studies*, 12(1): 1–18.

Pellegrino, A. (2001) Trends in Latin American skilled migration: 'brain drain' or 'brain exchange'? *International Migration*, 39(5): 111–132.

Pernia, E. M. (1976) The question of the brain drain from the Philippines, *International Migration Review*, 10(1): 63–72.

Phillips, N. (2011) Migration and development in Latin America and the Caribbean. In N. Phillips (Ed.), *Migration in the Global Economy*. Boulder, CO: Lynne Rienner Publishers (pp. 167–189).

Pieke, F. N., Van Hear, N., and Lindley, A. (2007) Beyond control? The mechanics and dynamics of 'informal' remittances between Europe and Africa, *Global Networks*, 7(3): 348–366.

Piper, N. (2004) Gender and migration policies in Southeast Asia and East Asia: legal protection and sociocultural empowerment of unskilled migrant women, *Singapore Journal of Tropical Geography*, 25(2): 216–231.

Portes, A. (1976) Determinants of the brain drain, *International Migration Review*, 10(4): 489–508.

Portes, A. and Zhou, M. (2012) Transnationalism and development: Mexican and Chinese immigrant organizations in the United States, *Population and Development Review*, 38(2): 191–220.

Raghuram, P. (2009a) Caring about 'brain drain' migration in a post-colonial world, *Geoforum*, 40(1): 25–33.

Raghuram, P. (2009b) Which migration, what development? Unsettling the edifice of migration and development, *Population, Space and Place*, 15(2): 103–117.

Ratha, D. (2007) Leveraging remittances for development. In J. Hollifield, P. Orrenius, and T. Osang (Eds.), *Migration, Trade, and Development*. Dallas, TX: Federal Reserve Bank of Dallas (pp. 173–186).

Rivera-Batiz, F. L. (1986) Can border industries be a substitute for immigration? *The American Economic Review*, 76(2): 263–268.

Rivera-Salgado, G. and Rabadán, L. E. (2008) Migration, collective remittances, and development: Mexican migrant associations in the United States. In T. van Naerssen, E. Spaan, and A. Zoomers (Eds.), *Global Migration and Development*. New York: Routledge (pp. 111–129).

Rodriguez, R. M. (2002) Migrant heroes: nationalism, citizenship and the politics of Filipino migrant labor, *Citizenship Studies*, 6(3): 341–356.

Rostow, W. W. (1950 [1990]) *The Stages of Economic Growth: A Non-Communist Manifesto*. Cambridge: Cambridge University Press.

Sako, S. (2002) Brain drain and Africa's development: a reflection, *African Issues*, 30(1): 25–30.

Saxenian, A. (2002) Brain circulation: how high-skill immigration makes everyone better off, *Brookings Review*, 20(1): 28–31.

Saxenian, A. L. (2005) From brain drain to brain circulation: transnational communities and regional upgrading in India and China, *Studies in Comparative International Development*, 40(2): 35–61.

Silvey, R. (2007) Mobilizing piety: gendered morality and Indonesian–Saudi transnational migration, *Mobilities*, 2(2): 219–229.

Skeldon, R. (2011) Reinterpreting migration and development. In N. Phillips (Ed.), *Migration in the Global Economy*. Boulder, CO: Lynne Rienner Publishers (pp. 103–119).

Sørensen, N. N. (2012) Revisiting the migration-development nexus: from social networks and remittances to markets for migration control, *International Migration*, 50(3): 61–76.

Tamis, A. (2005) *The Greeks in Australia*. Cambridge: Cambridge University Press.

Taylor, J. E. (1999) The new economics of labour migration and the role of remittances in the migration process, *International Migration*, 37(1): 63–88.

Taylor, S., Singh, M., and Booth, D. (2007) Migration, development and inequality: Eastern Punjabi transnationalism, *Global Networks*, 7(3): 328–347.

Touray, K. S. (2008) Final evaluation of the support project to the implementation of the Rwanda TOKTEN volunteer program. Retrieved from http://erc.undp.org/evaluationadmin/downloaddocument.html?docid=1814 (accessed 29 May 2015).

Tseng, Y. (2000) The mobility of entrepreneurs and capital: Taiwanese capital-linked migration, *International Migration*, 38(2): 143–168.

Tyner, J. (1999) The global context of gendered labor migration from the Philippines to the United States, *American Behavioral Scientist*, 42(4): 671–689.

United Nations (2006) Report of the Secretary General: international migration and development, A/60/871. United Nations General Assembly, Sixtieth Session, Agenda item 54(c): globalization and interdependence: international migration and development. Retrieved from http://www.un.org/en/development/desa/population/migration/generalassembly/reports/index.shtml (accessed 28 May 2015).

Upadhya, C. (2004) A new transnational capitalist class? Capital flows, business networks, and entrepreneurs in the Indian software industry, *Economic and Political Weekly*, 39(48): 5541–5151.

Walton-Roberts, M. (2004) Returning, remitting, reshaping: non-resident Indians and the transformation of society and space in Punjab, India. In P. Crang, C. Dwyer, and P. Jackson (Eds.), *Transnational Spaces*. London; New York: Routledge (pp. 78–103).

World Bank (2011) *Migration and Remittances Factbook* (2nd edition). Washington, DC: The International Bank for Reconstruction and Development/World Bank (p. 13). Retrieved from http://www.worldbank.org/prospects/migrationandremittances (accessed 1 September 2014).

World Bank (2014) Migration and remittances: recent developments and outlook, migration and development brief, number 23 (Oct 6, 2014). Retrieved from http://econ.worldbank.org/WBSITE/EXTERNAL/EXTDEC/EXTDECPROSPECTS/0,,contentMDK:21125572~pagePK:64165401~piPK:64165026~theSitePK:476883,00.html (accessed 28 May 2015).

World Bank (2015) Bilateral Remittance Data Matrix. Migration and Remittances Data. Retrieved from http://econ.worldbank.org/WBSITE/EXTERNAL/EXTDEC/EXTDECPROSPECTS/0,,contentMDK:22759429~pagePK:64165401~piPK:64165026~theSitePK:476883,00.html.

Yarnall, K. and Price, M. (2010) Migration, development, and a new rurality in the Valle Alto, Bolivia, *Journal of Latin American Geography*, 9(1): 107–124.

Yeates, N. (2009) Production for export: the role of the state in the development and operation of global care chains, *Population, Space and Place*, 15(2): 175–187.

5

Refugees

Introduction

The previous chapters have dealt primarily with labour migrations, which we have connected to complex assemblages of employer demands, state policies, and individual and household decision-making, among other factors. In this chapter, we turn to migrations that are tied less clearly to wages and labour markets than to episodes of political upheaval, warfare, and violence. We can

Plate 5.1 Syrian boy on a truck
Source: Andrew McConnell/Panos

speak of these as forced, or involuntary, migrations. It is important to recognize from the outset that in the real world there is no clear dividing line between 'voluntary' and 'involuntary' migrations, or between economic and political migrations. Many economic migrations involve some element of compulsion—most obviously in the case of slavery and trafficking, but also in the case of 'ordinary' migrations where difficult local circumstances make migration necessary for household survival. By the same token, many of those fleeing political instability and violence may also be in search of economic opportunity and may choose their destinations accordingly. All migrations, in this sense, are produced through some combination of economic and political factors and through interactions between human agency and structural forces beyond the immediate control of ordinary people. Yet, it is also apparent that some migrations involve more human agency than others and are motivated more obviously by the immediate threat of violence and conflict than by economic interests. Thus, we can begin to speak in more specialized terms about forced migrations and the specific politics that these migrations produce.

This chapter will examine the phenomenon of forced migration with a focus on refugees. Many contemporary discussions of refugees rely on the United Nations definition of a refugee as any individual who,

> owing to a well-grounded fear of being persecuted for reasons of race, religion, nationality, membership of a particular social group or political opinion, is outside of his country of nationality and is unable or, owing to such fear, is unwilling to avail himself of the protection of that country.

As we explain later in this chapter, the UN definition is narrow and individualistic and seems at odds with the reality of large-scale displacement caused by civil conflict and war. We prefer a broader definition, such as that offered by Gibney (2004, 7),

who describes refugees as 'those people in need of a new state of residence, either temporarily or permanently' because returning home or remaining where they are would 'seriously jeopardize their physical security or vital subsistence needs'.

While all migrants are perceived as problematic in a world organized around territorially bounded nation-states, refugees are particularly troublesome from the perspective of recipient countries. The world of refugees, some suggest, is almost a separate 'limbo world' (Walzer, 1970, cited in Malkki, 1995, 9) that exists on the outside of the 'normal', legitimate world of territorially bounded nations. Refugees enter other countries without any kind of invitation and are rendered fundamentally out-of-place. While at times treated with compassion, they are more often met by wariness or even outright hostility by their hosts, especially if they become a political liability for ruling elites. It is for this reason that states seek to control the movement of refugees, even as they voice their commitments to humanitarian assistance.

This chapter begins by explaining the phenomenon of refugee flows. Recapitulating some of the historical discussion in Chapter 2, we draw out the relationship between nation-state formation and refugees. We then explain the creation of modern, legal categories of refugee and **asylum seeker** during the Cold War era and consider the contemporary politics of refuge and asylum in the Global North. Here we explain that while countries of the Global North receive only a tiny fraction of those who flee across state boundaries due to civil conflict and ethnic or religious persecution, they have treated asylum seekers—that is, those requesting official refugee status from a foreign government—as a threat to national sovereignty and security and have created elaborate systems to control and to deter them. We then shift our attention to refugee politics in the Global South, emphasizing the ways in which refugees accommodate, subvert, and negotiate efforts by humanitarian organizations and host countries to control and manage them.

In concluding this chapter, we return to the distinctions made between voluntary (economic) migrants and involuntary (political) migrants. The distinction between those who are forced to migrate and those who migrate voluntarily for economic gain is central to migration policy in the Global North, and it underpins many contemporary humanitarian practices and policies. Yet, as we will see, this distinction increasingly serves to exclude the very people it is meant to assist by requiring them to prove that they, as individuals, face imminent persecution and that they are not motivated in any way by economic needs. This is a nearly impossible task for those seeking asylum in wealthy countries. We ask, then, whether there is an alternative to refugee policies in the Global North and whether those fleeing conflict might be better served by the elimination of strict distinctions between voluntary and involuntary migrants.

Refugees in historical perspective

The concept of 'refugee crisis' today conjures up images of throngs of people in the Global South displaced by violent conflicts and seeking a better life in wealthier countries. The dominant image of the 'Third World' refugee, however, is quite misleading. Until fairly recently, the forced movement of millions of people across borders has been a more constant feature of life in the Global North than in the Global South. European history, in particular, has been punctuated by massive forced migrations. Consider, for instance, the religiously motivated expulsions of the Reformation era, the political dislocations wrought by liberal revolutions of the late 18th and early 19th centuries, the exclusionary nationalisms of the late 19th century, and the upheavals of the first and second World Wars. As recently as the 1990s, Europe experienced a major refugee crisis with the collapse of the former Yugoslavia. Given the contentiousness of asylum in countries of the Global North and

the frequent exaggeration of the scale of refugee flows to these countries, it is helpful to provide some historical perspective and to explain how the modern categories of refugee and asylum seeker have emerged in an international system devised largely by powerful states.

Refugee flows and the formation of the modern nation-state system

Historically, refugee crises are closely connected to the formation of the modern nation-state system in Europe, a lengthy and complex process that began (roughly) in the 16th century with the consolidation of feudal kingdoms into cohesive, centralized territorial states (Wallerstein, 2004). This process of state-building and centralization shaped, and was shaped by, the Protestant Reformation, which generated new ideas about sovereignty and authority, as well as new modes of collective consciousness (Anderson, 1983). The Reformation also bred significant political discord and prompted the persecution of religious non-conformists—a notable example being the expulsion of half a million Protestants from France in 1685 (Marfleet, 2007). English-language dictionaries trace the origins of the word 'refugee'—from the French *refugié*, or one who seeks refuge or safety—to the expulsion of the Protestants from France.

French Protestants, known as **Huguenots**, were welcome in Protestant Britain, not least because of their artisanal skills and mercantile savvy. The British Parliament in 1709 passed a naturalization law that granted foreign Protestants British citizenship, requiring only that they convert to the Anglican Church, take an oath, and pay a fee (Bade, 2003). Thereafter, through the 18th and 19th centuries, Britain became a magnet for all kinds of political exiles and refugees. During the era of liberal revolutions in Europe—beginning with the French Revolution of 1789 and continuing for several decades—London was abuzz with dissidents from the Continent, especially from Germany, France, Hungary, Italy, and Belgium (Sassen, 1999). Later, these liberal dissidents were joined by growing numbers of socialists. Thousands of anarchists, especially from Germany, also settled in the United States, where they formed a radical subculture in big industrial cities (Goyens, 2007).

As the 19th century wore on, refugees from Europe's political upheavals were more tolerated than embraced by the British state and the British public. While many of the refugees were skilled artisans or intellectuals, others were destitute and unable to cope with exile. Anxiety about refugees in Britain and elsewhere in Europe increased significantly as the composition of refugee populations shifted in response to the emergence of ethno-national movements in the late 19th century. The nation-state, as we have seen, was an historically novel form of political-territorial organization predicated on the enclosure of populations and the integration of these populations into 'homogenous' nations (Hobsbawm, 1990). It presented what Malkki (1995, 6) describes as 'a powerful regime of classification, an apparently commonsensical system of ordering and sorting people into national kinds and types' (see also Mavroudi, 2010). While relatively open borders remained the norm in many major European countries (notably France and Britain) through the 19th century, the modern nation-state had at its disposal ever greater means to monitor and to regulate populations, to distinguish more clearly between citizens and aliens, and to exclude or eliminate those deemed undesirable.

If the age of revolutions in Europe produced a kind of refugee that was persecuted for what he or she said or did, the era of nationalism produced 'a type of refugee who was persecuted for something the persecutor viewed him or her as being' (Bade, 2003, 148). One of the most important refugee dramas of the late 19th century was connected to the persecution of Jews in Russia. Starting in the 1880s, millions of Jews (as well as Gypsies)—who had long been subject to discrimination and territorial containment in the Russian Empire—were targeted on multiple occasions by violent, rioting mobs. These violent attacks, called **pogroms**, led tens of thousands of Russian Jews to migrate westward. Most of these transited through Germany on the way to the United States, but thousands remained in Germany, adding to what was a sizable German Jewish population. The German state (and indeed, many assimilated German Jews) viewed these newcomers with alarm, leading to a new citizenship law in 1913 that codified an ethnic principle of descent, effectively barring Eastern European Jews from citizenship (Bade, 2003). This same westward movement of Jews also precipitated the end of Britain's relatively open-door immigration policies. Britain initially had tolerated the settlement of Jews, but as numbers of Jewish refugees reached 120,000, Britain abandoned its traditional liberalism. The Aliens Act of 1905 'empowered landing officers to prohibit the immigration of certain aliens traveling on certain ships'—namely, ships large enough to have a steerage class in which most Jewish refugees travelled (Paul, 1997, 66). The 1905 legislation also 'provided for the registration of all aliens within Britain, and imposed restrictions on aliens' freedom of movement' (ibid.). Foreshadowing contemporary political discourse, the debates leading up to the Aliens Act portrayed Eastern European Jews as 'economic migrants' rather than as 'real' refugees, thereby justifying their exclusion from Britain (Marfleet, 2006). In this sense, the British state posited asylum as an act of charity to be granted by British officials on a discretionary basis, and it encouraged a narrow conceptualization of 'refugee' as an individual political exile (we return to this theme in a moment).

Mounting rivalries between Europe's Great Powers in the early 20th century led to the outbreak of World War I and the subsequent displacement of millions of civilians. Large-scale displacement, linked to the post-war reorganization of territorial borders, continued long after the cessation of hostilities. The waning years of the Ottoman Empire offer an instructive example. During World War I, the Ottoman Empire, increasingly under the influence of Turkish nationalism, began the systematic expulsion of minority groups—most notably Armenians and Pontic Greeks—whom it accused of collaborating with its European rivals and of harbouring claims of self-determination. The Armenian community, which had lived in the Ottoman Empire for 500 years, was forced on what was essentially a death march from Anatolia into the Syrian desert in order to cleanse the Turkish heartland of non-Turkish people (Akçam, 2006). An estimated one million people died, and many others fled into Persia and Russia. The Pontic Greeks, as well, were subjected to death marches and were forced to leave the only homes they had known (Halo, 2001). After World War I, the Ottoman Empire dissolved, and its constituent parts were occupied by various European states. Greece participated in the partition and occupation of the Ottoman Empire in the hope of reclaiming historically Greek areas along the coast of Anatolia, in what is now Turkey (Hirschon, 2003a). Turkish nationalists led by Mustafa Kemal (later Atatürk), however, defeated the Greek army in the summer of 1922, leading to the flight of thousands of Greeks from their homes (Milton, 2008). Following the logic of nationalism, which strives for ethnic purity within territorial borders, the peace settlement between Turkey and Greece stipulated a population exchange between the two countries. In one of the most dramatic examples of ethnic cleansing in modern history, an estimated 1.3 million Anatolian Greeks were forced to resettle in Greece, while 350,000 Muslims in Greece were forced to move to Turkey (Hirschon, 2003b).

The post-World War I period also saw the continuation of anti-Semitism in Europe. The persecution of Jews reached new levels in Germany, where the National Socialist Party, driven by pseudo-scientific theories of racial superiority, embarked on a programme of territorial expansion and demographic purification, which led eventually to the extermination of six million Jews, Gypsies, communists, homosexuals, and other 'undesirables'. Large numbers of Jews fled from Nazi Germany and Central and Eastern European states in the 1930s but faced serious obstacles in the search for sanctuary in countries like Britain, France, and the US, which had been introducing more restrictions and controls on immigrants since the late 1800s, partly motivated in each case by anti-Semitism. Governments welcomed some prominent Jews, and there were some broader advocacy efforts on behalf of Jewish refugees; but governments, in general, balked at the prospect of resettling hundreds of thousands of Central and Eastern European Jews, even though their plight was well understood. Around 250,000 Jews in the 1930s managed to migrate to Palestine, a territory created from former Ottoman lands and placed under British 'mandate' rule in 1922 by the League of Nations. Faced with growing unrest among the local Arab population, British mandate rulers eventually limited Jewish migration to Palestine. Eventually Britain relaxed its own domestic controls, and 50,000 Jewish refugees entered the UK, albeit on temporary visas (Marfleet, 2006; see also Caron's (1999) discussion of policies towards refugees and immigrants in France in the 1930s).

Refugees at mid-century

In the aftermath of the Second World War some 40 million people were displaced across Europe. These included approximately 14 million ethnic Germans who had resided for generations in Czechoslovakia, Poland, Hungary, and elsewhere in Eastern Europe, but who were expelled following the Nazi defeat and forced to 'return' to Germany. There were also approximately 11 million displaced people who had been forced labourers in Germany's war economy (Bade, 2003). Many displaced persons remained in refugee camps for years after the war, unable or unwilling to return home in the face of Soviet occupation of their countries or due to fear of retribution from former enemies. As we saw in Chapter 3, some of these refugees were resettled as part of labour migration programmes in Western Europe, including the European Volunteer Workers programmes, which brought thousands of refugees from the Soviet-occupied Baltic republics to Britain.

As Europe struggled with its post-war refugee crisis, new refugee crises were brewing in Europe's colonial possessions as they transitioned to independent statehood. A notable example was the partition between Pakistan and India, largely along religious lines, following India's independence from Britain in 1947. Involving 10–15 million people, the population transfer that took place as Muslims fled to Pakistan and Hindus to India dwarfed even the epic population transfers between Turkey and Greece in the 1920s (Pandy, 2001). Another post-colonial refugee crisis took place in Palestine, where, as we have seen, the growth of the European Jewish population in the interwar years was opposed by the indigenous Arab population. The British government, which had expressed its commitment to a Jewish homeland while simultaneously promising Arabs an independent state, found itself unable to manage the situation it had created. Shortly after World War II, Britain withdrew from Palestine and turned the situation over to the newly created United Nations. A partition plan drawn up by the United Nations in 1947, which would have given a disproportionate share of Palestine's land to a proposed Jewish state, was rejected by the Arabs. The ensuing war between Jewish and Arab forces caused the displacement of approximately 750,000 Palestinian Arabs, most of whom fled to neighbouring Arab countries, where the UN set up refugee camps under the auspices of the **United Nations Relief and Works Agency (UNRWA)** (Chatty and Hundt, 2005). The new state of Israel declared its independence in 1948 and granted citizenship to the Arabs who had remained in place during the war between Jewish and Arab forces (approximately

20 percent of Israel's citizens today are Arabs). Israeli authorities, however, refused to readmit those Palestinian Arabs who had fled the war and proceeded to raze dozens of Palestinian villages to prevent any future return (Falah, 1996). The exiled Palestinians became one of the world's largest stateless populations, and their presence has had significant—and sometimes destabilizing—impacts on domestic politics in Lebanon and Jordan. For further discussion of the social and political marginalization of Palestinian refugees, see Mason (2007) and Ramadan (2009b).

Defining refugees in the Cold War era

The creation of the Palestinian refugee problem gives us pause to consider the legal construction of 'refugees' after World War II and the central role of the United Nations in defining and managing refugees. The massive destruction and dislocation of the first half of the 20th century provided the impetus for the creation of the United Nations as an international organization designed to foster stability and cooperation in the interstate system. At the end of the war, the United Nations began the process of drafting international agreements and conventions to govern the behaviour of member states and to enable collective action in times of international crisis. From the start, refugees were an important focal point of the United Nations. In 1946 the UN created the International Refugee Organization (IRO), the main objective of which was the **repatriation** of the millions of Europeans displaced by World War II—that is, the return of refugees to their countries of origin. But as the Cold War took shape, the IRO shifted its focus from repatriation to the **resettlement** of refugees in third countries. Resettlement remained a priority of the office of the **United Nations High Commissioner for Refugees (UNHCR)**, which replaced the IRO in 1950.

In 1951 the United Nations adopted the UN Convention Relating to the Status of Refugees (hereafter the 1951 Refugee Convention); this document, along with a 1967 Protocol that broadened the Convention's remit beyond Europe, laid out the international system's legal obligations to those seeking refuge in another country. Among the key legal principles articulated in the 1951 Refugee Convention was **non-refoulement**, which bars signatory states from refusing entry to refugees and returning refugees to places they have fled. The 1951 Refugee Convention also offered the first, systematic, legal definition of a refugee (stated in the introduction to this chapter). The highly individualistic nature of the UN's definition is striking given the reality of mass displacement and dislocation that instigated the creation of the IRO and the UNHCR after World War II. A refugee in this formulation is a single person who seeks protection from persecution, not a whole population fleeing violence, destruction, or ethnic cleansing.

Regardless of this individualistic definition, UNHCR continued to manage mass refugee flows in the decades after World War II. In 1972, for instance, the UNHCR, along with other international agencies, arranged for the resettlement of 40,000 Asians who had been expelled from Uganda by the post-colonial regime of Idi Amin (these were the descendants of Indian workers who had been brought to Africa by the British in the late 19th century). Even more dramatic was the resettlement of over 700,000 refugees in the 1970s in the aftermath of the Vietnam War. Many Vietnamese refugees had fled by boat to nearby Southeast Asian countries, most notably Malaysia, with some making it as far as Australia. While some of the Vietnamese '**boat people**' (as they came to be known) were given asylum, many were turned away, and some reportedly were towed back out to sea by hostile governments (Bronée, 1993). The UN intervened to prevent a humanitarian crisis, negotiating the safe landing of the boat people in Southeast Asian countries and arranging their resettlement in third countries (UNHCR, 2011b).

The Vietnamese refugee crisis demonstrated very clearly the prerogative exercised by individual nation-states in accepting or rejecting those seeking asylum. In other words, the UN, despite its international mandate, relied on the cooperation and goodwill of national governments for the protection and resettlement of refugees. The involvement of national governments in determining refugee status opened up humanitarian practice to significant politicization during the Cold War. This politicization was blatant during the Salvadoran civil war, which grew in the late 1970s from an internal conflict into a major theatre of the Cold War. The conflict was fuelled by the Reagan Administration (1981–8), which financed the Salvadoran government's suppression of left-wing insurgents. Through the 1980s, around a half million displaced Salvadoran civilians made their way to the United States, where they were promptly denied refugee status. Administration officials consistently classified Salvadoran refugees as self-interested 'economic migrants' and ordered the deportation of thousands of Salvadorans caught at the US–Mexico border (Macekura, 2011; see also Marfleet, 2011). The experiences of Salvadorans stood in stark contrast to the experiences of Cubans, who, as exiles from a communist regime, were generally welcomed by the US government. Western European governments were similarly welcoming towards hundreds of thousands of Eastern Europeans fleeing communist regimes—hence Gibney's (2004, 3) observation that 'liberal democratic states could be highly responsive to the claims of necessitous outsiders when responding to their needs also served to demonstrate the moral bankruptcy of communism'. (Some non-democratic states also welcomed refugees from communist countries; Box 5.1 presents an interesting case of Cold War-era refugee flows to Saudi Arabia.)

BOX 5.1 THE UIGHURS, SAUDI ARABIA, AND POST-COLD WAR GEOPOLITICS

The far western Chinese province of Xinjiang has long been home to a large Turkic-Muslim population, including a group known today as Uighurs. The historical relationship between the Uighurs and the Chinese state has been punctuated by episodes of submission, cooperation, and resistance since the late 18th century, with resistance becoming a more common state of affairs since the early 20th century. The communist takeover in China in 1948 and a violent crackdown on separatist movements in the 1960s caused tens of thousands of Uighurs and other minority groups to flee the region (Harris, 1993). A small but significant number of Uighurs ended up in Saudi Arabia, which was eager to exercise its leadership in the global Muslim community by welcoming Muslims fleeing from communist regimes. Uighur refugees, along with other Central Asian refugees in Saudi Arabia, identified themselves as *muhajirun*—a term applied to the Prophet Mohammed and his followers who fled persecution in Mecca in 622 CE (Balci, 2007). In the 1980s, economic and political opening in China made it possible for Uighur refugees to return to Xinjiang as missionaries in order to 're-Islamicize' China's Muslim population; at the same time, Uighurs in Xinjiang were permitted to make the pilgrimage to Mecca, thus gaining exposure to the puritanical form of Islam practised in Saudi Arabia. Chinese authorities, however, soon grew anxious about the Uighurs' engagements with Saudi Arabia and other conservative Muslim countries, viewing Islamic ideologies as fanning the flames of separatism in Xinjiang (Harris, 1993). Thus began another phase of repression by the Chinese state. The US found itself embroiled in this situation when it captured 22 Uighurs during the US invasion of Afghanistan in 2001. After detaining the Uighur captives in Guantanamo Bay for several years, the US government determined that they were not a threat to the US and ordered them to be released. Unable to send the Uighurs back to China due to humanitarian concerns, and barred from resettling them in the US by unsympathetic politicians, the administration negotiated the resettlement of the Uighurs with six different countries, including Albania and Slovakia. This episode illustrates well the prerogative exercised by states in accepting displaced and exiled groups. It illustrates, as well, the ambiguous ways that national governments perceive and deal with such groups. While some have cast the Uighurs as dangerous extremists, others treat them as freedom fighters escaping oppression. Humanitarian practice, it seems, rarely remains separate from the political and ideological agendas of individual nation-states.

Refugee crises and the politics of asylum since the Cold War

The end of the Cold War in the late 1980s did not diminish the politicization of refugees. Instead, the surfacing of ethnic and sectarian tensions in post-colonial and post-communist states—most notably the former Yugoslavia, Somalia, Afghanistan, Rwanda, and Sudan—ushered in a new period of refugee politics. In the wake of the Vietnamese refugee crisis, the UNHCR's commitment to resettlement had waned significantly and had shifted once again towards repatriation, or the return of refugees to their places of origin (UNHCR, 2011b; Chimni, 2002; Bakewell, 2002). Those unwilling or unable to return to their own countries increasingly chose (or were compelled) to find their own way to safe countries and to claim asylum from foreign governments. Wealthy countries, in turn, pursued ever more aggressive measures to restrict asylum claims within their borders.

After nearly two decades of imposing restrictions on labour migration and post-colonial settlement, European countries faced thousands—even hundreds of thousands—of asylum applications. Asylum applications in Germany, for instance, soared from 35,300 in 1984 to more than 121,000 in 1989 and peaked in 1992 at 438,200. In France, asylum applications increased at a more modest but still impressive rate, from 21,700 in 1984 to 61,400 in 1989; after levelling off for a time, asylum applications in 2004 once again crossed the 61,000 threshold. Britain saw applications rise from 4,200 in 1984 to 32,800 in 1994, and then to 71,100 in 1999. In 2002, new asylum applications in Britain reached 103,100 (Juchno, 2007; UNHCR, 2001a; 2001b) (see Table 5.1).

As signatories of the 1951 Refugee Convention, European states were obligated to review the cases of asylum seekers and to determine whether they merited official refugee status. But as numbers of applications swelled through the 1990s, bureaucratic systems quickly became overwhelmed, creating a sense of crisis in Europe. Sensationalist media reports in the 1990s and 2000s fixed public attention on asy-

lum seekers and seemed to confirm perceptions that European countries were being overrun by fraudulent asylum seekers. A good example is the media's coverage of the 'Sangatte affair' in the early 2000s. This incident unfolded as hundreds of asylum seekers—mostly young, single men from Kosovo, Afghanistan, Iraq, and Somalia—began to congregate near the entry point to the Channel Tunnel in the port of Calais in northwestern France. The French government had permitted the conversion of a disused warehouse in nearby Sangatte into a Red Cross shelter for asylum seekers, many of whom had been sleeping in parks and on beaches. It soon became obvious that the asylum seekers were using the camp as a staging ground for their bold (and extremely dangerous) efforts to sneak aboard lorries and trains en route to England via the Channel Tunnel. Media coverage provided numerous images of destitute young men plotting their entry into Britain via the Channel Tunnel. These images fed into existing

Table 5.1 First-time asylum applications in select European countries, 1985–2000

Country	1985	1985–1989	1990	1990–1994	1995	1995–1999	2000
Austria	6,724	64,441	22,789	76,160	5,919	53,530	18,280
Belgium	5,299	32,109	12,963	87,018	11,420	93,386	42,690
Denmark	8,698	42,171	18,992	76,442	10,055	36,044	10,080
France	28,925	178,661	54,813	184,593	20,170	112,257	38,590
Germany	73,832	455,254	193,063	1,337,190	127,937	542,414	78,760
Greece	1,398	23,986	6,166	12,804	1,312	11,812	3,000
Netherlands	5,644	46,355	21,208	151,141	29,258	170,388	43,890
Norway	829	23,199	3,962	30,024	1,460	24,042	10,320
Spain	2,360	15,710	8,647	53,100	5,678	30,442	7,040
Sweden	14,500	97,144	29,420	197,012	9,047	48,537	16,370
United Kingdom	4,389	28,549	26,205	150,850	43,965	223,265	97,860

Source: UNHCR (2001a) Asylum Applications in Industrialized Countries: 1980–1999. UNHCR Population Data Unit, Population and Geographic Data Section. Geneva: UNHCR

UNHCR (2001b) Asylum Applications Submitted in Europe, 2000. UNHCR Registration and Statistics Unit. Geneva: UNHCR

Plate 5.2 A sign, in Calais, France, produced by Eurotunnel, which warns about the dangers of trying to illegally travel through the Channel Tunnel, 2015

Source: Jenny Matthews/Panos

discourses of invasion and insecure borders, and prompted the British government to shed its image as a 'soft touch' by making the asylum process in Britain as difficult and unattractive as possible (Schuster, 2003; Koser, 2001). (For further discussion of the role of the media in reinforcing negative perceptions of asylum seekers, see Pickering (2001) and Gale (2004); for a more recent account of the situation in Sangatte, which was once again in the news at the time this book went to press, see Rigby and Schlembach, 2013).

The Sangatte case highlights the widespread presumption in Europe (and elsewhere) that asylum seekers are 'bogus'—that is, that their claims of persecution and personal endangerment are unfounded—even though the origins of asylum seekers correspond closely with major conflict zones (Sales, 2002). As we saw with the US response to the Salvadoran refugee crisis in the 1980s, governments have been quick to label asylum seekers 'economic migrants' desiring a better life, rather than people in need of a safe haven. Assumed to be undeserving of admittance, asylum seekers have been frequently accused of 'freeloading' and 'sponging' off of state welfare systems (Fletcher, 2008). While there is very little empirical evidence that asylum seekers move to wealthy countries to take advantage of welfare services (Crawley, 2010; Gilbert and Koser, 2006), states have offered them dwindling levels of financial support while awaiting decisions on their cases—a move that enjoys wide electoral support in Europe (Sales, 2002).

Plate 5.3 General view of a mostly Eritrean sector of the main so-called 'Jungle Camp' on the northern outskirts of Calais, 2015

Source: Chris Stowers/Panos

The reform of Britain's welfare system in the late 1990s and 2000s illustrates the growing consensus around the notion of asylum seekers as undeserving migrants. This reform began with the Immigration and Asylum Act of 1999, which removed asylum seekers in Britain from the mainstream welfare system and placed them in a separate benefits system called the National Asylum Support Service (NASS) (Hynes, 2011). NASS continued to provide subsistence support for asylum seekers but at a lower level than the regular welfare system. The most notable element of NASS—and one that made plain the increasingly punitive nature of government policy towards asylum seekers—was the shift from cash payments to vouchers that could be used in designated shops. With vouchers in hand,

asylum seekers would be publicly exposed every time they made a purchase. Critics charged that the vouchers stigmatized asylum seekers and, in making visible their status, made them vulnerable to attack. These concerns led to the suspension of the vouchers in 2002, though legislation passed in that same year denied support in the form of housing or state benefits to asylum seekers who lodged their claims for asylum more than 72 hours after arrival—a policy attacked by asylum advocates for contributing to destitution. This Act also ended the right of asylum seekers to work, forcing asylum seekers to depend on meagre NASS benefits or to work illegally.

To justify its withdrawal of the right to work for asylum seekers, the British government argued that asylum processing time would be significantly reduced so as to make employment unnecessary. And indeed, the government in the early 2000s introduced various fast-tracking procedures and curtailed the right for asylum seekers to appeal court decisions (Mulvey, 2011). Tightened restrictions on appeals meant that the fate of asylum seekers typically hung on the judgement of a single (usually overwhelmed) bureaucrat (Bohmer and Shuman, 2007; see also Gill, 2009; Blitz and Otero-Iglesias, 2011). Compounding the precariousness of asylum seekers' situation in Britain, legislation in 2006 withheld indefinite leave to remain (i.e. legal permanent residency), even from those granted formal refugee status. Since the passage of this bill, the British state has required that refugee cases be reviewed after five years, after which time refugees can be granted permanent residency or be deported back to countries of origin (Stewart and Mulvey, 2014). The turn away from international humanitarian obligations was equally dramatic in Germany, where lawmakers took the controversial step of amending the country's constitution to grant greater discretion to the state in hearing asylum cases (Gibney, 2004).

Asylum seekers and securitization

With so few recognized as 'genuine' refugees, asylum seekers, much like undocumented immigrants, have become the object of securitization, with governments pouring resources into the monitoring and detention of applicants (Anderson and Rogaly, 2005; Diez and Squire, 2008). Welch and Schuster (2005) remark on the criminalization of asylum seekers and the tendency for states to subject them to harsh penal systems. In the United States, where asylum has not been as salient a political issue as in Europe, more than 15,000 asylum seekers were detained between September 11, 2001, and December 2003 at US airports and border crossings, from which they were 'transported to jail, often in handcuffs, and usually without any clear understanding of why they were being detained' (ibid., 335). In 2003, on the eve of the US invasion of Iraq, the Department of Homeland Security initiated 'Operation Liberty Shield', which required detention of asylum seekers from dozens of countries where the terrorist network Al Qaeda had been known to operate. That same year, the Attorney General's office issued a directive stating that asylum seekers, along with illegal immigrants, could be held indefinitely if they were deemed to present a risk to national security. Press reports have surfaced about the deplorable conditions in detention facilities, some of which are converted prisons operated by private security corporations (e.g. Talbot, 2008; Frontline, 2011). In France, where the courts have steadily increased the amount of time that foreigners (asylum seekers or otherwise) can be detained prior to release or deportation, the conditions in detention centres are similarly deplorable, 'with people being held in overcrowded conditions, without access to sanitation or adequate food' (Welch and Schuster, 2005, 340). Migrant advocates have documented numerous acts of violence by border control officers in French detention centres, particularly at Paris's Charles De Gaulle airport, where the vast majority of asylum applications are lodged.

Detention has also featured prominently in the state's management of asylum seekers in Australia. The Migration Legislation Amendment Act 1989, to illustrate, allowed officers to arrest and detain anyone suspected of entering Australia illegally. Later legislation made detention mandatory for those entering without a valid visa until immigration status could be determined. In some cases, this process took several months or even years. Conveniently, the 1992 Migration Reform Act removed the nine-month time limit on detention, making indefinite detention permissible under Australian law. In the words of Minister for Immigration Gerry Hand, mandatory detention was intended to send a message that 'migration to Australia may not be achieved by simply arriving in this

Plate 5.4 A man enters through the gates of the Refugee Processing Centre at Lombrum, Manus Island
Source: Vlad Sokhin/Panos

country and expecting to be allowed into the community' (cited in Phillips and Spinks, 2011). Soon, stories surfaced of hunger strikes, demonstrations, and suicide attempts at various detention facilities, which were often located in remote areas (Silove, et al., 2007).

Increasingly, the governments of wealthy countries have sought to control asylum seekers by preventing them from entering national territory in the first place. Hyndman and Mountz (2008, 250) have coined the term **neo-refoulement** to refer to the 'return of asylum seekers and other migrants to transit countries or regions of origin before they reach the sovereign territory in which they could make a claim'. Australia again stands out as an exemplar of these practices with its decision in 2001 to off-shore

asylum processing. This decision was instigated by a Norwegian freighter's rescue of 433 asylum seekers aboard a sinking vessel en route to Australia. Australian officials refused entry to the freighter and warned the captain that he would be charged with people smuggling if he defied these orders (Hyndman and Mountz, 2008). Eventually, the asylum seekers were detained, but rather than being sent to Australia for processing, they were sent to the Pacific island of Nauru, which received an aid package of Aus$20 million in return (Hatton and Lim, 2005). Following this incident, in what became known as the 'Pacific Solution', a number of Australian island territories were 'excised'—cut out— from Australia's 'migration zone'. Boat arrivals intercepted in this excised area would be transferred to offshore processing centres located on Nauru, Manus Island (Papua New Guinea), and the excised Australian territory of Christmas Island. Those detained offshore could be denied legal assistance, the right to make a visa application, or judicial review of negative decisions (Phillips and Spinks, 2011). Those who *were* found to have legitimate refugee claims were eventually resettled, though the Australian government strived to relocate these individuals to a third country.

The Australian parliament subsequently eliminated or amended some of the more punitive components of Australian asylum policy. However, the Pacific Solution was never fully abandoned, and unauthorized boat arrivals continued to be processed on Christmas Island, which remained excised from Australia's

'migration zone'. While the proportion of those detained for more than 12 months declined as more asylum seekers were granted temporary 'bridging visas', long-term detention did not end entirely. Following a spike in boat arrivals from Afghanistan and Sri Lanka, the government revived the policy of transferring asylum seekers to offshore processing centres in Nauru and Papua New Guinea (see Laughland, 2013). The Australian government has also signed bilateral agreements with South Asian and Pacific countries to intercept boats en route to Australia in exchange for aid money (Hyndman and Mountz, 2008; Koser, 2010). A 2013 arrangement, for instance, allowed for the transfer of boat arrivals to Papua New Guinea for processing; those found to be refugees would be offered

Plate 5.5 Refugees waiting to get on the ferry to Athens from Kos

Source: Francois Razon

permanent settlement in Papua New Guinea and would not have permission to seek asylum or to settle in Australia.

Like Australia, the EU has sought aggressively to move its 'asylum problem' offshore by securing poor countries' cooperation in intercepting and detaining potential asylum seekers. By linking development aid to asylum policing, Europe effectively excludes asylum seekers without engaging in large-scale expulsions or 'directly violating liberal norms' (Gibney, 2008, 146). In addition to bilateral agreements with poorer neighbours, the EU has imposed visa requirements on the nationals of certain countries while implementing carrier sanctions to penalize airlines and shipping companies for transporting people to the EU who do not have proper documentation (Hatton, 2012; see also Collinson, 1996). Such measures effectively bar nationals of certain countries from EU space. Finally, the EU

has designated 'safe third countries' to which an asylum seeker can be returned if it is determined that he or she transited through one of those countries on the way to an EU member state. Thus, an asylum seeker must lodge an application not in the state he or she wishes, but the first 'safe' country he or she reaches. This provision, in short, permits EU member states to expel asylum seekers to other member states or to non-EU states, and it relieves 'all but one state of the duty to examine a claim' (Schuster, 2011, 1395).

The safe-third-country provision, Schuster (2011) notes, has placed an especially heavy burden on southern European countries, like Greece, Italy, and Spain, which are the first countries of arrival for many asylum seekers, and which have seen significant increases in numbers of asylum seekers as a result of EU policy harmonization. These countries generally lack the

BOX 5.2 CONTEMPORARY RESETTLEMENT POLITICS

The UNHCR in recent decades has prioritized repatriation over the resettlement of refugees in third countries. While the US, Canada, Australia, and other wealthy countries continue to receive thousands of resettlement cases each year, these cases represent only a small fraction (currently around 1 percent) of the world's refugees. Levels of refugee admittance in wealthy countries have not kept up with demand. Most problematic from the UNHCR's perspective has been the declining number of refugees accepted for resettlement in the US—long the top recipient of resettlement cases. In the late 1980s and early 1990s, the US routinely accepted over 100,000 refugees annually for resettlement. This number began to fall in the late 1990s and then dropped precipitously after the terrorist attacks of September 11, 2001 (Inkpen and Igielnik, 2014). Fewer than 30,000 refugees were admitted in 2002 and 2003 due to stringent screening policies. While admission numbers have recovered somewhat in recent years, the US government has typically failed to meet the refugee admission quota that is set annually by Congress and that has ranged between 70,000–80,000 per year since 2002 (Burt and Batalova, 2014). The UNHCR has compensated for lower admissions in the US by encouraging other countries to participate in resettlement programmes either on a formal or ad hoc basis. In recent years, a number of Eastern European and Latin American countries have begun to work with the UNHCR to resettle refugees. Efforts to broaden participation, though, are hampered by the high cost of resettling refugees, which is borne entirely by recipient countries. Still, some countries are willing to bear this cost if their cooperation with the UNHCR fulfils broader foreign policy objectives and confers the prestige that comes with participation in international humanitarian efforts (Nicholson, 2012). Yet again, we see the ways in which international humanitarian practice is mediated by the interests of individual nation-states.

Table 5.2 Total asylum applications submitted in selected industrialized countries, 2005–2014, with percent change from previous five years

Country	Total 2000–2004	2005	2006	2007	2008	2009	Total 2005–2009	% Change from previous 5 years	2010	2011	2012	2013	2014	Total 2010–2014	% Change from previous 5 years
Australia	38,700	3,200	3,520	3,980	4,770	6,170	21,640	−44.1%	12,640	11,510	15,790	11,740	8,960	60,640	180.2%
Austria	144,810	22,460	13,350	11,920	12,840	15,830	76,400	−47.2%	11,010	14,420	17,410	17,500	28,060	88,400	15.7%
Belgium	118,350	15,960	11,590	11,120	12,250	17,190	68,110	−42.5%	21,760	26,000	18,530	12,500	13,870	92,660	36.0%
Canada	175,230	19,740	22,910	28,340	36,900	33,250	141,140	−19.5%	23,160	25,350	20,500	10,380	13,450	92,840	−34.2%
Denmark	38,590	2,260	1,920	1,850	2,360	3,750	12,140	−68.5%	4,970	3,810	6,190	7,560	14,820	37,350	207.7%
France	279,190	49,730	30,750	29,390	35,400	41,980	187,250	−32.9%	48,070	52,150	55,070	60,230	59,030	274,550	46.6%
Germany	324,150	28,910	21,030	19,160	22,090	27,650	118,840	−63.3%	41,330	45,740	64,540	109,580	173,070	434,260	265.4%
Greece	26,890	9,050	12,270	25,110	19,880	15,930	82,240	205.8%	10,270	9,310	9,580	8,220	9,450	46,830	−43.1%
Netherlands	118,330	12,350	14,470	7,100	13,400	14,910	62,230	−47.4%	13,330	11,590	9,660	14,400	23,850	72,830	17.0%
Norway	67,010	5,400	5,320	6,530	14,430	17,230	48,910	−27.0%	9,220	8,680	10,690	13,280	12,640	54,510	11.4%
Spain	35,020	5,250	5,300	7,660	4,520	3,000	25,730	−26.5%	2,740	3,410	2,580	4,510	5,900	19,140	−25.6%
Sweden	127,350	17,530	24,320	36,370	24,350	24,190	126,760	−0.5%	31,820	29,650	43,890	54,260	75,090	234,710	85.2%
United Kingdom	393,830	30,840	28,320	28,300	31,320	29,840	148,620	−62.3%	22,640	25,900	27,980	29,880	31,260	137,660	−7.4%
United States	411,660	48,770	51,880	50,720	49,560	49,020	249,950	−39.3%	49,310	70,030	78,410	84,400	121,160	403,310	61.4%

Sources: UNHCR (2010) Asylum levels and trends in industrialized countries, 2009. Geneva: UNHCR. (Table 1. Asylum applications submitted in Europe and selected non-European countries, 2005–2009, p.13)

UNHCR (2005) Asylum levels and trends in industrialized countries, 2004. Geneva: UNHCR. (Table 1. Asylum applications submitted in Europe and non-European industrialized countries, 2000–2004, p. 8)

UNHCR (2015a) Asylum trends 2014: levels and trends in industrialized countries. Geneva: UNCHR (Table 1. Asylum applications submitted in Europe and selected non-European countries, 2010–2014, p. 20)

Table 5.3 Initial decisions on asylum applications (with percentages), select EU countries, 2008,

2008					2010		
Country	Applications processed	Acceptances, formal refugee status	Subsidiary/ humanitarian status	Applications rejected	Applications processed	Acceptances, formal refugee status	Subsidiary/ humanitarian status
Belgium	13,625	3,040 (22.3%)	470 (3.4%)	10,115 (74.2%)	16,665	2,700 (16.2%)	805 (4.8%)
Denmark	1,245	200 (16.1%)	525 (42.2%)	520 (41.8%)	3,300	660 (20.0%)	690 (20.9%)
Germany	19,335	7,310 (37.8%)	560 (2.9%)	11,465 (59.3%)	45,400	7,755 (17.1%)	2,690 (5.9%)
Greece	29,580	15 (0.1%)	40 (0.1%)	29,525 (99.8%)	3,460	60 (1.7%)	50 (1.4%)
Netherlands	10,920	515 (4.7%)	5,160 (47.3%)	5,245 (48.0%)	17,575	810 (4.6%)	7,190 (40.9%)
Sweden	29,545	1,695 (5.7%)	6,150 (20.8%)	21,700 (73.4%)	27,715	1,935 (7.0%)	6,575 (23.7%)
United Kingdom	23,790	4,780 (20.1%)	2,305 (9.7%)	16,705 (70.2%)	26,695	4,495 (16.8%)	2,000 (7.5%)

Source: Eurostat (2015) First instance decisions on applications by type of decision—annual aggregated data (online database).

Retrieved from http://ec.europa.eu/eurostat/web/asylum-and-managed-migration/data/main-tables

2010, 2012, 2014

2012				2014				
Applications rejected	Applications processed	Acceptances, formal refugee status	Subsidiary/ humanitarian status	Applications rejected	Applications processed	Acceptances, formal refugee status	Subsidiary/ humanitarian status	Applications rejected
13,160 (79.0%)	24,640	3,990 (16.2%)	1,565 (6.4%)	19,085 (77.5%)	20,410	6,470 (31.7%)	1,585 (7.8%)	12,355 (60.5%)
1,950 (59.1%)	4,695	1,035 (22.0%)	665 (14.2%)	2,995 (63.8%)	8,090	3,765 (46.5%)	1,715 (21.2%)	2,610 (32.3%)
34,955 (77.0%)	58,765	8,765 (14.9%)	8,375 (14.3%)	41,625 (70.8%)	97,415	33,310 (34.2%)	7,250 (7.4%)	56,855 (58.4%)
3,350 (96.8%)	11,190	30 (0.3%)	65 (0.6%)	11,095 (99.2%)	13,310	1,270 (9.5%)	705 (5.3%)	11,335 (85.2%)
9,575 (54.5%)	13,670	630 (4.6%)	4,875 (35.7%)	8,165 (59.7%)	18,810	2,485 (13.2%)	10,065 (53.5%)	6,260 (33.3%)
19,205 (69.3%)	31,570	3,745 (11.9%)	8,655 (27.4%)	19,170 (60.7%)	40,015	10,245 (25.6%)	20,405 (51.0%)	9,365 (23.4%)
20,200 (75.7%)	22,045	6,555 (29.7%)	1,295 (5.9%)	14,195 (64.4%)	26,055	8,990 (34.5%)	1,065 (4.1%)	16,000 (61.4%)

bureaucratic capacity to cope with large numbers of refugees, and the situation for asylum seekers in these countries is particularly bleak. Greece stands out for its especially dismal record of managing asylum cases. The European Court of Human Rights in 2011 ruled that the Belgian government had violated the human rights of an asylum seeker by deporting him to Greece and exposing him to the degrading treatment typical of Greek detention facilities. Since this time, several EU member states have barred asylum seekers from being deported to Greece. Greece, however, continues to be responsible for more than 40,000 asylum seekers, and Greek islands in the Eastern Mediterranean such as Lesvos are currently bearing the brunt of thousands of arrivals of asylum seekers from Syria and elsewhere in the Middle East (Day, 2015; UNHCR, 2015b; also Karamanidou and Schuster, 2012; Skordas and Sitaropoulos, 2004; Fekete, 2011).

Asylum today, in sum, is treated as a concession to be granted reluctantly. In most cases, governments will grant refugee status only to the small percentage of asylum seekers who can directly prove persecution (Bohmer and Shuman, 2007). Humanitarian organizations and refugee advocacy groups routinely criticize wealthy countries for their punitive treatment of asylum seekers and their reluctance to grant refugee status. Some wealthy countries counter such criticism by highlighting their continued participation in UNHCR resettlement programmes (Box 5.2 explains the contemporary resettlement process). Germany, likewise, can point to the fact that it

Plate 5.6 Words on a wall at Shatila Refugee Camp, Lebanon

Source: Francois Razon

Plate 5.7 Young Syrian refugees play in a dry riverbed at the Fayda informal settlement in the Bekaa Valley, Zahle, Lebanon

Source: Andrew McConnell/Panos

continues to be one of the largest recipients of asylum seekers in the world. Wealthy countries can also show that while they may deny formal refugee status, they will often grant some kind of humanitarian status or temporary leave to remain to those fleeing dangerous and violent conditions.

But if wealthy countries continue to fulfil their humanitarian commitments in a variety of ways, they clearly have become far less welcoming to uninvited entrants (De Wenden, 2011). Through the 2000s, efforts to discourage asylum seekers led to a significant decline in the number of asylum applications and acceptance rates—a 'success' in the eyes of policymakers (see Tables 5.2 and 5.3). As asylum applications have begun to climb again in the wake of the Syrian

civil war, European member states have begun to take extraordinary measures to divert Syrian refugees to Turkey.

Refugee politics in the Global South

The Global North's fears of being overrun by the victims of Third World conflicts belies the fact that wealthy countries since the 1980s have contended with only a small fraction of the world's forcibly displaced people. The overwhelming majority of people displaced by conflict and violence remain in the Global South—either within their own country, where they are known as **internally displaced persons** (IDPs), or in neighbouring countries, where they are recognized *en masse* by the UNHCR to be refugees based on the obvious fact that they have fled a conflict situation (the legal term used is *prima facie*, meaning, roughly, 'at first sight'). We take note here once again of the mismatch between the UN's definition of refugees as individual victims and the UNHCR's actual remit to protect and to assist entire populations displaced by conflict. Of the roughly 43 million 'persons of concern' under UNHCR protection in 2014, only around 1.2 million were seeking asylum from a foreign government; of these asylum seekers, only around half were found in wealthy countries of the Global North (South Africa has long received far more asylum seekers than most European countries) (UNHCR, 2015b). Until very recently the world's largest recipients of refugees have been Pakistan and Iran, which together hosted approximately 2.5 million people in 2013, most of them from Afghanistan (see Table 5.4). Today's most pressing refugee crisis is the civil war in Syria, which by the middle of 2014 had displaced an estimated 9.6 million

people. The Syrian crisis is being felt not in the Global North, but in Syria itself, which has an IDP population of 6.5 million people, and in neighbouring Jordan, Turkey, and Lebanon (UNHCR, 2015b). These three countries are currently among the top ten refugee-receiving countries in the world (Turkey reached the number one position in 2014). Lebanon, as a result of successive crises in the region (the Israeli-Palestinian conflict, the Iraq war, and now the Syrian civil war), has more refugees per 1,000 inhabitants than any country in the world. If Palestinian refugees under the protection of UNRWA are counted, then one in four people living in Lebanon in 2013 was a refugee. The presence of so many refugees in Lebanon has stretched the country's already fragile infrastructure to its limits.

Viewed in this broader, global context, the anxieties surrounding asylum seekers in the Global North seem wildly inflated. Displacement is a much more immediate and pressing problem in the Global South than in the Global

Table 5.4 Top ten refugee hosting countries, 2005, 2010, 2014

2005		2010		2014	
Country	Number of refugees	Country	Number of refugees	Country	Number of refugees
Pakistan	1,084,700	Pakistan	1,900,600	Turkey	1,600,000
Iran	716,400	Iran	1,073,400	Pakistan	1,500,000
Germany	700,000	Syria	1,005,500	Lebanon	1,150,000
Tanzania	548,800	Germany	594,300	Iran	982,000
United States	379,300	Jordan	450,900	Ethiopia	659,500
China	301,000	Kenya	402,900	Jordan	654,100
United Kingdom	293,500	Chad	347,900	Kenya	551,400
Chad	275,400	China	301,000	Chad	452,900
Uganda	257,300	United States	264,600	Uganda	385,500
Kenya	251,271	United Kingdom	238,100	China	301,000

Sources: UNHCR (2006) Global Refugee Trends, 2005. Geneva: UNHCR (p. 4; Table 1, pp. 11–14)
UNHCR (2011a) Global Trends, 2010. Geneva: UNHCR (p. 13)
UNHCR (2015c) Global Trends, 2014. Geneva: UNHCR (pp. 11–13)

North. To gain a more complete understanding of refugee crises therefore requires that we shift our attention from asylum politics in wealthy countries to refugee politics in poor countries and that we bring into focus the varied roles of aid organizations, international donors, and state institutions in shaping (and often limiting) the options available to those displaced by conflict. Bakewell's (2002) account of Angolan refugees in Zambia provides a glimpse into the dynamics through which national and international institutions manage refugee flows and shape the realities of refugees' lives. Angolan refugees first arrived in Zambia in the late 1960s in the midst of Angola's struggle for independence from Portugal. The Zambian government, fearing that the Portuguese would use the flow of refugees over the border as a pretext for invading Zambia, began to move refugees to settlements in relatively underpopulated regions in the Zambian interior. This policy continued into the 1980s, and by the early 2000s, the largest settlement housed around 4,000 people. The term 'settlement', as opposed to 'camp', indicated that residents would be responsible for their own subsistence rather than dependent on international aid (though international aid agencies did provide schools and healthcare). Refugees were given 2.5-hectare plots of land on which to build houses and to cultivate crops. Bakewell notes, however, that self-sufficiency did not relieve Angolan settlers from oversight by Zambian officials. The Zambian government allowed only refugees to live in the settlements, and it placed various restrictions on the mobility of settlement residents. As a result, the settlements were (and remain) quite isolated from surrounding communities.

Bakewell observes that by the 1990s, the UNHCR had begun to implement repatriation plans, reflecting the general shift in the organization in favour of returning refugees to countries of origin. Repatriation plans in the 1990s involved transporting refugees from the settlements in Zambia back to Angola and enticing returnees with offers of food aid, seeds, and agricultural tools. Repatriation plans, however, soon proved cumbersome, requiring bureaucratic efforts to distinguish between returned refugees from all other kinds of people (including 'economic migrants')—a process much easier said than done. In the end, the collapse of the Angolan peace process in the late 1990s caused the UNHRC to abandon repatriation plans, but not after some of those in the settlements had sold their assets and failed to cultivate their land. Reflecting on this experience, Bakewell questions the wisdom of the UNHCR's emphasis on returning refugees to countries of origin, noting that repatriation fails to recognize the ability of refugees to adjust to new circumstances and their desire to build their lives anew. At a more practical level, critics charge, expensive repatriation projects siphon off precious resources to a very specific group of people rather than using these resources more broadly to support regional economic development (Chimni, 2002).

Criticism of the wastefulness of repatriation schemes can be extended to refugee aid more generally, and the literature abounds with examples of the corrupting effects of massive infusions of aid on local economies and governance (e.g. Fluri, 2009). Jordan's response to refugees in the wake of the 2003 US invasion of Iraq illustrates well the perverse incentives created by international donors and the tendency for crisis assistance to sideline longer-term problems of economic development. Shortly after the US invasion of Iraq, the Jordanian government began voicing concerns to the international donor community about the growing presence of Iraqi 'guests' in the country, citing the fact that they had already shouldered the burden of the Palestinian refugee situation after 1967 (Mason, 2011). Major Western donors agreed to step up the flow of aid and to arrange for the resettlement of a portion of the Iraqis to third countries. In return, Jordanian authorities assured donors that they would not deport Iraqi refugees and that they would give refugees access to local institutions. Between 2007 and 2009, Jordan (which, interestingly, is not a signatory to the 1951 Refugee Convention) received close to $400 million that went either directly to the Jordanian government or was used to finance USAID projects (Seeley, 2010).

It soon became evident, however, that estimates of the Iraqi refugee population in Jordan had been wildly exaggerated, and aid agencies reported that far more Jordanians than Iraqis were coming to them for assistance. Critics charged that the Jordanian government had done very little in exchange for its massive aid windfall and that it had squandered untold millions of dollars on aid projects for a population it knew did not exist. Others suggested that Jordan was simply securing development assistance for its own population, which has been saddled with high unemployment, poverty, and high rates of demographic growth. The fact that many services funded by refugee aid were used almost entirely by Jordanians, from this perspective, was not a problem per se, but an indication that donors should have been targeting Jordanians in the first place (Seeley, 2010).

Refugee experiences

This critical perspective on the workings of humanitarian aid in the Global South raises many questions about the ways refugees negotiate the political realities created by displacement

Plate 5.8 Palestinian holding symbolic key

Source: Francois Razon

and the ways they respond to efforts by humanitarian organizations and host states to control and manage them. We can imagine that those who flee from violence and civil conflict across nation-state borders are exercising comparatively less agency than those who make a well-planned choice to seek economic opportunity elsewhere. Indeed, it is the very idea that refugees are forcibly displaced—that they have no choice but to leave their homes—that underpins modern humanitarianism, and especially the work of the UNHCR. Yet some scholars (e.g. Turton, 2003) have questioned the tendency among humanitarian organizations to cast refugees as helpless, passive victims of circumstances—as the objects of intervention rather than the authors of their own lives. Media images of humanitarian crises further obscure the ways refugees actively adjust to, subvert, or transform whatever situation they find themselves in. Even as the refugee experience is marked by compulsion, those living as refugees may participate in the shaping of outcomes and conditions in their places of origin, while also negotiating new forms of identity and membership in the places they have settled.

In drawing attention to the complexity of refugees' experiences, identities, and strategies, we can begin by considering the ways in which refugees, even within the highly controlled space of the refugee camp, can challenge the agendas of donor organizations and can insert their own politics into international humanitarian efforts. As we have described earlier, the UNHCR in recent decades has prioritized the

Plate 5.9 Mural in a school at Shatila refugee camp, Lebanon

Source: Francois Razon

return of refugees to their homelands. Israel, however, has vehemently opposed the repatriation of Palestinian refugees, which Israelis fear would dilute the country's Jewish identity. The seeming political impossibility of return has led international donors to nudge Palestinians to accept permanent settlement in third countries. This tension between Palestinians' political ambitions and their status quo as exiles continuously surfaces in their dealings with UNRWA. While viewing UNRWA assistance as a right borne of their dispossession, Palestinian refugees have also resisted efforts by UNRWA and other outside agencies to improve the camps, viewing such efforts as indicative of the international community's abandonment of the Palestinian right of return. Gabiam (2012) observes the ways in which Palestinian refugees in camps in Northern Syria contest and undermine the international community's 'development' agenda and its efforts to depoliticize Palestinian identity. Gabiam notes, in particular, the presence in the camps of multiple parties and grassroots organizations whose commitment to return and to Palestinian statehood remains strong. These organizations, as well as individual residents, continuously find ways to insert 'their political claims within the dehistoricizing and depoliticizing discourse of international aid', often in the form of political murals and graffiti (Gabiam, 2012, 104; see also Ramadan's (2009a) analysis of the multiple political claims found in murals in Palestinian refugee camps in Lebanon).

The Palestinian case speaks more broadly to the mismatch between official policies towards refugees and refugees' own methods of adjusting to their situation. We return to Bakewell's (2002) account of Angolan refugees in Zambia, which illustrates the ways in which refugees resist efforts by states and international organizations to contain them, to categorize them, and to dictate where they will go. As we have seen, the Zambian state tried to draw Angolan refugees to settlements away from the border to discourage Portuguese incursions. Some Angolans were willing to reside in these settlements and to accept their status as refugees in return for access to education and other services. Many others, however, resisted the settlement scheme. Their kinship ties with border villages along with the remoteness of these villages from state authority allowed many Angolan refugees to establish new livelihoods in Zambia and to become completely integrated into village life. Many described themselves as refugees only in the past tense, and there seemed to be little distinction between refugees and non-refugees in the border villages. 'Refugee', in short, had become a meaningless social category for those who avoided the settlements. Later UNHCR policies to encourage repatriation of Angolans therefore had limited impact. While some refugees did intend to return to Angola, Bakewell notes that they did not frame their return as 'going home', since 'home' had never been completely tied to Angola in the first place.

Liisa Malkki's (1995) ethnographic account of Burundian Hutu refugees in western Tanzania illustrates further the processes by which refugees make and unmake identities and produce multiple social and political realities in the context of displacement. Malkki identified distinctive responses to displacement among Hutus living in an organized refugee camp and those dispersed in towns outside the refugee camp. Camp dwellers, Malkki observed, passionately embraced their identity as Hutus and sought to reconstruct their history as 'a people' and the camp refugees responded to displacement by finding meaning in their status as exiles and by recreating Burundian nationhood in the camp. But other Hutu refugees subverted the categories imposed on them both by the international community and by Hutu nationalists. Town-dwelling Hutu refugees, in particular, sought ways to integrate into their surroundings, shifting and borrowing identities as circumstances dictated. This, Malkki argues, represented a rejection of an exclusive, totalizing national identity in favour of a 'lively cosmopolitanism'. Malkki's account reveals the choices that refugees make about political identity and belonging: while some respond to displacement by recreating a national order in exile, others refuse categorization and fixed identities.

Extending this analysis of refugee experiences to those seeking asylum in the Global North, scholars in recent years have sought to convey the capacity of asylum seekers to navigate difficult circumstances and to make decisions and choices. Scholars note that the decision to seek asylum from a foreign government is, in the first instance, an act of agency that involves considerable planning and strategizing. While asylum seekers may not have detailed knowledge of destinations or of asylum procedures in those destinations (Koser and Pinkerton, 2002), they, like other kinds of migrants, can use transnational social networks to select destinations where they have some connections, however weak or tenuous (Day and White, 2002; Collyer, 2005). Hiring a smuggler might also be interpreted in terms of human agency. The use of smugglers, in some respects, represents a relinquishment of control over one's migration path, insofar as asylum seekers may have only a limited idea of where they are being taken (Gilbert and Koser, 2006; Crawley, 2010) and may be vulnerable to exploitation by their smugglers. But smuggling can also be understood as a deliberate act of circumventing visa restrictions and as a purposeful response to new border control policies (Koser, 2001; Van Liempt and Doomernik, 2006). Van Liempt and Doomernik, in their research on asylum seekers in the Netherlands, note the very conscientious ways in which asylum seekers seek out a 'good' and 'trustworthy' smuggler who is likely to provide food and shelter and who 'knows the routes, has good contacts at borders, and provides good documents' (2006, 176). Smugglers, in a sense, become substitutes for social networks based on kinship and ethnicity, providing the knowledge and relationships necessary for migration to take place.

Once they reach their destination, asylum seekers (some of whom acquire formal refugee status or other humanitarian status) continue to exercise agency by using advocacy services, by building social relationships and networks with other asylum seekers and refugees, and by participating in both local and homeland politics (e.g. Antwi-Boateng, 2012; Al-Ali, et al., 2001). Asylum seekers may also manipulate their identities for pragmatic reasons, concealing their legal status or using this very identity to claim societal membership (e.g. Stewart, 2012; Bowes et al., 2007; Williams, 2006; Spicer, 2008). Finally, they develop strategies to stay in the country if their applications are denied. This might involve seeking recourse in the legal system or becoming undocumented immigrants (Bloch, et al., 2011). The latter strategy, in this instance, must be viewed as a rational, logical strategy given the migrants' investment in being smuggled across the border and the risks involved in returning to a conflict zone.

The ability of asylum seekers and refugees to control certain components of the migration process does not diminish the vulnerability they experience as a result of displacement and the increasingly harsh asylum policies in the Global North. Plenty of scholarly works document the stress and exclusion that asylum seekers face in the UK, Australia, and other countries due to detention, isolation, and punitive social policies (e.g. Fiddian-Qasmiyeh and Qasmiyeh, 2010; Correa-Velez et al., 2012). The point is simply that asylum seekers and refugees are not passive figures in forced migrations; rather, they have an active, if subordinate, role in shaping these migrations and in negotiating identity and belonging in countries of destination (Stewart, 2012).

Conclusions

As we move from this discussion of forced migrants to a more general discussion of immigration and border control policies in Chapter 6, it is important to reflect upon the consequences of distinguishing between refugees and other types of migrants. The legal concept of refugee (and the related concept of asylum seeker) was borne of major humanitarian crises in the 20th century. To treat the millions of people displaced by war, conflict, and extreme nationalisms in the 20th century simply as migrants would have been to ignore the violent circumstances compelling their migration. By creating a special refugee category and by extending humanitarian protection to those within this category, the international community recognized that some migrations are less voluntary than others—that for some, the 'choice' to leave is not much of a choice at all.

At the same time, however, the concept of refugee and the politics of refugee crises have always reflected the rigidity of the nation-state system and of nation-state-centred thinking. The modern notion of a refugee is based on an understanding of the world as divided into clearly defined nation-states. Those displaced by state violence and forced to live outside the boundaries of their own country are fundamentally out-of-place in the nation-state system. They become a problem to be solved by states and international agencies, preferably by returning them to wherever they 'belong'. In recent decades, the rather narrow legal definition of refugee has served as a convenient excuse for countries in the Global North to deny refugee status to asylum seekers. Asylum seekers, while protected in theory by international humanitarian norms, are increasingly viewed simply as undocumented immigrants. Harkening to a theme raised in Chapter 3 with respect to migrant labour, we can think about states *illegalizing* asylum seekers and forcing them into certain channels of entry that put them at risk of detention and deportation. Turton (2003, 14) notes the paradox that while wealthy states view the separation of refugees and economic migrants as essential to the management of cross-border flows, it has become

increasingly difficult in practice to distinguish between the two.

Some commentators have questioned the wisdom of continuing to define 'refugee' in narrow, legalistic terms and of creating such a complicated, expensive, and inhumane system to maintain distinctions between 'genuine' refugees and 'economic migrants' (Schuster, 2011). One solution is *not* to differentiate between economic and humanitarian migrants, but instead to make it easier for foreign workers to enter wealthier, more stable countries legally and to give them the flexibility to move back and forth across nation-state borders depending on political and economic circumstances (Koser, 2010). This, Bakewell (2002) notes, has been the de facto situation in parts of Africa where boundaries created in the colonial era have never fully contained 'national' populations. This approach recognizes that while forced migration is a very real phenomenon, migrants are often migrating for a variety of reasons and that political upheaval usually goes hand-in-hand with economic distress (Turton, 2003, 14). It also recognizes the uncomfortable fact that, especially in Europe, asylum *has* become an important route of entry for low-skilled migrants to wealthy labour markets. It is not a mere coincidence that numbers of asylum seekers in Europe began to increase at the same time that European countries began to close off formal labour migration channels. In short, the distinction between refugee and economic migrant is an arbitrary one—or, at least, an unhelpful one—that is ineffective in dealing either with humanitarian crises or with structural demands for migrant workers.

The need for a more flexible response to asylum seekers is all the more pressing in light of growing concerns about climate change. Millions of people each year are displaced by flooding, drought, and other natural hazards, and some scholars believe that these numbers will increase as global temperatures rise. As with those displaced by political crises and civil conflict, some of those displaced by climate events undoubtedly will cross borders and even make their way to the Global North. It seems highly unlikely that the governments of rich countries would broaden the definition of refugee to include those fleeing from climate change, though it can be argued that wealthy countries bear much of the responsibility to those in poor countries displaced by climate change given their role in generating greenhouse gas emissions. Wealthy countries could go about creating yet more migrant categories to distinguish between 'legitimate' and 'illegitimate' environmental refugees, thereby replicating the problems with the asylum system. Alternatively, wealthy states could recognize the complex interrelationships between political, economic, and environmental causes of migration, and could liberalize their migration systems accordingly.

There are, of course, all kinds of political reasons why border liberalization is unlikely to be adopted. In a world of nation-states, the privileges of membership are protected through strict border controls. The production of labour market segmentation, moreover, depends partly on the construction of legal categories, as we saw in Chapter 3. Even as many scholars urge open labour markets to match the broader globalization of capitalist economy, national governments produce ever more elaborate systems of control and management. These implications of the state's restrictionist impulses for those who endeavour to move across territorial boundaries is the subject of the following chapter.

Key terms in this chapter

asylum seeker	neo-refoulement
boat people	non-refoulement
Huguenots	pogroms
internally displaced persons (IDPs)	repatriation
	resettlement

United Nations High Commissioner for Refugees (UNHCR)   United Nations Relief and Works Agency (UNRWA)

Further reading

Betts, A. and Loescher, G. (Eds.) (2011) *Refugees in International Relations*. Oxford, UK; New York: Oxford University Press.

Gibney, M. (2010) *Global Refugee Crisis: A Reference Handbook*. Santa Barbara, CA: ABC-CLIO.

Kushner, T. and Knox, K. (1999) *Refugees in an Age of Genocide: Global, National, and Local Perspectives*. Abingdon; New York: Frank Cass.

Marfleet, P. (2006) *Refugees in a Global Era*. Basingstoke: Palgrave Macmillan.

UNHCR.org (this website provides the most up-to-date statistical information on refugees, asylum seekers and other populations of concern; it also includes numerous publications that explain UNHCR activities worldwide).

References

Akçam, T. (2006) *A Shameful Act: The Armenian Genocide and the Question of Turkish Responsibility*. New York: Henry Holt and Company.

Al-Ali, N., Black, R., and Koser, K. (2001) Refugees and transnationalism: the experience of Bosnians and Eritreans in Europe, *Journal of Ethnic and Migration Studies*, 27(4): 615–634.

Anderson, B. (1983) *Imagined Communities*. London; New York: Verso.

Anderson, B. and Rogaly, B. (2005) Forced labour and migration to the UK. Report prepared for Centre on Migration, Policy and Society (COMPAS—University of Oxford) in collaboration with the Trades Union

Congress. Retrieved from https://www.compas.ox.ac.uk/publications/reports-and-other-publications/forced-labour-and-migration-uk/.

Antwi-Boateng, O. (2012) After war then peace: the US-based Liberian diaspora as peace-building norm entrepreneurs, *Journal of Refugee Studies*, 25(1): 93–112.

Bade, K. J. (2003) *Migration in European History* (translated by Allison Brown). Malden, Oxford: Blackwell.

Bakewell, O. (2002) Returning refugees or migrating villagers? Voluntary repatriation programmes in Africa reconsidered, *Refugee Survey Quarterly*, 21(1–2): 42–72.

Balci, B. (2007) Central Asian refugees in Saudi Arabia: Religious evolution and contributing to the re-Islamicization of their motherland, *Refugee Survey Quarterly*, 26(2): 12–21.

Blitz, K. and Otero-Iglesias, M. (2011) Stateless by any other name: refused asylum-seekers in the United Kingdom, *Journal of Ethnic and Migration Studies*, 37(4): 657–573.

Bloch, A., Sigona, N., and Zetter, R. (2011) Migration routes and strategies of young undocumented migrants in England: a qualitative perspective, *Ethnic and Racial Studies*, 34(8): 1286–1302.

Bohmer, C. and Shuman, A. (2007) *Rejecting Refugees: Political Asylum in the 21st Century*. London: Routledge.

Bowes, A., Ferguson, I., and Sim, D. (2007) Asylum policy and asylum experiences: interactions in a Scottish context, *Ethnic and Racial Studies*, 32(1): 1–21.

Bronée, S. A. (1993) The history of the Comprehensive Plan of Action, *International Journal of Refugee Law*, 5(4): 534.

Burt, L. and Batalova, J. (2014) Refugees and asylees in the United States, Migration Information Source (Migration Policy Institute). Retrieved from http://www.migrationpolicy.org/article/refugees-and-asylees-united-states (accessed on 23 March 2015).

Caron, V. (1999) *Uneasy Asylum: France and the Jewish Refugee Crisis, 1933–1942*. Stanford, CA: Stanford University Press.

Chatty, D. and Hundt, G. L. (2005) *Children of Palestine: Experiencing Forced Migration in the Middle East*. Oxford, UK: Berghahn Books.

Chimni, B. S. (2002) Refugees and post-conflict reconstruction: a critical perspective, *International Peacekeeping*, 9(2): 163–180.

Collinson, S. (1996) Visa requirements, carrier sanctions, 'safe third countries', and 'readmission': the development of an asylum 'buffer zone' in Europe, *Transactions of the Institute of British Geographers*, 21(1): 76–90.

Collyer, M. (2005) When do social networks fail to explain migration? Accounting for the movement of Algerian asylum-seekers to the UK, *Journal of Ethnic and Migration Studies*, 31(4): 699–718.

Correa-Velez, I., Spaaij, R., and Upham, S. (2012) 'We are not here to claim better services than any other': social exclusion among men from refugee backgrounds in urban and regional Australia, *Journal of Refugee Studies*, 26(2): 163–186.

Crawley, H. (2010) 'No one gives you a chance to say what you are thinking': finding space for children's agency in the UK asylum system, *Area*, 42(2): 162–169.

Day, K. (2015) These are refugees, no migrants, arriving in their thousands on Greek shores, *Guardian* (27 July). Retrieved from http://www.theguardian.com/global-development/2015/jul/27/refugees-not-migrants-arriving-thousands-greece-shores (accessed 5 August 2015).

Day, K. and White, P. (2002) Choice or circumstance: the UK as the location of asylum applications by Bosnian and Somali refugees, *GeoJournal*, 56(1): 15–26.

De Wenden, C. W. (2011) The case of France. In G. Zincone, R. Penninx, and M. Borkert (Eds.) *Migration Policymaking in Europe: The Dynamics of Actors and Contexts*. Amsterdam: Amsterdam University Press (pp. 61–93).

Diez, T. and Squire, V. (2008) Traditions of citizenship and the securitisation of migration in Germany and Britain, *Citizenship Studies*, 12(6): 565–581.

Eurostat (2015) First instance decisions on applications by type of decision—annual aggregated data (online database). Retrieved from http://ec.europa.eu/eurostat/web/asylum-and-managed-migration/data/main-tables.

Falah, G. (1996) The 1948 Israeli-Palestinian war and its aftermath: the transformation and de-signification of Palestine's cultural landscape, *Annals of the Association of American Geographers*, 86(2): 256–285.

Fekete, L. (2011) Accelerated removals: the human cost of EU deportation policies, *Race & Class*, 52(4): 89–97.

Fiddian-Qasmiyeh, E. and Qasmiyeh, Y. M. (2010) Muslim asylum-seekers and refugees: negotiating identity, politics and religion in the UK, *Journal of Refugee Studies*, 23(3): 294–314.

Fletcher, E. (2008) Changing support for asylum seekers: an analysis of legislation and parliamentary debates, Sussex Centre for Migration Research, Working Paper 49. Retrieved from https://www.sussex.ac.uk/webteam/gateway/file.php?name=mwp49.pdf&site=252 (accessed 23 March 2015).

Fluri, J. (2009) 'Foreign passports only': geographies of (post) conflict work in Kabul, Afghanistan, *Annals of the Association of American Geographers*, 99(5): 986–994.

Frontline (2011) Lost in detention (television broadcast). Public Broadcasting Service. Retrieved from http://www.pbs.org/wgbh/pages/frontline/lost-in-detention/ (accessed 28 May 2015).

Gabiam, N. (2012) When 'humanitarianism' becomes 'development': the politics of international aid in Syria's Palestinian refugee camps, *American Anthropologist*, 114(1): 95–107.

Gale, P. (2004) The refugee crisis and fear: populist politics and media discourse, *Journal of Sociology*, 40(4): 321–340.

Gibney, M. J. (2004) *The Ethics and Politics of Asylum: Liberal Democracy and the Response to Refugees*. Cambridge: Cambridge University Press.

Gibney, M. J. (2008) Asylum and the expansion of deportation in the United Kingdom, *Government and Opposition*, 43(2): 146–167.

Gilbert, A. and Koser, K. (2006) Coming to the UK: what do asylum-seekers know about the UK before arrival? *Journal of Ethnic and Migration Studies*, 32(7): 1209–1225.

Gill, N. (2009) Presentational state power: temporal and spatial influences over asylum sector decisionmakers, *Transactions of the Institute of British Geographers*, 34(2): 215–233.

Goyens, T. (2007) *Beer and Revolution: The German Anarchist Movement in New York, 1880–1914*. Urbana-Champaign: University of Illinois Press.

Halo, T. (2001) *Not Even My Name: A True Story*. Basingstoke: Macmillan.

Harris, L. C. (1993) Xinjiang, Central Asia and the implications for China's policy in the Islamic world, *The China Quarterly*, 133: 111–129.

Hatton, T. J. (2012) Asylum Policy in the EU: the Case for Deeper Integration, ANU Centre for Economic Policy Research, Discussion Paper No. 660, March.

Hatton, T. J. and Lim, A. (2005) Australian asylum policy: the Tampa effect, *Agenda*, 12(2): 115–130.

Hirschon, R. (Ed.) (2003a) *Crossing the Aegean: An Appraisal of the 1923 Compulsory Population Exchange between Greece and Turkey*. New York: Oxford, UK: Berghahn Books.

Hirschon, R. (2003b) 'Unmixing peoples' in the Aegean region. In R. Hirschon (Ed.), *Crossing the Aegean: An Appraisal of the 1923 Compulsory Population Exchange between Greece and Turkey*. New York; Oxford, UK: Berghahn Books (pp. 3–12).

Hobsbawm, E. (1990) *Nations and Nationalism since 1780*. Cambridge: Cambridge University Press.

Hyndman, J. and Mountz, A. (2008) Another brick in the wall? Neo-refoulement and the externalization of asylum by Australia and Europe, *Government and Opposition*, 43(2): 249–269.

Hynes, P. (2011) *The Dispersal and Social Exclusion of Asylum Seekers: Between Liminality and Belonging*. Bristol: The Policy Press.

Inkpen, C. and Igielnik, R. (2014) Where refugees to the U.S. come from, FactTank (Pew Research Center). Retrieved from http://www.pewresearch.org/fact-tank/2014/07/28/where-refugees-to-the-u-s-come-from/ (accessed 23 March 2015).

Juchno, P. (2007) Demandes d'asile dans l'Union européenne, Statistiques en bref: Population et conditions sociales (1 October 2007). Retrieved from http://epp.eurostat.ec.europa.eu/cache/ITY_OFFPUB/KS-SF-07-110/FR/KS-SF-07-110-FR.PDF (accessed 23 March 2015).

Karamanidou, L. and Schuster, L. (2012) Realizing one's rights under the 1951 convention 60 years on: a review of practical constraints on accessing protection in Europe, *Journal of Refugee Studies*, 25(2): 169–192.

Koser, K. (2001) New approaches to asylum? *International Migration*, 39(6): 85–102.

Koser, K. (2010) Responding to boat arrivals in Australia: time for a reality check. Lowy Institute for International Policy Analysis Paper. Retrieved from http://www.lowyinstitute.org/publications/responding-boat-arrivals-australia-time-reality-check (accessed 21 January 2015).

Koser, K. and Pinkerton, C. (2002) The social networks of asylum seekers and the dissemination of information about countries of asylum. Retrieved from http://webarchive.nationalarchives.gov.uk/20110314171826/http://rds.homeoffice.gov.uk/rds/pdfs2/socialnetwork.pdf (accessed 23 March 2015).

Laughland, O. (2013) UN refugee agency condemns Australia's offshore detention regime, *Guardian* (26 November 2013). Retrieved from http://www.theguardian.com/world/2013/nov/26/un-refugee-agency-condemns-australias-offshore-detention-regime (accessed 23 March 2015).

Macekura, S. (2011) 'For fear of persecution': Displaced Salvadorans and US refugee policy in the 1980s, *The Journal of Policy History*, 23(3): 357–381.

Malkki, L. (1995) *Purity and Exile: Violence, Memory, and National Cosmology among Hutu Refugees in Tanzania*. Chicago: University of Chicago Press.

Marfleet, P. (2006) *Refugees in a Global Era*. Basingstoke: Palgrave Macmillan.

Marfleet, P. (2007) Refugees and history: why we must address the past, *Refugee Survey Quarterly*, 26(3): 136–148.

Marfleet, P. (2011) Understanding 'sanctuary': faith and traditions of asylum, *Journal of Refugee Studies*, 24(3): 440–455.

Mason, V. (2007) Children of the 'Idea of Palestine': negotiating identity, belonging and home in the Palestinian diaspora, *Journal of Intercultural Studies*, 28(3): 271–285.

Mason, V. (2011) The im/mobilities of Iraqi refugees in Jordan: pan-Arabism, 'hospitality', and the figure of the 'refugee', *Mobilities*, 6(3): 353–373.

Mavroudi, E. (2010) Nationalism, the nation and migration: searching for purity and diversity, *Space and Polity*, 14(3): 219–233.

Milton, G. (2008) *Paradise Lost: Smyrna 1922*. New York: Basic Books.

Mulvey, G. (2011) Immigration under new labour: policy and effects, *Journal of Ethnic and Migration Studies*, 37(9): 1477–1493.

Nicholson, M. (2012) Refugee resettlement needs outpace growing number of resettlement countries, Migration Information Source (Migration Policy Institute). Retrieved from http://www.migrationpolicy.org/article/refugee-resettlement-needs-outpace-growing-number-resettlement-countries (accessed 23 March 2015).

Pandy, G. (2001) *Remembering Partition*. Cambridge: Cambridge University Press.

Paul, K. (1997) *Whitewashing Britain: Race and Citizenship in the Postwar Era*. Ithaca, NY: Cornell University Press.

Phillips, J. and Spinks, H. (2011) Boat arrivals in Australia since 1976, Parliament of Australia Research Publications. Retrieved from http://www.aph.gov.au/About_Parliament/Parliamentary_Departments/Parliamentary_Library/pubs/BN/2011-2012/BoatArrivals (accessed 23 March 2015).

Pickering, S. (2001). Common sense and original deviancy: news discourses and asylum seekers in Australia. *Journal of Refugee Studies*, 14(2): 169–186.

Ramadan, A. (2009a) A refugee landscape: writing Palestinian nationalism in Lebanon, *ACME*, 8(1): 69–99.

Ramadan, A. (2009b) Destroying Nahr el-Bared: sovereignty and urbicide in the space of exception, *Political Geography*, 28(3): 153–163.

Rigby, J. and Schlembach, R. (2013) Impossible protest: noborders in Calais, *Citizenship Studies*, 17(2): 157–172.

Sales, R. (2002) The deserving and the undeserving? Refugees, asylum seekers, and welfare in Britain, *Critical Social Policy*, 22(3): 456–478.

Sassen, S. (1999) *Guests and Aliens*. New York: New Press.

Schuster, L. (2003) Asylum seekers: Sangatte and the Tunnel, *Parliamentary Affairs*, 56(3): 506–522.

Schuster, L. (2011) Turning refugees into 'illegal migrants': Afghan asylum seekers in Europe, *Ethnic and Racial Studies*, 34(8): 1392–1407.

Seeley, N. (2010) The politics of aid to Iraqi refugees in Jordan, *Middle East Report*, 256 (on-line). Retrieved from http://www.merip.org/mer/mer256/politics-aid-iraqi-refugees-jordan (accessed 21 January 2015).

Silove, D., Austin, P., and Steel, Z. (2007) No refuge from terror: the impact of detention on the mental health of trauma-affected refugees seeking asylum in Australia, *Transcultural Psychiatry*, 44(3): 359–393.

Skordas, A. and Sitaropoulos, N. (2004) Why Greece is not a safe host country for refugees, *Journal of Refugee Studies*, 16(1): 25–52.

Spicer, N. (2008) Places of exclusion and inclusion: asylum-seeker and refugee experiences of neighbourhoods in the UK, *Journal of Ethnic and Migration Studies*, 34(3): 491–510.

Stewart, E. (2012) UK dispersal policy and onward migration: mapping the current state of knowledge, *Journal of Refugee Studies*, 25(1): 25–49.

Stewart, E. and Mulvey, G. (2014) Seeking safety beyond refuge: the impact of immigration and citizenship policy upon refugees in the UK, *Journal of Ethnic and Migration Studies*, 40(7): 1023–1039.

Talbot, M. (2008) The lost children: What do tougher detention policies mean for illegal immigrant families? *New Yorker* (3 March 2008) Retrieved from http://www.newyorker.com/reporting/2008/03/03/080303fa_fact_talbot_(accessed 23 March 2015).

Turton, D. (2003) Conceptualising forced migration. Refugee Studies Centre Working Paper Series, 12. Oxford: University of Oxford.

UNHCR (2001a) Asylum applications in industrialized countries: 1980–1999. UNHCR Population Data Unit, Population and Geographic Data Section. Geneva: UNHCR.

UNHCR (2001b) Asylum applications submitted in Europe, 2000. UNHCR Registration and Statistics Unit. Geneva: UNHCR.

UNHCR (2005) Asylum levels and trends in industrialized countries, 2004. Geneva: UNHCR.

UNHCR (2006) Global refugee trends, 2005. Geneva: UNHCR (p. 4; Table 1, pp. 11–14).

UNHCR (2010) Asylum levels and trends in industrialized countries, 2009. Geneva:

UNHCR (Table 1. Asylum applications submitted in Europe and selected non-European countries, 2005–2009, p. 13).

UNHCR (2011a) Global trends, 2010. Geneva: UNHCR (p. 13).

UNHCR (2011b) *UNHCR Resettlement Handbook*. Geneva: UNHCR.

UNHCR (2015a) Asylum trends, 2014: Levels and trends in industrialized countries. Geneva: UNCHR (Table 1. Asylum applications submitted in Europe and selected non-European countries, 2010–2014, p. 20).

UNHCR (2015b) Country profiles database. Retrieved from http://www.unhcr.org/ (accessed 23 March 2015).

UNHCR (2015c) Global trends, 2014. Geneva: UNHCR (pp. 11–13).

Van Liempt, I. and Doomernik, J. (2006) Migrant's agency in the smuggling process: the perspectives of smuggled migrants in the Netherlands, *International Migration*, 44(4): 165–190.

Wallerstein, I. (2004) *World Systems Analysis: An Introduction*. Durham, NC: Duke University Press.

Welch, M. and Schuster, L. (2005) Detention of asylum seekers in the US, UK, France, Germany, and Italy: a critical view of the globalizing culture of control, *Criminal Justice*, 5(4): 331–355.

Williams, L. (2006) Social networks of refugees in the United Kingdom: tradition, tactics and new community spaces, *Journal of Ethnic and Migration Studies*, 32(5): 865–879.

6

Immigration control and border politics

Introduction

This chapter builds upon Chapter 5 by examining more broadly the policies through which nation-states grant or deny entry to foreigners. As Coleman and Kocher (2011) note, the formulation of entry policies is fundamentally a *bordering* process through which state authorities exercise sovereignty over territory. Entry policies set the terms by which 'strangers' and 'aliens' may cross borders and may be given leave (or not) to remain within national space. As such, these policies must be situated among many kinds of bordering practices, including the fortification of physical frontiers and the surveillance and control of those living *within* national space (ibid.). We might imagine that globalization, which has been marked by the diminishment of barriers to trade, investment, and market exchange, would reduce the significance of territorial boundaries for people. After all, labour mobility is a key feature of the globalized economy, and there are hundreds of millions of people on the move in the world today. Borders of even the wealthiest countries are porous, making possible the integration of capital, commodity, and labour markets. Yet nation-state boundaries continue to matter. Even in a globally integrated world, states exercise significant control over the crossing of borders and the allocation of rights and privileges to those residing within their borders. As they open themselves up to global economic flows, states maintain a vested interest in regulating who comes and goes and managing distinctions between citizens and strangers (Hollifield, 2004). They have, moreover, greatly increased their technological capacity to do so.

This chapter explores the exercise of state power and state authority over human mobility. Our preceding discussions of labour migrants and refugees have revealed some of the ways that states open themselves to flows of migrants *and* the ways they create barriers to these flows. States, as we have seen, may loosen visa restrictions to encourage inflows of workers with certain skills; they may eliminate racial barriers to encourage population growth and economic vitality; they may welcome (or just grudgingly accept) those fleeing conflicts elsewhere in countries of origin; and they may tolerate or ignore the presence of unauthorized immigrants. Equally, they may limit numbers of visas, erect walls and fences to prevent unauthorized border crossings, and pursue aggressive detention and deportation policies to discourage would-be labour migrants and asylum seekers. Scholars differ over which tendency dominates: some academics have highlighted the increasing militarization of borders and the fortress mentality that seems to guide many wealthy countries' immigration policies; others, in contrast, argue that nation-states have lost or relinquished control of their borders due to a variety of political and economic pressures operating within and beyond nation-states (see Favell and Hansen, 2002; Joppke, 1998; Freeman, 1995; Sassen, 1999; Megoran, 2005;

Plate 6.1 Mexican migrants on the border with the USA at Tijuana
Source: Clive Shirley/Panos

Casey, 2010). In this chapter, we eschew either/ or arguments and suggest instead that entry and border control policies are inherently contradictory—that states *simultaneously* open and close themselves to mobile populations. In doing so, they create multiple kinds of citizen-subjects who are positioned differently—some more marginally than others—within the body politic.

This chapter begins with an historical overview of border control regimes in Europe and the New World settler societies in the 19th and early 20th centuries. From this historical discussion we develop a theoretical framework for understanding the work that borders perform in terms of regulating populations, producing segmented labour markets, and protecting the privileges of national citizenship. Borders,

we emphasize, are not necessarily about keeping people out; they are also about creating and preserving distinctions among those who reside within those borders, whether on an authorized or unauthorized basis. We then consider in greater detail three phenomena that have been salient in recent years in wealthy immigrant-receiving societies: the proliferation of migrant categories, the securitization of migration, and the expansion of border-control practices beyond the border zone itself. Finally, in our concluding thoughts, we explore the ethics of contemporary entry and border control policies and consider the argument for a borderless world.

Entry policies and border control in historical perspective

Many contemporary discussions of entry policies and border control take for granted the existence of nation-state borders and assume that the purpose of these borders is to keep foreigners out. In this brief historical overview, we try to set aside these assumptions in order to understand more fully how and why immigration and border control measures first emerged in the European context and then in European settler societies.

We begin with the gradual development in Europe from the 16th century onward of a system of mutually recognized, sovereign territorial states. While territorial boundaries shifted continuously into the 20th century, states came to function as containers of economies, politics, and societies, with state bureaucracies exercising administrative control over populations residing within state borders (Taylor, 1994). Early modern Europe was dominated by mercantilist thinking, which considered populations to be a source of wealth and military power. States therefore had a considerable interest in preventing emigration or at least limiting it. With the expansion of commerce and trade, states were also interested in controlling entry of foreign merchants and commodities. Documents of origin and identity 'were demanded as a matter of course from ever expanding groups of people in the 16th century' (Groebner, 2001, 16), and **passports** came into wider use as a means to authenticate the origins of those arriving in ports and to combat smuggling (Salter, 2003). Finally, states sought to exercise control over *internal* mobility through vagrancy laws and 'poor laws' that prevented impoverished rural labourers from seeking relief outside of their town or village of origin (Torpey, 2000).

Mercantilist attitudes declined in the 19th century and were superseded by a liberal agenda that emphasized free trade, open markets, and the primacy of individual free will. Through the 19th century, European states began to relax restrictions on internal movement and emigration, repealing vagrancy laws and granting greater legal freedom of movement to the lower classes. Poor relief gradually shifted from localities to the state with the beginning of social welfare systems, and European states moved to abolish **visa** and passport requirements on entry and exit and to remove residual limitations on the rights of citizens to seek work and settle in other parts of their own country (Torpey, 2000) (see Box 6.1 for an explanation of the difference between a visa and a passport). This reflected several intersecting imperatives: European states, first, were eager to rid themselves of problematic groups, including the growing ranks of poor, landless workers. Second, in a context of political unrest, revolution, and continental warfare, states needed to secure the support and loyalty of populations; this encouraged (slow) democratization and the (limited) extension of rights to lower classes. And third, they had an interest in supporting the development of industrial capitalism, which demanded labour mobility.

As we saw in Chapter 2, the liberalization of the global capitalist economy in the 19th century ushered in an era of massive flows of workers between European states and between Europe and the New World. Mobility, in one sense, was problematic in a world of mutually exclusive national populations and monopolistic states. But this same mobility was central to the formation and solidification of modern, capitalist, national societies. The state partly resolved this tension between control and mobility through the active management of populations and borders. As movement within and across borders became more liberalized, the state continued to exert its policing power over populations by instituting elaborate systems of personal identification—not so much to hinder migration as to distinguish more clearly between citizens and non-citizens. Liberal migration regimes thus rested upon the exclusive authority of the state to confer identities of citizen and 'alien'—

BOX 6.1 A NOTE ON TERMINOLOGY: VISAS AND PASSPORTS

The difference between a passport and a visa warrants some explanation. A passport is a legal document issued by the country of origin. This document is recognized internationally and applies to only one individual. All passports contain 'a written request by a representative of the sovereign asking on the behalf of his or her sovereign to allow the national to pass through the territory of another sovereign' (Salter, 2004, 73). In principle the passport assures the destination state that the bearer of a passport can be returned to the country that issued the passport—though states have been known to deny re-entry to troublesome nationals. A visa supplements a passport; it is granted by the country of destination and indicates that the country has scrutinized the potential entrant. Visas typically must be arranged *before* travel, though some countries grant visas at the border for a small fee, mainly as a means of raising revenue. Visas often specify the purpose of the visit and the period of time in which the traveller is permitted to remain in the country. In some cases, visas may be valid for a few weeks or a few months; in other cases, visas may permit a person to reside legally in a country for an entire year or more.

As Neumeyer (2010) demonstrates, visa restrictions can be a significant deterrent to potential entrants (whether visitors, asylum seekers, or workers) due to the cost and hassle of applying for a visa at an embassy or consulate—a process that does not always result in an actual visa. As might be expected, travellers from poor countries face far more restrictions—especially when planning travel to wealthy countries—than do travellers from wealthy countries. While some countries have eased visa requirements in recent years to promote tourism and trade, visa requirements in most cases have become more stringent. Even travellers who are not subject to visa restrictions face a growing number of hurdles to entry in wealthy countries (ibid.). The United States, for instance, today requires visitors from visa-waiver countries to apply for Electronic Travel Authorization, which checks applicants' names against criminal databases.

authority exercised through new technologies, including photography and fingerprinting, the precursors to biometric passports and iris scans (Torpey, 2000; also Walters, 2002).

This tension between liberalization and control became more pronounced in the late 19th century as states began to impose stricter immigration controls on specific groups. In the United States, for instance, the imposition of stricter controls began in 1882 with the first of a series of Chinese Exclusion acts that were passed in response to **nativist** unrest among white workers in the American West. These acts barred the further entry of Chinese workers (the first time a specific racial group was targeted by immigration legislation) and later compelled all Chinese residents in the US to register themselves, to be photographed, and, when asked, to present evidence of their lawful presence in the US (Ngai,

2003; King, 2000). The legislative action against the Chinese was part of a broader trend of bureaucratic control over immigration that was designed explicitly to separate desirable from undesirable immigrants and thereby to shape the racial character of the nation (Lee and Yung, 2010). This control regime included the installation of permanent border inspection stations (including Ellis Island in New York and Angel Island in San Francisco), the creation of a full-fledged Bureau of Immigration in 1891, and new literacy requirements for entry aimed primarily at Southern and Eastern Europeans (King, 2000). Similar processes took place in Australia and Canada, which passed 'white-only' immigration legislation targeted against Chinese immigrants, as well as Indian immigrants, who at the time shared the status of British subjects with white Canadians and Australians (see Anderson, 1991; Mongia, 1999).

France also saw new laws that sharpened distinctions between natives and foreigners, even as the country became increasingly reliant on foreign workers in its manufacturing, construction, and mining sectors. While industrialists welcomed foreign workers, others resented the labour market competition they created. The state, moreover, was keen to maintain some control over foreigners who lived in France but had no obligation to serve the French state in the event of war. Starting in 1888, the French state imposed a new identification system on all foreigners, albeit with limited effectiveness; this was followed in 1893 by legislation mandating the registration of foreign workers, and further legislation in 1912 requiring itinerant foreign workers to carry identity documents with fingerprints. A similar pattern of events was seen in Germany amid growing fears of being overwhelmed by Polish workers (Bade, 2003). Starting in the late 19th century, Germany imposed new restrictions and identification-card requirements on foreign workers. In the lead-up to World War I, many European states began to impose ever more stringent restrictions and to revive passport requirements. In Britain, for instance, passport requirements were reimplemented in 1905 in response to the influx of Eastern European Jewish refugees (discussed in Chapter 5).

World War I definitively ended the liberal migration regime of the late 19th century. Commentators at the time saw the imposition of strict border controls as a temporary state of affairs. After the war, the League of Nations urged the removal of passport controls and the return to freedom of movement, which it saw as crucial to peace and economic recovery. But if anything, the interwar period saw the solidification of state surveillance and border policing regimes. A notable example was the creation of the US Border Patrol in 1924, which, as Ngai (2003) describes, was made necessary by the passage the same year of National Origins quotas restricting Southern and Eastern European migration. The restrictionist impulses of the

early 20th century reflected several interrelated concerns. First were ongoing concerns about spies and enemy infiltrators in a context of deep distrust among Europe powers. Second were heightened desires to protect native workers from competition due to fears of labour unrest and revolution (for the same reason, the state began to take a more active role in the provision of social welfare at this time). And third were racist ideologies and societal anxieties about unassimilable 'degenerate' races. Overall, as Torpey (2000, 121) argues, the tighter connection between citizens and states that developed in the early 20th century 'led to an intensified preoccupation with determining who is "in" and who is "out" when it came to enjoying the benefits—both political and economic—of membership in those states'.

The key features of the restrictionists regime—passport controls, border patrols and checkpoints, and race-based restrictionism—remained firmly in place after World War II, albeit disrupted by the immense refugee crisis in Europe (see Chapter 5). At the midpoint of the 20th century, anyone wishing to cross borders would need a valid passport with a photograph to establish his or her nationality and status. Nonetheless, migration flows picked up significantly in the decades after the war. The Australian government, for instance, eager for economic growth and development, created the Department of Immigration in 1945 to attract settlers, assuring a sceptical public that the great majority of immigrants would be British and the rest white and European (Walsh, 2008). Two decades later, Australia, the US, and Canada would all repeal racial restrictions, paving the way (albeit not intentionally) for high levels of non-white immigration (King, 2000; Hugo, 2014). Meanwhile, Europe in the post-war period also experienced the renewal of high levels of immigration, as described in Chapter 2. Included among the immigrants were millions of guestworkers from Europe's periphery, who entered in the 1950s and 1960s through bilateral labour agreements, and post-colonial migrants, many of whom had settlement rights in Europe's former imperial metropoles.

The picture hereafter becomes very complicated. The traditional settler societies are generally regarded as embracing expansionary immigration policies from the mid-1960s onward. In contrast, European countries are often described as pursuing more restrictionist regimes, ending post-war labour recruitment, reworking citizenship laws to restrict the right of post-colonial migrants from settling (Paul, 1997), and striving to limit asylum seekers. But there are many cross-currents flowing through entry and border control policies that make it difficult to characterize any country's immigration system as unequivocally expansionary or restrictive. Canada and Australia, for instance, while welcoming in hundreds of thousands of permanent settlers every year, have become increasingly selective in their admission policies, favouring skills over either family or humanitarian considerations (Hugo, 2014). The US has been less selective with its legal immigration, and has tolerated, as well, the growth of a large population of undocumented families. But since the 1990s, the country has spent billions of dollars securing the US–Mexico border to impede unauthorized entry (Andreas, 2000) and in recent years has focused resources on deporting and detaining thousands of undocumented immigrants (Hagan, et al., 2011). Meanwhile, Western European countries, while going to great lengths to restrict labour migration and asylum, as well as family reunification and foreign marriages, have opened themselves to relatively low-skilled Eastern European immigration through EU integration. As well, Southern European countries like Greece and Spain have largely tolerated (or perhaps failed to manage) the inflow of hundreds of thousands of unauthorized labour migrants from outside the EU who fill labour needs in the construction, caring, and agricultural sectors (Lazaridis and Koumandraki, 2007; Iosifides et al., 2007).

As we saw in Chapter 3, European countries have also courted highly skilled workers, making it possible for them to seek work without employer sponsorship. There are, then, multiple stories to be told about immigration and border control in the Global North—stories that speak to control, restriction, and the assertion of state sovereignty, on the one hand, and mobility, fluidity, and openness on the other hand. What can these disparate stories tell us in more general terms about the nature of contemporary entry policies and border control politics?

Theorizing immigration control in contemporary liberal democracies

Characterizations of contemporary immigration policies and border control measures vary widely. As alluded to in the introduction, some scholars view borders primarily as sites of exclusion, emphasizing the power of state borders to hinder migration and to create what Salter (2008) calls a 'permanent state of exception' that excludes certain individuals and groups from basic rights and legal protections. This view highlights the (re)assertion of state sovereignty in a context of globalization and punctuates many current discussions of border militarization, the proliferation of deportation and detention policies, and the use of biometric technologies to create a 'virtual border' (see, for instance, Van Houtum, 2010; Van Houtum and Pijpers, 2007; Walters, 2002; Bloch and Schuster, 2005; Muller, 2010; Mountz et al., 2013; Bosworth and Kaufman, 2011). Others, in contrast, have highlighted the *failure* of borders to control migration flows, pointing to substantial flows of immigrants across borders in spite of tightened border-control measures and public opposition to immigration. We give particular attention to this latter set of arguments, exploring the position that borders are subordinate both to labour-market forces and to domestic political pressures. We then consider an alternative conceptualization of border control as working not so much to restrict mobility (though borders can and do have this effect) as to differentiate between citizens and aliens. Entry policies and physical borders, in other words, are about creating and maintaining spheres of privilege and 'belonging' in which migrants are variously placed or excluded (Walters, 2002).

The limits of borders: global integration and domestic politics

For some scholars, contemporary borders and entry policies are notable for their inability to control flows of migrants. As much as states try to keep out immigrants, from this perspective, they largely fail to do so. The incapacity of states to control migration flows is at times attributed partly to the dynamics of globalization. Multinational corporations and the expanding service sector, on the one hand, have generated demands for highly mobile workers that supersede the interests of states to control flows of workers across their borders; global inequalities, on the other hand, have created an enormous supply of workers seeking opportunities and higher wages elsewhere. There is, in short, a powerful supply-and-demand mechanism at work that is not easily harnessed by states (De Haas, 2008). The social dynamics of migration, moreover, are such that population flows have a self-sustaining quality to them: the settlement of migrants invariably lowers the cost of migration for their friends, relatives, and compatriots, setting chain migrations into motion despite state efforts to control these processes (see, for instance, Castles, 2004b; also Cornelius and Tsuda, 2004; Guiraudon, 2008).

Other scholars have offered a different analysis, suggesting that states act contrary to their stated interests of controlling migration by promoting free-trade and economic-liberalization policies. States, in a sense, have not so much lost control as relinquished control over their borders. Durand and Massey (2003) and Cornelius (2005), for instance, attribute the seeming ineffectiveness of the fortification of the US–Mexico border to the US government's own free-trade policies, and especially NAFTA. Far from absorbing surplus labour in Mexico, NAFTA has exposed ever more Mexican workers to market forces, creating greater labour market instability and promoting further migration (for a broader discussion of the unintended consequences of US legislation for Mexican immigration, see Massey and Pren, 2012). Favell and Hansen (2002) offer a similar analysis of the European context, emphasizing the role of state policy in producing and sustaining migration flows. By actively participating in the project of European integration and expansion, they suggest, European states have deliberately fostered a fluid labour regime marked by high levels of cross-border flows between Eastern and Western Europe and between the EU and its periphery. In addition to liberalizing labour mobility within Europe, European states have sought out non-EU migrants through an array of work permits for skilled and unskilled workers, while simultaneously tolerating undocumented immigrants who have made their way into European labour markets (De Haas, 2008). The latter has been especially pronounced in Southern Europe countries, where **regularization** programmes extending temporary legal status to undocumented workers have been a common feature of immigration policy since the 1990s (Triandafyllidou and Ambrosini, 2011).

The seeming primacy of economic interests and imperatives in driving migration flows draws our attention to domestic politics in wealthy immigrant-receiving societies, and especially to the tensions that exist between those who support tighter control over cross-border flows and those who advocate greater openness. Gary Freeman (1995), for instance, argues that despite widespread animus towards immigrants among electorates, there is an expansionary bias in liberal democracies that can be attributed to the workings of organized groups who have a vested and well-articulated interest in immigration and the resources to influence policy (see also Sassen, 1999; Facchini and Mayda, 2008). Employers and business interests are the obvious 'culprits' here, but Freeman also notes the growing influence of minority activists and civil-rights groups in promoting expansionary immigration policies. Freeman, like Favell and Hansen (2002), is largely dismissive of far-right anti-immigrant groups, like the Lega Nord in Italy and the Front National in France, who frequently appear on the political scene in many liberal democracies; their influence in bringing about restrictionist policies, he suggests, tends to be cyclical and ephemeral. Of more importance, according to Freeman, is the broad consensus about immigration that exists among political elites, who typically negotiate entry policies with little public oversight.

The US Immigration Control and Reform Act of 1986 (IRCA) often serves as the paradigmatic example of the influence of special interest groups on immigration policy. Initiated in a context of growing public animosity towards Mexican 'illegal aliens', the legislation required employers for the first time to check the legal status of their employees, and it introduced sanctions on employers for knowingly hiring undocumented workers. But in the course of legislative deliberation, these provisions were significantly watered down as agribusiness lobbyists pressed lawmakers to remove the requirement that employers actually verify the authenticity of documents presented to them. At the same time, pro-immigrant forces, including Latino and civil-rights activists, mobilized in support of an amnesty for the millions of undocumented immigrants resident in the country. After a great deal of wrangling and compromise, the amnesty was incorporated into the legislation, providing a path of legalization for approximately three million undocumented immigrants (for a fuller discussion, see Joppke, 1998). Meanwhile, continued lobbying by agribusiness interests ensured that only a miniscule percentage of the federal budget would be dedicated to the enforcement of laws against hiring undocumented workers (Andreas, 2000).

Freeman (1995) argues that while these special-interest politics and expansionary tendencies are especially evident in traditional settler societies like the US, they are also present in European societies. European politics, he argues, have become increasingly like those in the US, with organized interest groups and elite consensus, rather than public opinion, driving immigration policies and the implementation of immigration laws. So, for instance, Boswell (2007) demonstrates that heightened public concern about security after the September 11, 2001, terrorist attacks had little substantive impact on immigration policy because immigration bureaucracies were relatively insulated from securitarian impulses by their own bureaucratic practices. Civil servants, in many European contexts, were able to operate largely as they had before and to follow their own (relatively liberal, pro-business) policy aims (also Lahav, et al., 2014). Joppke (1998) offers a related analysis of expansionary immigration policies in Europe. Observing that 'only liberal states are plagued by the problem of unwanted immigration', Joppke argues that positive net migration in Europe is driven primarily by the liberal-democratic principles and humanitarian norms that were inscribed in European constitutions after World War II. Joppke suggests that the enforcement of liberal values by independent judiciaries, in particular, has prevented legislatures from acting upon their restrictionist instincts and from summarily ejecting unwanted groups like asylum seekers and unauthorized immigrants. The German state's efforts to stop the permanent settlement of Turkish guest workers, for instance, were hindered by the German court system, which repeatedly ruled in favour of the fundamental right of guest workers to remain in Germany and to reunite with their families.

Like Freeman, Joppke, and others cited here, we are sceptical of claims that states have become impenetrable fortresses and are equally sceptical that states have lost control over immigration.

Yet we hesitate to pin the uneasy coexistence between anti-immigrant sentiment and actual mobility on any single mechanism operating either within or outside of nation-states. All of these analyses, in one manner or another, assume that the primary purpose of borders is to keep out immigrants, so that if borders are not keeping out immigrants, it is due to some peculiarity of state practice or policy enforcement: states for a variety of reasons are not acting upon their sovereign capacity to keep out those whom they, or their electorates, do not want. But this view obscures the work that borders perform in a world of nation-states and minimizes the very real power that states exercise over people's mobility. Borders, we wish to emphasize, are doing *something*. Certainly, one might imagine that patterns of mobility would look far different if there were no borders at all.

The purpose of state bordering practices, as Walsh (2008, 791) explains, 'is not to obstruct human movement but, rather, to regulate it and define the conditions under which it may legitimately occur'. The state, in this sense, is 'a central mediator, manager, and intervening variable that tightly defines and limits the admissible paths of movement'. We have seen historically that passports and border checkpoints in the emerging nation-state system functioned not to stop migration flows, per se, but to manage and to monitor flows and to maintain distinctions between nationals and non-nationals, citizens and non-citizens. In the following sections, we set aside the question of whether borders work, focusing instead on *how* they work—that is, the ways they continuously produce differences between insiders and outsiders and differentiated regimes of mobility. We consider the complex and often contradictory functions and workings of contemporary entry policies and border control regimes by focusing on three key phenomena: migration management and the proliferation of migrant categories; the securitization of immigration policy; and the creation of complex geographies of border enforcement.

Migration management and the proliferation of migrant categories

The modern state has always sought to manage migration—that is, to control and to shape flows of people over borders. States, as we have seen, routinely have encouraged some migrations—for instance, through direct recruitment or through non-enforcement of migration policies—while closing off other migration channels. Moreover, states have sought to maintain control over migrants *within* their borders, and to distinguish them from members of the national community, through visas, passports, and other forms of identity. The concept of **migration management**, then, speaks to the essence of modern state practice (Hollifield, 2004). Here, however, we use 'migration management' in a more specific sense to refer to more recent articulations of state authority over human mobility. According to Geiger and Pécoud (2010), the term gained currency in the 1990s through international initiatives—led by international organizations like the IOM— to coordinate cross-border mobility and to make this mobility orderly and predictable, as well as fair. Those leading such initiatives have argued that migration, rather than a threat, should be viewed as beneficial to all 'stakeholders' involved—receiving states, sending states, and migrants themselves. In Castles' (2004a, 874) idealized terms, migration management represents

a cooperative process in which all participants have a voice, including the governments and civil societies of the sending countries, the receiving populations and above all the migrants themselves. To be effective, policies need to be fair and to be perceived as fair by all the groups involved.

Migration management emphasizes organization and optimization over restriction, and it revolves around 'best practices' that pursue several goals simultaneously: the circulation of flexible labour; respect for migrants' human rights; and the protection of state sovereignty.

To some extent, this concept offers a somewhat kinder and gentler alternative to the zero-immigration policies and the xenophobic political rhetoric that crop up in most immigrant-receiving societies (Layton-Henry, 2004). Administered by the proceduralist, bureaucratic state, migration management programmes have the air of depoliticized neutrality; those charged with implementing the programmes view themselves as acting fairly, transparently, and firmly according to clearly defined entry rules and criteria in welcoming certain immigrants while excluding others (see Balch (2009) for a discussion of the formulation of managed migration policy in Britain). But the technocratic rhetoric of migration management masks highly political actions. Geiger and Pécoud (2010) note, for instance, that measures to stop unauthorized migration or to prevent refugees from claiming asylum may be framed as 'necessary' to combat human trafficking, while campaigns to discourage would-be migrants may be justified in terms of 'protecting' the potential victims of smugglers, though they come with few commitments to secure migrants' rights. Despite claims to promote the interests of all stakeholders, critics charge, migration management primarily serves the interests of particular actors within wealthy states.

A notable component of migration management has been the production of sociolegal

Plate 6.2 A French customs officer discovers four Romanian immigrants stowed away in a truck heading for the UK, Calais, France

Source: JB Russell/Panos

categories that vary in terms of the rights and privileges allocated to them. Again, this is nothing new, but what distinguishes today's migration management systems from those of the past is the sheer volume and complexity of categories. The growth of bureaucracies and the development of new technologies have greatly facilitated management practices and have allowed states to monitor and to enforce immigration rules (however imperfectly) for millions of people with variable immigrant statuses (Kofman, 2002). Critics argue that the production of migrant categories has come to revolve almost entirely around concepts of economic competitiveness rather than justice or humanitarianism (Hyndman and Mountz, 2008). These critics point to the role of business interests and neoliberal ideology in shaping contemporary migration management and in driving, in particular, the expansion of visas for skilled migrants (Flynn, 2005). This has been evident in the EU and individual member states, which, as we have seen, liberalized visa policies in the 2000s to encourage the migration of highly-skilled workers in technology, finance, and other fields.

Referring to the British context, Mulvey (2011) contends that the legacy of neoliberal migration management since the 2000s has been to sharpen the distinction between 'wanted' and 'unwanted' migrants and to legitimize public intolerance of asylum seekers, undocumented migrants, and family migrants. But it is important to note that the distinction between desirable and undesirable shifts over time and that even the privileged few can find themselves increasingly shut out. For instance, we have recently seen limits placed on skilled migration, especially in Britain and the United States, to calm voter anxiety about labour-market competition. Britain's Conservative–Liberal Democrat Coalition government, elected in the midst of a severe economic slowdown in 2010, has delivered on a campaign pledge to reduce UK net immigration to 'tens of thousands' by imposing an annual limit on skilled immigrants from non-

European Economic Area (EEA) countries and by terminating post-study work visas, which had allowed non-EEA graduates of UK universities to work in the UK for up to two years after graduation (UK Border Agency, 2010; Conservative Party, 2010; see also Semmelroggen's (2011) account of efforts by German policymakers to give preferential labour market access to German workers). Meanwhile, in the United States, the legislature has repeatedly resisted calls from high-tech firms to eliminate the cap on H-1B visa holders. Skilled labour flows, in short, are subject to state intervention and control as much as unskilled flows, and entry policies can be difficult to negotiate even for those with high levels of human capital (Mavroudi and Warren, 2013).

Migration management, then, is a complex phenomenon that speaks to states' recognition of the need for, and reality of, mobility and the desire to control and to channel that mobility. It is, at its core, an exercise of state power that reflects assumptions about the neat division of humanity into distinct territories and the prerogative of states to invite (or disinvite) aliens and to set the criteria for their stay (Walters, 2002). Managed migration programmes, we wish to suggest, should not be evaluated solely in terms of their ability to keep 'undesirable' migrants out while allowing 'desirable' migrants in; clearly, there are gaps between the stated aims of managed migration and actual outcomes and consequences of policies (Cornelius and Tsuda, 2004; Lahav and Guiraudon, 2007). Rather, these programmes should be assessed in terms of the ways in which they distinguish between citizens and aliens, as well as among aliens, and parse out rights and privileges accordingly. We consider questions of citizenship and rights in greater detail in Chapter 7.

The securitization of migration

Migration management, despite its air of technocratic rationality, is closely associated with

securitization, a term that hints at paranoia towards external 'threats'. Securitization, as we use it here, refers to the tendency of modern nation-states to construct migration as a security risk and to link migration discursively and in practice to a range of other security problems like terrorism and trafficking. It refers, as well, to the state's efforts to build up the technological capacity to control cross-border flows. Like migration management, what Faist (2006) calls the 'migration-security nexus' is deeply rooted in the history of the modern nation-state, as we have seen with the pioneering use of biometrics in the early 20th century. Contemporary modes of securitization have taken shape since the 1980s with the development of new sur-

veillance technologies, the vast expansion of data-collection capabilities, and the formation of new modes of information sharing (Muller, 2010; Duran, 2010; Broeders, 2007; Wilson and Weber, 2008; Warren and Mavroudi, 2011).

The European Union exemplifies these trends (Van Houtum, 2010). As seen in Chapter 5, the increase in numbers of asylum seekers in the 1990s provided the impetus to harmonize immigration control policies among EU member states through the implementation of safe third-country provisions, carrier sanctions, and the like (Foster, 2008). The ability to track asylum seekers (and other third-country nationals) through EU space, in turn, hinged on new information and data-gathering systems, including

Plate 6.3 A US border patrol agent fingerprints a recently arrested immigrant at a detention facility, Nogales, Arizona, USA

Source: Yannis Kontos/Polaris/Panos

the Schengen Information System, which border authorities and police across Europe could use to access information about asylum claimants, human traffickers, drug smugglers, and other undesirables. Through the 1990s and early 2000s, the EU prepared for the accession of post-socialist republics in Central and Eastern Europe by fortifying the EU's new eastern border and by incorporating Eastern European states into the harmonized asylum regime. This harmonization process culminated with the creation in 2005 of **Frontex**, the European border policing agency, which was strategically headquartered in Poland (see Box 6.2).

A similar process of securitization has taken place along the US–Mexico border over several decades. The precursor to contemporary border enforcement policies along the US–Mexico border was the unfortunately-named Operation Wetback, which apprehended over one million undocumented immigrants in the 1950s, many of whom were sent deep into Mexico's interior (Hernández (2006) notes that Mexican authorities at this time were even more eager than the US authorities to control undocumented immigration, viewing outflows of Mexican workers as impeding Mexico's modernization). In the 1990s, the federal government responded to a groundswell of popular hostility towards undocumented immigration with Operation Hold the Line and Operation Gatekeeper, which involved the construction of 13-foot high security walls

BOX 6.2 FRONTEX: EUROPE'S BORDER AGENCY

The European Agency for the Management of Operational Cooperation at the External Borders of the Member States of the European Union, also known as Frontex, was created in 2004 after several years of ad hoc border-control ventures among EU member states. The creation of Frontex took place amidst the European Union's expansion eastward and reflected deepening concerns about the capacity of new EU members, as well as older EU members in Southern Europe, to control trafficking, international crime, and undocumented immigration. The agency does not replace national-level border agencies, but rather, provides support for them. Among Frontex's early creations was the 'Rapid Border Intervention Team' (RABIT), which was first deployed in Greece in 2010 to stem the tide of unauthorized entries along the Greek–Turkish border using dogs, a helicopter, multiple patrol cars and buses, thermo-vision vehicles, and 175 agents (Carrera and Guild, 2010). The RABIT programme has since been replaced by a variety of other 'joint operations' to patrol Europe's land and sea borders and to control **transit** movement—that is, passage of people through one or more countries en route to a final destination. Collyer et al. (2012) note that the EU has intensified pressure on transit countries both within and outside Europe to monitor and to preempt the inflow of migrants and asylum claimants. These efforts have been aided by numerous 'smart border' technologies and cooperation between Frontex the eu-LISA, the EU's new information technology agency. While Frontex seems eager to demonstrate its capacity to stop unwanted flows of immigrants through new smart-border technologies, it also draws on humanitarian discourses to explain its mission. The agency's press releases tend to focus on the rescue of migrants and to highlight the abusive behaviour of smugglers. And indeed, Frontex operations in the Mediterranean have saved tens of thousands of migrants from drowning. But the agency's humanitarian discourses belie the European policies that have forced migrants and asylum seekers to undertake increasingly dangerous land and sea crossings. Further, as Pallister-Wilkins (2015) notes, those being rescued, having lost all of their savings to reach Europe's shores, in many cases are detained and/or sent back to poor, unstable countries through bilateral readmission agreements.

along the border in Texas and California, a significant increase in the number of border patrol agents, and the implementation of technologies used during the first Gulf War, including unmanned aerial surveillance (i.e. drones), video and night-vision scope surveillance, electronic ground sensor systems, and vehicle-mounted infrared telescopes (Koskela, 2010; Andreas, 2000). The monitoring of mobile populations at and beyond the physical frontiers of the US and of other wealthy countries has intensified since the terrorist attacks of 2001 (Adey, 2004; Salter, 2004; Wilson and Weber, 2008; Salter and Zureik, 2005). Moreover, a growing proportion of the work of securitization—including visa application processing, fingerprint collection, cell-phone monitoring, and the detention and deportation of migrants—is carried out by private corporations, creating what some scholars call the 'surveillance-industrial complex' (Hayes, 2012; also Amoore, 2006).

As alluded to earlier, however, some scholars question whether securitization practices and discourses lead to any meaningful reduction of migration flows (Boswell, 2007; Lahav et al., 2013). Peter Andreas (2000) has argued that border securitization primarily serves a political purpose: to convince anxious publics that states have control over borders and that state sovereignty remains intact. But even if it is partly a public-relations gesture, we cannot dismiss the very real effects that securitization has on mobility and migrants. Amped-up borders, it is clear, do not completely stop the flow of migrants (Salter, 2004); indeed, the seeming mismatch between 'get tough' policies and persistent cross-border mobility leads many scholars to question the efficacy of borders and entry policies. But even if they do not stop migratory flows, securitization measures profoundly shape migration channels and the conditions under which migrants live and labour in receiving societies (De Haas, 2008; Triandafyllidou and Ambrosini, 2011; Staeheli and Nagel, 2008).

As borders become more exclusionary, more fortified, and riskier to cross, they greatly increase the vulnerability of those who cross them with or without authorization. Unauthorized border-crossers, in the first instance, are more likely to turn to smugglers to assist them in getting across the border, and they are more likely to take perilous routes (De Haas, 2008; Fernández-Kelly and Massey, 2007; Cornelius, 2005; Van Houtum, 2010). Carling and Hernández-Carretero's (2011) research on the flow of small boats from West Africa to the Canary Islands of Spain, for instance, highlights that while Frontex has had mixed success in terms of impeding flows, its actions have been more successful in pushing irregular migration into more dangerous channels through the Sahara, Libya, Malta, and Italy (Lutterbeck, 2006). In the case of the US, aggressive interdiction policies and the militarization of the border zone over the past few decades has meant the growing reliance on **coyotes**, or smugglers, and highly risky crossings in remote stretches of the desert Southwest, leading to thousands of deaths in recent years (Andreas, 2003).

Dangerous crossings, detention, and deportation are also increasingly common features of migration to countries in the Global South, like Saudi Arabia, Malaysia, South Africa, and Israel, all of which rely heavily on immigrant workers to perform menial and difficult jobs (Vigneswaran et al., 2010). Israel's Holot detention facility, built in 2013 to hold up to 3,000 migrants, illustrates well the prevalence of detention and deportation policies and the impacts of these policies on migrants. Most of those detained at Holot have been Eritreans and Sudanese who have crossed into Israel from the Sinai desert with the intention of claiming asylum. Reminiscent of Joppke's (1998) arguments about the role of liberal norms and institutions in limiting the state's capacity to stop 'unwanted' immigration, the Israeli High Court of Justice ordered the Holot facility to close in 2014; as well, the High Court overturned highly punitive

Plate 6.4 Memorial crosses in Nogales, left for people who perished in the Arizona Desert near the Mexican–USA border, 2010

Source: Markel Redondo/Voces Mesoamerica/Panos

legislation which would have allowed the Israeli state to detain unauthorized migrants for up to three years, arguing that this legislation violated the human rights and dignity of migrants (Lior, 2014). But by the time the court made its ruling, state policies, including the summary rejection of asylum applications, had already led to a precipitous decline in the number of asylum claimants. Moreover, despite the court's order to close Holot, the facility remained open as of April 2015, and the Israeli government had

ordered detainees to leave within thirty days or to face indefinite imprisonment (Zonszein, 2015; for further discussion of Israeli politics vis-à-vis unauthorized immigration, see Kalir, 2015).

Those unauthorized migrants who do manage to cross borders and to avoid detention, as we described in Chapter 3, labour under the constant threat of deportation (De Genova, 2002). Securitization, from this perspective, is more than a spectacle of state policing power or a political ploy. It is a means by which the state produces and reproduces migrant insecurity (Coleman and Kocher, 2011). Ultimately, then, we can understand contemporary border regimes as doing what borders have always done—dividing people and territory, channelling mobility, and demarcating the terms of entry and membership. These bordering processes, we reiterate, take place even as economies become more integrated and as the volume of trade and human mobility mushrooms. Very few states today strive for autarky; if anything, the past four decades have seen an ever stronger commitment in the international system to a neoliberal agenda that supports the free flow of goods, services, and indeed, workers across borders. But wealthy states at the same time have insisted upon exercising control over individual migrant bodies through the maintenance of 'hard' borders and through the threat (and actual practice) of deportation and expulsion. Capitalist logic and nationalist anxiety are thus tightly interwoven in state immigration and border control policies, creating different classes of mobile bodies, ranging from 'hyper-kinetic' business elites whose border crossings involve first-class lounges and fast-passes through airport security lines, to unauthorized migrants who spend their life savings to be smuggled across the desert or the sea to destinations only partly known (Sparke, 2006; Muller, 2010).

Rethinking the geography of borders: interior surveillance and the off-shoring of immigration control

As states have increased their capacity to monitor and to manage borders, they have produced particular geographies of power and territorial control. The process of bordering creates a stark geography of 'us' and 'them', foreigner and citizen, home and abroad. This is most evident at the physical frontiers of nation-states. But bordering practices are not limited to territorial boundaries—or as Salter (2004, 80) remarks,

borders are not just lines in the sand. Rather, states produce many complicated geographies as they implement security measures *within* their own territory and as they expand their reach *beyond* their own territorial boundaries. Borders, in this sense, function more as geographically diverse networks than as simple lines, confronting migrants (and potential migrants) at every turn (Coleman, 2007).

Border control and surveillance, to be sure, has never been confined to the perimeter of the nation-state. Both past and present, states have exercised their authority to find, detain, and deport undesirables within their territory and to surveille foreigners living within the boundaries of the nation-state. State power, in this sense, saturates territory and operates through national space. Scholars today detect an intensification of internal control practices in a context of securitization. Many discussions of internalized immigration enforcement have focused on the US context, with its large population of undocumented immigrants and its complex, multi-layered system of government (Varsanyi et al., 2012). Federal immigration authorities in the US have sole power to police immigration—a power they wrested from the states in the late 19th century (Zolberg, 2003). Since the late 1990s, however, federal authorities have increasingly devolved enforcement capabilities to local proxies. **Section 287(g)** of the 1996 Illegal Immigration Reform and Immigrant Responsibility Act, for instance, authorizes the director of Immigration and Customs Enforcement (ICE) to enter into agreements with local and state law enforcement. Through Section 287(g), ICE can effectively deputize officers to carry out federal immigration enforcement directives. This is but one component of a broader set of cooperative agreements between ICE and local law enforcement designed to combat various criminal threats (see US Immigration and Customs Enforcement, 2015). Critics argue that this devolution of federal authority to local law enforcement has diverted resources from community policing, intensified the profiling of Latinos, and soured relationships between Latinos and police (Varsanyi et al., 2012; Coleman, 2012) (see Box 6.3 on the **Secure Communities** programme for further discussion of the devolution of immigration policing to localities in the US).

At the same time that the federal government has devolved authority to localities, individual state and local governments in the US have taken it upon themselves to create and to enforce their own immigration statutes in response to

the alleged inaction of the federal government on immigration control. One early manifestation of local state action was Proposition 187, a 1994 ballot initiative in the state of California that barred undocumented immigrants from state social services, including the public education system and emergency medical care, and required teachers, healthcare workers, and other state employees to report undocumented immigrants to the authorities (Zolberg, 2007). This initiative (called 'S.O.S.' or 'Save Our State' by its supporters) was struck down by the Supreme

BOX 6.3 SECURE COMMUNITIES

The Secure Communities programme in the United States exemplifies the pervasiveness of immigration enforcement across national space. Secure Communities was created in 2008 to increase 'deportation capacity' through the sharing of information between local, state, and federal law enforcement agencies. Upon arresting and booking a suspected criminal, local and state police run the arrestee's fingerprints against various federal immigration and criminal databases. Immigration and Customs Enforcement (ICE) is immediately notified if there is a 'hit', whether or not any crime has actually been committed. ICE then takes over the case and may initiate deportation—a process that in many cases does not involve any hearing before a judge, much less any legal assistance. Federal officials have consistently described Secure Communities as targeting criminal aliens who have committed serious felonies and those repeatedly violating immigration laws. But in practice, the programme has rounded up tens of thousands of undocumented immigrants guilty of little more than minor traffic violations or what were previously considered civil violations or misdemeanours. In the programme's first few years, millions of names were submitted to ICE, leading to a sharp increase in the number of people held in detention facilities and deported (Bosworth and Kaufman, 2011) (see Table 6.1). Advocacy groups have accused local law enforcement of racially profiling Latinos and arresting them on flimsy pretexts in order to run their fingerprints through the ICE database. Such practices, advocates charge, have sown distrust between the police and Latinos, hampering efforts to address serious crimes. Advocacy groups also decry the break-up of hundreds of thousands of mixed legal-status families due to deportation. Concerns about the programme have led several states and municipalities to limit participation in Secure Communities, mainly by curtailing the authority of local police to hold deportable immigrants on behalf of federal agents (Henderson, 2014). Facing local resistance and pressure from Latino activists, the Obama administration in 2012 implemented a 'deferred action' policy to protect undocumented immigrants brought to the US as children; subsequently, the Obama administration scaled back Secure Communities altogether (Preston, 2015). This shift reflects the ability of different interest groups and actors in liberal democracies to temper restrictionist impulses. Still, it must be noted that cooperative arrangements between federal and local authorities, the proliferation of random traffic checkpoints, and the long-term erosion of immigrants' civil liberties continue to make the lives of many migrants highly precarious (Stuesse and Coleman, 2014; see also Moore, 1999).

Table 6.1 Immigrant removals from the US, 1983–2013

Year	Number of removals
1983	19,211
1984	18,696
1985	23,105
1986	24,592
1987	24,336
1988	25,829
1989	34,427
1990	30,039
1991	33,189
1992	43,671
1993	42,542
1994	45,674
1995	50,924
1996	69,680
1997	114,432
1998	174,813
1999	183,114
2000	188,467
2001	189,026
2002	165,168
2003	211,098
2004	240,665
2005	246,431
2006	280,974
2007	319,382
2008	359,795
2009	391,597
2010	382,265
2011	387,134
2012	418,397
2013	438,421

Source: Department of Homeland Security, Yearbook of Immigration Statistics, 2013; http://www.dhs.gov/yearbook-immigration-statistics-2013-enforcement-actions

Court. Subsequent state-led initiatives, however, have been more successful. In 2010, for instance, the Arizona legislature passed **Senate Bill 1070** (Support Our Law Enforcement and Safe Neighborhood Act), which authorized state and local officers to arrest any person suspected of committing a deportable crime. SB 1070 also required officers conducting a stop, detention, or arrest to verify the immigration status of persons suspected of being in the country illegally (a provision critics refer to as 'Stop and show me your papers'). The Supreme Court struck down elements of the law deemed to infringe on the supremacy of the federal government in immigration matters, but the Court upheld the requirement for state and local law enforcement officers to verify immigration status. This emboldened other states, including South Carolina, Georgia, and Alabama (states, it should be noted, that do not share a border with Mexico), to pass similar or even harsher legislation. These state laws have been accompanied by scores of county and municipal laws directed more or less explicitly against immigrants, including English-only laws and ordinances limiting numbers of unrelated people cohabiting in a single housing unit (see Winders, 2007; Brettell and Nibbs, 2011; Vicino, 2013; Leerkes, Leach, and Bachmeier, 2012; Varsanyi, 2008).

The case of South Africa, which has a large population of migrants from Zimbabwe and other sub-Saharan African countries, provides further illustration of the power of local authorities to produce and to enforce borders in the spaces of everyday urban life. Scholars note that local police officers in South Africa have enormous discretion to implement immigration laws and to decide which forms of human mobility will be permitted to take place (Klaaren and Ramji, 2001; Vigneswaran et al., 2010). In some instances, lax law enforcement behaviour can work to create a permissive environment for undocumented immigrants; but law enforcement practices more often work to assert state sovereignty and authority (Vigneswaran et al.,

2010). The policing of migrants has been especially harsh in the city of Johannesburg, where a police crackdown on crime has led to the arbitrary arrest of migrants and the raiding of buildings and neighbourhoods known to have high concentrations of migrants. Policing in the inner city, according to Vigneswaran et al. (2010, 479), 'has come to resemble a vast immigration control exercise', with the fortunes of migrants dependent on the dispositions of police officers at any given moment. Police officers are not the only state officials who enforce borders on a day-to-day basis. Those migrants who attempt to regularize their status often encounter state officials who transform application procedures into major bureaucratic obstacles. Officials, for instance, can make migrants wait for an appointment longer than the duration of their transit permits, withhold information about their rights, or interfere with efforts to fill out forms (ibid.; Landau, 2010). These examples illustrate how the border presents itself to migrants not just at the physical boundaries of the state, but in the face-to-face, everyday interactions between migrants and those endowed with some measure of state authority. These include, most obviously, police officers and immigration bureaucrats, but we must also consider how teachers, social workers, public transport workers, healthcare workers, and others might work to enforce state power and to reproduce distinctions between citizens and foreigners (for further illustration of internal policing practices in the context of Italy and Greece, see Triandafyllidou and Ambrosini, 2011).

As state authorities saturate national territory with borders, they simultaneously expand bordering functions beyond their territorial limits, exercising authority over mobile bodies even before these bodies enter national space. Once again, we can see important historical precedents to the geographical extension of borders—what Zolberg (2007) calls 'remote border control'. For instance, the Immigration Act of 1924 charged American consulates overseas with keeping track of national-origins quotas and distributing immigration visas accordingly (Torpey, 2000). Thus, prospective immigrants, long before setting foot on American soil, could be vetted through police checks, medical inspections, and assessments of fiscal responsibility and political views. More recent examples of remote-control border enforcement practices abound. We have seen in Chapter 5, for instance, how key elements of EU harmonization—safe third-country provisions, visa requirements, and carrier sanctions—have been designed to push responsibility for asylum claimants away from EU territory and onto overseas consulates, neighbouring countries, and transport companies.

As they seek to push immigration and border control outward, states in many cases foster strategic partnerships with neighbouring states that are points of origin or transit for unauthorized migrants (Boswell, 2003). Such partnerships, indeed, are a key component of managed-migration 'best practice' (Geiger and Pécoud, 2010). These relationships are typically asymmetrical, involving promises of foreign assistance in return for stricter policing of immigrant transit routes. For instance, Australia, as described in Chapter 5, has negotiated agreements with the impoverished Pacific island of Nauru to receive and process asylum seekers intercepted at sea in return for economic development aid (described in Chapter 5). There has also been significant cooperation between Mexico and the United States on migration control, especially since the 2001 terrorist attacks on the US. After 2001, for instance, the Mexican government reportedly deployed a group of Israeli- and US-trained border enforcement officers to its southern border and installed new computer systems to track unauthorized migrants and to detect false documents (Andreas, 2003; also Meyers, 2003).

The EU, meanwhile, has created for itself an extensive buffer zone through numerous bilateral and multilateral partnerships with North African and Middle Eastern countries, including the euphemistically named European Neighbourhood Policy (ENP). Such partnerships, as Del Sarto (2010) explains, have sought to secure, in particular, the borders of North African countries in order to prevent migrants from sub-Saharan Africa from transiting through the Maghreb. Partnerships often involve **readmission agreements**, whereby North African countries agree to readmit migrants who have been intercepted en route to Europe or deported from Europe. Partnerships between Europe and North African countries typically rest on a principle of conditionality that rewards cooperating countries with various benefits: loosened visa restrictions, higher quotas for migrant workers, development assistance, and the transfer of border-management technology from Europe to the Mediterranean periphery (De Haas, 2008). Del Sarto (2010) suggests that the creation of partnerships and the extension of border control beyond physical boundaries produce a complex, overlapping border geometry—more a 'borderlands' than a clearly demarcated territorial boundary (see also Bialasiewicz, 2012).

The outsourcing of policing functions to poor, politically unstable neighbours might seem like a dubious strategy for wealthy nation-states to pursue. Yet these practices of co-opting poorer neighbours through foreign aid greatly expand the policing capacity of wealthy states (Geiger and Pécoud, 2010). Whether poor countries benefit from these partnerships is a matter of some debate. On the one hand, poor countries exercise some leverage in their negotiations with European states and can extract various resources from Europe in return for their cooperation. On the other hand, poor countries can become dumping grounds for intercepted and deported migrants. Trauner and Deimel (2013), for instance, show that thousands of migrants detained and deported at the behest of European governments by the impoverished Sahelian state of Mauretania have been absorbed by the even more impoverished Sahelian state of Mali. With the Malian state unable or unwilling to deal with these returned (or more often, refouled) migrants, non-governmental organizations have taken it upon themselves to alleviate the suffering caused by Europe's restrictive entry policies and its partnerships with African states.

Conclusions

We have tried to demonstrate in this chapter that while it is problematic to assume that states fully control migration flows, it is equally problematic to assume that states have somehow lost, or given up, control over their borders. The increasing integration of the global economy—of production systems, commodity and capital markets, and labour forces—has taken place through the diligent management of borders and the intensive application of new technologies to monitor and to control mobility. Borders, we have emphasized, have multiple functions, only one of which is to keep people out. Borders can be rigid in some respects and permeable in others, but regardless of whether borders are functioning in a rigid or permeable fashion at any given moment, we can say unequivocally that borders matter at, within, and beyond geographical frontiers of the nation-state. Borders stretch across and saturate space in ways that produce different kinds of mobility for different kinds of people.

Borders are a taken-for-granted feature of the modern world, yet they raise a variety of ethical and moral questions. For some political philosophers like Michael Walzer (1983), borders are justifiable insofar as they are conducive to the formation of political communities and hence to the practice of democracy. Territorial and political closure, in other words, generates membership, mutual obligation, and sense of common life; these characteristics, in turn, are a prerequisite for the provision of goods and services to meet mutual needs—what Walzer calls the 'sphere of security and welfare'. Without closure, there are no communities at all, and thus no political inclusiveness. From this perspective, nation-states—as the primary form of political community in the modern world—have a moral right to choose the composition of the political community through admission and exclusion. These practices, Walzer insists, are at the core of communal independence and self-determination.

Other political philosophers have taken a different tack. Joseph Carens (1987, 252) argues that 'citizenship in Western liberal democracies is the modern equivalent of feudal privilege—an inherited status that greatly enhances one's life chances'. Because borders serve primarily to preserve systems of privilege and power and to prevent individuals from exercising individual rights and freedoms, they can have no moral justification. Carens's ideas rest on the liberal ideal of the equal moral worth of the individual and the priority of the individual over any kind of community. Carens notes that liberal democracies today view restrictions on *internal* mobility to be reprehensible; if that is the case, then why do they continue to tolerate restrictions on *international* mobility? What justifies treating the nation-state as a special kind of community that warrants such illiberal measures? All liberal communities, Carens insists, must be open to those who wish to join (see also Johnson, 2003).

Other scholars make even more impassioned arguments about the moral intolerability of borders and immigration restrictions. Nick Megoran (2005) and others emphasize the ways in which borders function to separate the poor from the rich, to criminalize immigrants, and to facilitate their exploitation. Megoran (2005, 641) elaborates this position:

Current immigration controls in Britain and other Western states are expensive to administer and cannot possibly achieve their desired effect. They hamper economic growth and perpetuate inequalities, undermine the welfare state, contradict formal commitments to liberal values and human rights, foster criminality, and condemn the vulnerable to exploitation and even death. They are the unfortunate heritage of a reprehensible chapter of twentieth century politics.

Megoran implores scholars like himself to take an active part in struggles 'to close that chapter by ending immigration controls' (ibid.). Insofar as global capitalism produces inequalities and wage differences through shifting patterns of investment, these commentators suggest, workers must have the right to respond to labour market signals and to seek a better standard of living elsewhere (Hayter, 2001; also Zolberg, 2012).

The idea of open borders, however, does present its own set of moral quandaries. Not all advocates of open borders, it should be noted, are driven by moral concerns or a passion for social justice; many libertarians and free-market advocates, for instance, see the removal of borders and immigration controls primarily in terms of economic efficiency, the smooth functioning of labour supply and demand, and the inevitability of global economic integration (Casey, 2010; for a fuller discussion of different positions on open borders, see Wellman and Cole, 2011). We must ask, who would actually benefit in a truly borderless, globalized labour market and capitalist economy: workers, corporations, consumers? Are labour rights and workplace protections sustainable in borderless societies? What effect would open labour markets have on low-skilled workers? Is it possible to create any sense of societal cohesion or democratic practice in an unbounded society? How would rights be guaranteed? These are difficult questions, and we do not pretend to have answers. Our aim in raising these kinds of questions is simply to encourage our readers to consider the complex moral questions that borders raise and to look beyond the often simplistic arguments that characterize public discourse in migrant-receiving societies.

Key terms in this chapter

coyotes	regularization
Frontex	Section 287(g)
migration management	Secure Communities
	securitization
nativist/nativism	Senate Bill 1070 (SB 1070)
passports	
readmission agreements	transit
	visa

Further reading

Collyer, M. (2012) Migrants as strategic actors in the European Union's Global Approach to Migration and Mobility, *Global Networks*, 12(4): 505–524.

Doty, R. L. (2009) *The Law into Their Own Hands: Immigration and the Politics of Exceptionalism*. Tucson: University of Arizona Press.

Fitzgerald, D. (2006) Inside the sending state: the politics of Mexican emigration control, *International Migration Review*, 40(2): 259–293.

Hampshire, J. (2013) *The Politics of Immigration*. Cambridge, UK; Malden, MA: Polity.

Vaughan-Williams, N. (2012) *Border Politics: The Limits of Sovereign Power*. Edinburgh, UK: University of Edinburgh Press.

Vigneswaran, D. (2008) Enduring territoriality: South African immigration control, *Political Geography*, 27: 783–801.

References

Adey, P. (2004) Surveillance at the airport: surveilling mobility/mobilising surveillance, *Environment and Planning A*, 36(8): 1365–1380.

Amoore, L. (2006) Biometric borders: governing mobilities in the war on terror, *Political Geography*, 25(3): 336–351.

Anderson, K. (1991) *Vancouver's Chinatown: Racial Discourse in Canada, 1875–1989*. Quebec City: McGill-Queen's University Press.

Andreas, P. (2000) *Border Games: Policing the US–Mexico Divide*. Ithaca, NY: Cornell University Press.

Andreas, P. (2003) A tale of two borders: the US–Mexico and US–Canada lines after 9/11, Working Paper number 77, Center for Comparative Immigration Studies. San Diego: University of California.

Bade, K. J. (2003) *Migration in European History* (translated by Allison Brown). Malden, Oxford: Blackwell.

Balch, A. (2009) Labour and epistemic communities: the case of 'managed migration' in the UK, *The British Journal of Politics & International Relations*, 11(4): 613–633.

Bialasiewicz, L. (2012) Off-shoring and outsourcing the borders of EUrope: Libya and EU border work in the Mediterranean, *Geopolitics*, 17(4): 843–866

Bloch, A. and Schuster, L. (2005) At the extremes of exclusion: deportation, detention and dispersal, *Ethnic and Racial Studies*, 28(3): 491–512.

Boswell, C. (2003) The 'external dimension' of EU immigration and asylum policy, *International Affairs*, 79(3): 619–638.

Boswell, C. (2007) Migration control in Europe after 9/11: explaining the absence of securitization, *JCMS: Journal of Common Market Studies*, 45(3): 589–610.

Bosworth, M. and Kaufman, E. (2011) Foreigners in a carceral age: immigration and imprisonment in the United States, *Stanford Law and Policy Review*, 22(1): 429–454.

Brettell, C. B. and Nibbs, F. G. (2011) Immigrant suburban settlement and the 'threat' to middle class status and identity: the case of Farmers Branch, Texas, *International Migration*, 49(1): 1–30.

Broeders, D. (2007) The new digital borders of Europe: EU databases and the surveillance of irregular migrants, *International Sociology*, 22(1): 71–92.

Carens, J. H. (1987) Aliens and citizens: the case for open borders, *The Review of Politics*, 49(2): 251–273.

Carling, J. and Hernández-Carretero, M. (2011) Protecting Europe and protecting migrants? Strategies for managing unauthorised migration from Africa, *British Journal of Politics and International Relations*, 13(1): 42–58.

Carrera, S. and Guild, E. (2010) 'Joint Operation RABIT 2010'–FRONTEX assistance to Greece's border with Turkey: revealing the deficiencies of Europe's Dublin asylum system, CEPS Liberty and Security in Europe, November 2010 (policy paper). Retrieved from http://aei.pitt.edu/15186/ (accessed 28 May 2015).

Casey, J. P. (2010) Open borders: absurd chimera or inevitable future policy? *International Migration*, 48(5): 14–62.

Castles, S. (2004a) The factors that make and unmake migration policies, *International Migration Review*, 38(3): 852–884.

Castles, S. (2004b) Why migration policies fail, *Ethnic and Racial Studies*, 27(2): 205–227.

Coleman, M. (2007) A geopolitics of engagement: neoliberalism, the war on terrorism, and the reconfiguration of US immigration enforcement, *Geopolitics*, 12(4): 607–634.

Coleman, M. (2012) The 'local' migration state: the site-specific devolution of immigration enforcement in the US South, *Law & Policy*, 34(2): 159–190.

Coleman, M. and Kocher, A. (2011) Detention, deportation, devolution and immigrant incapacitation in the US, post 9/11, *The Geographical Journal*, 177(3): 228–237.

Collyer, M., Düvell, F., and De Haas, H. (2012) Critical approaches to transit migration, *Population, Space and Place*, 18(4): 407–414.

Conservative Party (2010) *Invitation to Join the Government of Britain: The Conservative Manifesto 2010*. London: Conservative Party.

Cornelius, W. (2005) Controlling 'unwanted' immigration: lessons from the United States, 1993–2004, *Journal of Ethnic and Migration Studies*, 31(4): 775–794.

Cornelius, W. A. and Tsuda, T. (2004) Controlling immigration: the limits of government intervention. In W. A. Cornelius, T. Tsuda, P. Martin, and J. Hollifield (Eds.), *Controlling Immigration: A Global Perspective* (2nd edition). Stanford, CA: Stanford University Press (pp. 3–14).

De Genova, N. P. (2002) Migrant 'illegality' and deportability in everyday life, *Annual Review of Anthropology*, 31: 419–447.

De Haas, H. (2008) The myth of invasion: the inconvenient realities of African migration to Europe, *Third World Quarterly*, 29(7): 1305–1322.

Del Sarto, R. (2010) Borderlands: the Middle East and North Africa as the EU's southern buffer zone. In D. Bechev and K. Nicolaidis (Eds.), *Mediterranean Frontiers: Borders, Conflicts and Memory in a Transnational World*. London: I. B. Tauris (pp. 149–167).

Department of Homeland Security (2013) Yearbook of Immigration Statistics, 2013. Retrieved from http://www.dhs.gov/yearbook-immigration-statistics-2013-enforcement-actions.

Duran, J. (2010) Virtual borders, data aliens, and bare bodies: culture, securitization, and the biometric state, *Journal of Borderland Studies*, 25(3–4): 219–230.

Durand, J. and Massey, D. (2003) The costs of contradiction: US border policy 1986–2000, *Latino Studies*, 1(2): 233–252.

Facchini, G. and Mayda, A. M. (2008) From individual attitudes towards migrants to migration policy outcomes: theory and evidence, *Economic Policy*, 23(56): 652–713.

Faist, T. (2006) The migration-security nexus: international migration and security before and after 9/11. In Y. M. Bodemann and G. Yurdakul (Eds.) *Migration, Citizenship, Ethnos*. Basingstoke: Palgrave Macmillan (pp.103–120).

Favell, A. and Hansen, R. (2002) Markets against politics: migration, EU enlargement and the idea of Europe, *Journal of Ethnic and Migration Studies*, 28(4): 581–601.

Fernández-Kelly, P. and Massey, D. (2007) Borders for whom? The role of NAFTA in Mexico–US migration, *The Annals of the American Academy of Political and Social Science*, 610(1): 98–118.

Flynn, D. (2005) New borders, new management: the dilemma of modern immigration policies, *Ethnic and Racial Studies*, 28(3): 463–490.

Foster, M. (2008) Responsibility sharing or shifting? 'Safe' third countries and international law, *Refuge*, 25(2): 64–78.

Freeman, G. (1995) Modes of immigration politics in liberal democratic states, *International Migration Review*, 29(4): 881–902.

Geiger, M. and Pécoud, A. (2010) The politics of international migration management. In M. Geiger and A. Pécoud (Eds.), *The Politics of International Migration Management*. Basingstoke; New York: Palgrave Macmillan (pp. 1–20).

Groebner, V. (2001) Describing the person, reading the signs in late medieval and renaissance Europe: identity papers, vested figures, and the limits of identification, 1400–1600. In J. Caplan and J. Torpey (Eds.), *Documenting Individual Identity*. Princeton, NJ: Princeton University Press (pp. 15–27).

Guiraudon, V. (2008) Moroccan immigration in France: do migration policies matter? *Journal of Immigrant & Refugee Studies*, 6(3): 366–381.

Hagan, J. M., Rodriguez, N., and Castro, B. (2011) Social effects of mass deportations by the United States government, 2000–2010, *Ethnic and Racial Studies*, 34(8): 1374–1391.

Hayes, B. (2012) The surveillance–industrial complex. In K. Ball, K. D. Haggerty, and D. Lyon (Eds.), *Routledge Handbook of Surveillance Studies*. Abingdon, Oxon; New York: Routledge (pp. 167–175).

Hayter, T. (2001) Open borders: the case against immigration controls. In T. Omoniyi and S. Gupta (Eds.), *The Cultures of Economic Migration: International Perspectives*. Aldershot; Burlington, VT: Ashgate (pp 17–26).

Henderson, T. (2014) More jurisdictions defying Feds on deporting immigrants. Stateline. Pew Charitable Trusts. Retrieved from http://www.pewtrusts.org/en/research-and-analysis/blogs/stateline/2014/10/31/more-jurisdictions-defying-feds-on-deporting-immigrants (accessed 28 May 2015).

Hernández, K. L. (2006) The crimes and consequences of illegal immigration: a cross-border examination of Operation Wetback, 1943 to 1954, *The Western Historical Quarterly*, 37(4): 421–444.

Hollifield, J. (2004) The emerging migration state, *International Migration Review*, 38(3): 885–912.

Hugo, G. (2014) Change and continuity in Australian international migration policy, *International Migration Review*, 48(3): 868–890.

Hyndman, J. and Mountz, A. (2008) Another brick in the wall? Neo-refoulement and the externalization of asylum by Australia and Europe, *Government and Opposition*, 43(2): 249–269.

Iosifides, T., Lavrentiadou, M., Petracou, E., and Kontis, A. (2007) Forms of social capital and the incorporation of Albanian immigrants in Greece, *Journal of Ethnic and Migration Studies*, 33(8): 1343–1361.

Johnson, K. R. (2003) Open borders, *UCLA Law Review*, 51: 193.

Joppke, C. (1998) Why liberal states accept unwanted immigration, *World Politics*, 50(2): 266–293.

Kalir, B. (2015) The Jewish state of anxiety: between moral obligation and fearism in the treatment of African asylum seekers in Israel, *Journal of Ethnic and Migration Studies*, 41(4): 580–598.

King, D. (2000) *Making Americans: Immigration,*

Race, and the Origins of the Diverse Democracy. Cambridge, MA: Harvard University Press.

Klaaren, J. and Ramji, J. (2001) Inside illegality: migration policing in South Africa after Apartheid, *Africa Today*, 48(3): 35–47.

Kofman, E. (2002) Contemporary European migrations, civic stratification and citizenship, *Political Geography*, 21(8): 1035–1054.

Koskela, H. (2010) Did you spot an alien? Voluntary vigilance, borderwork and the Texas virtual border watch program, *Space and Polity*, 14(2): 103–121.

Lahav, G. and Guiraudon, V. (2007) Actors and venues in immigration control: closing the gap between political demands and policy outcomes. In V. Guiraudon and G. Lahav (Eds.), *Immigration Policy in Europe: The Politics of Control*. Abingdon, UK; New York: Routledge (pp. 1–25).

Lahav, G., Messina, A. M., and Vasquez, J. P. (2014) Were political elite attitudes toward immigration securitized after 11 September? Survey evidence from the European Parliament, *Migration Studies*, 2(2): 212–234.

Landau, L. B. (2010) Loving the alien? Citizenship, law, and the future of South Africa's demonic society, *African Affairs*, 109(435): 213–230.

Layton-Henry, Z. (2004) Britain: from immigration control to migration management. In W. A. Cornelius, T. Tsuda, P. Martin, and J. Hollifield (Eds.), *Controlling Immigration: A Global Perspective* (2nd edition). Stanford, CA: Stanford University Press (pp. 297–333).

Lazaridis, G. and Koumandraki, M. (2007) Albanian migration to Greece: patterns and processes of inclusion and exclusion in the labour market, *European Societies*, 9(1): 91–111.

Lee, E. and Yung, J. (2010) *Angel Island: Immigrant Gateway to America*. Oxford: Oxford University Press.

Leerkes, A., Leach, M., and Bachmeier, J. (2012) Borders behind the border: an exploration of state-level differences in migration control and their effects on US migration patterns, *Journal of Ethnic and Migration Studies*, 38(1), 111–129.

Lior, I. (2014) High Court orders closure of detention facility for African asylum seekers, *Haaretz* (22 September). Retrieved from http://www.haaretz.com/news/national/.premium-1.617143 (accessed 29 May 2015).

Lutterbeck, D. (2006) Policing migration in the Mediterranean, *Mediterranean Politics*, 11(1): 59–82.

Massey, D. S. and Pren, K. (2012) Unintended consequences of US immigration policy: explaining the post-1965 surge from Latin America, *Population and Development Review*, 38(1), 1–29.

Mavroudi, E. and Warren, A. (2013) Highly skilled migration and the negotiation of immigration policy: non-EEA postgraduate students and academic staff at English universities, *Geoforum*, 44: 261–270.

Megoran, N. (2005) The case for ending migration controls, *Antipode*, 37(4): 638–642.

Meyers, D. W. (2003) Does 'smarter' lead to safer? An assessment of US border accords with Canada and Mexico, *International Migration*, 41(4): 5–44.

Mongia, R. V. (1999) Race, nationality, mobility: a history of the passport, *Public Culture*, 11(3): 527–556.

Moore, K. (1999) A closer look at anti-terrorism law: *American-Arab Anti-Discrimination Committee v. Reno* and the construction of aliens' rights. In M. Suleiman (Ed.), *Arabs in America: Building a New Future*. Philadelphia: Temple University Press (pp. 84–99).

Mountz, A., Coddington, K., Catania, R. T. and Loyd, J. M. (2013) Conceptualizing detention: mobility, containment, bordering, and exclusion, *Progress in Human Geography*, 37(4): 522–541.

Muller, B. J. (2010) Unsafe at any speed? Borders, mobility and 'safe citizenship', *Citizenship Studies*, 14(1): 75–88.

Mulvey, G. (2011) Immigration under New

Labour: policy and effects, *Journal of Ethnic and Migration Studies*, 37(9): 1477–1493.

Neumeyer, E. (2010) Visa restrictions and bilateral travel, *Professional Geographer*, 62(2): 171–181.

Ngai, M. (2003) The strange career of the illegal alien: immigration restriction and deportation policy in the United States, 1921–1965, *Law and History Review*, 21(1): 69–108.

Pallister-Wilkins, P. (2015) The humanitarian politics of European border policing: Frontex and border police in Evros, *International Political Sociology*, 9(1): 53–69.

Paul, K. (1997) *Whitewashing Britain: Race and Citizenship in the Postwar Era*. Ithaca, NY: Cornell University Press.

Preston, J. (2015) Republicans resist Obama's move to dismantle apparatus of deportation, *New York Times* (January 15). Retrieved from http://www.nytimes.com/2015/01/16/us/secure-communities-immigration-program-battle.html?_r=0 (accessed 1 June 2015).

Salter, M. B. (2003) *Rights of Passage: The Passport in International Relations*. Boulder, CO: Lynne Rienner Publishers.

Salter, M. B. (2004) Passports, mobility, and security: how smart can the border be? *International Studies Perspectives*, 5(1): 71–91.

Salter, M. B. (2008) When the exception becomes the rule: borders, sovereignty, and citizenship, *Citizenship Studies*, 12(4): 365–380.

Salter, M. and Zureik, E. (Eds.) (2005) *Global Surveillance and Policing: Borders, Security, Identity*. Cullompton: Willan Publishing.

Sassen, S. (1999) Beyond sovereignty: immigration policy making today. In S. Jonas and S. D. Thomas (Eds.), *Immigration: A Civil Rights Issue for the Americas*. Wilmington, DE: Scholarly Resources (pp. 15–26).

Semmelroggen, J. (2011) A critical discourse analysis of the policy formation process of the 2009 action programme on skilled labour migration in Germany. Doctoral Thesis, Loughborough University. Available at https://dspace.lboro.ac.uk/dspace-jspui/bitstream/2134/9910/2/Thesis-2011-Semmelroggen.pdf.

Sparke, M. B. (2006) A neoliberal nexus: economy, security and the biopolitics of citizenship on the border, *Political Geography*, 25(2): 151–180.

Staeheli, L. A. and Nagel, C. R. (2008) Rethinking security: perspectives from Arab–American and British Arab activists, *Antipode*, 40(5): 780–801.

Stuesse, A. and Coleman, M. (2014) Automobility, immobility, altermobility: surviving and resisting the intensification of immigrant policing, *City & Society*, 26(1): 51–72.

Taylor, P. J. (1994) The state as container: territoriality in the modern world-system, *Progress in Human Geography*, 18: 151–162.

Torpey, J. (2000) *The Invention of the Passport: Surveillance, Citizenship and the State*. Cambridge: Cambridge University Press.

Trauner, F. and Deimel, S. (2013) The impact of EU migration policies on African countries: the case of Mali, *International Migration*, 51(4): 20–32.

Triandafyllidou, A. and Ambrosini, M. (2011) Irregular immigration control in Italy and Greece: strong fencing and weak gate-keeping serving the labour market, *European Journal of Migration and Law*, 13(3): 251–273.

United Kingdom Border Agency (UKBA) (2010) Annual limit for Tier 1 and Tier 2 visa applications (24 November). Retrieved from http://www.ukba.homeoffice.gov.uk/sitecontent/ newsfragments/35-t1-t2-annual-limits (accessed 19 June 2012).

US Immigration and Customs Enforcement (2015) Delegation of immigration authority, Section 287(g) Immigration and Nationality Act. Retrieved from http://www.ice.gov/factsheets/287g (accessed 2 June 2015).

Van Houtum, H. (2010) Human blacklisting: the global apartheid of the EU's external border regime, *Environment and Planning D: Society and Space*, 28(6): 957–976.

Van Houtum, H. and Pijpers, R. (2007) The European Union as a gated community: the two-faced border and immigration regime of the EU, *Antipode*, 39(2): 291–309.

Varsanyi, M. W. (2008) Immigration policing through the backdoor: city ordinances, the 'right to the city', and the exclusion of undocumented day laborers, *Urban Geography*, 29(1): 29–52.

Varsanyi, M., Lewis, P. G., Provine, D. M., and Decker, S. (2012) A multilayered jurisdictional patchwork: immigration federalism in the United States, *Law & Policy*, 34(2): 138–158.

Vicino, T. J. (2013) *Suburban Crossroads: The Fight for Local Control of Immigration Policy*. Lanham, MD: Lexington Books.

Vigneswaran, D., Araia, T., Hoag, C., and Tshabalala, X. (2010) Criminality or monopoly? Informal immigration enforcement in South Africa, *Journal of Southern African Studies*, 36(2): 465–481.

Walsh, J. (2008) Navigating globalization: immigration policy in Canada and Australia, 1945–2007, *Sociological Forum*, 23(4): 786–813.

Walters, W. (2002) Deportation, expulsion, and the international police of aliens, *Citizenship Studies*, 6(3): 265–292

Walzer, M. (1983) *Spheres of Justice: A Defense of Pluralism and Equality*. New York: Basic Books.

Warren, A. and Mavroudi, E. (2011) Managing surveillance? The impact of biometric residence permits on UK migrants, *Journal of Ethnic and Migration Studies*, 37(9): 1495–1511.

Wellman, C. H. and Cole, P. (2011) *Debating the Ethics of Immigration: Is There a Right to Exclude?* Oxford: Oxford University Press.

Wilson, D. and Weber, L. (2008) Surveillance, risk and preemption on the Australian Border, *Surveillance and Society*, 5(2): 124–141.

Winders, J. (2007) Bringing back the (b)order: post-9/11 politics of immigration, borders, and belonging in the contemporary US South, *Antipode*, 39(5): 920–942.

Zolberg, A. (2003) The archaeology of 'remote control'. In A. Fahrmeir, O. Faron, and P. Weil (Eds.), *Migration Control in the North Atlantic World: The Evolution of State Practices in Europe and the United States from the French Revolution to the Inter-War Period*. New York: Berghahn Books (pp. 195–220).

Zolberg, A. (2007) Immigration control policy: law and implementation. In M. C. Waters, R. Ueda, and H. B. Marrow (Eds.), *The New Americans*. Cambridge, MA: Harvard University Press (pp. 29–42).

Zolberg, A. (2012) Why not the whole world? Ethical dilemmas of immigration policy, *American Behavioral Scientist*, 56(9): 1204–1222.

Zonszein, M. (2015) Israel to deport Eritrean and Sudanese asylum seekers to third countries, *Guardian* (31 March). Retrieved from http://www.theguardian.com/world/2015/mar/31/israel-to-deport-eritrean-and-sudanese-asylum-seekers-to-third-countries (accessed 2 June 2015).

7

The politics of citizenship and integration

Introduction

In Chapter 6 we argued that bordering policies and practices serve not so much to keep out immigrants as to differentiate between citizens and 'aliens'. Border control and entry policies, in this sense, have a key role in producing citizenship in modern nation-states and in defining its contours (Mongia, 1999). In this chapter, we explore this idea further, examining how the configuration of citizenship and belonging continues to take place after immigrants have established a presence in destination societies. Dominant groups and institutions, we suggest, continuously differentiate between foreigners and nationals, as well as among various categories and classes of immigrants. This differentiation takes place both through informal social practices in workplaces, schools, and neighbourhoods and through formal policies and laws.

Our aim in this chapter is to investigate the political dynamics through which immigrant-receiving societies define who belongs and on what terms. Whether they view themselves as countries of immigrants or as the unwitting recipients of unwanted 'guests', national societies—legislators, bureaucrats, political parties, corporations, educators, and voluntary organizations—must decide how, to what degree, and under what conditions newcomers are to be incorporated into the life of the nation-state. They must decide which rights and privileges should be extended to aliens, which procedures

immigrants must follow to become formal members, and which measures, if any, should be taken to accommodate cultural and linguistic differences. We refer to the process of incorporating and extending societal membership to foreigners as the politics of integration and citizenship. This process is invariably contentious and fraught with ambiguities. As with entry and border control policies, citizenship and integration politics involve numerous judgements about the relative worth of particular groups and their social, cultural, and racial characteristics. Such judgements about 'others' and outsiders, in turn, require the continuous evaluation and articulation of national identity and 'we-ness'—that is, the core characteristics and values that define the nation and the conditions under which outsiders might become one of 'us' (Antonsich, 2012).

Immigrants constantly confront particular configurations of we-ness and otherness in their encounters and interactions with employers, government agents, neighbours, teachers, and law enforcement officials. Immigrants are not passive figures in the politics of integration and citizenship. On the contrary, they actively negotiate their membership in receiving societies, at times by politically mobilizing to claim formal rights and inclusion in national narratives. We save such immigrant-centred discussions for the following chapter. Here, we keep the focus mainly on the ways receiving societies respond to immigrants and on the political discourses that frame these responses. Our analysis begins with a discussion of the concepts of integration and citizenship and the connections between these terms. We then explore the ways in which citizenship and integration politics flow from 'civic' or 'ethnic' conceptions of national membership. Finally, we examine forms of openness and closure, as well as inclusion and exclusion, that cut across national contexts. Our argument here is that tensions and contradictions with respect to the position of immigrants exist in all immigrant-receiving societies, regardless of whether these are classified as civic or ethnic polities. We suggest, as well, that the proliferation of immigrant classifications and the geographical unevenness of policies towards settled immigrant populations have rendered citizenship increasingly differentiated and fragmented. Citizenship and integration, we conclude, must be understood in all national contexts as multiple, shifting, and contingent on local circumstances.

Conceptualizing citizenship and integration

Citizenship and integration are complex terms with multiple meanings. Scholars have long debated what these terms mean, why they are important, and whether they remain meaningful in a globalizing era. We attempt to peel back some of these conceptual layers to better understand why ideas of citizenship and integration have been so central to scholarly and public debates about immigration.

The term 'citizenship' refers, first of all, to legal membership in modern nation-states. The fact that legal citizenship is often used interchangeably with 'nationality' reflects the assumed congruity between the political community (or **polity**) and the nation in modern nation-states—a congruity that developed fitfully (and often incompletely) through political struggle, first in Europe and later in post-colonial societies. Citizenship confers a legal identity on the individual that is recognizable in the context of the interstate system. Citizenship also provides the individual, at least in theory, with a set of rights and legal protections guaranteed by the state. Some political theorists, following T. H. Marshall's (1950) classic treatise on citizenship, have viewed citizenship rights in liberal democratic societies as having *expanded* over the course of centuries to encompass civil rights (personal liberties and freedoms of expression, religious belief, and the like), political rights (the ability to select members of governing bodies through an electoral system), and, in the post-World War II era, social rights (access to a social safety net provided by the state). Theorists have also viewed citizenship rights as becoming more *inclusive* over time, extending from a small class of property-holding white men to working classes, women, and racialized minorities. But as we will discuss below, citizenship does not march inevitably towards full inclusion. Rights can be curtailed, reversed, or even eliminated for citizens and non-citizen residents alike. At the same time, the state can increase the obligations and responsibilities that it places on citizens and non-citizens living within the nation-state (for a fuller discussion of the structure of citizenship in modern nation-states, see Turner, 1993).

Along with these more formal and legalistic meanings, citizenship refers to values, virtues, and norms attached to membership in a polity (Smith, 2002; also Dagger, 2002). One can practise 'good citizenship', for instance, by participating actively in civic organizations and by taking care of one's community. Conversely, one can be seen to fall short of citizenship ideals, for instance, by evading taxes or relying on welfare. Citizenship also conveys a sense of belonging in the political community, which, in the modern nation-state system, is commensurate with the national community. Modern citizenship, in this sense, while expressed and codified in legalistic terms, rests upon highly subjective narratives of who 'we' are as a people—what Smith (2003) calls 'constitutive stories'. As a citizen, one is expected to feel a sense of allegiance to the wider community of citizens and to express some degree of solidarity with that community. Receiving societies can and do weave newcomers into narratives of the national community, as seen with the 'melting pot' metaphor commonly used in the United States to describe the supposed blending together of different cultural groups to form a distinctively American society. But receiving societies can equally invoke ideas of community to exclude particular groups from the body politic, as seen in US, Australian, and Canadian policies that for decades prohibited Asian immigrants from joining the national community through **naturalization**.

Resting as it does on the idea of community, citizenship thus encompasses both legalistic and emotive elements that are difficult, if not impossible, to separate (Staeheli, 2008; Ho, 2009). Debates about citizenship are by no means limited to the issue of immigration. Liberal-democratic societies continuously debate the meaning of equality and societal membership for a variety of groups including women, gays, religious and linguistic minorities, and indigenous people. But by bringing into the polity those who are formally 'aliens' and foreigners, immigration raises particularly thorny questions about the nature of rights, the requirements of membership, and the content of community norms and values (Mavroudi, 2010). States and societies must decide how, whether, and under what conditions immigrants may become legal members of the polity and the national community.

Integration, like citizenship, is a complex concept with many layers of meaning. At the most basic level, integration refers to the incorporation of immigrants into societies of settlement, and it can be analyzed both as a *process* of adjustment, adaptation, and acceptance, and as an *end state* in which immigrants are no longer distinguishable from non-immigrants in terms of economic opportunities, residential choices, and cultural behaviours. Theories of integration have been articulated and debated most fully among US sociologists under the purview of 'assimilation' studies. This scholarship springs from Park and Burgess' (1921, 735–736) definition of assimilation as 'a process of interpenetration and fusion in which persons and groups acquire the memories, sentiments, and attitudes of other persons and groups and, by sharing their experience and history, are incorporated with them in a common cultural life'. Classic assimilation scholarship has been closely tied to the concept of the 'race-relations cycle', which describes a sequence of contact, competition, accommodation, and assimilation between immigrant and host-society groups (Park, 1950; Lyman, 1968). The idea of a race-relations cycle suggests that the presence of a new group will lead initially to tension, struggle, and sometimes pronounced residential segregation (i.e. the formation of **ghettos**) but that this will give way to accommodation and eventually, with more interpersonal interaction, to the reduction, if not the disappearance, of distinctions between groups. (Box 7.1 elaborates on the concept of the ghetto.)

BOX 7.1 THE GHETTO

Scholars have long been intrigued by patterns of residential segregation and the formation of ghettos—a term that comes from the island where the Jews of Venice were compelled to live in the 16th century. In his classic treatise on the ghetto, University of Chicago sociologist Lewis Wirth (1928) compared the Jewish quarters of mediaeval and early modern European cities with the Jewish neighbourhoods of America's industrial cities in the early 20th century. As an urban ecologist, Wirth viewed certain social traits, behaviours, and customs as emerging from particular sociospatial environments. For Jews, spatial isolation in the ghetto generated distinctive cultural norms, skills, and community bonds that persisted over generations. Wirth, however, viewed the American ghetto as distinct from the European ghetto. While European Jews were forced to live in the ghetto, Jewish immigrants in cities like Chicago could choose to live beyond it, and Wirth believed that with greater economic opportunity many Jews would leave the ghetto. Wirth's understanding of the inevitable demise of the Jewish ghetto reflected a relatively optimistic view of the acculturation of immigrants to American society and the waning over time of discrimination.

Kay Anderson's (1991) work on Vancouver's Chinatown offers a different analysis of the ghetto that focuses on the ways dominant groups perceive ghetto space and the people living in ghettos. Anderson argues that white Canadians, perceiving Chinese immigrants to be unassimilable into what was imagined to be an Anglo-Saxon nation, actively produced the space of the Chinese ghetto through municipal policies and housing market discrimination. Once they had contained Chinese immigrants and starved them of municipal services, the white population of Vancouver represented Chinatown as a foreign space of disease, filth, and vice. Chinatown thus served as the visible 'other' against which white Canadians could define their own national and racial identity.

Ghettos continue to elicit the anxieties of dominant groups, who sometimes describe immigrant neighbourhoods as lawless, no-go areas seething with criminal activity. Scholars have sought to dispel misconceptions about immigrant residential concentrations, in the first instance, by more clearly defining what does or does not constitute a 'ghetto'. Massey and Denton (1993, 19), in their influential work on residential segregation in the US, defined a ghetto as 'a set of neighbourhoods that are exclusively inhabited by members of one group, within which virtually all members of that group live'. According to this definition, no group in US history other than African Americans has ever been truly ghettoized. This more specific definition of a ghetto has been used by scholars in other contexts to question the extent to which immigrant groups are living an isolated, self-segregating existence, as many policymakers suppose (see, for instance, Peach, 2009; Shon, 2010).

While generally recognizing spatial clustering to be the outcome of discriminatory practices and the limited economic resources of immigrant and minority groups, scholarly analyses at times can reinforce stereotypes of immigrant and minority neighbourhoods by treating them as sites of social pathology (Wacquant, 1997). As with urban ecologists in the past, scholars today sometimes describe the ghetto as a causal agent in creating and reinforcing disadvantage by concentrating the negative social effects of joblessness and disconnecting people from job-finding networks. The notion of 'neighbourhood effects' has informed dispersal programmes in some countries that attempt to remove poor, racialized groups from areas of concentrated poverty in order to break the cycle a social dysfunction (for a critical discussion, see Slater, 2013). Certainly the link between neighbourhoods and social outcomes cannot be dismissed, but it is unclear that moving racialized groups outside of particular neighbourhoods can solve structural inequalities that manifest themselves in segmented labour and housing markets. At the same time, by viewing immigrant and minority neighbourhoods as problems in and of themselves, there is a tendency to ignore the ways in which they might be sites of community, identity, social capital, and rich cultural production (Philips et al., 2007; also Gilroy, 1993). There is, it seems, a balance to be struck between viewing immigrants as victims of discrimination and as agents who exercise some degree of choice in where they live and with whom they associate.

It should be noted that many scholars have grown uncomfortable with the term 'assimilation'—a term that has sometimes been associated with a belief that the disappearance of distinctive immigrant identities is not only inevitable but desirable. For some, 'integration' is a more politically neutral term that makes no judgement about the desirability of immigrants' adoption of dominant cultural norms. Whether they are using the term 'assimilation' or 'integration', however, scholars are generally interested in assessing the extent to which cultural 'others' are becoming more like the **mainstream** (a concept that relates to middle-class whites in most Global North contexts) in terms of education level, residential patterns, civic engagement, employment, and cultural practices. Scores of empirical studies attempt to uncover the varying levels of integration among different immigrant groups and to identify which characteristics of immigrants and host societies seem to promote or to hinder the incorporation of immigrants into various spheres of mainstream life.

There is significant consensus today among scholars that integration (or assimilation, if you prefer) takes place along highly differentiated or 'segmented' trajectories that are shaped, on the one hand, by immigrant traits and resources (e.g. human and social capital), and, on the other hand, by the political, economic, and social characteristics of receiving societies (e.g. local labour market structures, racial and ethnic hierarchies, and naturalization policies) (see for instance, Portes and Zhou, 1993; Ellis and Almgren, 2009; Neckerman, et al., 1999; Portes, et al., 2005). Depending on the particular confluence of variables and circumstances, immigrants and their descendants can experience upward mobility into the dominant socioeconomic group, or they can be pushed downward into a racialized, ghettoized underclass.

Integration studies, in short, focus on the ways in which place- and group-specific characteristics combine to produce measurable social outcomes. What, then, is the relationship between integration and citizenship? How are contexts of settlement—the constraints placed on immigrants and the opportunities afforded to them—shaped by citizenship policies that define the boundaries of the community of citizens? How might the particular regime of rights, privileges, and legal status that exists in a given host society shape immigrants' access to the privileged spaces, spheres, and pathways of dominant groups?

Even a cursory look within immigrant-receiving societies suggests that these relationships are not always clear-cut. Israel, for instance, has an expansionary immigration policy inscribed in the 1950 Law of Return, which grants formal citizenship to any Jew who wishes to settle in Israel. Yet despite their inclusion in the structures of citizenship and in national narratives of Jewish return, some Jewish immigrant groups have been treated as outsiders and have experienced high levels of deprivation. For instance, Mizrahi (Middle Eastern) Jews, who began to immigrate to Israel in the 1950s, were widely viewed as culturally backward by the established Ashkenazi (European) Jewish population. Ashkenazi Jews sought to limit the settlement of Mizrahi Jews in Israel's larger cities, reasoning that such settlement would inevitably lead to zones of poverty and crime. The Israeli state, dominated by Ashkenazi Jews, therefore embarked on a programme of planned housing settlements in frontier regions as a means to assimilate Mizrahi Jews and to secure Israel's territory. Ashkenazi Jews generally shunned these settlements, and the 'development towns' soon became isolated spaces of deprivation containing an almost entirely Mizrahi population (Yiftachel, 2000; see also Elias and Kemp, 2010).

Formal citizenship for Mizrahi Jews therefore does not necessarily signify full inclusion in the community of citizens, and conditions of exclusion—racial segregation, educational disparities, and the like—can persist for generations. Still, formal membership is not meaningless. Mizrahi Jews, while socially marginalized, do have access to state protection and state resources, as well as legal status; they, unlike Palestinian exiles, and unlike the thousands of non-Jewish low-skilled migrant workers from Africa and Asia who reside in Israel, are entitled to land, housing, job training, formal employment, and social services (Minghuan, 2012). They also have a clear political stake in Israeli society, and they have achieved an influential political voice in Israel in recent years (Acosta, 2014). In the following section,

Plate 7.1 A welcome sign and an Israeli flag hang at Ulpan Etzion in Jerusalem
Source: © RONEN ZVULUN/Reuters/Corbis

we consider in more general terms how systems of rights and entitlements associated with membership in the community of citizens can shape integration outcomes in particular contexts.

Citizenship and integration in national contexts

Relationships between citizenship and integration undoubtedly are complicated, yet scholars have noted some broad tendencies among immigrant-receiving societies and have sought to link certain citizenship regime types to distinctive integration outcomes. Some scholars suggest that states and societies tend to follow relatively stable policy trajectories rooted in forma-

tive national experiences—a tendency scholars call 'path dependency' (Favell, 1998). From this view, past policy decisions and approaches inform future ones, and current policies bear the imprint of previous policy debates and formulations. Scholars working from this perspective have most commonly distinguished between countries founded upon ethnic conceptions of nationhood, in which societal membership is based on blood-ties and lineage, and those founded upon civic conception of nationhood, in which membership is based upon commitment to foundational or constitutional principles rather than descent (Brubaker, 1990; Koopmans and Statham, 1999; Greenfeld, 1992; Reeskens and Hooghe, 2010). **Ethnic politics** are seen to adopt more exclusionary policies towards immigrants, often restricting formal citizenship to those with blood ties to the national community (known as **jus sanguinis**, or rule of blood) and in some cases by denying the very existence of settled minority communities. Meanwhile, societies founded upon civic conceptions of nationhood are regarded as more accepting of immigrants as potential citizens, often granting formal membership based solely on birth on national territory (known as **jus soli**, or the rule of soil).

There is some validity to these distinctions. Take, for example, Germany, which, up until the late 1990s, was an exemplar of ethnic constructions of nationhood and citizenship. For decades, Germany refused to recognize itself as a country of immigration despite its long history of reliance on immigrant labour. While denouncing Nazi ideologies of racial supremacy, the (West) German state after World War II nonetheless maintained an ethnic conception of citizenship that guided its policy of granting automatic citizenship to ethnic Germans fleeing from (or expelled by) communist regimes in Eastern Europe. At the same time that it prioritized the immigration of ethnic Germans, the government treated post-war immigrant workers from Turkey, North Africa, and Eastern and Southern Europe as *guests*. The state reinforced the temporary status of guest workers by placing them in dormitory-type housing, limiting the length of labour contracts, and discouraging the entry of dependents. Even as the permanent settlement of guest workers and their reunification with their family members became evident by the mid-1970s, the German government continued to treat them as foreigners, offering incentives to repatriate, limiting naturalization rights, and, in some Länder, financing schools where Turkish-origin children would learn their 'mother tongue' to aid their presumed reintegration back into Turkish society (Smolicz, 1990). Changes to these policies and the extension of German citizenship to 'foreigners' came only gradually and after intervention by the German

courts (Joppke, 1999). Even with the growing inclusiveness of key state and labour-market institutions (including access to Germany's robust vocational training and apprenticeship system), the Turkish community continued to experience high levels of unemployment, welfare dependency, and poor academic achievement. Faist (1993) noted the persistent tendency in the 1980s and 1990s to view Turkish-origin youth as a 'problem group' and to relegate them to special programmes for the 'disadvantaged' in which there was little hope of acquiring an apprenticeship. The participation of Turkish-origin youth in 'dead-end' training programmes 'turned immigrant school-leavers into foreigners, a stigmatized minority' (Faist, 1993, 321; also Smolicz, 1990).

Many other countries fit the ethnic citizenship mould. Greece, for instance, adheres to a jus sanguinis system of citizenship that has made it extremely difficult for migrants to gain legal status or for the Greek-born children of migrants to access Greek citizenship. Greek society as a whole has tended to view migrants not as potential citizens but as expendable, temporary, cheap labour, and there have been few efforts to extend formal rights or privileges to this group. Since 2009, when Greece plunged into a major financial crisis, violent attacks on migrants have become increasingly common. Some of this violence has been supported by a virulently anti-immigrant political party known as Golden Dawn, which gained several seats in the Greek Parliament in the wake of the financial crisis and has since become Greece's third largest political party (Ayiomamitis, 2015; Koronaiou and Sakellariou, 2013). Like Greece, Japan has practised a form of xenophobic ethno-nationalism evident in the country's reluctance to recognize and extend full membership to its sizable immigrant population. The state's treatment of the 600,000 Koreans residing in Japan today illustrates how state policies and practices tied to ethnic models of citizenship can hinder the incorporation of foreign residents into the body politic. As described in Chapter 2, colonial policies and labour recruitment strategies during Japan's occupation of Korea (1910–45) led to the settlement of around two million Koreans in Japan. Under the Japanese occupation, Koreans had Japanese nationality, albeit with the inferior political and social status of colonial subjects. With the collapse of Japan's empire, Koreans in Japan lost their Japanese nationality, and the Japanese state sought to repatriate them. Many, in fact, did return to Korea, but some stayed because of insecure political and economic conditions in Korea. These became known as 'zainichi' (meaning 'staying in Japan'). Japan in subsequent years offered permanent residency and some social benefits to Koreans (many of whom registered as South Korean citizens). But despite some measure of legal security, Koreans existed in a social climate shaped by ideologies of mono-ethnicity and by 'the colonial legacy of contempt for Koreans' (Tai, 2004, 359). Their inferior status manifested itself in labour- and housing-market discrimination and in inequalities in the educational sector. Interestingly, and in contrast to Greece and Germany, the Japanese state has permitted and even expected Korean residents to naturalize. But until recently, naturalization was burdensome and expensive, and it required Koreans essentially to reject their Korean identity by adopting Japanese names and accepting Japanese norms. Many Koreans therefore declined to naturalize, and they have tended to identify strongly with either North or South Korean political organizations (Chapman, 2004).

As disadvantaged as their position has been, the Koreans in Japan have had a relatively privileged position compared to migrants from the Philippines, Thailand, China, and other Asian countries. These migrants began to arrive in large numbers in the 1980s despite severe legal restrictions in Japan on unskilled labour migration—restrictions that employers circumvented through state-sanctioned 'training programmes' for foreign workers. Negative attitudes towards Asian migrants and the state's commitment to principles of ethnocultural homogeneity informed efforts in the 1980s and 1990s to recruit Japanese-origin workers from South America to fill low-end jobs in the manufacturing sector. Unlike Asian workers, these Japanese-Brazilians and Japanese-Peruvians (the descendants of late 19th-century contract labourers) were given legal residency permits and access to the labour market, though this preferential treatment did not fully compensate for their unfamiliarity with Japanese language and social norms (Yamanaka, 1996; see also Tsuda, 1999).

Societies built upon civic conceptions of nationhood and citizenship pose a different set of problems and issues with respect to immigrant integration. To reiterate, **civic polities** are those in which membership does not hinge primarily on ethnic membership, but rather, on the individual's commitment to the laws and constitutional principles of the polity. In theory, anyone, regardless of race or ethno-national origins, can become a member of the polity, often by birth on national territory. Civic polities, therefore, are relatively willing to accept (and even eager to attract) immigrants from a wide array of backgrounds as potential members of the polity. This has been the case in historic settler societies like the United States, Australia, Canada, Argentina, and Brazil. It has also been the case in France, which has absorbed millions of migrants from the rest of Europe and from its (former) colonies over the past century and a half. The United States continues to be the single largest recipient of immigrants in the world, and Australia, Canada, and France are also among the top ten immigrant recipients today. These societies have very distinctive histories and political systems, but common to them is the elevation of liberal constitutional ideals of equality, liberty, and individualism to the level of civic religion. For many immigrants, full formal membership has been a possibility and a reality, and prominent voices within these societies have upheld the idea that people from different national and religious backgrounds can join the community of citizens.

The relative openness of the civic polity comes with many caveats. France and the United States, for instance, have often insisted on a degree of conformity to societal norms and a visible commitment to a common national identity, which is typically construed as culturally neutral or 'universal'. Debates in France since the 1980s over the wearing of Islamic head coverings can be understood in this light. French politicians and public intellectuals treated the public display of religious identity through the Islamic headscarf as an assault on French egalitarianism and **laïcité**. Laïcité is a concept borne of many struggles between the Catholic Church and the French state throughout the 19th century and historically has denoted the subordination of religious authority to secular authority. Increasingly, laïcité has also come to signify the (supposed) neutrality of the public sphere and public spaces, which demands that citizens confine personal religiosity within the private realm. In practice, the concept of laïcité has been deployed almost entirely in relation to Islam, which many non-Muslims in France associate with fundamentalism, extremism, and the oppression of women (see Bowen (2007) for a detailed discussion of public discourses surrounding headscarves). The hostility towards the headscarf and the desire to expel religious signifiers to the private sphere speaks more broadly to a profound distrust of any form of 'communalism', or the assertion of group identities. This wariness towards ethnic self-consciousness can be seen in the French state's long-standing efforts to control immigrant voluntary organizations (especially those associated with Arabs and Muslims) and to steer them toward particular assimilatory ends (Nicholls, 2012). It is evident, as well, in the state's reluctance to collect census data on the basis of race or religion. Silverman (2007, 635) notes the irony that in politicizing 'certain differences (considered unacceptable in the public sphere) while depoliticizing others (considered "neutral" and "value-free")', the French

state fixes ever more firmly the boundaries of otherness in French society.

This aversion to group specificity is less pronounced in the United States, which recognizes different racial categories in the census and which has instituted 'affirmative action' programmes to compensate for past discrimination against certain groups, especially African Americans. But even in the United States, group recognition has its limits, and there has been fierce opposition to affirmative action and the consideration of race in university admissions and hiring decisions. Recent US Supreme Court decisions have upheld the viewpoint that racial preferences run contrary to principles of egalitarianism and individualism, though universities and other institutions may continue to implement policies designed to increase diversity. More generally, there is a strong current of thought that political mobilization along the lines of race and ethnicity—what critics call 'identity politics'—threatens to fragment the polity and to undermine national unity, especially when it influences school and university curricula (e.g. Schlesinger, 1998). (See Box 7.2 for a discussion of the terms 'race' and 'ethnicity'.)

Civic and ethnic polities, then, have distinctive politics that stem from particular conceptualizations of nationhood and citizenship. They also have some distinctive immigration outcomes: while ethnic polities often host large populations of non-citizens who are politically and economically marginalized, civic polities provide pathways for legal membership but make full, substantive membership contingent on newcomers' adoption of dominant values and norms. Yet even as we draw some meaningful distinctions between ethnic and civic polities, we need to recognize that few societies operate purely as civic or ethnic citizenship regimes and that in reality, the lines between regime types are very blurry (Bloemraad, et al., 2008; Brubaker, 1999; Yack, 1996). Nation-building, we are reminded, requires the constant articulation of who 'we' are as a people, and such articulations often

BOX 7.2 A NOTE ON TERMINOLOGY: RACE VERSUS ETHNICITY

Concepts of **race** and **ethnicity** come up frequently in discussions of citizenship and integration. The term 'ethnicity' comes from the Greek word 'ethnos', meaning a group of individuals of the same kind or type. The word refers to a group whose members are bound together by common identity, norms, social practices, and ways of life that we often describe as 'culture'. Contemporary scholars generally recognize ethnicity to be socially constructed—something that people create and foster—rather than an immutable or inheritable set of traits (Nagel, 1994). Migration scholars have long understood immigrant ethnicity to fade over time and/or to be transformed or 'reinvented' in receiving contexts (e.g. Park and Burgess, 1921; Conzen et al., 1992). This idea of ethnicity as a set of voluntary and changeable social bonds is central to the concept of assimilation.

The term 'race' has been used in the West since the 16th century to describe groups of people with common hereditary traits or common descent. In the 19th and early 20th centuries, the term came to reflect a belief in the separate biological origins of various groups (though it was also commonly used in early sociological scholarship in a way that more closely resembles contemporary usage of 'ethnicity' or 'nationality'). Such beliefs in the separate origins of human communities have been thoroughly refuted, but the term 'race' has maintained its currency. Today, scholars use 'race' to refer to groups who are stigmatized by their visible, physical differences and who are subject to various forms of discrimination and subordination. Scholars, in this sense, understand race to be more persistent and less voluntaristic than ethnicity.

It is important to note that the distinction between ethnicity and race can be somewhat arbitrary. In other words, scholars (and societies in general) apply these terms in ways that reflect their own perceptions of the differences associated with particular groups. One example of this can be seen in the US census, which has superimposed an 'ethnic' Hispanic category atop existing 'racial' categories of 'black' and 'white'. By treating Hispanic as an ethnic category, the census glosses over the immense social diversity that exists in Latin America, while ignoring the significant, persistent discrimination experienced especially by Mexican-Americans, who constitute 65 percent of so-called Hispanics. The term 'racialization' can help us to avoid the problems that arise when scholars treat race and ethnicity as objective categories and attempt to place groups in one or the other. Racialization refers to the *process* by which dominant groups denigrate, stigmatize, and subordinate others based on any number of traits, including not only skin colour but also religion, language, and other cultural practices. From this perspective, social ideologies and practices produce a material reality of race, but race itself is not an explanation for social patterns (Anthias and Yuval-Davis, 2005). Unfortunately, the concept of racialization raises its own set of thorny questions. How, for instance, can scholars evaluate the material outcomes of racialization processes without using the same racial categories that they reject? Is it possible or desirable to avoid racial categories when these have such profound social meaning? Such quandaries are not easily resolved, but they do indicate that categories of race and ethnicity should not be taken as givens. For further discussion of ethnicity and race, see Back and Solomos (2000), Omi and Winant (2014), and Gilroy (2013).

rest on assumptions about fundamental differences between ethnic and racial groups, even in countries that adhere to civic conceptions of citizenship (Glenn, 2011). Most societies combine elements of jus soli and jus sanguinis citizenship regimes, linking formal membership both to residency and to inheritance, and most societies express a greater or lesser degree of ambivalence towards foreigners that plays out in formal and informal practices towards immigrants. So while the link between ethnicity and societal membership may be more pronounced in those societies associated with ethnic citizenship regimes, even those countries that have been seemingly most open to immigrant settlement have often connected membership to notions of ethnicity and race, as seen with historical bars on Asian migration and naturalization in Australia, Canada, and the US.

The fact that those racial bars were eventually lifted highlights that the character of citizenship and integration policies can change quite dramatically over time, path-dependency notwithstanding. A recent example of such a dramatic shift can be seen in Greece, where the left-wing government elected in 2015 has promised to implement a new citizenship law that will allow the children of long-term residents the opportunity to naturalize as Greek citizens. Of course, policy shifts can move in the direction of greater closure, as seen with the 'Pasqua Laws' in France, which sought in the 1990s to restrict automatic jus soli citizenship by requiring children born in France to foreign parents to declare their intention to acquire French citizenship (Hamilton, et al., 2004). In the following sections, we set aside typologies of citizenship and integration to consider some broad trends that cut across national contexts. As we have seen with entry and border control politics, liberal-democratic societies are constituted by different interests and voices that can push and pull policies in different directions. Moreover, nation-states are not self-contained entities, but rather are influenced by shifting circumstances in other countries and, increasingly, by global human rights norms. Looking across immigrant-receiving contexts today, we see a complex mix of policies, laws, and public discourses that indicate both the inclusion and exclusion of long-term immigrant residents.

The opening up of societal membership

We begin by considering some of the ways in which societal membership has become more accessible to and inclusive of immigrants across national contexts. First, while some contemporary societies hold immigrants in a subordinate position and offer few opportunities to join formally the body politic, many receiving societies have extended at least some of the rights and protections associated with citizenship to non-citizen immigrants. The extension of substantive rights to non-citizens living within state borders is often described as a form of **post-national citizenship**, a term that encompasses both the attachment of rights to personhood regardless of nationality and the organization of political life beyond nation-state boundaries (Soysal, 1994). Post-national citizenship has been attributed to the increasing salience of international human rights norms since World War II and the development of international institutions, as well as transnational social movements, committed to the implementation of these norms (Sassen, 2002).

The phenomenon of post-national citizenship has been discussed most extensively in the context of European countries, where long-term residents typically enjoy most of the rights of citizens—a status that Hammar (1990) terms **denizenship**. In Germany, for instance, guest workers were generally ineligible for naturalization until the late 1990s, yet constitutional court rulings in the 1970s and 1980s affirmed their access to civil and social rights and guaranteed their rights to family reunification (Joppke, 1999). In some cases, like Sweden, Denmark, Ireland, and Luxembourg, long-term residents have been granted local voting rights in addition to civil and social rights (Bauböck, 2005; Groenendijk, 2008). The adoption of post-national citizenship norms has been especially remarkable in some newer immigrant-receiving societies, like Spain and Italy, where laws passed from the 1980s onward guaranteed basic equality between (legal) immigrants and non-immigrants, barred discrimination in housing and labour markets, and guaranteed access to some or all of the state welfare system. In 2000, the Spanish state went further by opening up access to the country's healthcare system—which had already granted all Spanish citizens, EU nationals, and legal immigrants the right to healthcare through enrollment in the social security system—to undocumented immigrants who registered in their local municipality as residents (Calavita, 2005). The extension of rights to non-citizens seen in European Union member states has been affirmed in various ways by the EU itself. While individual member states have preserved their role as gatekeepers of legal permanent residency (as well as citizenship), the EU has stipulated that those who *do* secure permanent residency in one EU state may have access to all EU states through a standard EU residency permit. Moreover, the EU specifies that permanent residents, regardless of where they are living in the EU, will enjoy equal treatment with EU nationals in terms of social and civil rights, workplace protections, and access to educational and employment resources (European Union, 2003; for a more normative discussion of residency-based rights, or **jus domicile**, see Bauder, 2014).

Second, in addition to extending citizenship rights to non-citizens, many immigrant-receiving societies have severed links between ethnicity/race and formal citizenship status, thereby opening up full membership to those formerly excluded from the body politic. As alluded to earlier, this decoupling of ethnicity/race and citizenship took place in Australia, Canada, and the US in the 1960s and 1970s when race-based restrictions and quotas were replaced with 'race-neutral' policies based on combinations of skills, family ties, and humanitarian needs. As a result of these new policies, Australia, Canada, and the US have experienced the significant diversification of their citizenry. More recently, we see this decoupling taking place in countries like Germany and Japan. Having extended most of the rights of citizenship to long-term residents, the German government in 1999 took the further step of granting automatic citizenship to the children born in Germany to foreign parents after January 1, 2000. The 1999 law specified that upon turning 23, these children would need to choose between their parents' citizenship and German citizenship, but this provision was significantly loosened in 2014, and young people today may retain dual citizenship provided they have lived in Germany for at least eight years. This new legislation permitting dual citizenship is widely regarded as having removed one of the major hurdles to naturalization among the descendants of guest workers, and supporters of citizenship reform argue that tolerance for dual citizenship will greatly increase young Turkish-German people's sense of belonging in German society (we return to the topic of dual citizenship in a moment).

Japan has also witnessed a de-linking of ethnicity and formal membership, though this process in Japan has been driven more by grassroots mobilization than by the state. As described above, the Japanese government for many years offered naturalization to long-term Korean residents, but placed such onerous conditions on naturalization that most Koreans maintained their status as foreign residents. Partly due to the influence of international human rights norms and partly the emergence of a civil rights movement in Japan, the Japanese government in the 1990s became more lenient in granting naturalization and removed the more burdensome requirements placed on Korean residents. Even more significant in promoting naturalization was the mobilization of young people against monocultural conceptions of nationhood and citizenship. These young people, more than the state, have given public validation to notions of cultural diversity and have made hyphenated identities more acceptable (these kinds of negotiations of societal membership by immigrants are the focus of Chapter 8) (Tai, 2004; Chapman, 2004).

The ideas espoused by young Koreans in Japan reflect broader intellectual trends associated since the 1970s with **multiculturalism**—a political philosophy that has advocated not only the decoupling of ethnicity and citizenship but also the formal acknowledgement and accommodation of differences within society. Multiculturalism has not been universally embraced, but it has had a significant influence on many major immigrant-receiving societies, including Canada, Australia, the US, and Britain. Multiculturalism takes many different forms, but in all cases involves a reimagining of the nation as a collection of distinctive cultural communities rather than as a homogenous cultural entity. For proponents of multiculturalism, recognition and

Plate 7.2 Immigrants on subway with citizenship poster in background, Toronto, Canada

Source: Aga Szewczyk

validation of cultural differences is fundamental to political liberalism and is a prerequisite to the full incorporation of immigrants and minorities into national societies (Kymlicka, 2007).

In practical policy terms, multiculturalism can involve the granting of linguistic and cultural rights to certain immigrant and minority groups, the extension of political representation to these groups, and/or the targeting of government assistance to foster social equality between groups. Such policies have been most salient in Australia and Canada, where the expansion of non-European immigration has been accompanied by new narratives of national identity and new policies to accommodate—and indeed, to celebrate—cultural differences. To illustrate, multiculturalist discourses and policies in Canada emerged from political efforts to recognize the ethno-linguistic rights of French-speaking Canadians; principles of linguistic and cultural recognition were then extended to include the country's growing population of immigrants (see Wood and Gilbert, 2005). Cultural pluralism has since been enshrined in the Canadian Charter of Rights and Freedoms, and public policy from the national to the municipal level protects cultural freedom and offers formal recognition to certain cultural groups (including aboriginal groups) as a means of fostering full and equal participation in public life. The enactment of the Employment Equity Act in 1995, for instance, required that employers increase the representation of women, people with disabilities, Aboriginal people, and 'visible minorities' (mainly from immigrant backgrounds). Some scholars credit Canadian multicultural policies and narratives and its active support for immigrant communities with creating a strong sense of inclusion among immigrants, evident in the country's relatively high levels of naturalization (Bloemraad, 2006; Wright and Bloemraad, 2012).

Finally, connected to the extension of rights to non-citizens, the decoupling of ethnicity and formal membership and the adoption of multicultural policies has been the growing acceptance of **dual citizenship** in many immigrant-receiving societies (Howard, 2005; Faist, 2007). The modern nation-state system has been predicated on an exclusive, one-to-one relationship between the individual and the state, and becoming a naturalized citizen has typically meant relinquishing citizenship in one's country of origin. But attitudes about dual citizenship both in sending and receiving societies have shifted significantly. As discussed in Chapter 4, major immigrant-sending countries, like Mexico, Turkey, and India, have changed citizenship laws in recent decades to permit dual citizenship among their émigrés, mainly as a strategy to garner migrant remittances. The idea here is that by becoming full-fledged citizens of countries of settlement, émigrés are more likely to have secure positions in the labour market and hence higher earnings and remittances (there are, of course, other political reasons why sending states support dual citizenship—see Whitaker, 2011). At the same time, immigrant-receiving states in the Global North have become more lenient towards dual citizenship, dropping, or not enforcing, the requirement that immigrants relinquish existing citizenships upon naturalization. The reasoning behind the acceptance of dual citizenship is that immigrants are more likely to integrate fully if they naturalize, and they are more likely to naturalize if they are not forced to relinquish their nationality of birth (see Spång (2007) for a discussion of this reasoning in Swedish policy debates). In addition to the interests of sending and receiving states in fostering immigrant integration (albeit for different ends), international human rights norms—especially those relating to the right to possess a nationality—have had some bearing on dual citizenship policies; so, too, has increasing gender equity in citizenship laws, which ensures that more female immigrants are able to pass their citizenship to their children when they marry someone of a different nationality (Faist, 2007).

As we have seen in Chapter 4, dual citizenship has facilitated migrants' continued political and economic participation in countries of origin.

Whether it also encourages integration in *receiving* societies in terms of civic engagement and upward socioeconomic mobility is difficult to say. Some scholars point to a certain instrumentalism among immigrants, whereby acquiring a second citizenship is a means of acquiring a desirable passport and access to wealthy labour markets (e.g. Mavroudi, 2008). Some commentators interpret this instrumentalism as evidence of immigrants' lack of meaningful affinity with their adopted country. Others, however, demonstrate that dual citizenship is wholly compatible with immigrants' civic participation and incorporation in immigrant-receiving societies (e.g. Escobar, 2004). Regardless of actual outcomes, dual citizenship signifies the erosion of nation-state exclusivity and signals the state's acknowledgement that members of the polity may have multiple allegiances and attachments.

Citizenship closure

The shift towards more open, expansive, and flexible citizenship regimes, marked by post-national rights, the decoupling of ethnicity and citizenship, and the growing acceptance of dual citizenship, has been remarkable. But it must be emphasized that the opening up of citizenship has not been a linear process; there are still major differences between nation-states, and major contradictions within them, in terms of attitudes towards immigrant populations. Regardless of their rhetorical commitments to international human rights norms and their seeming acceptance of migrants' transnational identities, nation-states continuously assert their authority over the lives of immigrants and determine the conditions under which immigrants live and labour. National societies today prioritize the management and control of immigrant populations and the regulation of access to welfare states, labour markets, and polities, and some states—especially those in the Arab Gulf region—severely restrict the labour-market and geographical mobility of immigrant populations. In some instances, like Japan and Israel, citizenship rights and state support continue to be offered to some immigrant groups but withheld from others. For those excluded from the privileged boundaries of citizenship (or denizenship), life can be characterized by severe economic and social vulnerability.

Insofar as citizenship regimes shift over time, they do not necessarily move along a single trajectory towards greater openness and accessibility. On the contrary, legislatures can restrict or claw back rights, often prompted by anti-immigrant sentiment among electorates and among political elites. So while we can identify examples of the decoupling of ethnicity and citizenship, we can also find instances in which the relationship between ethnicity and citizenship, has, in fact, become stronger. For example, at the very moment when Britain was devising a multicultural system of integration, it was also contriving to limit what had been a broadly conceived ideal of British citizenship linked to the British Empire (see Box 7.3). More specifically, the concept of **patriality**, which worked its way into British immigration legislation in the 1960s and 1970s, reinforced settlement rights of those with at least one grandparent born or naturalized in Britain (i.e. a form of jus sanguinis). In practice, patriality worked to strip citizens of the New Commonwealth (i.e. Britain's former colonies in Asia, Africa, and the Caribbean) of their right to settle in Britain, since those citizens were unlikely to have a grandparent born or naturalized in Britain. At the same time, it affirmed the settlement rights, and hence the essential Britishness, of the descendants of whites who settled Britain's semi-autonomous dominions (i.e. Australia, Canada, New Zealand, and South Africa) and who colonized Zimbabwe and Kenya (Paul, 1997).

BOX 7.3 BRITISH MULTICULTURALISM AND THE 'RACE RELATIONS' PARADIGM

Multicultural philosophies emerged in the 1970s in several wealthy immigrant-receiving societies. In some instances these built upon and reworked much older systems of cultural recognition. British multiculturalism, for instance, grew out of colonial policies that generally eschewed the assimilation of subject populations and that often reinforced or even fabricated communal identities as a method of rule. In the early 20th century, as ideas of self-determination gained momentum worldwide, the British political elite worked to reconceptualize the British Empire as a multinational 'commonwealth' whose members enjoyed (at least in theory) equal status (Mongia, 1999). After World War II, notions of equality among citizens of the British Commonwealth remained central to Britain's imperial identity and prestige, even as its formal empire collapsed in the face of anti-colonial movements. This liberal commonwealth ideology led for a time to liberal settlement policies in Britain despite misgivings among state elites about the desirability of non-white immigration (Paul, 1997).

As these misgivings grew more pronounced through the 1950s and 1960s, the British state began to impose ever stricter limits on the immigration of people from South Asia, Africa, and the Caribbean, while instituting multiculturalist policies to facilitate the inclusion of those already settled. Limitations on immigration, in this sense, were seen to be crucial to the success of multiculturalism. British multiculturalism developed through the 1970s under the rubric of 'Race Relations'. The Race Relations model centred on an ethic of 'tolerance' that was first given public expression in 1966 by the British Home Secretary, Roy Jenkins, who described integration 'not as a flattening process of assimilation but as equal opportunity, accompanied by cultural diversity, in an atmosphere of mutual tolerance'. A decade later, the British state created the Commission for Racial Equality to investigate and to enforce anti-discrimination statutes, partly through

Plate 7.3 Numerous Jamaicans disembarking the MV Empire Windrush in 1948
Source: © Hulton-Deutsch/Hulton-Deutsch Collection/Corbis

the careful monitoring of 'equal opportunity' hiring practices in local governments, universities, and businesses. On a more quotidian level, multiculturalism involved the ad hoc, pragmatic accommodation of cultural differences in everyday life—for instance, the provision of halal lunches for Muslim school children, and modifications of workplace uniforms for those wearing headscarves and turbans for religious reasons (Favell, 1998).

Multiculturalism always had its detractors on the political right and the political left, and, as we describe later in this chapter, multicultural policies increasingly came under attack starting in the late 1980s over concerns with the supposed non-integration of South Asian Muslims. Reflecting a growing disenchantment with a race-based model of multiculturalism, the British government replaced the Commission for Racial Equality in 2006 with the Equality and Human Rights Commission, which addresses multiple forms of discrimination, not just those based on official racial categories. For further discussion of political challenges to contemporary British multiculturalism, see Modood (2005).

In some instances the racially restrictive implications of changing citizenship laws are not immediately evident. For instance, a 2008 amendment to the Canadian Citizenship Act was widely hailed for extending (or restoring) citizenship to those who had previously been ineligible for or had lost their Canadian citizenship for a variety of reasons under earlier citizenship laws—in many cases because of the marital status of parents or because parents had acquired another citizenship while living abroad. Such individuals had come to be known in the Canadian media as 'Lost Canadians' (Harder, 2010). At the same time, the 2008 legislation restricted the inheritability of citizenship by second and subsequent generations born overseas to Canadian citizens. In other words, those inheriting Canadian citizenship when born abroad would no longer be entitled to pass on that citizenship to children not born on Canadian soil (previous laws had permitted second and subsequent generations to apply for the retention of Canadian citizenship before their 28th birthday) (Winter, 2014).

On the surface, both of these provisions seemed to represent a further liberalization of Canadian citizenship. The first provision rectified past injustices that had denied citizenship to people based on patriarchal norms and non-recognition of dual citizens, while the second provision represented the further de-linking of formal citizenship status from blood ties and inheritance. Upon closer inspection, however, these provisions have tended to reinforce particular, racialized ideas about what counts as an 'authentic' connection to Canada and which groups are deserving of liberal treatment (Winter, 2014). Many Lost Canadians are the descendants of white, European-origin Canadians who had naturalized in the United States. Despite living abroad, these Lost Canadians were accepted as 'real' Canadians who had been denied their rightful place in Canadian society. In sharp contrast, those targeted by new restrictions on citizenship inheritance tend to be those who

have acquired Canadian citizenship since the 1970s—most of them from Asian and Middle Eastern countries. This restriction was conceived in the wake of a military conflict in Lebanon in 2006, which required the evacuation of hundreds of Canadian citizens residing in or visiting Lebanon at the time. There was 'a widespread assumption that [*these*] dual citizens had a thin allegiance to Canada, and yet they imposed a heavy burden on the Canadian government and taxpayer when they made rights claims' (Nyers, 2010, 54, quoted in Winter, 2014). Unlike the Lost Canadians, whose dual citizenship and lack of residency in Canada was viewed as non-threatening, the Lebanese-Canadian dual citizens were portrayed as free riders and people lacking a 'real connection' with Canada (for further discussion of discriminatory trends in Canada's citizenship and integration policies, see Tonon and Raney, 2013).

Changes such as those seen in Canada reflect a renewed emphasis in many wealthy immigrant-receiving countries on the connection between formal membership, rights, and national identity (Joppke, 2004). In the United States, for instance, welfare reform legislation passed in 1996 (called, rather tellingly, the Personal Responsibility and Work Opportunity Reconciliation Act, or **PRWORA**) revoked the rights of legal permanent residents to means-tested federal benefits during their first five years of residence and barred them from some benefits altogether. This legislation was passed in a context of mounting claims (mostly exaggerated) that immigrants were abusing the welfare system and placing an excessive burden on the federal budget (Gerken, 2013). PRWORA, along with a series of congressional acts that greatly expanded the government's power to deport non-citizens, led to an uptick in naturalization rates among those who had previously been content with denizenship—a phenomenon that scholars call 'defensive' or 'protective' naturalization (Massey and Pren, 2012; Gilbertson and Singer, 2003).

Meanwhile, political discourse in European

countries has swung decidedly away from multicultural inclusion and towards notions of conformity, cohesion, and immigrants' responsibilities to the body politic (Alexander, 2013; Kofman, 2005; Mitchell, 2003; Vertovec and Wessendorf, 2010). This shift can be linked to a string of urban disturbances and terrorist incidents, starting in the late 1980s, involving European Muslims. In the wake of these incidents (the latest being a terrorist attack on Brussels in March 2016), a growing chorus of voices from the media, government, and civil society has argued that multiculturalist ideals of tolerance and diversity have fostered religious extremism. Opposition to multiculturalism and the renewed insistence on immigrants' conformity to national norms has come from across the political spectrum. Indeed, some of the strongest advocates of assimilatory policies, especially with reference to Muslim communities, are former advocates of multiculturalism (Kundnani, 2008).

In the case of Britain, the backlash against multiculturalism began to build in the late 1980s, when groups of British Muslims staged public burnings of Pakistani-British author Salman Rushdie's controversial book *The Satanic Verses* (1988)—an incident that many commentators interpreted as evidence of Muslims' inherent illiberalism (Muslim leaders involved in the book burnings countered that they wished to be protected equally by Britain's anti-blasphemy laws—see Asad (1990) and Cottle (1991) for further discussion). The '**Rushdie Affair**' was followed by other incidents involving British Muslims, including urban disturbances in 2001 and the bombing of the London Underground in 2005, prompting the formulation of a new 'social cohesion' agenda. Advocates of the social cohesion agenda have described Muslims as leading 'parallel lives' isolated from the British mainstream, and they have increasingly required British Muslims to demonstrate their full commitment to British society (for a critical overview, see Finney and Simpson, 2009). Legislative efforts in Britain against arranged marriages and the importation of brides and grooms from South Asia must be interpreted in light of assumptions about Muslim non-integration. (Kalra and Kapoor (2009), Phillips (2006), and Meer, et al. (2010) provide detailed accounts of social cohesion discourses and policies in Britain.)

In the Netherlands, disenchantment with multiculturalism led to the reinstatement of a requirement that immigrants relinquish existing citizenship as a condition for naturalization (though the Dutch state continues to grant exceptions to this requirement). The Netherlands, along with Germany, Britain, Belgium, and other European countries, have in recent years imposed more stringent language and cultural requirements on those wishing to immigrate, especially the foreign-born spouses of long-term residents or naturalized citizens, to demonstrate sufficient integration (Vasta, 2007; Entzinger, 2006). The Dutch government even produced a video to explain to potential immigrants (mainly foreign-born spouses of ethnic-minority Dutch citizens) the core values of Dutch culture, including the acceptance of homosexuality and public nudity; newcomers presumably are required to accept these core values if they wish to join Dutch society, though one might reasonably ask if there is unanimity among Dutch citizens on these issues (see Joppke, 2004).

Uneven landscapes of citizenship and integration

It is therefore difficult to speak unequivocally of a shift to a post-national mode of citizenship, the decoupling of ethnicity and citizenship, or the increasing inclusiveness of national societies. For every instance of societal opening, we can find an example of the reassertion of more bounded conceptions of societal belonging. In most cases, policies towards settled immigrant communities pull in different directions simultaneously, reflecting diverse political pressures and a deep ambivalence towards immigrants. States increasingly make distinctions between those who are wanted and unwanted, desirable and undesirable, and in doing so parse rights and privileges, multiplying and fragmenting the forms of citizenship possible in a given national context. It is perhaps more apt to speak of citizenship*s* in the plural, rather than citizenship in the singular, in recognition of the divergent ways that immigrants can become incorporated into the structures and spheres of social membership (Kofman, 1995, 2002).

The multiplication and fragmentation of citizenship within national contexts is reflected in the uneven geographical landscape of belonging in immigrant-receiving contexts. Citizenship and integration policies, while usually formulated at a national level, are often interpreted and implemented at a subnational level—in regions, provinces, and municipalities, all of which have varying levels of autonomy from central governments (Kofman, 1995; García, 2006). Citizenship, in this sense, is geographically contingent—that is, immigrants' access to rights and societal resources, their social and economic mobility, and their experiences of inclusion or exclusion will reflect localized combinations of policies, practices, and sociopolitical orientations (Varsanyi, 2007). In the US, for instance, the 1996 PRWORA legislation both restricted immigrant access to social welfare and devolved the administration of welfare programmes to state governments. The result has been a very complicated patchwork of welfare benefits and eligibility across the country, with some states providing relatively generous benefits for immigrants—even dedicating state funds for those not eligible for federal programmes— and other states withholding key benefits even from legal immigrants who have fulfilled the five-year moratorium (for a detailed discussion, see Bitler and Hoynes, 2011). In Italy, as well, one finds significant differences between regions, with some, like Emilia-Romagna and Veneto, launching innovative initiatives in the 1990s to improve immigrants' access to healthcare, housing, employment, and other social services, while other regions have done very little to foster immigrant incorporation or equality (Calavita, 2005).

Focusing on the uneven geographical landscape of citizenship draws our attention to the multiple state and non-state actors who shape the experience of citizenship and integration on a day-to-day basis through frequent interactions with immigrants. Of particular importance are actors in the voluntary sector—including philanthropies, non-governmental organizations (NGOs), and civic, labour, and religious groups—who do the everyday work of integration and who mediate relationships between dominant groups and immigrants in particular local contexts. Tsuda (2006) demonstrates in the case of Japan that NGOs, often in partnership with municipal governments, have assumed responsibility for integrating immigrants in the absence of any proactive government policies. NGO engagement with immigrants in Japan, Tsuda suggests, creates a kind of local citizenship that validates the presence of immigrants in particular municipalities. Japanese NGOs have had an especially important role with respect to undocumented workers, whom municipal governments are forbidden by law from assisting. Volunteer groups in Japan assist the undocumented in resolving labour disputes, in accessing medical service, education, and housing, and in regularizing legal status. NGOs also have a crucial role in Southern Europe because of deliberate policies by central governments to subcontract integration activities to the voluntary sector. In Spain, for example, labour unions and advocacy organizations in major cities help immigrants to secure documents, to find jobs, to access healthcare, and to secure shelter (Calavita, 2005; also Merrill, 2006). Likewise, in the United States, the federal government has long relied on voluntary organizations at the local level to assist in the settlement of refugees and to provide English-language instruction and citizenship preparation for immigrants. Many faith-based voluntary organizations advocate on behalf of the most marginalized of immigrants and promote universalistic conceptions of social justice that push against exclusionary nationalisms (Hondagneu-Sotelo, 2006; also Stuesse, 2010).

To be sure, the local voluntary sector is not always a site of progressive, inclusive politics. The local politics of citizenship and integration can also involve the mobilization of citizens' groups against the presence of immigrants. Such has been the case with opposition to the construction of mosques in cities and towns across Europe. Saint-Blancat and Schmidt di Friedberg (2005) describe one such incident in Lodi, a small city in the Lombardy region of Italy, where the municipal council in 2000 granted local Muslims a plot of land to build a new mosque. Local activists affiliated with Lega Nord, a right-wing political organization, responded to this decision by organizing an anti-mosque march through the city and by circulating a petition demanding a stop to the construction plans. Lodi's mosque controversy soon became a national issue—a flashpoint in wider societal debates about the capacity of Italian society to absorb 'foreigners' and to accept cultural and religious differences. Lodi's mayor sought to defuse the situation by recommending another location for the mosque outside the city limits, even though the more distant location would prevent local Muslims from fulfilling their religious obligations. Four years later, the mosque still had not been built, and Lodi's Muslim community was rendered almost entirely invisible.

Many other kinds of spaces besides mosques become sites of contestation over the inclusion of immigrants in the community of citizens. Even relatively privileged immigrant groups can face local opposition when their differences become visible in the urban landscape. Wealthy Chinese immigrants living in Canada and the US, for instance, have faced opposition from local homeowners' associations when

they have attempted to alter or to rebuild their homes in line with their particular family needs and cultural beliefs and practices. For instance, in the Shaughnessy Heights neighbourhood of Vancouver—an exclusive residential enclave with older English-style homes—the construction of so-called 'monster houses' by wealthy Chinese immigrants (intended to accommodate extended families) prompted long-term white residents in the 1980s and 1990s to fight for stricter zoning regulations and for the preservation of the character of the neighbourhood (Mitchell, 1997). Public hearings with local planning officials were highly contentious, pitting the property rights of Chinese newcomers against the interests of long-term Anglo residents. As Mitchell (ibid.) describes, the arguments put forward by white homeowners reflected fears about the loss of a particular Anglo-Canadian way of life to the Chinese newcomers, who were often described as overly competitive and as not conforming to the Anglo-Canadian model of the nuclear family. Lung-Amam (2013) describes a similar series of events in the affluent and increasingly diverse suburban town of Fremont, California. In Fremont, Lung-Amam (ibid.) observes, arguments in favour of restrictive zoning were almost always framed in race-neutral terms, referring to neighbourhood aesthetics and the desire to maintain homeowners' views of Fremont's surrounding hills. But the implication was that Chinese immigrants were out-of-step with local norms and that they should not be permitted to redefine the character of the neighbourhood.

These examples reveal how rights, a sense of belonging, and incorporation into mainstream social spheres are structured and experienced in localities and in the spaces of everyday life (Staeheli et al., 2012). Citizenship and integration are embodied processes that take shape through complex interactions and negotiations between immigrants and citizens. So while we can speak, at one level, of national citizenship regimes that produce particular patterns of integration, we must also recognize that citizenship is not a uniform status and that the relationship between citizenship and integration varies significantly across the national landscape. The attitudes and actions of real people in cities and neighbourhoods, as much as national-level policies, continuously shape and reshape the contours of immigrants' experiences: their access to rights, their physical and socioeconomic mobility, and their ability to negotiate a place for themselves in the community of citizens.

Conclusions

The categories that scholars often use to describe citizenship and integration, while helpful in identifying and comparing patterns of immigrant incorporation across national contexts, tend to obscure the fluidity of citizenship and the dynamics of inclusion and closure that operate within and between national contexts. The incorporation of immigrants, as indicated by their social and economic mobility, their access to housing and other societal resources, and their participation in societal decision-making, hinges at least partly on the roles that dominant groups reserve for immigrants within societies. It hinges, as well, on the extent to which dominant groups view immigrants—with their varying 'racial' characteristics, cultural practices, and levels of human capital—as potential members of the body politic. The extension or withholding of membership, however, is never a clear-cut process (Glenn, 2011). All national societies are replete with contradictions and complexities that produce, simultaneously, patterns of inclusion and exclusion and of downward and upward mobility.

Our discussion in this chapter has focused mainly on the roles of dominant groups— both state and non-state actors—in producing the discursive, institutional, and policy frameworks in which immigrant incorporation takes place. Leading into our final chapter, we wish to emphasize that immigrants, despite their subordinate status in national societies, play a significant role in shaping these frameworks and contesting their strictures (Sassen, 2002; Glenn, 2011). While sometimes silenced by exclusionary practices, immigrants do not passively accept the dictates of dominant groups. Rather, immigrants actively negotiate the rules of membership that they encounter in their everyday interactions with state bureaucrats, teachers, language instructors, social workers, and so on. Immigrants make strategic decisions to conform to dominant norms and practices or to resist, challenge, and rework the terms of membership in the community of citizens. A focus on immigrant agency and everyday interactions between immigrants and non-immigrants helps to shed light on the many inconsistencies in integration outcomes that we see within and across national contexts. For instance, while mosque construction has been a highly contentious issue in many Global North contexts, there are instances in which established communities have accepted or even welcomed mosques (Gale, 2004). And while in many instances dominant groups treat the residential clustering of immigrants as cause for alarm, in other instances, they interpret immigrant neighbourhoods as an asset to cities and an indicator of the overall health of cities. There are many reasons for these differences, but in all cases, immigrants' efforts to develop relationships with established groups and to frame their differences as compatible with local ways of life play an important role in creating particular outcomes (Ehrkamp, 2012). As much as we can point to official citizenship and integration policies as shaping the incorporation of immigrants into receiving societies, we must also consider how immigrants actively lay claim to membership in localities and polities. In the final chapter, we highlight these complexities and focus on the ways in which immigrants shape and transform national societies and national space.

Key terms in this chapter

civic polity

denizenship

dual citizenship

ethnic policy

ethnicity

ghettos

jus domicile

jus sanguinis

jus soli

laïcité

mainstream

multiculturalism

naturalization

patriality

polity

post-national
citizenship

PRWORA

race

Rushdie Affair

Further reading

Alba, A. (2005) Bright vs. blurred boundaries: second generation assimilation and exclusion in France, Germany, and the United States, *Ethnic and Racial Studies*, 28(1): 20–49.

Brubaker, R. (2001) The return of assimilation? Changing perspectives on immigration and its sequels in France, Germany, and the United States, *Ethnic and Racial Studies*, 24(4): 531–548.

Dobrowolsky, A. and Tastsoglou, E. (Eds.) (2013) *Women, Migration and Citizenship: Making Local, National and Transnational Connections*. London: Ashgate.

Kashiwazaki, C. (2013) Incorporating immigrants as foreigners: multicultural politics in Japan, *Citizenship Studies*, 17(1): 31–47.

Ong, A. (1999) *Flexible Citizenship: The Cultural Logics of Transnationality*. Durham, NC: Duke University Press.

Phillips, D. (2010) Minority ethnic segregation, integration and citizenship: a European perspective, *Journal of Ethnic and Migration Studies*, 36(2): 209–225.

Vasta, E. (2013) Do we need social cohesion in the 21st century? Multiple languages of belonging in the metropolis, *Journal of Intercultural Studies*, 34(2): 196–213.

Winders, J. (2013) *Nashville in the New Millennium: Immigrant Settlement, Urban Transformation, and Social Belonging*. New York: Russell Sage Foundation.

References

Acosta, B. (2014) The dynamics of Israel's democratic tribalism, *The Middle East Journal*, 68(2): 268–286.

Alexander, J. C. (2013) Struggling over the mode of incorporation: backlash against multiculturalism in Europe, *Ethnic and Racial Studies*, 36(4): 531–556.

Anderson, K. J. (1991) *Vancouver's Chinatown: Racial Discourse in Canada, 1875–1980*. Quebec City: McGill-Queen's Press.

Anthias, F. and Yuval-Davis, N. (2005) *Racialized Boundaries: Race, Nation, Gender, Colour and Class and the Anti-Racist Struggle*. Abingdon; New York: Routledge.

Antonsich, M. (2012) Exploring the demands of assimilation among white ethnic majorities in Western Europe, *Journal of Ethnic and Migration Studies*, 38(1): 59–76.

Asad, T. (1990) Multiculturalism and British identity in the wake of the Rushdie Affair, *Politics & Society*, 18(4): 455–480.

Ayiomamitis, P. (2015) Trial of far-right Golden Dawn leaders starts in Greece, *Guardian* (20 April). Retrieved from http://www.theguardian.com/world/2015/apr/20/greece-far-right-golden-dawn-nikos-michaloliakos-trial-start (accessed 21 June 2015).

Back, L. and Solomos, J. (Eds.) (2000) *Theories of Race and Racism: A Reader*. Abingdon; New York: Routledge.

Bauböck, R. (2005) Expansive citizenship: voting beyond territory and membership. *Political Science and Politics*, 38(4): 683–687.

Bauder, H. (2014) Domicile citizenship, human mobility and territoriality, *Progress in Human Geography*, 38(1): 91–106.

Bitler, M. and Hoynes, H. W. (2011) Immigrants, welfare reform, and the US safety net, National Poverty Center and Russell Sage Foundation. Retrieved from http://www.socsci.uci.edu/~mbitler/papers/Bitler-Hoynes-Immigrants-Safety-Net-ver-5-1.pdf (accessed 21 June 2015).

Bloemraad, I. (2006) Becoming a citizen in the United States and Canada: structured mobilization and immigrant political incorporation, *Social Forces*, 85(2): 667–695.

Bloemraad, I., Korteweg, A., and Yurdakul, G. (2008) Citizenship and immigration: multiculturalism, assimilation, and challenges to the nation-state, *Annual Review of Sociology*, 34: 153–179.

Bowen, J. R. (2007) *Why the French Don't Like Headscarves: Islam, the State, and Public Space.* Princeton, NJ: Princeton University Press.

Brubaker, W. R. (1990) Immigration, citizenship, and the nation-state in France and Germany: a comparative historical analysis, *International Sociology*, 5(4): 379–407.

Brubaker, W.R. (1999) The Manichean myth: rethinking the distinction between 'civic' and 'ethnic' nationalism. In H. Kriesi, K. Armingeon, H. Siegrist, and A. Wimmer (Eds.), *Nation and National Identity: The European Experience in Perspective.* Zurich: Verlag Ruegger (pp. 55–72).

Calavita, K. (2005) *Immigrants at the Margins: Law, Race, and Exclusion in Southern Europe.* Cambridge; New York: Cambridge University Press.

Chapman, D. (2004) The third way and beyond: *Zainichi* Korean identity and the politics of belonging, *Japanese Studies*, 24(1): 29–44.

Conzen, K. N., Gerber, D. A., Morawska, E., Pozzetta, G. E., and Vecoli, R. J. (1992) The invention of ethnicity: a perspective from the USA, *Journal of American Ethnic History*, 12(1): 3–41.

Cottle, S. (1991) Reporting the Rushdie Affair: a case study in the orchestration of public opinion, *Race & Class*, 32(4): 45–64.

Dagger, R. (2002) Republican citizenship. In E. Isin and B. S. Turner (Eds.), *The Handbook of Citizenship Studies.* London; Thousand Oaks, CA: Sage (pp.145–158).

Ehrkamp, P. (2012) Migrants, mosques, and minarets: reworking the boundaries of liberal democracy in Switzerland and Germany. In M. Silberman, K. Till, and J. Ward (Eds.), *Walls, Borders, Boundaries: Spatial and Cultural Practices in Europe.* New York: Berghahn Books (pp. 153–172).

Elias, N. and Kemp, A. (2010) The new second generation: Non-Jewish Olim, Black Jews and children of migrant workers in Israel, *Israel Studies*, 15(1): 73–94.

Ellis, M. and Almgren, G. (2009) Local contexts of immigrant and second-generation integration in the United States, *Journal of Ethnic and Migration Studies*, 35(7): 1059–1076.

Entzinger, H. (2006) Changing the rules while the game is on: from multiculturalism to assimilation in the Netherlands. In Y. M. Bodemann and G. Yurdakul (Eds.), *Migration, Citizenship, Ethnos: Incorporation Regimes in Germany, Western Europe and North America.* Basingstoke: Palgrave Macmillan (pp. 121–144).

Escobar, C. (2004) Dual citizenship and political participation: migrants in the interplay of United States and Colombian politics, *Latino Studies*, 2(1): 45–69.

European Union (2003) Council Directive 2003/109/EC concerning the status of third-country nationals who are long-term residents (25 November). Retrieved from http://eur-lex.europa.eu (accessed 21 June 2015).

Faist, T. (1993) From school to work: public policy and underclass formation among young Turks in Germany during the 1980s, *International Migration Review*, 27(2): 306–331.

Faist, T. (2007) The fixed and porous boundaries of dual citizenship. In T. Faist (Ed.), *Dual*

Citizenship in Europe: From Nationhood to Societal Integration. Aldershot: Ashgate (pp. 1–44).

Favell, A. (1998) *Philosophies of Integration: Immigration and the Idea of Citizenship in France and Britain*. Basingstoke: Macmillan.

Finney, N. and Simpson, L. (2009) *'Sleepwalking to Segregation'?: Challenging Myths about Race and Migration*. Bristol: Policy Press.

Gale, R. (2004) The multicultural city and the politics of religious architecture: urban planning, mosques and meaning-making in Birmingham, UK, *Built Environment*, 30(1): 30–44.

García, M. (2006) Citizenship practices and urban governance in European cities, *Urban Studies*, 43(4): 745–765.

Gerken, C. (2013) *Model Immigrants and Undesirable Aliens: The Cost of Immigration Reform in the 1990s*. Minneapolis: University of Minnesota Press.

Gilbertson, G. and Singer, A. (2003) The emergence of protective citizenship in the USA: naturalization among Dominican immigrants in the post-1996 welfare reform era, *Ethnic and Racial Studies*, 26(1): 25–51.

Gilroy, P. (1993) *The Black Atlantic: Modernity and Double Consciousness*. Cambridge, MA: Harvard University Press.

Gilroy, P. (2013) *Between Camps: Nations, Cultures and the Allure of Race*. Abingdon; New York: Routledge.

Glenn, E. N. (2011) Constructing citizenship exclusion, subordination, and resistance, *American Sociological Review*, 76(1): 1–24.

Greenfeld, L. (1992) *Nationalism: Five Roads to Modernity*. Cambridge, MA: Harvard University Press.

Groenendijk, K. (2008) *Local Voting Rights for Non-Nationals: What We Know and What We Need to Learn*. Washington, DC: Migration Policy Institute.

Hamilton, K., Simon, P., and Veniard, C. (2004) The challenge of French diversity, *Migration Information Source*. Retrieved from http:// www.migrationpolicy.org/article/challenge-french-diversity (accessed 21 June 2015).

Hammar, T. (1990) *Democracy and the Nation State: Aliens, Denizens and Citizens in a World of International Migration*. Aldershot: Avebury.

Harder, L. (2010) 'In Canada of all places': national belonging and the lost Canadians, *Citizenship Studies*, 14(2): 203–220.

Ho, E. L. E. (2009) Constituting citizenship through the emotions: Singaporean transmigrants in London, *Annals of the Association of American Geographers*, 99(4): 788–804.

Hondagneu-Sotelo, P. (Ed.) (2006) *Religion and Social Justice for Immigrants*, New Brunswick: Rutgers University Press.

Howard, M.M. (2005) Variation in dual citizenship policies in the countries of the EU, *International Migration Review*, 39(3): 697–720.

Joppke, C. (1999) *Immigration and the Nation-State: The United States, Germany, and Great Britain*. Oxford: Oxford University Press.

Joppke, C. (2004) The retreat of multiculturalism in the liberal state: theory and policy, *The British Journal of Sociology*, 55(2): 237–257.

Kalra, V. S. and Kapoor, N. (2009) Interrogating segregation, integration and the community cohesion agenda, *Journal of Ethnic and Migration Studies*, 35(9): 1397–1415.

Kofman, E. (1995) Citizenship for some but not for others: spaces of citizenship in contemporary Europe, *Political Geography*, 14(2): 121–137.

Kofman, E. (2002) Contemporary European migrations, civic stratification and citizenship, *Political Geography*, 21(8): 1035–1054.

Kofman, E. (2005) Citizenship, migration and the reassertion of national identity, *Citizenship Studies*, 9(5): 453–467.

Koopmans, R. and Statham, P. (1999) Ethnic and civic conceptions of nationhood and the differential success of the extreme right in Germany and Italy. In M. Guigni, D. McAdam, and C. Tilly (Eds.), *How Social Movements Matter*, Minneapolis: University of Minnesota Press (pp. 225–252).

Koronaiou, A. and Sakellariou, A. (2013) Reflections on 'Golden Dawn', community organizing and nationalist solidarity: helping (only) Greeks, *Community Development Journal*, 48(2): 332–338.

Kundnani, A. (2008) Islamism and the roots of liberal rage, *Race & Class*, 50(2): 40–68.

Kymlicka, W. (2007) *Multicultural Odysseys: Navigating the New International Politics of Diversity*. Oxford: Oxford University Press.

Lung-Amam, W. (2013) That 'monster house' is my home: the social and cultural politics of design reviews and regulations, *Journal of Urban Design*, 18(2): 220–241.

Lyman, S. M. (1968) The race relations cycle of Robert E. Park, *Pacific Sociological Review*, 11(1): 16–22.

Marshall, T. H. (1950) *Citizenship and Social Class and Other Essays*. Cambridge: Cambridge University Press. (Excerpt reprinted in C. Pierson and F. C. Castles (Eds.) (2006) *The Welfare State Reader* (2nd edition). Cambridge: The Polity Press.)

Massey, D. S. and Denton, N. A. (1993) *American Apartheid: Segregation and the Making of the Underclass*. Cambridge, MA: Harvard University Press.

Massey, D. S. and Pren, K. A. (2012) Unintended consequences of US immigration policy: explaining the post-1965 surge from Latin America, *Population and Development Review*, 38(1): 1–29.

Mavroudi, E. (2008) Palestinians and pragmatic citizenship: negotiating relationships between citizenship and national identity in diaspora, *Geoforum*, 39(1): 307–318.

Mavroudi, E. (2010) Nationalism, the nation and migration: searching for purity and diversity, *Space and Polity*, 14(3): 219–233.

Meer, N., Dwyer, C., and Modood, T. (2010) Embodying Nationhood? Conceptions of British national identity, citizenship, and gender in the 'Veil Affair', *The Sociological Review*, 58(1): 84–111.

Merrill, H. (2006) *An Alliance of Women: Immigration and the Politics of Race*. Minneapolis: University of Minnesota Press.

Minghuan, L. (2012) Making a living at the interface of legality and illegality: Chinese migrant workers in Israel, *International Migration*, 50(2): 81–98.

Mitchell, K. (1997) Conflicting geographies of democracy and the public sphere in Vancouver BC, *Transactions of the Institute of British Geographers*, 22(2): 162–179.

Mitchell, K. (2003) Educating the national citizen in neoliberal times: from the multicultural self to the strategic cosmopolitan, *Transactions of the Institute of British Geographers*, 28(4): 387–403.

Modood, T. (2005) *Multicultural Politics: Racism, Ethnicity, and Muslims in Britain*. Minneapolis: University of Minnesota Press.

Mongia, R. V. (1999) Race, nationality, mobility: a history of the passport, *Public Culture*, 11(3): 527–556.

Nagel, J. (1994) Constructing ethnicity: creating and recreating ethnic identity and culture, *Social Problems*, 41(1): 152–176.

Neckerman, K. M., Carter, P., and Lee, J. (1999) Segmented assimilation and minority cultures of mobility, *Ethnic and Racial Studies*, 22(6): 945–965.

Nicholls, W. (2012) Governing immigrants and citizenship regimes: the case of France, 1950s–1990s, *Citizenship Studies*, 16(3–4): 511–530.

Omi, M. and Winant, H. (2014) *Racial Formation in the United States*. Abingdon; New York: Routledge.

Park, R. E. (1950) *Race and Culture*. Glencoe, IL: The Free Press.

Park, R. E. and Burgess, E. W. (1921) *Introduction to the Science of Sociology*. Chicago: University of Chicago Press.

Paul, K. (1997) *Whitewashing Britain: Race and Citizenship in the Postwar Era*. Ithaca, NY: Cornell University Press.

Peach, C. (2009) Slippery segregation: Discovering or manufacturing ghettos?

Journal of Ethnic and Migration Studies, 35(9): 1381–1395.

Phillips, D. (2006) Parallel lives? Challenging discourses of British Muslim self-segregation, *Environment and Planning A,* 24(1): 25–40.

Phillips, D., Davis, C., and Ratcliffe, P. (2007) British Asian narratives of urban space, *Transactions of the Institute of British Geographers,* 32(2): 217–234.

Portes, A. and Zhou, M. (1993) The new second generation: segmented assimilation and its variants, *The Annals of the American Academy of Political and Social Science,* 530(1): 74–96.

Portes, A., Fernández-Kelly, P., and Haller, W. (2005) Segmented assimilation on the ground: the new second generation in early adulthood, *Ethnic and Racial Studies,* 28(6): 1000–1040.

Reeskens, T. and Hooghe, M. (2010) Beyond the civic–ethnic dichotomy: investigating the structure of citizenship concepts across thirty-three countries, *Nations and Nationalism,* 16(4): 579–597.

Saint-Blancat, C. and Schmidt di Friedberg, O. (2005) Why are mosques a problem? Local politics and fear of Islam in northern Italy, *Journal of Ethnic and Migration Studies,* 31(6): 1083–1104.

Sassen, S. (2002) Towards post-national and denationalized citizenship. In E. Isin and B. S. Turner (Eds.), *The Handbook of Citizenship Studies.* London; Thousand Oaks, CA: Sage (pp. 277–292).

Schlesinger, A. M. (1998) *The Disuniting of America: Reflections on a Multicultural Society.* New York: WW Norton & Company.

Shon, J. P. K. (2010) The ambivalent nature of ethnic segregation in France's disadvantaged neighbourhoods, *Urban Studies,* 47(8): 1603–1623.

Silverman, M. (2007) The French Republic unveiled, *Ethnic and Racial Studies,* 30(4): 628–642.

Slater, T. (2013) Your life chances affect where you live: a critique of the 'cottage industry' of neighbourhood effects research, *International*

Journal of Urban and Regional Research, 37(2): 367–387.

Smith, R. M. (2002) Modern citizenship. In E. Isin and B. S. Turner (Eds.), *The Handbook of Citizenship Studies.* London; Thousand Oaks, CA: Sage (pp. 105–116).

Smith, R. M. (2003) *Stories of Peoplehood: The Politics and Morals of Political Membership.* Cambridge: Cambridge University Press.

Smolicz, J. J. (1990) The mono-ethnic tradition and the education of minority youth in West Germany from an Australian multicultural perspective, *Comparative Education,* 26(1): 27–43.

Soysal, Y. N. (1994) *Limits of Citizenship: Migrants and Postnational Membership in Europe.* Chicago: University of Chicago Press.

Spång, M. (2007) Pragmatism all the way down? The politics of dual citizenship in Sweden. In T. Faist (Ed.), *Dual Citizenship in Europe: From Nationhood to Societal Integration.* Aldershot: Ashgate (pp. 103–126).

Staeheli, L. A. (2008) Citizenship and the problem of community, *Political Geography,* 27(1): 5–21.

Staeheli, L. A., Ehrkamp, P., Leitner, H., and Nagel, C. R. (2012) Dreaming the ordinary: daily life and the complex geographies of citizenship, *Progress in Human Geography,* 36(5): 628–644.

Stuesse, A. (2010) What's 'justice and dignity' got to do with it? Migrant vulnerability, corporate complicity, and the state, *Human Organization,* 69(1): 19–30.

Tai, E. (2004) 'Korean Japanese': a new identity option for resident Koreans in Japan, *Critical Asian Studies,* 36(3): 355–382.

Tonon, L. and Raney, T. (2013) Building a conservative nation: an examination of Canada's new citizenship guide, Discover Canada, *International Journal of Canadian Studies,* 47(1): 201–219.

Tsuda, T. (1999) The permanence of 'temporary' migration: the 'structural embeddedness' of Japanese–Brazilian immigrant workers in

Japan, *The Journal of Asian Studies*, 58(3): 687–722.

Tsuda, T. (2006) Localities and the struggle for immigrant rights: the significance of local citizenship in recent countries of immigration. In T. Tsuda (Ed.), *Local Citizenship in Recent Countries of Immigration: Japan in Comparative Perspective*. Lanham, MD: Lexington Books (pp. 3–36).

Turner, B. S. (1993) Contemporary problems in the theory of citizenship. In B.S. Turner (Ed.), *Citizenship and Social Theory*. London; Thousand Oaks, CA: Sage Publications (pp. 1–18).

Varsanyi, M. W. (2007) Documenting undocumented migrants: the *Matriculas Consulares* as neoliberal local membership, *Geopolitics*, 12(2): 299–319.

Vasta, E. (2007) From ethnic minorities to ethnic majority policy: multiculturalism and the shift to assimilationism in the Netherlands, *Ethnic and Racial Studies*, 30(5): 713–740.

Vertovec, S. and Wessendorf, S. (Eds.) (2010) *Multiculturalism Backlash: European Discourses, Policies and Practices*. Abingdon; New York: Routledge.

Wacquant, L. J. (1997) Three pernicious premises in the study of the American ghetto, *International Journal of Urban and Regional Research*, 21(2): 341–353.

Whitaker, B. E. (2011) The politics of home: dual citizenship and the African diaspora, *International Migration Review*, 45(4): 755–783.

Winter, E. (2014) (Im)possible citizens: Canada's 'citizenship bonanza' and its boundaries, *Citizenship Studies*, 18(1): 46–62.

Wirth, L. (1928) *The Ghetto*. Chicago: University of Chicago Press (reprinted in 1998 by Transaction Publishers, New Brunswick, NJ).

Wood, P. K. and Gilbert, L. (2005) Multiculturalism in Canada: accidental discourse, alternative vision, urban practice, *International Journal of Urban and Regional Research*, 29(3): 679–691.

Wright, M. and Bloemraad, I. (2012) Is there a trade-off between multiculturalism and socio-political integration? Policy regimes and immigrant incorporation in comparative perspective, *Perspectives on Politics*, 10(1): 77–95.

Yack, B. (1996) The myth of the civic nation, *Critical Review*, 10(2): 193–211.

Yamanaka, K. (1996) Return migration of Japanese–Brazilians to Japan: the Nikkeijin as ethnic minority and political construct, *Diaspora: A Journal of Transnational Studies*, 5(1): 65–97.

Yiftachel, O. (2000) Social control, urban planning and ethno-class relations: Mizrahi Jews in Israel's 'Development Towns', *International Journal of Urban and Regional Research*, 24(2): 418–438.

Migrant identities, mobilizations, and place-making practices

Introduction

In the previous chapter we called attention to the complexity of integration and citizenship, highlighting the often ambiguous and contradictory ways that nation-states and localities manage the incorporation of immigrants into 'mainstream' life. In all immigrant-receiving contexts, state officials, journalists, activists, and ordinary citizens continuously debate the economic, social, and cultural impacts of newcomers: Are they capable of integrating into the nation? Are their beliefs and ways of life compatible with the societal mainstream? Are they adhering to societal rules and norms? Affirmative responses to such questions can lead to a relatively welcoming environment for immigrants, including access to rights and privileges of citizenship; negative responses can contribute to the long-term marginalization or exclusion of these groups from mainstream spaces and spheres. In either case, it is the prerogative of dominant, host-society groups to define the terms of integration and citizenship and to lay out the procedures and rules for becoming a full-fledged member of society.

Dominant groups thus have a critical role in shaping the experiences of immigrant groups in all spheres of life. But immigrants are not passive figures in the politics of citizenship and integration. Immigrants produce their own **social fields**—consisting of interpersonal networks, community institutions, and norms—that intersect with the social fields of dominant groups.

These social fields provide immigrant communities with the resources and capacities needed to respond to the opportunities and constraints that present themselves through the process of migration and settlement. Through their social fields, immigrants can engage with, or buffer themselves from, the hostility of dominant groups, and they can negotiate membership within mainstream social spheres, sectors, and institutions.

In this final chapter, we focus on immigrant social fields, highlighting the institutions and social practices through which immigrants construct community life and group identities, and through which they engage with dominant groups in societies of settlement. Scholars have long expressed an interest in immigrant identities, social practices, and communal institutions. We begin this chapter, therefore, by exploring the early US-centred literature on immigrant communities and by identifying within it key themes of community solidarity, generational transition, and assimilation. This early literature provides a basis from which to examine more contemporary (and more geographically diverse) accounts of identity, youth cultures, political mobilization, and place-making practices that highlight the dynamic negotiation of group boundaries.

From there, we give more careful consideration to the geography of immigrant social fields, and we evaluate theoretical perspectives that have moved discussions of immigrant identities and experiences beyond the receiving-society context. More specifically, we explore the concepts of transnationalism and diaspora, both of which emphasize that immigrants' social fields straddle nation-state boundaries and encompass multiple localities. Our terminology will change at this point from 'immigrant' to 'migrant', reflecting a shift in focus from bounded national societies to more complex social and spatial configurations. How, we ask, do migrants' transnational and diasporic practices alter our understandings of integration, identity, and belonging?

Immigrant experiences through the lens of Assimilation Theory

As described in Chapter 7, the sociologists of the University of Chicago provided some of the earliest theorizations of the transformations experienced by immigrants in settlement contexts. These sociologists in many cases were immigrants themselves, or the children of immigrants, and as such, they were acutely aware of the nativist sentiment that was rife in the US in the early 20th century. In writing about the lives of immigrant communities, they were keen to demonstrate to the dominant population that immigrants could and would assimilate into mainstream life—that if given time and adequate prodding, immigrants would lose those characteristics that, from the perspective of dominant groups, marked them as inferior and backwards, and would assume the traits, behaviours, and social memories of the 'mainstream' (Kivisto, 1990; 2004). In this sense, Chicago School theorists recognized community identities and structures as dynamic, being shaped both by the agency of immigrants and by the discriminatory attitudes and practices of dominant groups.

Early sociological ruminations on immigrant communities reflected the main intellectual trends of the day. Scholars were especially influenced by the biological sciences, likening cities to ecological, organic communities shaped by group competition and succession. They also drew on theories of modernization and urbanism, typified by the work of German theorist Georg Simmel, who posited the breakdown of traditional societies with the advent of industrialization and urbanization and the replacement of primary, kinship-based bonds with more impersonal and instrumental relationships. The Chicago School's detailed, ethnographic studies of immigrant communities thus often characterized assimilation as a social-psychological process that unfolded as immigrants—most of them coming from rural, peasant backgrounds—interacted with the dominant, urbanized, individualistic society. Immigrants were seen to arrive in America, as Pauline Young (1928, 238) put it, with a 'distinctive culture, a set of social attitudes and values which are deeply rooted, long cherished, and sanctioned by religion'. Over time, from this perspective, immigrants could be expected to distance themselves from traditional European modes of thinking to embrace new, individualistic ways associated with urbanized, American lifestyle. As articulated by Peter Speek (1926, 248), himself an immigrant, 'The European people have the habit of herd life, of dependence upon others, of following the leader, the hero. Here an immigrant has soon to learn to depend upon himself, to think with his own head, and act according to his own ideas and resolves. . .'

However 'natural' and ultimately liberating this process might be, scholars understood it as generating significant psychological distress. Robert Park (1928, 893) described adjustment to life in a new land as a time of 'inner turmoil', 'intense self-consciousness', and personal crisis. Likewise, Thomas and Znaniecki (1920) described the process of transition as one marked by many instances of social disorganization, deviancy, and delinquency as those from traditional, peasant backgrounds become unmoored from community norms. For Thomas and Znaniecki, immigrant institutions and associations formed an important, if partial, buffer to the upheaval of immigration—a site where immigrants could find social stability and solidarity in the absence of intimate, meaningful relationships with dominant groups. Ultimately, though, they and other scholars viewed immigrant associations as incapable of holding back the tide of social transformation.

The transition to the second generation was viewed as pivotal in this regard. Scholars saw immigrants' clubs, religious institutions, and mutual aid societies as being constantly undermined by their children's acquisition of the habits and traits of the surrounding society. Rather dramatically, Julius Drachsler (1920, 79–80) likened the second generation to a 'fatal disease gnawing at the vitals of the immigrant community'. Within every immigrant home, Drachsler suggested, there was a 'death struggle between two worlds, two cultures, two civilizations', each embracing a different language, different points of reference, and different manners and customs. Scholars also observed these generational changes within immigrants' places of worship, where monolingual immigrant congregations gave way to bilingual and predominantly English-speaking faith communities (e.g. Speek, 1926). Others focused on public schools as the crucible of generational transition. Young (1928), for instance, argued,

> The children learn a new and different moral code through their associations at public school. They begin to live simultaneously in two different worlds: their home, their religious and communal life, represent one culture, and the public school and the larger community represent another. To the child, however, the English language is a native tongue, he learns it during his childhood simultaneously imbibing American customs which become second nature to him at an early age.

Importantly, scholars recognized that even with assimilation, social barriers could remain firmly in place for immigrants and their descendants, thereby reinforcing distinctive identities. Young (1928) took note of the fact that young American-born Jews were more often tolerated than accepted and found it difficult to develop warm, intimate friendships with the dominant group. As a result, they were typically compelled to identify with their own group. Similarly, Robert Park (1928) described the barriers faced by those visibly different from the majority population, including Chinese and Japanese immigrants—groups, as we have seen, who were barred from naturalization at the time Park was writing. Park concluded that 'assimilation and the accompanying amalgamation of racial stocks does not proceed with the same ease and the same speed in all cases' (1928, 890). (See Box 8.1 for further discussion of Park's ideas on assimilation.)

This idea of assimilation as an incomplete and differentiated process was further developed and systematized by Milton Gordon (1964) in what has sometimes been called the canonical account of assimilation theory (Alba and Nee, 1997). Gordon understood assimilation to be a multi-dimensional process involving the conformity of immigrants to the social and cultural practices and norms of dominant groups—conformity needed in order for immigrants to participate and advance in the receiving society. He characterized this as a stepwise, progressive process, with each dimension following from the other. Yet he also suggested that while some degree of acculturation among immigrant and minority groups was inevitable, full, 'structural' assimilation, whereby a minority group enters into 'the social cliques, clubs, and institutions of the core society' (Gordon, 1964, 71), was *not* inevitable; that whether by choice or by the discriminatory practices of the Anglo-Saxon, Protestant middle class, many in the United States would remain outside the core society and would need to form their own institutions. Gordon thus rejected the popular characterization of the United States as a 'melting pot', or an amalgam of different

BOX 8.1 ROBERT PARKS' 'THE MARGINAL MAN'

Through much of the 20th century, Robert Park was one of the most influential theorists of the individual and social transformations wrought by migration. Works like 'The Marginal Man', published in 1928 in the *American Journal of Sociology*, provide important insights into the debates that raged in the early 20th century about the outcomes of mass immigration. Park describes migration as a process that is at once catastrophic and exhilarating—that leads simultaneously to the breakdown of societal order and the creation of new types of personalities. According to Park, 'contact and collision with a new invading culture' causes the traditional organization of society to break down, thereby emancipating the individual from former social norms and ties' (Park, 1928, 887). Over the course of time, people are reintegrated into a new social order, but in the process, their character changes: they become 'not merely emancipated, but enlightened' and the emancipated individual 'learns to look upon the world in which he was born and bred with something of the detachment of a stranger' (ibid., 888). In other words, the individual becomes a cosmopolitan urbanite.

In 'The Marginal Man', Park addresses the problem of 'race' that preoccupied many of his contemporaries. Park in some respects understood race to be a biological, inherited category. Yet he denied that biological traits had any bearing on 'culture' or 'mentality', and he argued that if assimilation did not take place, it was not because of any inherent faults on the part of racial groups, but because of the way others responded to their physical traits. In Parks' own words, 'the chief obstacle to the cultural assimilation of races is not their different mental, but rather their divergent physical traits. It is not because of the mentality of the Japanese that they do not so easily assimilate as do the Europeans' (ibid., 890). The condition of non-acceptance and racial prejudice, according to Park, produces the 'marginal man'—a 'hybrid' person who lives and shares 'intimately in the cultural life and traditions of two distinct peoples' but who is neither willing nor able to break with his past. Parks' ideas, concerns, and concepts are very much a product of his era, yet it is important to recognize that he was pushing against scholars who treated race as tied immutably to 'culture'. To Park, culture, more than race, was at the heart of scholarly enquiry into migration and assimilation, and Park insisted that the intermingling and 'interbreeding' of people would lead eventually to cooperation and social progress. Parks' ideas about the constant transformation of societal order and culture through the encounters between different groups, and his engagements with concepts of hybridity, in-betweenness, and marginality, continue to resonate with contemporary cultural theory.

elements resulting in an entirely new society. Instead, he described the United States as a collection of relatively self-contained sub-societies based primarily on broad socioreligious categories (Catholic, Protestant, or Jewish) in which people would live their lives from cradle to grave.

Other American sociologists, perennially dissatisfied with the 'melting pot' analogy, homed in on 'ethnicity' as a key dimension of social organization in the US. (As described in Chapter 7, scholars use ethnicity to denote voluntaristic forms of group identity and solidarity, often based on national or regional origins; 'race', in contrast, typically describes more rigid and permanent social divisions based on physiognomic differences.) Advocates of the 'ethnic retention' position argued that the ethnic affiliations of European immigrant groups would not easily fade away, but rather, would be transformed and mobilized in a context of competitive urban and neighbourhood politics (Glazer and Moynihan, 1963; Yancey, et al., 1976). Other scholars, however, countered that ethnic identities among the descendants of European immigrants were becoming largely symbolic and optional—something to be rolled out on special occasions rather than an integral part of everyday life (Gans, 1979; Waters, 1990). Indeed, analyses of the 1980 census revealed that a growing number of European-origin Americans viewed themselves simply as 'white' and were not members of any discernible ethnic group (Lieberson, 1985). This broad group of whites socialized and intermarried with each other and lived in the same neighbourhoods; in short, they had achieved the sameness that is the crux of assimilation (a sameness largely denied to African Americans) (Gans, 1992).

Questions about how and whether immigrants become part of mainstream societies took on a new sense of urgency in the 1990s, in the context of renewed large-scale immigration to the US. Since this time, American scholars have debated whether contemporary immigrants—most of whom hail from Latin America and Asia—are following the same trajectory of group change supposedly followed by their European predecessors (Portes and Zhou, 1993; Perlmann and Waldinger, 1997; Zhou, 1997; Alba and Nee, 1997). As described in Chapter 7, scores of empirical studies—many of them based on large-scale survey data—have attempted to measure objectively the different trajectories of assimilation that exist among immigrants and to disentangle the complex relationships between immigrant traits (e.g. education levels, social capital), host-society structures, and patterns of economic and residential mobility. Such studies (in the US and elsewhere) have called attention to the diversity of incorporation pathways, and they have at times served to dispel negative stereotypes of immigrants (e.g. Peach, 1996). But they reveal relatively little about the everyday politics through which immigrants negotiate their belonging within a 'mainstream' that is actively constructed by dominant groups. In other words, by focusing on assimilation as a measurable and clearly defined end state, this literature tends to miss the shifting and contested ideas and practices that generate sameness and difference in immigrant-receiving contexts (Nagel, 2009).

Immigrant lives through the lens of 'difference'

While some scholars have focused on measuring assimilation, others have taken a different approach that focuses not so much on adaptation and acculturation as on the cultural subordination of immigrant and minority groups. Especially influential in developing this perspective were Cultural Studies scholars in Britain, who in the 1980s offered trenchant critiques of public discourses that cast immigrants as a social 'problem' and that pathologized immigrants' family structures and cultural practices. The consistent portrayal of non-white people as lacking in the essential qualities of Britishness, Cultural Studies scholars argued, was the means through which white British politicians fabricated ideas of British nationhood (Gilroy, 1987). More abstractly, Cultural Studies perspectives challenged the taken-for-granted quality of social categories like black, white, and Asian, and they explored the ways in which these categories were produced and reproduced through everyday social discourses and practices (Hall, 1992; Hall and du Gay, 1996). In questioning the common-sense nature of social categories, and in exposing the power relations embedded in them, Cultural Studies perspectives intersected with diverse theoretical influences—including Gramscian concepts of ideological hegemony; Foucauldian ideas on discourse, power, and the production of knowledge; and Edward Said's (1978) theorization of Orientalism, among others. This theoretical cross-pollination has produced a diverse collection of critical scholarship on identity and social difference that continues to inform migration research today.

One important element of this work has been the critical appraisal of **whiteness** as a dominant social category. Scholars have argued that understanding the racialization of minorities requires that we interrogate the formulation of dominant identities and the social practices through which whites preserve their privilege vis-à-vis racialized Others (Bonnett, 1997; Frankenburg, 1997). This interest in whiteness has produced revisionist histories that have interpreted the assimilation of European immigrants in settler societies as the whitening of immigrants and their descendants and a widening of the boundaries of white privilege—a process that required the continued exclusion of certain racialized Others (e.g. indigenous groups, Asians, etc.) from full membership in the polity and nation (see Jacobson, 1999; Roediger, 2005; also Hickman and Walter, 1995).

Such scholarship has been concerned with the ways that immigrant groups have negotiated racial hierarchies both through acts of resistance and through accommodation of dominant norms and ideologies. Gualtieri (2009) for instance, explores how Syrian immigrants, a group precariously situated in the racial hierarchies of the early 20th century, actively positioned themselves as part of the white mainstream and were complicit in the racialization of others. In the early 1900s, a series of cases were brought before federal courts questioning the racial identity of Syrians. If they were determined to be Asians, Syrians, like the Chinese, would be ineligible for naturalization. The Syrian community leaders (and their lawyers) responded to the imminent threat of racial exclusion not by challenging racial hierarchies but by strenuously defending their community's whiteness. They did this, in part, by using (now discredited) anthropological theories linking the Semitic peoples of the Eastern Mediterranean to Christianity and hence to Western civilization.

The insights of this critical scholarship have also been brought to bear on the study of generational transitions in immigrant communities. While assimilation scholarship continues to focus on the adoption of mainstream outlooks and behavioural patterns by second-generation groups

(see Chafetz and Ebaugh, 2000; Rumbaut and Portes, 2001), a growing body of literature is more concerned with young people's ongoing (and often ambiguous) engagement with racialized identities and their role in creating entirely new cultural forms. Mary Waters' (1996) exploration of the identities of second-generation Afro-Caribbean youths in New York City, for instance, illustrates how the children of immigrants navigate the racial hierarchies that they encounter in their everyday lives. Waters explains that many of the young people she interviewed assert their Caribbean ancestry as a means of distinguishing themselves from African Americans, thereby avoiding the stigmatization of being black. In doing so, they (like the early Syrian American community) tend to reinforce racial hierarchies, even as they contest their own racialization. Les Back's (1996) groundbreaking study of working-class youths in London, meanwhile, traces the emergence of an urban 'multiculture' on London's housing estates. Back examines how young working-class people experience racism from dominant British society but also create new cultural forms that transcend locality and racial/cultural differences, especially in the realm of music. Back emphasizes, however, that while these young people reject racism and seek common identity in neighbourhood, they continue to understand themselves in racial terms and to produce and reproduce racial identities and stereotypes.

These accounts push well beyond traditional discussions of second-generation youth 'caught between two worlds' and emphasize the ways that young people negotiate different social categories and meanings and actively produce new cultures, new social norms, and new identities (another good example is Dwyer's (1999) description of British Muslim girls' use of fashion to assert and to negotiate identities in school settings). With this said, the issue of intergenerational tensions within families has not entirely fallen by the wayside, though current literature is more attuned to the complex dynamics of race and gender that are central to conflicts between immigrants and their children. Nadine Naber (2005), for instance, details the familial rifts that occur as young Muslim Arab Americans engage with their faith in new ways. The second-generation Muslim Arab Americans Naber interviewed describe themselves as 'Muslims first, Arabs second', and they reject what they feel are their parents' un-Islamic cultural practices and beliefs. In embracing the pure tenets of Islam, these young people challenge their parents' patriarchal norms and racist beliefs, defending, in particular, interracial marriage and women's equality and autonomy. Such positions can generate significant conflict between these young people and their parents, as well as between men and women, as the young women Naber interviewed tend to push the argument of women's equality much farther than their male counterparts do. Yeh and Lama's (2006) account of Tibetan youth cultures offers another example of the complexities of race, gender, and intergenerational conflict. The second-generation Tibetan refugees in California and Colorado interviewed by Yeh and Lama challenge and subvert their relatively privileged status as 'deserving victims'—a status their parents have cultivated by gaining the support of white converts to Buddhism. Bristling against what they view as their parents' deferential attitudes towards whites and sense of superiority vis-à-vis other Asian groups, some young Tibetans have adopted the hip-hop style associated with African Americans—complete with tattoos, heavy chains, and baggy trousers. Elders, in turn, read these 'black' styles and behaviours as the loss of 'traditional culture' and as a significant threat to white support for Tibet's liberation from China.

Immigrants' place-making practices

Another important theme to emerge within this broad body of critical scholarship has been immigrants' production and negotiation of place. Immigrants historically have formed residential clusters or 'colonies' in societies of settlement—a process described in great detail by early assimilation scholars, who interpreted clustering as a natural outcome of social heterogeneity and group competition in urban environments (see Wirth, 1938). Dominant groups, as we have seen, have frequently viewed immigrant neighbourhoods as spaces of disease, vice, and deviance and have endeavoured to isolate them or, alternatively, to 'cleanse' them through public-policy interventions like slum clearances (Anderson, 1991; also Farrar, 2008). Immigrants, however, have rarely been passive in political debates about their residential and communal spaces. On the contrary, they have sought actively to validate their physical presence in the space of the nation.

Kay Anderson's (1991) account of Vancouver's Chinatown, mentioned in Chapter 7, illustrates the ways that immigrants have responded to social and spatial marginalization and have reconfigured dominant meanings attached to immigrant spaces. Having struggled against severe discrimination by white Canadian society in the late 19th and early 20th centuries, Chinese civic and business organizations participated in the reimagining of Chinatown in the 1920s and 1930s from a space of vice and deviance to one of Oriental quaintness. The Chinese Benevolent Association, Anderson shows, embarked on a project to erect Chinese-style buildings in the area, while the city's merchant elite encouraged images that promoted Chinatown's exoticness. Such efforts, Anderson (1991, 156) suggests, 'demonstrated strategic awareness of the reward to be had from "re-orienting" Chinatown in conformity with European images'. These commercial endeavours were not enough to stop urban renewal plans in the 1960s, which targeted Chinatown as a 'blighted' area. The community, however, mobilized in full force to prevent the construction of a freeway that would have obliterated the neighbourhood. Again, in contesting the characterization of their neighbourhood as

Plate 8.1 Muslim man praying next to his hot dog stand, US
Source: Jacob Silberberg/Panos

expendable, they emphasized the importance of this space as a tourist destination in need of preservation. Anderson highlights the ambiguities that surfaced through this process. That is, as Chinese community groups deployed narratives of Chinese-ness that reconfigured racialized categories and stereotypes, they did little to challenge or to undermine racist ways of thinking in Canada. (For complementary analyses, see Glasman's (1991) account of late 19th-century synagogue construction in London and Karafilis' (2010) discussion of 19th-century immigrant narratives of life in the Jewish ghetto.)

In recent years, many discussions about immigrant space have centred on the growing presence of immigrants in suburban areas. In the US, Britain, Canada, and Australia, suburbs

have typically been dominated by middle-class whites. Since the 1990s, however, demographers have taken note of the direct settlement of many immigrants in suburban areas (Singer, et al., 2009; Chiang and Hsu, 2005). Scholars have coined the term **ethnoburb** (Li, 1998) to describe both ethnic residential and business clusters outside of the urban core and multi-ethnic suburban neighbourhoods. Scholars have noted, as well, the construction of large community centres and places of worship on the outskirts of many cities that serve as focal points of community life for immigrant groups scattered across sprawling metropolitan areas (Dwyer, et al., 2013; Waghorne, 1999). Shifting residential patterns, in addition to confounding tidy assumptions about urban residential

Plate 8.2 Religious book stall outside Birmingham central mosque, UK

Source: Heidi Bradner/Panos

structure, have added a new twist to the spatial politics of belonging in immigrant-receiving societies. The presence of immigrants outside of their 'natural' place in the urban landscape (i.e. densely populated inner-city ghettos) and the encroachment of immigrant Others on spaces of essentialized whiteness generate a particular set of politics. We described these politics in our discussion in Chapter 7 of 'monster house' controversies in Vancouver, Canada, and Fremont, California. Similar examples of these politics abound in the literature. Trudeau (2006), for instance, describes neighbourhood opposition to a Hmong-owned abattoir, used by various immigrant groups for the ritual slaughter of animals, in a predominantly white semi-rural town on the outskirts of Minneapolis, Minnesota.

Bugg (2013), likewise, discusses opposition to the construction of a Hindu temple on the outskirts of Sydney, Australia, on the basis that the proposed temple, with its foreign smells and exotic festivals, would not be in keeping with the semi-rural, English-settler character of the area. These cases demonstrate the ways in which existing residents conceive of space as belonging inherently to one group, and the ways residents use seemingly neutral zoning regulations to 'defend' the essential character of places against the encroachment of foreign Others (also Duncan and Duncan, 2003; Nelson, 2008). Importantly, these cases also indicate the ways that immigrants contest their exclusion and claim belonging within the residential spaces of white privilege, at times by emphasizing the compatibility of immigrant cultural practices and aesthetics with the existing cultural landscape, and at other times by asserting their right to be culturally different. Returning to the case of the 'monster mansions' in Vancouver, Mitchell (1997a) explains that the Chinese community responded to white opposition by allying itself with pro-growth real-estate developers and by forming their own ad hoc committee to contest proposed zoning restrictions. This committee made public allegations of racism against those supporting new zoning regulations and supported its own position by extolling the virtues of the Chinese community—their respect for elders, their family orientation, and their industriousness. This combination of strategies ultimately was successful in stopping proposed regulations and in disrupting the sense of entitlement that Shaughnessy's white residents

maintained in defining neighbourhood character and the 'common good'.

Amanda Wise's (2005) ethnographic work on the everyday practices of living with difference in Ashfield, a multiethnic suburb of Sydney, reveals even more complex and ambiguous negotiations in a context of suburban diversification. Wise explores the anxieties expressed by the shrinking white population towards newcomers—mainly Greek, Italian, Turkish, and Lebanese immigrants who arrived in the 1960s, 1970s, and 1980s, and a more recent group of Chinese and Indian immigrants whose commercial and social establishments have come to dominate the local built environment. But she also explores the acts of cooperation, neighbourliness, and reciprocity that punctuate daily life in multiethnic neighbourhoods. Wise emphasizes that there is no neat division between 'good multiculturalists'

Plate 8.3 Greek–Australian festival at Mornington Park, near Melbourne, January 2012
Source: Chris Phutully

and 'bad racists'; rather, people's perceptions and assessments of the Other are inevitably fluid and contextual. She suggests that it is through small, almost invisible, exchanges that we can witness the reconfiguration of belonging in immigrant-receiving contexts and that we can observe the creation of forms of community that are not bounded by clear divisions between 'us' and 'them'. (For other rich accounts of neighbourhood interactions, see Horton, 1995; Naylor and Ryan, 2002.)

Immigrant political mobilization

Immigrants' interactions with planning boards, zoning councils, and neighbours in claiming and creating spaces of belonging in cities and neighbourhoods prompt us to consider more broadly the political mobilization of immigrant groups and their engagements with formal political systems, both as opponents of those systems and as potential participants within them. Despite, or perhaps because of, their economic vulnerability and their lack of formal rights, immigrants historically have engaged in numerous forms of political participation and activism. As might be expected given the crucial role of migrants as workers, a great deal of immigrant activism has been oriented around labour issues. Historians have commented extensively on the role of immigrants in working-class movements and labour radicalism in Europe, Latin America, and North America (Goyens, 2007; also Streeby, 2007). This historical scholarship has often noted the tensions between native and immigrant workers and the tendency for native workers to support restrictions on immigration in order to protect their own wages and working conditions (Higham, 1955). Native labour activists, however, have at times mobilized immigrants and have sought justice on their behalf, reasoning that the exploitation of immigrants ultimately hurts all workers. Such was the case in France in the 20th century, when periodic xenophobic outbursts among unionists gave way to sustained

efforts to achieve political and social rights for immigrants (see Lloyd, 2000).

Labour activism, of course, is not a thing of the past, though the context and tenor of labour mobilization has changed. Contemporary labour activism tends to draw upon international human rights discourses and to tie local conditions to broader patterns of neoliberal globalization; it also tends to take place as much through non-governmental organizations (NGOs) as through labour unions (Hsia, 2009). An example of contemporary labour activism is the Consulate Hopping Protest that took place in Hong Kong in 2005. The protest, as described by Constable (2009), involved female domestic workers from Nepal, the Philippines, Indonesia, Thailand, and Malaysia, who presented mock awards to their respective consular officials, criticizing their authoritarian behaviours and their willingness to 'sell out' their female citizens to foreign employers. The multinational groups of protestors moved on to Hong Kong's government office to protest a decision to cut wages and benefits to foreign domestic workers and to impose a levy on them. Finally, the protestors marched on the US consulate to express their opposition to the World Trade Organization and its support of economic globalization. Labour unions, notes Constable (2009), had a role in these mobilizations, but even more visible were numerous non-governmental organizations that advocate on behalf of migrant domestic workers in Hong Kong. Indeed, Constable notes that many of the participants in the Consulate Hopping Protest were unemployed migrant domestic workers temporarily living in shelters run by NGOs and migrant activists. These activists were responsible for raising domestic workers' consciousness about political and labour issues and encouraging them to be politically involved.

Importantly, participants in the Consulate Hopping Protest did not make claims to legal membership in the polity. Such claims would perhaps seem unrealistic given the strict system of labour permits in Hong Kong that limit workers to two-year contracts and that forbid entry to workers' family members. Yet there are cases in which immigrant-worker activism does involve more assertive claims of societal membership, even by those in a precarious legal situation. A dramatic example of such claims-making could be seen in the massive street demonstrations that took place in Chicago, Los Angeles, and other large US cities in 2006. These demonstrations involved hundreds of thousands of undocumented immigrants and their advocates who publicly demanded comprehensive immigration reform in the US and a pathway to legal citizenship. Aware of scepticism among US citizens about the deservingness of unauthorized workers, demonstrators did not simply demand legal status, but rather attempted to explain why they merited membership in the polity and why current immigration entry and enforcement policies unjustly discriminated against them (Nicholls, 2013; Glenn, 2011).

While immigrant mobilization often relates in some manner to workers' rights, activism can also revolve around less tangible issues of cultural representation. This is especially the case in societies where multicultural discourses and policies have validated the public expression of cultural differences and have made group recognition a prerequisite for access to some state resources. In the United States, the emergence of 'identity politics' in the 1980s and 1990s (a product of long-standing forms of ethnic-based pluralist politics and new multiculturalist discourses) encouraged the formation and public assertion of new identity categories, like Latino, Asian American, and Arab American. In this political context, activists regarded the management of their groups' public image as being of the utmost importance in gaining a seat, so to speak, at America's 'multicultural table' (Kurien, 2007). Kurien (2007), to illustrate, describes the formation of a public Indian-American identity in the 1990s and the mobilization of Indian-American activists against what they viewed as negative, Euro-centric portrayals of India and

Plate 8.4 A plea for racial tolerance and strength in diversity, Cape Town, South Africa, 2008

Source: Eric Miller/Panos

Hinduism in the media and elsewhere. In 2005, when the California Board of Education offered the new sixth-grade world-history textbook for community review, Indian- and Hindu-American organizations quickly proposed over 100 edits to the text and demanded the redaction of references to the worship of multiple deities, the relationship between Hinduism and the caste system, and the unequal treatment of women in Indian society. Around the same time, activists within Indian community attempted to build clout in the American political system by creating a lobbying group called the US–India Political Action Committee—modelled on a powerful pro-Israeli lobbying group—that could unite the community and put forward a common platform on issues ranging from trade with India to civil rights violations against Indian immigrants.

Another example of group formation and mobilization in contexts of competitive pluralism can be seen in the case of Latino activists in Canada. Veronis (2006) describes efforts among activists to build a coherent 'Latin American community' from disparate South and Central American groups as a means of gaining voice and representation within Canada's multicultural political system. Veronis focuses on the Hispanic Day Parade in Toronto, an event that today attracts tens of thousands of people from across the metropolitan area. Veronis reads this parade as a practice of Canadian citizenship, whereby immigrants lay claim to societal membership through their use of public space. Latin American community leaders, she notes, have purposefully routed the parade through a relatively low-income, predominantly immigrant suburban neighbourhood in order to affirm Latin American identities, to challenge mainstream representations of disadvantaged groups, and to call attention to their place—literally and figuratively—in Canadian society.

Both Kurien and Veronis emphasize the many ambiguities and complications surrounding immigrants' participation in pluralist-multicultural politics. Kurien indicates that prominent South Asian scholars, as well as secular Indian-American organizations, came out against Hindu-Indian activists' efforts to revise California's world-history textbooks, arguing that proponents of the revisions were allied with the virulently nationalist Hindutva movement in India (we discuss these kinds of transnational connections in greater detail below). Secular Indian-American groups, moreover, have accused Hindu-Indian groups of allying themselves with right-wing groups in the United States, espousing anti-Muslim sentiment and not speaking out against the assault on civil liberties

that took place in the US in the aftermath of the September 11, 2001, terrorist attacks. In the case of the Latin American community in Toronto, Veronis suggests that while the Hispanic Day Parade is an important show of solidarity, it also supports a neoliberal agenda that has reframed multiculturalism as a business strategy. Many of the organizers of the parade, Veronis notes, are business leaders who are not particularly inclined to raise uncomfortable questions about the lack of affordable housing and high levels of unemployment among immigrants. Clearly, then, the mobilization of 'community' is problematic: while it can redress oppression by dominant groups, it can equally replicate social inequalities and subordinate particular voices and interests within the community.

These cases make clear that the boundaries of community are always contested and are never stable or static. While immigrants often conform to the logic of pluralistic political systems that require them to coalesce around particular identities and interests, they just as often bristle against categories imposed upon them by dominant groups and so-called community leaders. The complexity and fluidity of multicultural politics can be seen in Britain, where the antiracist movement in the 1980s brought forth a politicized 'Black' community, the boundaries of which were subsequently contested by Muslims of South Asian origin. Through the 1990s, 'British Muslims' formed national organizations and mobilized around a variety of issues, including state funding for Muslim schools (Meer, 2009). Yet the category of British Muslim itself has been just as contentious as that of 'Black'. British-Arab community members, for instance, have tended to distance themselves from the British-Muslim category, which they view both as stigmatized and as overly politicized (Nagel and Staeheli, 2011). Following the logic of multiculturalism, British-Arab activists have attempted to build solidarity among Britain's fractured Arab-origin population and have advocated for the creation of an independent British-Arab census category.

We have tried to convey here the complexity of immigrant identities and experiences and the often tortuous paths that immigrants follow in negotiating a place for themselves in receiving societies. The ongoing preoccupation with measuring assimilation only gets us so far in understanding immigrants' engagements with dominant groups, their use of space, their formulation of group identities and narratives, and their political participation and mobilization. Attention to immigrants' experiences reveals a tangle of social processes: the creation and re-creation of group solidarities; the contestation and accommodation of existing power arrangements; the negotiation and reconfiguration of membership and belonging. These processes are fluid, contentious, and never predetermined in their outcomes. The identification of empirical patterns—where immigrants live, how much they earn, what level of education they achieve, and so on—is meaningful only when we situate them in the social production of 'us' and 'them', sameness and difference, in immigrant-receiving contexts.

In adopting this critical perspective on immigrants' identities, place-making practices, and political participation, however, we might ask whether it is enough to focus exclusively on dynamics within immigrant-receiving contexts, or whether understanding immigrant experiences also requires us to consider the more complex geographies in which immigrants' lives are situated. What happens when we think about migrants' social fields not as contained in one location, but as stretching across boundaries and as linking together multiple locations?

Migrant transnationalism and the formation of diasporas

Scholars of immigration, perhaps understandably, have often been primarily interested in what immigration means for their own societies: whether immigrants are 'successfully' acculturating and adapting to 'mainstream' life or whether they are becoming a 'problem' for national cohesion. Early assimilation scholars *were* cognizant of the importance of immigrants' connections to their places of origin (see, for instance, Thomas and Zaniekci, 1920), but there was an assumption that immigrants' connections with places of origin—like their efforts to preserve traditional cultural practices—were ephemeral. Later sociologists made note of instances of ethnic 'reactivation', whereby the second- and third-generation descendants of immigrants became interested once again in homeland-based identities, often in light of political events taking place in their parents' or grandparents' homelands. But, again, this reactivation of identity was seen to be largely symbolic and to have little substantive effect on the assimilation process (Gans, 1979).

Scholars began to rethink their assumptions about the containment of immigrants' lives within immigrant-receiving societies in the early 1990s (e.g. Basch, et al., 1994). These scholars argued that the study of migration had for too long been confined by 'methodological nationalism'—an assumption that the nation-state and national society is the natural sociopolitical unit in the modern world (Wimmer and Glick Schiller, 2002, 302). They proposed a new transnational framework that would more accurately reflect the fluidity and border-crossing nature of social reality, and especially of migrants' lives. Drawing on elements of World Systems Theory and anthropological theories of culture and globalization, their conceptualization of **transnationalism** highlighted the enmeshment of migration within a global capitalist economy that had rendered boundaries porous and permeable. In a context of constant cross-border movement of people, money, goods, and ideas—all of it facilitated by new communications and transport technologies—the concept of discrete 'sending' and 'host' societies seemed hopelessly outmoded. So, too, did the concept of 'immigrant', with its implication of the more-or-less permanent settlement in a receiving nation-state.

In its stead, proponents of the transnational perspective offered the term 'transmigrant', which in their view captured the indeterminacy and circuitousness of migration flows (as mentioned in Chapter 1, we find this term redundant, so we simply use 'migrant' in the following discussion).

In rethinking migrant experiences to capture cross-border relationships, scholars also revived the concept of **diaspora**. Diaspora has been applied to groups that have been scattered or dispersed from an original homeland and that form distinctive, persistent minorities in their places of settlement. Definitions of diaspora have often centred on diasporas' sense of alienation from the society of settlement, their idealization of their homeland, and their commitment to returning to and/or to restoring their original homeland (see Safran, 1991). Jews are typically seen as the archetypal diaspora owing to their spiritual attachment to an historical homeland and their outsider status in places of settlement. More recently, however, scholars have applied the term more broadly to the lives, social networks, social imaginaries, and political activities of a variety of groups who, in various ways and to varying degrees, long for, recreate, and remain engaged with homelands (e.g. Cohen, 2008; Jöns, et al., 2015; for a critical overview, see Brubaker, 2005).

Scores of publications appeared in the 1990s and early 2000s offering rich descriptions of migrants' border-spanning practices and their diasporic identities. This early scholarship illustrated that migrants' connections with homelands do not end when they settle in a new destination. Rather, migrants participate actively in communities of origin, maintain strong financial connections with hometowns, and communicate daily with family members from afar. Portes (1997, 812) described this transnational condition in terms of 'dual lives', suggesting that 'participants are often bilingual, move easily between different cultures, frequently maintain homes in two countries and pursue economic, political and cultural interest that require their presence in both'. Similarly, Michael Peter Smith (1994, 20) spoke of cultural 'bifocality', arguing that migrants were 'involved simultaneously in more than one culture but fully living in neither'. According to Smith, migrants assembled household and community networks across borders as a means of surviving in an integrated global economy that relied on migrant labour but that rendered migrants' lives increasingly precarious. On a more sanguine note, Smith suggested that transnationalism had created new possibilities for the orchestration of political action across a 'variety of institutional and geographical scales' and had facilitated the formation of new 'global grassroots movements' (ibid., 31).

Indicative of this bold new perspective was Roger Rouse's (1992) analysis of migration between Mexico and the US. Mexico–US migration, Rouse argued, had traditionally been interpreted in terms of movement between two completely autonomous, mutually exclusive communities. Within this framework, it had been assumed that 'settlement' was a process through which migrants shifted their attention and the locus of social ties from one location to the other. Rouse, however, used the case of migration between the *municipio* of Aguililla in west-central Mexico and Redwood City, California, to illustrate that even long-term settlement did not lead to a complete break of ties with places of origin, and that migrants remained orientated towards the *muncipio*—not least through the sending of remittances—even as they situated themselves in Redwood City. The constant back-and-forth movement across borders along with the circulation of money, goods, and services, Rouse argued, had 'woven together' the *municipio* and settlements in the US so tightly that 'in an important sense, they had come to form a single community spanning the various locales' (Rouse, 1992, 45).

As Rouse's account indicates, ideas of transnationalism intersected with the growing interest in migrant remittances and hometown associations, which we covered in Chapter 4. What had been the topic of rather dry economic and policy analyses became part of an exciting discussion about the complex trans-border lives of contemporary migrants. The interest in remittances, in turn, brought greater attention to the role of states in facilitating migrants' connections with their homelands. In this respect, while theorists of transnationalism had been eager to move beyond nation-state-centric understandings of migrant experiences, and while many early discussions described the nation-state as 'unravelling' under the pressures of globalization (Smith, 1994), the literature increasingly recognized the key role of the (sending) nation-state in transnational phenomena. The state could institutionalize ties with communities abroad, facilitate the flow of remittances, and incorporate diasporas into the political life of the homelands through new forms of citizenship and representation (Itzigsohn, 2000; Guarnizo, et al., 2003; Smith, 2003).

In keeping with the new interest in the role of the nation-state in transnational social fields, scholars focused attention on migrants' active participation in long-distance nationalism, state formation, and citizenship politics through various forms of collective action. Glick Schiller and Fouron (1999), for instance, described how people of Haitian descent in Canada and the US imagined themselves as part of a diasporic, transnational nation—a phenomenon that coincided with efforts by the Haitian state to claim all people of Haitian origin as members of the nation regardless of their formal citizenship. The Haitian diaspora, Glick Schiller and Fouron suggested, had adopted a language of immutable blood ties to the Haitian nation, which they expressed through their continuous engagement with Haitian politics and economic development, as well as through transnational kinship networks. Smith and Bakker's (2005) account of the political campaign of Andres Bermudez, a Mexican immigrant residing in California, for the mayor's office in his home city of Jerez, Mexico, also uncovered migrants' engagements with

state institutions and state authority. Bermudez deployed a narrative of the heroic Mexican migrant to subvert Mexico's entrenched political elite and to mobilize ordinary Mexicans to reform political life in Mexico. Forging alliances with influential migrant organizations in the state of Zacatecas, Bermudez pressed for, and eventually succeeded in, instituting state-level constitutional reforms to recognize 'bi-national residency'. This recognition, in turn, facilitated the candidacies of émigrés for popular municipal elections.

At the same time that they re-centred the nation-state in analyses of transnationalism, scholars of transnationalism began to grapple in earnest with the less positive aspects of transnational communities. As alluded to above, scholars tended initially to hype diaspora and transnationalism as a mode of empowerment, liberation, and cultural hybridity (e.g. Basch, et al., 1994; Clifford, 1994; Smith, 1994; for a critique, see Mitchell, 1997b). But they soon took note of the oppressive social norms through which diasporas reproduce themselves and the sometimes troubling ideologies that sustain transnational solidarity (Anthias, 1998; 2008; also Yeoh and Willis, 1999). Many of these critical discussions have focused specifically on the role of unequal gender relations in the production and reproduction of diaspora and transnationalism (Werbner, 2004). Salih's (2001) ethnographic research on Moroccan women in Italy, for instance, sheds light on the ways in which gender-specific obligations to family members impinge on women's transnational lives. Salih's research reveals that women's decisions to move, to return, or to stay put often hinge on caregiving requirements, and that women commonly experience the back-and-forth movement across borders (a particular challenge when finances are tight or when legal status is insecure) in order to respond to the competing needs of children, aging parents, and spouses. Salih refers to these patterns collectively as the 'transnational sphere of reproductive and care activities'. Participation in this sphere, she notes, can confer status and respect on migrant women as providers, but can equally generate anxiety and stress as women struggle to meet the demands and expectations of disparate family members. Such mixed emotions are especially salient in cases where migrant women leave their children in the care of family members and friends while they care for families in the Global North (for instance, Hondagneu-Sotelo and Avila, 1997; Parreñas, 2001; Spitzer et al., 2003).

As scholars have come to understand transnationalism as mediated by gender, class, and other dimensions of social difference, they have also come to acknowledge the variability of migrants' understandings of and attachments to 'home'. If early scholarship tended to assume a uniform commitment to a national homeland among diasporas, subsequent research has emphasized that migrants' relationships to places of origin are complicated and often ambivalent. Mavroudi (2008), to illustrate, argues that while Palestinian exiles in Greece are deeply committed to the idea of a Palestinian homeland, not all feel an equal sense of empowerment from engaging in diasporic politics. Indeed, for some, political demonstrations and other homeland-oriented activities are a constant reminder of loss and of the seemingly endless conflict between Israel and the Palestinians. Disenchantment with Palestinian politics, in turn, can fuel a sense of guilt and detachment. So while they are politicized as Palestinians, they experience tensions between idealized notions of Palestinianness and the realities of exile (Mavroudi, 2007). The Lebanese community in Senegal provides further illustration of the complexities of relationships with 'home'. The Lebanese began to migrate to Senegal over a century ago for economic opportunity, and many continue to visit and to send remittances to Lebanon even after three or four generations in Senegal. Yet community members describe themselves as something other than 'Lebanese', and they have not always welcomed newcomers from Lebanon, who are

viewed as bringing Lebanon's fractious politics to Senegal (Leichtman, 2005). Moreover, as the cost of living has skyrocketed in Lebanon and the prospect of 'return' has become more remote, Leichtman (2005, 671) notes, many Lebanese in Senegal have chosen 'to distance themselves from Lebanon, pour scorn on its way of life, and define themselves more strongly with what they are most familiar and where they can best succeed: Senegal'. These cases demonstrate that home is not a fixed location, but a shifting topography of commitments, emotional attachments, and material relationships, the coordinates of which stretch across time and space (Werbner, 2002; Staeheli and Nagel, 2006).

Some scholars have attempted to analyze the variable intensity of transnationalism in a systematic fashion and to identify specific factors that lead to or discourage transnational orientation. Guarnizo et al. (2003), for instance, surveyed Dominican, Colombian, and Salvadoran immigrants in the United States and found that levels of political transnationalism varied widely within and between these groups. Many had some loose or sporadic connections, but only a small percentage of immigrants had meaningful, sustained engagement. This study indicates that migrants' human capital (e.g. education level and economic resources) combined with political circumstances in the country of origin influence levels and types of political transnationalism among different migrant groups (also Østergaard-Nielsen, 2003). Complementing this research is Moran-Taylor and Menjívar's (2005) study on the transnational orientations of Guatemalan and Salvadoran migrants in Phoenix, Arizona. Moran-Taylor and Menjívar observe that while some migrants fully intend to return to places of origin, others are far more ambivalent about 'home', and still others express no desire to return at all. These different attitudes about the prospect of returning to cities and countries of origin appear to hinge on where migrants' immediate families, and particularly children, are located. Having one's children close by, Moran-Taylor and Menjívar suggest, may allow migrants to be 'at home' wherever they are located and may mitigate against transnational orientations (see also Morawska, 2004).

In an ironic twist, this growing recognition of the unevenness and variability of transnational behaviours and orientations has brought research on transnationalism full circle to questions of assimilation and integration—that is, to migrants' negotiations of belonging in countries of settlement. While early theorizations of transnationalism treated questions of assimilation and integration as somewhat outmoded or passé, current scholarship explicitly considers how processes of integration and transnationalism

operate both in tandem and in tension with each other (see Box 8.2 for a discussion of the role of historical scholarship in theorizations of transnationalism). The current literature suggests the nature of interactions between transnationalism and the negotiation of membership in receiving societies are rarely straightforward or intuitive. In some cases, secure legal status, economic mobility, and high rates of naturalization in the receiving society seem to encourage stronger transnational ties; those transnational ties, in turn, can further migrants' civic and political incorporation in societies of settlement as they begin to engage with host-society political systems on behalf of home-country causes (Pantoja, 2005; Portes et al., 2008). In other

BOX 8.2 HISTORICAL PERSPECTIVES ON TRANSNATIONALISM AND DIASPORA

Scholars of transnationalism have often posited that intense, persistent, cross-border activity among migrants is a new phenomenon borne of late-20th century globalization and advancements in transport and communication technologies. Some scholars, however, have raised objections to this basic premise of transnational theory, pointing to the intensity of global flows in the 19th century and the involvement of migrants at this time in a range of transnational politics and practices. While they may not have had access to jet travel or the internet, migrants of the 19th century took advantage of the plummeting cost of rail and steamship travel to move back and forth across borders, and they communicated regularly with compatriots by post and telegraph. Local mother-language presses circulated information about goings-on back home and provided migrants with forums in which to participate in national debates (e.g. Gualtieri, 2009). Radical labour movements, which shook industrialized societies to their core in the late 19th and early 20th century, were fuelled by trans-Atlantic and cross-border flows of revolutionary ideas, radical leaders, and funds (Goyens, 2007). Nationalist movements at the turn of the century also relied on émigré communities for financial, political, and even military support, as seen in the struggle for Italian unification (Gabaccia, 2001) and in the development of Arab nationalism in post-Ottoman Syria (Gualtieri, 2009).

These histories pose an important challenge to theories of transnationalism, as well as to theories of assimilation. On the one hand, if transnationalism is not new, then how do we interpret the patterns and processes of migrant incorporation that took place in major settler societies like Canada, Australia, Argentina, Brazil, and the US? Did these migrants, in fact, simply assimilate into these societies as is commonly assumed? On the other hand, can we assume that contemporary migrants will maintain their transnational orientations across multiple generations? Will their connections with places of origin diminish, as happened (apparently) with their forebears? These difficult questions force us to move past the now-and-then dichotomy that characterized initial theorizations of transnationalism and to think more carefully of the ways in which material and emotional connections with far-off 'homelands' intersect with and shape migrants' engagements with societies of settlement in different historical and geographical contexts.

cases, transnational orientations seem to be a response to racialization, downward mobility, or marginalization. That is, the denial of access to membership in societies of settlement seems to encourage some migrants to attach themselves more firmly to places of origin (Mazzucato, 2008). And yet we have also seen (as in the case of undocumented workers in the US) that precariousness and exclusion can have the opposite effect, prompting migrants to mobilize to claim rights of membership. Trajectories of migrants' identities, engagements, and mobilizations, in short, do not seem to conform to any predetermined path, but rather, like many other aspects of migrants' lives, seem contingent on unique combinations of place-based circumstances, local histories, and migrant characteristics—such as their economic resources and skills; their position in class, gender, age, and racial hierarchies; and their familial situations.

Conclusions

We conclude this chapter and this book purposefully on a note of open-endedness and indeterminacy. Like many questions relating to migration—e.g. are migrants good for the economy? Do borders work? Does citizenship matter?—questions about the transformative effects of migration on people's identities and lives do not lend themselves to clear-cut answers. In this chapter, as in other chapters, we have urged our readers to eschew simple models and formulas and to embrace instead the complexities and ambiguities of social relationships as they unfold over time and space. It is not easy to categorize migrants, to pigeonhole their experiences, or to impose some orderly trajectory on their lives. Migrants are at once victims of exploitation and exploiters of others. They are subject to social hierarchies and inequalities and they reproduce and reinforce social hierarchies and inequalities in their families and communities. Migrants are excluded by ideologies of race, but

they can rework these same ideologies to gain inclusion in dominant spheres, sometimes at the expense of other migrants or minority groups. Migrants can enthusiastically maintain ties with homelands, but their spouses, children, and friends can just as easily reject those ties and create alternative social fields and ideas of home. This kind of messiness is not incidental to migration but central to it.

Unfortunately, most of the media reports we see about migration and migrants, while sometimes sympathetic to migrants, tend to ignore all of this messiness. What we get instead are certain stock images of migrants as toiling farmworkers, as asylum seekers stranded at sea, or as refugees languishing in UN camps. These images are not inaccurate, per se, but they greatly oversimplify who migrants are and the processes and relationships that shape their mobility and their experiences. Take, for instance, the case of Filipinos in Saudi Arabia. We often hear about the terrible exploitation of Filipino workers in Saudi Arabia, and for good reason. Yet a closer look at this group reveals many factors that complicate the dominant image of oppressed Filipino workers. Filipinos in Saudi Arabia are not a homogenous group. Some Filipinos—especially those who are Muslim—have in fact experienced upward mobility by migrating to Saudi Arabia. These Muslim Filipinos tend to work in more skilled occupations and in many cases are able to migrate as families, making it possible for them to view their time in Saudi Arabia as a long-term commitment rather than a temporary sojourn (Johnson, 2010). But while in some ways they feel more 'at home' in Saudi Arabia than in the Philippines, they are routinely confronted with Saudi racism towards Filipinos and by a multitude of limitations on their rights and freedoms. This, in turn, generates a sense of camaraderie with other Filipinos that cuts across both class and religious divides. In addition to participating in local Filipino migrant organizations and in transnational networks, some middle-class Filipino families have taken in lone Filipina domestic workers who have run away from abusive employers and who have therefore lost their legal status. The complexities of the situation do not end here. In extending assistance to runaways, middle-class Filipino migrants are not acting in an entirely altruistic manner. Indeed, taking in a runaway is one of the only means by which middle-class Filipinas can secure the domestic help needed if they are to engage in paid employment (thereby avoiding an isolated, home-bound existence). Solidarity between Filipinos, then, is tempered by the need of middle-class Filipinas to affirm their class status in a context in which they themselves are often mistaken for servants (ibid.).

What does this brief account, with all of its twists and turns, tell us about the category of 'Filipino migrant worker'? Filipino at one level is an identity category that facilitates labour exploitation in Saudi Arabia and that, at the same time, serves as a source of local and transnational solidarity. Underlying that solidarity, though, are very distinctive sets of opportunities and constraints. Some Filipinos are highly exploited domestic workers, while others are less exploited skilled workers. Some are lone workers supporting families back 'home' in the Philippines, while others are part of family units intent on creating 'home' in the country of settlement. The Filipinos described here are citizens and foreigners, subjects and agents, documented and undocumented. There is no simple way to explain this scenario, and it does not provide any clear answers to the kinds of either/or questions that animate public debate about immigration in wealthy receiving societies.

This is not to say, however, that there are no generalizations to be made about migration. The case of Muslim Filipinos returns us to a number of key themes and perspectives that have appeared throughout this book. We see in this case, for instance, the segmentation of labour markets by race, gender, and other markers of social difference, and we can take note of the specificity of migration processes in terms of places of origin and destination and social

characteristic of migrants. We see the continued salience of the nation-state in the management of population flows, the selectivity of borders, and the assignment of rights and privileges to particular groups. We see the simultaneous rigidity and fluidity of national polities and institutions. We see, as well, the interplay of structure and agency—that is, migrants' negotiation and accommodation of, or outright resistance to, the institutions, social orders, and power arrangements that they encounter on a day-to-day basis. Embracing the messiness of migration, then, is not about miring ourselves in the details of every single migration case study. Rather, it involves using the details of specific cases in a focused way to explore the power dynamics, located in states, economies, families, and households, that drive and shape human mobility.

Key terms in this chapter

diaspora	transnationalism
ethnoburb	whiteness
social fields	

Further reading

Blunt, A. and Bonnerjee, J. (2013) Home, city and diaspora: Anglo–Indian and Chinese attachments to Calcutta, *Global Networks*, 13(2): 220–240.

Cheng, W. (2010) 'Diversity' on Main Street? Branding race and place in the new 'majority-minority' suburbs, *Identities: Global Studies in Culture and Power*, 17(5): 458–486.

Christou, A. and Mavroudi, E. (Eds.) (2015) *Dismantling Diasporas: Rethinking the Geographies of Diasporic Identity, Connection and Development*. London: Ashgate.

Dwyer, C. and Bressey, C. (Eds.) (2008) *New Geographies of Race and Racism*. Aldershot: Ashgate.

Jackson, P., Crang, P., and Dwyer, C. (Eds.) (2004) *Transnational Spaces*. London: Routledge.

Kitiarsa, P. (2008) Thai migrants in Singapore: state, intimacy and desire, *Gender, Place and Culture*, 15(6): 595–610.

Law, L. (2001) Home cooking: Filipino women and geographies of the senses in Hong Kong, *Cultural Geographies*, 8(3): 264–283.

Vertovec, S. (2001) Transnationalism and identity, *Journal of Ethnic and Migration Studies*, 27(4): 573–582.

Willis, K. D. and Yeoh, B. S. (2000) Gender and transnational household strategies: Singaporean migration to China, *Regional Studies*, 34(3): 253–264.

References

Alba, R. and Nee, V. (1997) Rethinking assimilation theory for a new era of immigration, *International Migration Review*, 31(4): 826–874.

Anderson, K. J. (1991) *Vancouver's Chinatown: Racial Discourse in Canada, 1875–1980*. Quebec City: McGill-Queen's Press.

Anthias, F. (1998) Evaluating diaspora: beyond ethnicity? *Sociology*, 32(3): 557–580.

Anthias, F. (2008) Thinking through the lens of translocational positionality: an intersectionality frame for understanding identity and belonging, *Translocations: Migration and Social Change*, 4(1): 5–20.

Back, L. (1996) *New Ethnicities and Urban Culture: Racism and Multiculture in Young Lives*. New York: St Martin's Press.

Basch, L., Schiller, N. G., and Blanc, C. S. (1994) *Nations Unbound: Transnational Projects, Postcolonial Predicaments, and Deterritorialized Nation-States*. Amsterdam: Gordon and Breach.

Bonnett, A. (1997) Geography, 'race' and whiteness: invisible traditions and current challenges, *Area*, 29(3): 193–199.

Brubaker, R. (2005) The 'diaspora' diaspora, *Ethnic and Racial Studies*, 28(1): 1–19.

Bugg, L. B. (2013) Citizenship and belonging in the rural fringe: a case study of a Hindu temple in Sydney, Australia, *Antipode*, 45(5): 1148–1166.

Chafetz, J. S. and Ebaugh, H. R. (Eds.) (2000) *Religion and the New Immigrants: Continuities and Adaptations in Immigrant Congregations*. Walnut Creek, CA: Altamira Press.

Chiang, L. H. N. and Hsu, J. C. R. (2005) Locational decisions and residential preferences of Taiwanese immigrants in Australia, *GeoJournal*, 64(1): 75–89.

Clifford, J. (1994) Diasporas, *Cultural Anthropology*, 9(3): 302–338.

Cohen, R. (2008) *Global Diasporas: An Introduction*. Abingdon: Routledge.

Constable, N. (2009) Migrant workers and the many states of protest in Hong Kong, *Critical Asian Studies*, 41(1): 143–164.

Drachsler, J. (1920) *Democracy and Assimilation: The Blending of Immigrant Heritages in America*. New York: MacMillan.

Duncan, J. and Duncan, N. (2003) Can't live with them, can't landscape without them: racism and the pastoral aesthetic in suburban New York, *Landscape Journal*, 22(2): 88–98.

Dwyer, C. (1999) Veiled meanings: young British Muslim women and the negotiation of differences, *Gender, Place and Culture*, 6(1): 5–26.

Dwyer, C., Gilbert, D. and Shah, B. (2013) Faith and suburbia: secularisation, modernity and the changing geographies of religion in London's suburbs, *Transactions of the Institute of British Geographers*, 38(3): 403–419.

Farrar, M. E. (2008) *Building the Body Politic: Power and Urban Space in Washington*. Urbana-Champaign: University of Illinois Press.

Frankenberg, R. (Ed.) (1997) *Displacing Whiteness: Essays in Social and Cultural Criticism*. Durham, NC: Duke University Press.

Gabaccia, D. (2001) Class, exile, and nationalism at home and abroad: the Italian Risorgimento. In D. Gabaccia and F. M. Ottannelli (Eds.), *Italian Workers of the World: Labor Migration and the Formation of Multiethnic States*. Chicago; Urbana: University of Illinois Press (pp. 21–40).

Gans, H. J. (1979) Symbolic ethnicity: the future of ethnic groups and cultures in America, *Ethnic and Racial Studies*, 2(1): 1–20.

Gans, H. J. (1992). Comment: ethnic invention and acculturation, a bumpy-line approach, *Journal of American Ethnic History*, 12(1): 42–52.

Gilroy, P. ([1987]2002) *There Ain't No Black in the Union Jack*. Abingdon, UK: Routledge.

Glasman, J. (1991) Assimilation by design: London synagogues in the nineteenth century, *Immigrants & Minorities*, 10(1–2): 171–211.

Glazer, N. and Moynihan, D. P. (1963) *Beyond the Melting Pot: The Negroes, Puerto Ricans, Jews, Italians and Irish of New York City*. Cambridge, MA: MIT Press.

Glenn, E. N. (2011) Constructing citizenship exclusion, subordination, and resistance, *American Sociological Review*, 76(1): 1–24.

Glick Schiller, N. and Fouron, G. E. (1999) Terrains of blood and nation: Haitian transnational social fields, *Ethnic and Racial Studies*, 22(2): 340–366.

Gordon, M. M. (1964) *Assimilation in American Life: The Role of Race, Religion and National Origins*. New York: Oxford University Press.

Goyens, T. (2007) *Beer and Revolution: The German Anarchist Movement in New York City, 1880–1914*. Urbana-Champaign: University of Illinois Press.

Gualtieri, S. (2009) *Between Arab and White: Race and Ethnicity in the Early Syrian American Diaspora*. Berkeley; Los Angeles: University of California Press.

Guarnizo, L. E., Portes, A., and Haller, W. (2003) Determinants of transnational political action among contemporary migrants, *American Journal of Sociology*, 108(6): 1211–1248.

Hall, S. (1992) Race, culture, and communications: looking backward and forward at Cultural Studies, *Rethinking Marxism: A Journal of Economics, Culture & Society*, 5(1): 10–18.

Hall, S. and Du Gay, P. (Eds.) (1996) *Questions of Cultural Identity*. London: Sage.

Hickman, M. J. and Walter, B. (1995) Deconstructing whiteness: Irish women in Britain, *Feminist Review*, 50 (summer): 5–19.

Higham, J. (1955) *Strangers in the Land: Patterns of American Nativism, 1860–1925*. New Brunswick, NJ: Rutgers University Press.

Hondagneu-Sotelo, P. and Avila, E. (1997) 'I'm there, but I'm there': the meanings of Latina transnational motherhood, *Gender & Society*, 11(5): 548–571.

Horton, J. (1995) *The Politics of Diversity: Immigration, Resistance, and Change in Monterey Park, California*. Philadelphia, PA: Temple University Press.

Hsia, H. C. (2009) The making of a transnational grassroots migrant movement: a case study of Hong Kong's Asian Migrants' Coordinating Body, *Critical Asian Studies*, 41(1): 113–141.

Itzigsohn, J. (2000) Immigration and the boundaries of citizenship: the institutions of immigrants' political transnationalism, *International Migration Review*, 34(4): 1126–1154.

Jacobson, M. F. (1999) *Whiteness of a Different Color*. Cambridge, MA: Harvard University Press.

Johnson, M. (2010) Diasporic dreams, middle-class moralities and migrant domestic workers among Muslim Filipinos in Saudi Arabia, *The Asia Pacific Journal of Anthropology*, 11(3–4): 428–448.

Jöns, H., Mavroudi, E., and Heffernan, M. (2015) Mobilising the elective diaspora: US–German academic exchanges since

1945, *Transactions of the Institute of British Geographers*, 40: 113–127.

Karafilis, M. (2010) The Jewish Ghetto and the Americanization of space in Mary Antin and her contemporaries, *American Literary Realism*, 42(2): 129–150.

Kivisto, P. (1990) The transplanted then and now: the reorientation of immigration studies from the Chicago School to the new social history, *Ethnic and Racial Studies*, 13(4): 455–481.

Kivisto, P. (2004) What is the canonical theory of assimilation? *Journal of the History of the Behavioral Sciences*, 40(2): 149–163.

Kurien, P. (2007) Who speaks for Indian Americans? Religion, ethnicity, and political formation, *American Quarterly*, 59(3): 759–783.

Leichtman, M. A. (2005) The legacy of transnational lives: beyond the first generation of Lebanese in Senegal, *Ethnic and Racial Studies*, 28(4): 663–686.

Li, W. (1998) Anatomy of a new ethnic settlement: the Chinese ethnoburb in Los Angeles, *Urban Studies*, 35(3): 479–501.

Lieberson, S. (1985) Unhyphenated whites in the United States, *Ethnic and Racial Studies*, 8(1): 159–180.

Lloyd, C. (2000) Trade unions and immigrants in France: from assimilation to antiracist networking. In R. Penninx and J. Roosblad (Eds.), *Trade Unions, Immigration, and Immigrants in Europe, 1960–1993*. Amsterdam: Berghahn Books (pp. 111–132).

Mavroudi, E. (2007) Learning to be Palestinian in Athens: constructing diasporic national identities, *Global Networks*, 7(4): 392–412.

Mavroudi, E. (2008) Palestinians in diaspora, empowerment and informal political space, *Political Geography*, 27(1): 57–73.

Mazzucato, V. (2008) The double engagement: transnationalism and integration. Ghanaian migrants' lives between Ghana and the Netherlands, *Journal of Ethnic and Migration Studies*, 34(2): 199–216.

Meer, N. (2009) Identity articulations, mobilization, and autonomy in the movement for Muslim schools in Britain, *Race, Ethnicity and Education*, 12(3): 379–399.

Mitchell, K. (1997a) Conflicting geographies of democracy and the public sphere in Vancouver BC, *Transactions of the Institute of British Geographers*, 22(2): 162–179.

Mitchell, K. (1997b) Different diasporas and the hype of hybridity, *Environment and Planning D: Society and Space*, 15: 533–554.

Moran-Taylor, M. and Menjívar, C. (2005) Unpacking longings to return: Guatemalans and Salvadorans in Phoenix, Arizona, *International Migration*, 43(4): 91–120.

Morawska, E. (2004) Exploring diversity in immigrant assimilation and transnationalism: Poles and Russian Jews in Philadelphia, *International Migration Review*, 38(4): 1372–1412.

Naber, N. (2005) Muslim first, Arab second: a strategic politics of race and gender, *The Muslim World*, 95(4): 479–495.

Nagel, C. R. (2009) Rethinking geographies of assimilation, *The Professional Geographer*, 61(3): 400–407.

Nagel, C. R. and Staeheli, L. A. (2011) Muslim political activism or political activism by Muslims? Secular and religious identities amongst Muslim Arab activists in the United States and United Kingdom, *Identities*, 18(5): 437–458.

Naylor, S. and Ryan, J. R. (2002) The mosque in the suburbs: negotiating religion and ethnicity in South London, *Social & Cultural Geography*, 3(1), 39–59.

Nelson, L. (2008) Racialized landscapes: whiteness and the struggle over farmworker housing in Woodburn, Oregon, *Cultural Geographies*, 15(1): 41–62.

Nicholls, W. J. (2013) Making undocumented immigrants into a legitimate political subject: theoretical observations from the United States and France, *Theory, Culture & Society*, 30(3): 82–107.

Østergaard-Nielsen, E. (2003) The politics of migrants' transnational political practices, *International Migration Review*, 37(3): 760–786.

Pantoja, A. D. (2005) Transnational ties and immigrant political incorporation: The case of Dominicans in Washington Heights, New York, *International Migration*, 43(4): 123–146.

Park, R. E. (1928) Human migration and the marginal man, *American Journal of Sociology*, 33(6): 881–893.

Parreñas, R. S. (2001) Mothering from a distance: emotions, gender, and intergenerational relations in Filipino transnational families, *Feminist Studies*, 27(2): 361–390.

Peach, C. (1996) Does Britain have ghettos? *Transactions of the Institute of British Geographers*, 21(1): 216–235.

Perlmann, J. and Waldinger, R. (1997) Second generation decline? Children of immigrants, past and present—a reconsideration, *International Migration Review*, 31(4): 893–922.

Portes, A. (1997) Immigration theory for a new century: some problems and opportunities, *International Migration Review*, 31(4): 799–825.

Portes, A. and Zhou, M. (1993) The new second generation: segmented assimilation and its variants, *The Annals of the American Academy of Political and Social Science*, 530(1): 74–96.

Portes, A., Escobar, C., and Arana, R. (2008) Bridging the gap: transnational and ethnic organizations in the political incorporation of immigrants in the United States, *Ethnic and Racial Studies*, 31(6): 1056–1090.

Roediger, D. R. (2005) *Working Toward Whiteness: How America's Immigrants Became White*. New York: Basic Books.

Rouse, R. (1992) Making sense of settlement: class transformation, cultural struggle, and transnationalism among Mexican migrants in the United States, *Annals of the New York Academy of Sciences*, 645(1): 25–52.

Rumbaut, R. G. and Portes, A. (Eds.) (2001) *Ethnicities: Children of Immigrants in America*. Berkeley; Los Angeles: University of California Press.

Safran, W. (1991) Diasporas in modern societies: myths of homeland and return, *Diaspora: A Journal of Transnational Studies*, 1(1): 83–99.

Said, E. (1978) *Orientalism: Western Representations of the Orient*. New York: Pantheon.

Salih, R. (2001) Moroccan migrant women: transnationalism, nation-states and gender, *Journal of Ethnic and Migration Studies*, 27(4): 655–671.

Singer, A., Hardwick, S. W., and Brettell, C. (Eds.) (2009) *Twenty-First Century Gateways: Immigrant Incorporation in Suburban America*. Washington, DC: Brookings Institution Press.

Smith, M. P. (1994) Can you imagine? Transnational migration and the globalization of grassroots politics, *Social Text*, 39(summer): 15–33.

Smith, M. P. (2003) Transnationalism, the state, and the extraterritorial citizen, *Politics & Society*, 31(4): 467–502.

Smith, M. P. and Bakker, M. (2005) The transnational politics of the Tomato King: meaning and impact, *Global Networks*, 5(2): 129–146.

Speek, P. A. (1926) The meaning of nationality and Americanization, *American Journal of Sociology*, 32(2): 237–249.

Spitzer, D., Neufeld, A., Harrison, M., Hughes, K., and Stewart, M. (2003) Caregiving in transnational context: 'My wings have been cut; where can I fly?' *Gender & Society*, 17(2): 267–286.

Staeheli, L. A. and Nagel, C. R. (2006) Topographies of home and citizenship: Arab-American activists in the United States, *Environment and Planning A*, 38(9): 1599–1614.

Streeby, S. (2007) Labor, memory, and the boundaries of print culture: from Haymarket to the Mexican Revolution, *American Literary History*, 19(2): 406–433.

Thomas, W. I. and Znaniecki, F. (1920) *The Polish Peasant in Europe and America: Monograph of an Immigrant Group* (Volume V: Organization and Disorganization in America). Boston: Richard G. Badger.

Trudeau, D. (2006) Politics of belonging in the construction of landscapes: place-making, boundary-drawing and exclusion, *Cultural Geographies*, 13(3): 421–443.

Veronis, L. (2006) The Canadian Hispanic Day Parade, or how Latin American immigrants practise (sub)urban citizenship in Toronto, *Environment and Planning A*, 38(9): 1653–1671.

Waghorne, J. P. (1999) The Hindu gods in a split-level world: the Sri Siva-Vishnu Temple in suburban Washington, DC. In R. A. Orsi (Ed.) *Gods of the City: Religion and the American Urban Landscape*. Bloomington: Indiana University Press (pp.103–130).

Waters, M. C. (1990) *Ethnic Options: Choosing Identities in America*. Berkeley; Los Angeles: University of California Press.

Waters, M. C. (1996) Ethnic and racial identities of second-generation black immigrants in New York City. In A. Portes (Ed.), *The New Second Generation*. New York: Russell Sage (pp. 171–196).

Werbner, P. (2002) The place which is diaspora: citizenship, religion and gender in the making of chaordic transnationalism, *Journal of Ethnic and Migration Studies*, 28(1): 119–133.

Werbner, P. (2004) Theorising complex diasporas: purity and hybridity in the South Asian public sphere in Britain, *Journal of Ethnic and Migration Studies*, 30(5): 895–911.

Wimmer, A. and Glick Schiller, N. (2002) Methodological nationalism and beyond: nation-state building, migration and the social sciences, *Global Networks*, 2(4): 301–334.

Wirth, L. (1938) Urbanism as a way of life, *American Journal of Sociology*, 44(1): 1–24.

Wise, A. (2005) Hope and belonging in a multicultural suburb, *Journal of Intercultural Studies*, 26(1–2): 171–186.

Yancey, W. L., Ericksen, E. P., and Juliani, R. N. (1976) Emergent ethnicity: a review and reformulation, *American Sociological Review*, 41(3): 391–403.

Yeh, E. T. and Lama, K. T. (2006) Hip-hop gangsta or most deserving of victims? Transnational migrant identities and the paradox of racialization in the USA, *Environment and Planning A*, 38: 809–829.

Yeoh, B. S. and Willis, K. (1999) 'Heart' and 'wing', nation and diaspora: gendered discourses in Singapore's regionalisation process, *Gender, Place and Culture: A Journal of Feminist Geography*, 6(4): 355–372.

Young, P. V. (1928) The reorganization of Jewish family life in America: a natural history of the social forces governing the assimilation of the Jewish immigrant, *Social Forces*, 7(2): 238–244.

Zhou, M. (1997) Segmented assimilation: issues, controversies, and recent research on the new second generation, *International Migration Review*, 31(4): 975–1008.

Index

Figures are shown by a page reference in *italics* and tables are shown in **bold**.

Africa: European migration to, 19th century 40; international migration 51–2; migrants to Israel 1; slave trade 32–3; sub-Saharan Africa 52, 104

agency of migrants: economic/political migration as voluntary/involuntary 118–19, 120; exploitation of stereotypes 79–80; integration and rules of membership 198; migration as a conscious choice 79; political mobilization of 81; of refugees 141–3; and social networks 21, 143; undocumented immigrants 80–1; worker negotiations 79

agriculture: differentiated wage structures 67, 79; vegetable pickers *60*

aid: for asylum policing 131–2; for economic development 91, 93, 95, 107; for refugee-receiving countries 139–40

Albania 67

Algeria 40

Anderson, K. 181, 211

Andreas, P. 164

Angola 139, 142

anti-immigrant groups 158

Araia, T. 169

Argentina 40

Asia: economic growth 49; female domestic workers from 51, 67, 70; migrant workers to Gulf Arab States 51; migration corridors, Southeast Asia 49–51; promotion of labour export 100–1; *see also individual countries*

assimilation studies: canonical accounts 207–8; Chicago School theorists 205; clustering of immigrants 211–12; criticism of 181–2; diaspora relationships 218; ethnicity and social organization 208–9; incorporation pathways 209; and the Marginal Man 208; multi-dimensional processes 207–8; overview of 180; psychological distress 206–7; and second generation immigrants 207; and transnationalism 222–3

asylum seekers: aid for asylum policing *130*, 131–2, 169; applications to Europe, post-Cold War 125–6, **126**; Australian policies 129–32, *130*, 169; as 'bogus' 127–8; definitions of 6–7, 144; discretionary status of 121, 136–7, 144; displacement due to climate change 144–5; to Europe, late 20th century 47; in France 126–7, *127*, 129; in Germany 137; in Greece *131*, 136; initial decisions on asylum applications, EU **134–5**; in Israel *2*, 6; Jungle Camp, Calais *128*; in Lebanon *136*, *137*, *141*; media coverage of 126–7; within national contexts 7; neorefoulement and 130–1; safe-third-country provisions 132–3; securitization of 129–37; term 119; total asylum applications, selected countries **133**; *see also* refugees

Australia: asylum seekers, detention of 129–30; Chinese immigrants, historical 35; convict labour 33; decoupling of ethnicity/race and citizenship 189; expansionary immigration policies 48–9, 156; foreign-born population 10; gateway cities 11; Greek community in 110; international tertiary education programmes 75–6; multiculturalism policies 190; nativist unrest and immigration controls 154; neorefoulement of asylum seekers (Pacific Solution) 130–2, *130*, 169; racially motivated immigration restrictions, early 20th century 42; skilled migration programme 75

Back, L. 210
Bakewell, O. 139, 142, 144
Bakker, M. 220
Bauder, H. 76
Beaverstock, J. 74, 77
Bhagwati, J. N. 98
Bonacich, E. 63
Booth, D. 110
border controls: as bordering practices 151, 159, 166; economic interests and migration flows 157–8; effects on remittances 109; European Union (EU) 157, *160*, 162–3, 169–70; exclusionary practices 156; failure of 156, 157; and global labour mobility 151; historical perspectives 153–6; and internal surveillance 166–9; nativist unrest and immigration controls 154–5; necessity of 170–1; outsourcing of 69, 130–2, *130*, 169–70; readmission agreements 170; remittances and 109; remote border controls 169–70; restrictionist regimes 154–5; role of nation-states 72–3, 156, 159; Sangatte affair, France 126–7, *127*; and separation of rich/poor 171; special interest groups influences 158; US–Mexico border controls 97, *152*, 155, 157, *162*, 163–4, *165*
Borjas, G. 82
Boswell, C. 158
Brazil: European migration to 30, 31, 40; slave trade and 33
Bruff, I. 79
Burgess, E. W. 180

Canada: changing citizenship laws 194; Chinatown, Vancouver 181, 211–12; Chinese immigrant 'monster houses' 197, 213, 214; decoupling of ethnicity/race and citizenship 189, 194; expansionary immigration policies 48–9, 156; foreign-born population 10; Latino activists 217; Live-In Caregiver programme 71; multiculturalism policies 190; nativist unrest and immigration controls 154; racially motivated immigration restrictions, early 20th century 42; skilled migrants in 75, 76
Cangiano, A. 5–6
capitalism: emergence of and migration flows 15, 41, 151, 153; geographical inequalities, need for 96; global capitalism and transnationalism 218–19; as goal of post-colonial nations 92, 93; labour/capital relationship 83; and neo-Marxist theories 19
Carens, J. 171
Caribbean states: emigrants by population percentage 12; immigration to the UK, 1950s 71, *193*; slave trade and 33
Carling, J. 164
Castles, S. 159
chain migration 40–1, 157
Chakravartty, P. 78
Chicago School theorists 205
China: Chinese exclusion acts, USA 154; Chinese ghetto, Vancouver 181, 211–12; Chinese immigrant 'monster houses' Canada/US 197, 213, 214; Chinese immigrants, historical 35, *35*, 154; Chinese students in Japan 77–8; cultivation of diasporic communities 102–3; indentured workers (coolie system) 34–5; internal migration 8; Uighur population 125
citizenship: changing citizenship laws 191–5; civic conceptions of 183–4, 185–8; concept of 179–80; decoupling of ethnicity/race from 187, 189–90, 194; denizenship 188; dual citizenship options 103, 189, 191; Eastern European Jews in Germany 121; ethnic conceptions of 183–5, 186–8; and

integration 178, 182–8; intensification
of ethnicity/race and citizenship 192; jus
domicile 189; jus sanguinis 184; jus soli
184, 187, 188; local politics of 196–8; of
Mizrahi Jews in Israel 182; multiculturalism
and 190, 195; nation-state control over
191–2; non-state actors and 196–7; path
dependency, policy trajectories 183;
post-national citizenship 188–9; rights
of 179; voting rights, émigrés 103; and
the wider community 179–80; *see also*
post-national citizenship
civic citizenship 183–4, 185–8
climate change 144–5
Cold War era: and development concept 92;
politicization of refugees 124–5; refugee
resettlement 123
Coleman, M. 151
colonialism: alternative labour sources 33–5;
colonial migrants to Europe 45–6; convict
labour 33; coolie system 34–5, 66; by
Europe 29; European migration to the
colonies 30, 31–2; indentured servitude 32;
migration flows 29–30; native population
decline 32; slave trade 32–3; in Spanish
America 29–30
Constable, N. 215
construction industry: migrant workers
in *3*, 13; Polish workers in the UK 80;
remittances for social and prestige items
108
coolie system 34, 66
core, term 16
Cornelius, W. A. 157
cottage industries 30–1, 35
coyotes 164
Cultural Studies 209

De Haas, H. 104–5
decolonialization: post-colonial development
92–3; state formation and refugee crises
123; *see also* colonialism
Deimel, S. 170
Del Sarto, R. 170
Delgado Wise, R. 110

denizenship 188
Denton, N. A. 181
deportation: Secure Communities
programme, USA 167; and securitization
policies 165–6; of undocumented
immigrants 73
destination countries *see* receiving countries
development: aid for economic development
91, 93, 95, 107; co-development
programmes 107, 108–9; concept of 92;
development aid and asylum policing *130*,
131–2, 169; intermediate development and
migration 95–6; migration as development
strategy 97–110; migration hump model
95–6, *95*; neoliberalist models of 96;
post-colonial development 92–3;
remittances to sending countries 99–103;
to retain potential migrants in sending
countries 94–7; sustainable development
93; term 92; underdevelopment, condition
of 93; uneven development patterns 107–8;
see also migration-development nexus
diaspora: in assimilation theories 218;
cultivation of diasporic communities 101–2;
definitions of 219; diasporic consciousness
101–3, 109–10; historical perspective 222;
long-distance nationalism 220; relationship
with places of origin 221; repressive
gender norms, reproduction of 220–1;
and trans-border lives 218–20; *see also*
transnationalism
domestic workers: Consulate Hopping
Protest 215–16; as female employment
66–7; Filipina workers *68*, 100, *101*; Gulf
Arab States 51; historical perspective 32;
Live-In Caregiver programme, Canada
71; occupational segmentation 70;
undocumented immigrants 72
Dominican Republic 102, 103, 105
Doomernik, J. 143
Drachsler, J. 207
dual labour market theory 65–6
Dubai, UAE *3*
Durand, J. 157
Dustmann, C. 82

economic processes: growth and skilled migrants 75; and migration flows 15–16, 157–8; migration for personal economic success 79; neoclassical approaches 18–19, 91, 94; role of migrants within 81–2; skills and education of migrants 59; social capital 59–61; structural readjustment policies, Global South 99; *see also* development; migration-development nexus

Ecuador 20

education: advanced systems of and brain drain 98; and earning potential 58; emigration of education population 12; and employment of African Americans 58–9; exploitation of foreign students 77–8; and human capital 58–9; international tertiary education programmes 75–6; of nurses, Philippines 101

El Salvador 12, 124

Ellis, M. 61

emigration, term 5

émigrés: diasporic consciousness 101–3, 109–10; dual nationality provisions 103, 191; term 5; ties with countries of origin 98; *see also* skilled migrants

entropy models 17

ethnic citizenship 183–4

ethnic economies 62; *see also* immigrant entrepreneurialism

ethnicity: concepts of 187; decoupling of ethnicity/race and citizenship 187, 189–90, 194; ethnicity and social organization 208–9

ethnoburbs 212–13

ethno-national conflict: First World War 41–2; inter-war years 42–3; Palestine/Israel 43; partition of India 43; Second World War 43

Europe: asylum applications, post-Cold War 125–6; asylum seekers, late 20th century 47; colonial settlers 45–6; commercial economy formation 30; complex migration policies 156; compulsory expulsions, inter-war years 43; cottage industries 30–1, 35; expansionary immigration policies in 158; feudal Europe 29; foreign-born population 10; indentured servitude 32; industrialization 35–8; inter-state migration, post-war years 44–5; knowledge workers 47; labour demands, war economies 41–2; low-skilled workers 47–8; mass migration to the New World 38–40; migration from 40; migration to the 'New World' 29–30; population growth, historical *36, 37*; proletarianization 30, 36; refugees, historical 120; refugees, post-WWII 123; rural-to-urban migration, 18th century 30–1, 35; slave trade 32–3; sovereign state, development of 29, 153; state formation and refugee flow 120–2; state policies and border controls 157; undocumented immigrants in Southern Europe 48; urbanization rates *31*

European Neighbourhood Policy (ENP) 170

European Union (EU): asylum policing and development aid 132; blue card (skilled migrants) 75, 78; changing citizenship law 194–5; employment opportunities in origin countries 95; Frontex 163, 164; initial decisions on asylum applications **134–5**; outsourcing of border controls 169–70; post-national citizenship 188–9; safe-third-country provisions 132–3; securitization of migration 162–3

European-centred world economy 28–30

exclusionary border controls 154, 156

expansionary immigration policies: Australia 48–9, 156; business interests and 158; Canada 48–9, 156; Europe 158; Israel 182; United States of America (USA) 46, 48, 156

Fabbri, F. 82

Faist, T. 162

Favell, A. 157, 158

Fawcett, J. 20

feudal Europe 29

Filipino Domestic Workers Association 81

First World War: border controls 155; foreign labour, Germany 42; refugees 121–2

Fitzgerald, D. 107

Fouron, G. E. 220
France: asylum seekers, detention of 129; border control, Calais *160*; civic conceptions of citizenship 185–6; immigrant workers, historical 36, 42, 185; the Islamic headscarf debates 186; laïcité 186; nativist unrest and immigration controls 155; Pasqua Laws 188; Sangatte affair 126–7, *127*
Freeman, G. 157–8
Frontex 163, 164

Gabiam, N. 142
gateway cities 10–12
Geiger, M. 159, 160
gender: hometown associations (HTA) as patriarchal 109; and intergenerational conflict 211; and segmented labour markets 66–9; social capital and gender disparities 64; *see also* domestic workers; women
geographical terminology 16
Germany: asylum seekers in 47, 137; citizenship of Eastern European Jews 121; decoupling of ethnicity/race and citizenship 189; dual citizenship options 189; ethnic citizenship policies 184; foreign labour, WWI 42; Germany–Turkey corridor 9, 163; Greek immigrants to *44*; guest workers 45, 70, 97, 103, 158, 184, 188; industrialization 35, 36; Jews and Nazi Germany 122; nativist unrest and immigration controls 155; net migration figures *14*; Polish immigrants, historical 36, 38; skilled migrant unemployment rates 76; undocumented immigrants 81
ghettos 180–1, 211–12
Gibney, M. J. 119, 124
Glick Schiller, N. 220
Global North: development and migration flows 94–7; refugees, historical 120; term 16
Global South: migration as development strategy 97–110; refugees within 137–40; structural readjustment policies 99; term 16
globalization: global capitalism and transnationalism 218–19; and industrial restructuring 83; and labour mobility 14, 151; patterns of 14–15
Goldring, L. 109
Grasmuck, S. 61
gravity models 17
Great Britain *see* United Kingdom
Greece: asylum seekers *131*, 136; Greek Cypriot community, UK 62–3; Greek-Australian communities 110; immigrants to Germany *44*; jus sanguinis system of citizenship 184; Palestinian community in 221; policy shift, migrants and citizenship 188; refugees asleep on the beach *6*; and Turkish state formation 122
Grillo, R. 108–9
Grosfoguel, R. 61
Gualtieri, S. 210
Guarnizo, L. E. 221
guest workers 45, 70, 97, 103, 184, 188
Gulf Arab States: Asian migrant workers 51, 67, 70; domestic workers 51, 67, 70; foreign-born population 10, 51; *see also* Saudi Arabia

Haiti 220
Haller, W. 221
Hammar, T. 188
Hansen, R. 157, 158
healthcare industry: and brain drain 98; as recipient of labour export strategies 100–1; skilled migrants in 74
Hernández-Carretero, M. 164
highly skilled migrants *see* skilled migrants
Hoag, C. 169
Huguenots 120
human capital: and education 58–9; and labour markets 58–9; skilled migrants 74; term 58
Human Development Index (UN) 93
Hyndman, J. 130

identity politics 216–17
illegal immigrants, term 7, 72; *see also* undocumented immigrants
immigrant, term 5

immigrant entrepreneurialism: as alternative to unemployment 65; Greek Cypriot community, UK 62–3; Korean community, Los Angeles 62; marginal enterprises 65; skilled migrants 74; and social capital 61–3; and transnational networks 63

immigrant institutions 206–7

immigration: complexity of migration policies 155–6; internalized immigration enforcement 166–9; term 5

indentured servitude/workers 32, 34–5, 66

India: brain circulation 105–6; indentured workers (coolie system) 34, 66; partition 43, 123; remittances 12; skilled workers in the USA 74, 78, 105–6; uneven development patterns 108

Indonesia 70

industrialization: Border Industrialization Program (BIP) (US–Mexico) 94, 96, 97; deindustrialization 65; for development 92–3, 94; and laws of migration 16–17; migration and 35–8; of the New World 38–41; and post-war development theories 92

integration: and citizenship 182–8; concept of 180, 181–2; into the mainstream 182, 206; of Mizrahi Jews in Israel 182; race-relations cycle 180; see also assimilation studies

internal migration: in China 8; links with international migration 8; term 4

internally displaced persons (IDPs) 137–9

International Bank of Development and Reconstruction, 92

International Monetary Fund (IMF) 92, 99

International Organization for Migration (IOM) 5

International Refugee Organization (IRO) 123

Ireland: foreign-born population 10; migration to England, historical 37, 41, 45, 96; skilled migrants 79

Israel: asylum seekers in 2, 6; crackdown on unauthorized immigrants 1, 2; expansionary immigration policies 182; formation of 43, 123; Holot detention facility 164–5; immigration, post-war years 43; Jewish immigrants to 2–3; migrants for low-paid jobs 3; repatriation of Palestinian refugees to 142; see also Jews

Italy: co-development programmes with Senegal 108–9; foreign workers, status of 3–4; foreign-born population 10; laws on authorized immigration 1–2; local politics of citizenship 196; Lodi mosque controversy 197; migration to the New World, 19th century 40, 95–6; migration within Europe, historical 36; undocumented immigrants 48

Japan: decoupling of ethnicity/race and citizenship 189; exploitation of foreign students 77–8; Japanese-origin workers 49, 185; Korean labour 50, 184–5, 189–90; net migration figures 14; NGO engagement with immigrants 196; unskilled labour migration to 49, 185; xenophobic ethnonationalism 184

Jerusalem 183

Jews: Ashkenazi (European) Jews 182; migration to Palestine 122, 123; Mizrahi Jews in Israel 182; Nazi Germany and 122; persecution of in Russia, historical 121; spatial isolation in the ghetto 180–1; see also Israel

Joppke, C. 158

Jordan: Iraqi refugees in 139–40; as refugee-receiving country 138

Jureidini, R. 67

jus sanguinis 184

Kassim, A. 73

Klaufus, C. 108

Kloosterman, R. 65

knowledge workers 47, 74; see also skilled migrants

Kocher, A. 151

Kogan, I. 76

Korea: Korean community, Los Angeles 62; Korean labour in Japan 50, 184–5, 189–90

Kurien, P. 216, 217

Kuwait 10

labour activism 215–16
labour markets: assessments of migrants in 82; clustering of workers 59–60; demand for unskilled workers 52; dual labour market theory 19, 65–6; gendered and racialized divisions of labour 66–7; globalization of 14, 151; human capital 58–9; medieval period mobility 29; and migration flows 15–16; occupational categories 58; piece rates 37; primary/secondary sectors and social coding 65–6; role of migrants within 81–2; role of the state 69–71; skilled migrants 73–9; social capital and 59–61; two-tiered markets 38; undocumented immigrants in 71–3; *see also* segmentation of labour
Lama, K. T. 211
Latapí, E. 109
Latin America: Chinese labour, historical 35; migration corridors 52
Lawson, V. 20
Lazaridis, G. 67
Lebanon: asylum seekers in *136, 137, 141*; Lebanese in Senegal 221; as sending and receiving country 13, 138; Shatila Refugee Camp *136, 141*
Lee, E. 17–18
legal processes: Aliens Act of 1905 (UK) 121; changing citizenship laws 103, 191–5; legal status of workers 70–1; oversight of, Malaysia 73, 80–1; Personal Responsibility and Work Opportunity Reconciliation Act (PRWORA) 194, 196; US Immigration Control and Reform Act of 1986 (IRCA) 158
Ley, D. 74
Lichter, M. 69
Lung-Amam, W. 197
Lutz, H. 81

mainstream assimilation 182, 206; *see also* assimilation studies; integration
Malaysia: as importer and exporter of labour 50–1; undocumented immigrants, oversight of 73, 80–1

Mali: Gidimaxa Jikké (co-development programme) 107; intercepted migrants stranded in 170
Malkki, L. 121, 142–3
the Marginal Man 208
Márquez Covarrubias, H. 110
Marshall, T. H. 179
Martin, P. L. 96
Massey, D. 157, 181
Mavroudi, E. 110, 221
McDowell, L. 70
McKay, S. C. 69–70
Megoran, N. 171
Menjívar, C. 221–2
Mexico: Border Industrialization Program (BIP) 94, 96, 97; bracero program 46, 70, 94; citizenship laws 103; debt peonage 33; Mexico–US migration corridor 9, 13; migrant flows from 9, 13; migration as detrimental to national economy 97; net migration figures *14*; remittances 12, 109; tres-por-uno program 103–4; uneven development patterns 107; US economic policies towards 94–5; US–Mexican border controls 97, *152*, 155, 157, *162*, 163–4, *165*; US–Mexican transnational migrants 219
middleman minority 62, 63
migrants: definitions of 5; as distinct from refugees 144; global numbers of 8
migration: definitions of 4–5; global scale of 8; internal migration 4; international migration 4; links with globalization 14, 151
migration data 5, 12–13
migration flows: and capitalism 15, 41, 151, 153; colonialism 29–30; destination countries *9, 11*; and economic interests 15–16, 157–8; foreign-born populations 9–10; into gateway cities 10–11; and labour markets 15–16; migration corridors 9; from poorer to wealthier countries 15–16, 94–7; receiving countries, regulation of 9, 70–1; sending countries 8–9, *10, 12*; state formation and refugee flow 120–2; sub-Saharan Africa 52

migration hump model 95–6, *95*
migration management: concept of 159–60; migrant categories 160–1; neutral administration of 160
migration theories: economic models 18; entropy models 17; feminist approaches 20–1; gravity models 17; migration systems approach 20; neo-Marxist theories 19; power relations 20–1; push-and-pull model 17–18; Ravenstein's laws 16–17; structuralist theories 18–19
migration-development nexus: co-development programmes 107, 108–9; complexity of 110–12; economic growth and 93; level of economic development, sending countries 94–7; migration as development strategy 70, 97–110; role of remittances 103–4; term 91–2; uneven development patterns 107–8; *see also* development
migration-security nexus 162–6
Mitchell, K. 197
mobility: and border controls 151; concept of 7; economic development and 96–7; global capitalism and mobility 41, 153; global scale of 8; international migration within 8–9; liberal migration regimes 153–4; medieval period mobility 8–9
modern period 28–9
Moran-Taylor, M. 221–2
Morocco 104–5
Moukarbel, N. 67
Mountz, A. 130
multiculturalism: backlash against, UK 195; and identity politics 216–17; policies of 190
Mulvey, G. 161
Muslims: the Islamic headscarf debates, France 186; Lega Nord 197; local opposition to mosques 197; Muslim man praying, US *212*; religious bookstall, Birmingham *213*; Rushdie Affair, UK 195
myths of return 63

Naber, N. 211
nationhood *see* citizenship
nation-state-centred perspectives 5–7

nation-states: acceptance of refugees 119, 124–5, 144; and border controls 72–3, 156, 159; and categorization of undocumented immigrants 72–3; changing citizenship laws 191–5; control of migration 73, 151; engagement with globalized migration flows 15, 151; increased population controls, 20th century 41; interstate system, creation of 29; promotion of labour export 69–70; state formation and refugee flow 120–2; *see also* receiving countries; sending countries
native workers: employment options 65–6; nativist unrest and immigration controls 154–5; skilled workers, opposition to 78–9; term 59
naturalization 180
neo-Marxist theories: criticism post-war development theories 93; on migration 19
net migration 13
Netanyahu, Benyamin 1
Netherlands 65, 195
Neumeyer, E. 154
Ngai, M. 72
non-government organizations (NGOs) 196
North American Free Trade Agreement (NAFTA) 94, 157

occupational segmentation 69–70; *see also* segmentation of labour
Ottoman Empire 122

Pakistan 123
Palestine: Jewish migration to 122, 123; Palestinian diaspora in Greece 221; partition 43; refugees 123, 142
Papua New Guinea 131–2
Park, R. 180, 206, 207, 208
passports 153, 154, 155
patterns of migration: chain migration 40–1, 157; and definitions of migration 5; and globalization 14–15; stepwise patterns of migration 17, 28; *see also* migration flows
Peace of Westphalia 29
Pécoud, A. 159, 160

periphery, term 16
Philippines: female domestic workers 67, 68, *68*, 71; Filipinos in Saudi Arabia 222–3; healthcare training programs 101; promotion of labour export 100, *101*; promotion of migration 69–70; unskilled workers, Japan 49
Piore, M. 19
place-making: Chinese immigrant 'monster houses' 197, 213, 214; ghettos 180–1, 211–12; reimagining of immigrant neighbourhoods 211–12; in the suburbs (ethnoburbs) 212–14
pogroms 121
Poland: mass migration from, 19th century 41; migration to Germany, historical 36, 38; Polish workers in the UK 79–80, *80*
political processes: labour activism 215–16; political mobilization of immigrant groups 215–18; regularization of undocumented workers 73, 81; securitization of border controls 164; through social remittances 105; and trans-border lives 220–2; voting rights, émigrés 103
political-economy perspectives 18–19
polity 179
Portes, A. 98, 219, 221
post-national citizenship 188–9; *see also* citizenship
post-war development theory 92–3; *see also* development; migration-development nexus
poverty constraint 18, 95
Preston, I. 82
proletarianization 30, 36

Qatar 10

race: concepts of 187; decoupling of ethnicity/ race and citizenship 187, 189–90, 194; and intergenerational conflict 211; whiteness as social category 209–10
racialization, term 187
racism: affirmative action programmes 186; and the Marginal Man 208; post-war

period 155–6; race-based restrictions, border controls 42, 46, 154–5; and second-generation migrants 210; and segmented labour markets 66–9; xenophobic ethnonationalism 184–5; *see also* slave trade
Rath, J. 65
Ravenstein, Ernst Georg 16–17
receiving countries: dual nationality provisions 103, 191; by number of immigrants *9*; occupational segmentation 70; by percentage of the population *11*; refugees as problematic 119; and regulation of migrant flows 9, 70–1; *see also* citizenship; integration
refugees: Cold War era politicization of 124–5; definitions of 119, 121, 144; distinction from economic migrants 144; from El Salvador 124; forced migration 119, 120–3, 144; within the Global South 137–40; historical perspective 120–3; Hutus in Tanzania 142–3; identity-formation 142–3; internally displaced persons (IDPs) 137–9; international institutions and 139–40; migrant agency and 141–3; non-refoulement 124; as problematic for receiving countries 119; repatriation of 123, 125, 139; resettlement of 123, 132, 142; Second World War 43; social networks 143; and state formation, historical 120–2; Syrian 138; top ten refugee hosting countries **138**; as undocumented immigrants 143; use of smugglers 143; Vietnamese boat people 124; *see also* asylum seekers
regularization: and border controls, Europe 157; of undocumented immigrants 73, 81
remittances: collective remittances 104; global flow of 12, 14, 104; hometown associations (HTA) 104, 105, 109; money transfer services *102*, 104; and poverty reduction 104–5; reliability of 109; sending country economic development and 99–103; and social and prestige items 108; state promotion of 103–4; stricter border controls and 109; and trans-border lives

219–20; uneven development patterns from 107–8; values of 99, **99**, *100*

restrictive immigration policies: anti-immigrant groups and 158; race-based restrictions, border controls 42, 46, 154–5; skilled migrants restrictions, UK 78

Reynolds, R. R. 79

Riccio, B. 108–9

Rogaly, B. 79

Rostow, W. W. 92

Rouse, R. 219

rural-to-urban migration 4, 30–1, 35, 36

Russia: net migration figures 13, *14*; persecution of Jews, historical 121

Rwanda 106

Saint-Blancat, C. 197

Salih, R. 220–1

Salter, M. B. 156

Saudi Arabia: Filipino workers in 222–3; foreign workers, status of 1, 3; foreign-born population 10; Indonesian domestic workers 70; Saudization policy 3; Uighur refugees in 125

Schmidt di Friedberg, O. 197

Schultz, T. 58

Schuster, L. 129, 132

second generation immigrants 207, 210–11

Second World War, refugees 122–3

securitization: of asylum seekers 129–37; and deportation policies 165–6; of EU borders 162–3; and increased risks to migrants 164; and internal surveillance 166–9; of migration 161–6; political purpose of 164; technological innovation 162; US–Mexican border controls *162*, 163–4, *165*

segmentation of labour: gendered and racialized divisions of labour 66–9; legal status of workers 70–1; occupational segmentation 69–70

selective immigration policies 59, 82

sending countries: cultivation of diasporic communities 101–2; dual nationality provisions 103, 191; economic development to retain potential migrants 94–7; migrant flows 8–9, *10*, *12*; migration as detrimental to national economics 97–8; migration as development strategy 97–110; by number of emigrants *10*, 95; occupational segmentation 69–70; by percentage of the population 12, *12*; promotion of labour export 69–70, 100–1; remittances and economic development 99–103

Senegal 221

service industries 67–9

settler societies: civic conceptions of citizenship 185–6; expansionary immigration policies 48, 75, 156; foreign-born population 9–10, 13; post-war period migration to 46; restrictive immigration policies 42; *see also* Australia; Canada; United States of America (USA)

sex industry 72

Silverman, M. 186

Silvey, R. 20, 70

Simmel, G. 205

Singh, M. 110

Skeldon, R. 92

skilled migrants: blue cards (EU) 75, 78; brain circulation 105–6, 108; as brain drain 12, 97–8, 108; in Canada 75, 76; deskilling of 76–7; economic desirability of 75; exploitation of 77–9; H-1B visas (USA) 78–9, 161; human capital 74; international tertiary education programmes 75–6; knowledge workers 47, 74; migration management policies and 161; native opposition to 78–9; professional association regulations 76; selective immigration policies 59, 82; skilled migration programmes 75; social capital 74; Transfer of Knowledge through Expatriate Nationals (TOKTEN) programme 106; in the UK 74, 75, 78, 161; unemployment rates 76

slave trade 32–3

Smith, M. P. 219, 220

smugglers, people 143, 164

social capital: clustering of workers 59–60; constraints of 63–5; critiques of 65; economic processes 59–61; and gender disparities 64; immigrant entrepreneurialism 61–3; kinship and co-ethnicity ties 61; segmentation of hotel workers 69; skilled migrants 74

social fields 205

social networks: and agency of migrants 21, 143; immigrant institutions 206–7; negative aspects of 63–4; and occupational segregation 60–1, 63, 64–5, 69; and social capital 60; of trailing spouses 77; as transnational 21, 63, 143

social remittances 105

sojourning 5

Somalia 109

South Africa: European migration to, 19th century 40; internalized immigration enforcement 168–9; racial tolerance march 216

Spain: colonialism 29–30; foreign-born population 10; migrant agricultural workers 60; net immigration figures 13; net migration figures 14; post-national citizenship 188–9; undocumented immigrants 48

Speek, P. 206

stepwise patterns of migration 17, 28

superdiversity 11–12

sustainable development 93

Switzerland 36–7

Syria 118

Tanzania 142–3

Taylor, S. 110

Thailand 50–1

Thomas, W. I. 206–7

tourism 8

training 58

Transfer of Knowledge through Expatriate Nationals (TOKTEN) programme 106

transmigrant, term 7

transnationalism: agency and social networks 21, 63, 143; and assimilation theories 222–3; historical perspective 222; and immigrant entrepreneurialism 63; and political orientations 220–2; and

reproduction of repressive gender norms 220–1; social networks and occupational segregation 60–1, 63, 64–5, 69; trans-border lives and the diaspora 218–20; see also diaspora

transoceanic exploration 29

transport: chain migration 40–1, 157; and ease of migration to the New World 39, 40

Trauner, F. 170

Tshabalala, X. 169

Tsuda, T. 196

Turkey: citizenship laws 103; compulsory expulsions, inter-war years 43; Germany–Turkey corridor 9, 163; guest workers, Germany 97, 103, 158, 184; as refugee-receiving country 138; remittances 12; state formation and refugee flow 122

Turton, D. 144

unauthorized immigrants, term 7

underdevelopment 93

undocumented immigrants: deportation of 73; to Europe, late 20th century 48; migrant agency 80–1; political mobilization of 81; refugees as 143; regularization of 73, 81; and regulation of migrant flows 70; role in the labour market 71–3; Secure Communities programme, USA 167; state categorization of 72–3; term 7; trafficking 72

United Arab Emirates 10

United Kingdom: Aliens Act of 1905 121; border control, Calais 160; Caribbean migrants, 1950s 71, 193; Cultural Studies 209; curry house kitchen 64; European labour, post-war years 44–5; European Volunteer Workers (EVWs) 70–1, 123; foreign-born population 9–10; gateway cities 11; Greek Cypriot community 62–3; group formation and mobilization 217–18; immigrant, term 5; International Passenger Survey (IPS) 5–6; Jewish migration to 122; migration data 5–6; multiculturalism policies 192, 195; National Asylum Support

Service (NASS) 128; patriality concept
192; Polish workers in 79–80, *80*; political
mobilization of undocumented workers
81; Race Relations model 192–3; refugee
populations, historical 120–1; refugees and
welfare reforms 127–9; Rushdie Affair 195;
Sangatte affair 126–7, *127*; skilled migrants
to 74, 75, 78, 161; workers from former
colonies 45
United Nations High Commissioner for
Refugees (UNHCR) 123, 124, 132, 138,
139, 141–2
United Nations Relief and Works Agency
(UNRWA) 123, 142
United Nations (UN): on benefits of migration
97; Convention Relating to the Status
of Refugees 124, 126; non-refoulement
principle 124; refugee definition 5, 119,
123, 124, 138; Transfer of Knowledge
through Expatriate Nationals (TOKTEN)
programme 106
United States of America (USA): affirmative
action programmes 186; African Americans,
education and employment 58–9; asylum
seekers, detention of 129; benefits/
negatives of migrants 82–3; Border
Industrialization Program (BIP) 94, 96,
97; bracero program 46, 70, 94;
categorization of undocumented
immigrants 72–3; Chinese immigrant
'monster houses' 197, 213, 214; Chinese
immigrants, historical 35, *35*, 154; civic
conceptions of citizenship 185, 186;
decoupling of ethnicity/race and citizenship
189; economic policies towards Mexico
94–5; European migration to, 19th century
39; expansionary immigration policies 46,
48, 156; foreign-born population 9–10,
39, 48; gateway cities 11; H-1B visas
78–9, 161; identity politics 216–17; illegal
immigrant, term 7; immigrant, term 5;
immigrant removals **168**; Immigration
and Customs Enforcement (ICE) 166,
167; Indian-American groups 216, 217;
internalized immigration enforcement

166–8; international tertiary education
programmes 75–6; Korean community,
Los Angeles 62; labour activism 216;
landing at Ellis Island *39*; meat packing
industry 82–3; Mexican migrants to
7, 9, 42, 219; Mexico–US migration
corridor 9, 13; migration data 5; mobility
into 8; nativist unrest and immigration
controls 154; net migration figures *14*;
NGO engagement with immigrants
196–7; Personal Responsibility and
Work Opportunity Reconciliation Act,
(PRWORA) 194, 196; racial categories,
US census 186, 187, 209; racially motivated
immigration restrictions 42, 46; refugees,
resettlement of 132; Section 287(g)
166–7; Secure Communities programme
167; Senate Bill 1070 (SB1070) 168;
skilled workers and migration management
161; social capital of migrant workers
61; Tibetan community, California 211;
undocumented immigrants 48; US Border
Patrol 155; US–Mexican border controls
152, 155, 157, *162*, 163–4, *165*
United We Dream (USA) 81
United Workers Association (UK) 81
US Immigration Control and Reform Act
of 1986 (IRCA) 158

Van Liempt, I. 143
Van Riemsdijk, M. 78
Veronis, L. 217
Vertovec, S. 11
Vietnam 124
Vigneswaran, D. 169
visas 154

Waldinger, R. 69
Walsh, J. 159
Walzer, M. 170
Waters, M. 210
Welch, M. 129
Wickham, J. 79
Wirth, L. 180–1
Wise, A. 214–15

women: deskilling of professional migrants 76–7; domestic workers, Gulf Arab States 51, 67, 70; domestic/caring work 20, 66–7; labour export strategies for 101; migration as a conscious choice 79; social capital as male-dominated 64; social networks and occupational segregation 60–1, 69; trafficking 72; as trailing spouses 77; *see also* gender
Wong, L. L. 74

World Bank 92, 93
Wright, R. 61

Yeates, N. 110
Yeh, E. T. 211
Young, P. 205, 207

Zambia 139, 142
Zin, R. H. M. 73
Znaniecki, F. 206–7